After Christianity

Daphne Hampson

TRINITY PRESS INTERNATIONAL
VALLEY FORGE, PENNSYLVANIA

Library of Congress Cataloging-in-Publication
data available
1-56338-196-6

First published 1996 by
SCM Press Ltd
9–17 St Albans Place, London N1 0NX

First North American edition published 1996 by
Trinity Press International
P.O. Box 851
Valley Forge, PA 19482

Trinity Press International is a division of the
Morehouse Publishing Group

Typeset by Regent Typesetting, London
Printed in Great Britain

Contents

Preface   v

Introduction: A Shift of Paradigm   1

I Christian Particularity   12

II Continuity and Discontinuity   51

III Feminist Ethics   84

IV Christian Idolatry   119

V Woman, the Other   169

VI A Future Theism   212

VII Spirituality and Praxis   254

Notes   286

Index   323

Every new age is unbelievable beforehand,
and after, inevitable

Marge Piercy, 'The Magician', *To Be of Use* (1973)

Preface

Within British society at least, a quiet revolution is underway. Many are saying that,while they do not credit orthodox Christianity, they count themselves spiritual persons. If I am not much mistaken it is mostly women who, on the media and elsewhere, are making such comments. I am such a woman. The only difference is that I am by profession a theologian!

Christianity faces crisis. People will say that, in its two thousand year history, Christianity has always faced crises. But there are reasons why this time it may not survive. It is important to recognize how fundamental the crisis is. The church cannot simply undergo a face-lift, bringing itself more up to date, for example through ordaining women as priests. It has tried that. While wishing those women well, many wonder why they bother further with the church. Feminist women, in particular, have for the most part moved on long ago.

The crisis with which Christianity is confronted is twofold. In the first place it has to do with the matter of the truth of Christian claims. Christianity has proclaimed a grand myth or story: that God created the world; humankind fell; 'he' sent his son, who died and rose, and who will come again at the end of time. Alternatively these claims have been conceptualized in the doctrinal language of Trinity and incarnation. Belief in these things has worn thin with this generation. When in 1963 John Robinson's *Honest to God* was published it came to many people – who were fascinated – as something of a shock. Since then, many books and innumerable radio discussions and articles in the press have familiarized the educated public with the fact that the foundations of Christian belief are decidedly shaky. In the last decade there has been a sea change. There was a time when it took much courage to say publicly in the media that one was not a Christian. Now it takes none at all.

But in the second place it has become apparent that there is an ethical crisis. People have come to think irrelevant the way in which Christians look back to the first century in arranging their thoughts on any number of issues. The ordination debate has only served to highlight how far the church lags behind the rest of society. Christianity appears to be wedded to a primacy of the male; its language for God is archaic. In large part it is the rise of feminism that has caused this ethical crisis. No longer confined by the church, women have begun to discover their own spirituality. Men have ceased to control what it is that women shall think.

The two issues, that of the truth of Christianity and that of whether it can be considered ethical, are profoundly related. Once people form the ethical judgment that Christianity is a masculinist religion, one which legitimizes patriarchy, they have clear eyes to see that Christianity cannot possibly be true. On the other hand, once people come to find Christian doctrine incredible, if they have no psychological investment in it, they will naturally leave Christianity behind. Yet many people – including, I note, virtually all my friends – have by no means ceased to be spiritual persons. The importance of there being a spiritual dimension to our lives seems more evident than ever. It is simply that Christianity can no longer be the vehicle for that spirituality. In a spirit of adventure, people are seeking a way forward.

In one sense I am attempting no more in this book than, as a theologian, to articulate and to think through this agenda. I commence, in Chapter I, by grasping the nettle as to why it is that Christianity cannot be true. Since at least the eighteenth century we have been aware of what has been called the 'scandal of particularity': that there cannot have been a one-off event such as a resurrection would constitute. But there has been much confusion surrounding this. In Chapter II, I continue by arguing that our relationship to the past must, in the sphere of our religion, be what it is in any other sphere (which is only possible if one does not credit that there could have been a particular revelation). This will solve the ethical dilemma involved in looking back to a patriarchal history, as Christians inevitably must. Readers who are cognizant of my *Theology and Feminism* (Basil Blackwell 1990) will recognize that here I build on themes which I have discussed before. I use this opportunity to answer critics and to explain myself more fully.

If we are to consider the depth to which the feminist critique of Christianity reaches, it will be necessary to explore the thinking which has taken place in the realm of feminist theory over the last decade and a half. This I attempt in some manner to do in Chapter III. Many educated people (particularly men, I surmise) have no idea what has transpired. Yet feminism is shaking the foundations of many academic disciplines and will yet shake theology. If we are to conceive of what it is with which theology must be commensurate, if it is to be considered ethical and relevant, it is imperative that we consider feminist thinking. In particular I try to articulate how feminists from different schools conceptualize the self-in-relation.

I turn in Chapters IV and V to a 'reading' of the Judaeo-Christian tradition, in particular Christianity. The insights and values which have emerged in the previous chapter prove a useful tool of analysis. In Chapter IV, I consider what have been major paradigms: transcendent monotheism; the theme of the relationship of God to humanity as exemplified by covenant, sacrifice and incarnation; and finally the doctrine of the Trinity. I show that they reflect what is a male reality, given male circumstances. In Chapter V, I focus on the masculinist construct of the idea of woman and femininity. I consider how this has governed the place which woman, symbolically or in actuality, has been accorded within the tradition – and the detrimental effect on the lives of women. 'Readings' of this nature are difficult to undertake. But I believe they are crucial if we are to gain insight into religion as we have known it.

In Chapter VI, I progress to what is perhaps the heart of the book. I think through how it is that I have come to conceptualize that dimension of reality which is God. I do this in dialogue with the great theologian of modernity, Friedrich Schleiermacher. I consider the nature of religious experience and questions of theodicy and prayer. This chapter forms at least an essay as to how we might find our way forward in Western religion. In the final chapter, Chapter VII, I consider the implications of this for the nature of the life which could be called spiritual. In particular I consider certain practices which may allow an awareness of that which is God.

Readers who know my former work will want to ask how my position may have changed since I wrote *Theology and Feminism*. I think that I have moved forward notably in two respects. In the first place it became crystal clear to me not long after writing *Theology and Feminism* that the basic incompatibility between feminism and Christianity lies in the fact that Christianity is necessarily heteronomous, in that it understands God as other than the self and known through revelation. Feminists must stand for human autonomy (though not isolation). I explore this theme in the essay which I have contributed to a book which I have edited in the meantime: *Swallowing a Fishbone? Feminist Theologians Debate Christianity* (SPCK 1996). It remains important to the present work. In the second place, at the time that I wrote *Theology and Feminism* I was hardly aware of French feminism. I now think it indispensable for analysing the Western tradition.

A few words on the type of book which this is may be useful. I have reason to think, from the feedback I receive, that my readers are very diverse. That is something in which I delight. This is a more academic book than *Theology and Feminism*. I participate in academic debates, as I must. But I endeavour not to write in such a way that the more general reader will be unable to follow me. More academic readers must therefore excuse me if I sometimes give what to them must seem unnecessary explanations, though I believe that the particular way in which I put things is probably crucial to my argument. Chapter III on feminist theory is specifically provided for those who have no previous knowledge. I also have reason to think that this book might serve well as a textbook. Although the chapters follow logically one from another, they are reasonably self-contained.

In completing this book I am aware of many debts of gratitude. In the first place I wish to thank my North American editor, Dr Harold (Hal) Rast, who has stood by me over many years, never doubting that this book would see the light of day. I must also thank my British editor, Dr John Bowden, for his theological expertise which has been so invaluable and the painstaking care that he has taken with my manuscript. I have to thank the Leverhulme Foundation for funds for replacement teaching which allowed me to spend the academic year 1988–89 back at Harvard Divinity School. I have always thought that going to Harvard for my theological training was the most important decision of my life and I am grateful for the vigour and the life of that community. I spent a sabbatical term in 1990 at Massey College in the University of Toronto, during which I carried out much of the preliminary research for this book. Knowing that I desperately needed more knowledge of Continental philosophy, I took a year's leave of absence from my position in 1992–93 and undertook a degree at the University of Warwick. It has made a world of difference.

On a personal level I have many to thank. I think of friends, interestingly many of them older than myself, whose lives have been an inspiration and who have helped me to envisage the ways forward which women may find. I think more especially of Kay Carmichael, Sarah Doering, Penelope Eckersley, Marion McNaughton and Ruth Robinson. Here in the St Andrews area I am grateful for friends who have encouraged and supported me during the final arduous months of writing. I thank Greta Arnott for long walks on the beach, Liz Wilson for her presence on the end of the telephone, and Roma Foster for her perspicacity and humour. I also want to express my gratitude to my new colleagues (exclusively male) with whom in recent months I have delighted to participate in first-rate intellectual discussion in a weekly seminar and lunch-time discussion group. But above all I have to thank my students. Over so many years now intellectual excitement has been generated in the classroom or round the seminar table. In particular I thank the following students, undergraduate and postgraduate, who have worked for me as research assistants: Naomi Higham, Guy Collins, Sarah Nicholson and Sue Waslin – and I remember also Helene

Deas who, in her will, left the funds to the staff of St Mary's College which have enabled them to be paid.

Last – but not least – I feel bound to recognize the debt that I owe to my parents. That is something which, the older one becomes, it is increasingly easier to acknowledge! My father, born into the optimism of Victorian Greater Manchester, had a no-nonsense attitude to any kind of obfuscation and a profound ethical sense. In some ways he had walked out of the Enlightenment, though his judgment was tempered by his experience of modern history. My mother, by contrast, has a strong sense of spirituality, acknowledging the efficacy of God's power, while not conforming to any traditional Christian doctrine. I realize that I owe it in part to her that, on leaving the Christian church, it did not so much as occur to me that I should become an atheist. In some ways I have needed to bring together my double inheritance. I could never evade issues of truth, while at the same time I was aware that this must include thinking about that reality which is God. For some years my parents forebore to have children, partly on account of the difference in their outlooks. Their firstborn became a theologian!

The final task in writing a book I have found the most perplexing: choosing a picture for the cover. Covers are symbolic, they give a first impression. My editor, John Bowden, in a moment of great insight told me that the book was about 'the nature of personhood'. So I wanted to put a human form on the cover; for the human form is the most powerful symbol. And since human beings are male or female and it should not be a man, it should be a woman (though I should gladly have had both a man and a woman). But then my friends warned me there was a problem: people would think it was a book 'about women'. How interesting that the most famous book published by my publishers (which I have already mentioned), Robinson's *Honest to God*, simply had a man on the cover – and no one thought it was a book about men! As Hegel said, man is the universal, woman the particular. In a nutshell, that was the problem which my book tackled.

So what of other options? Something 'spiritual' – a beautiful sunset or clouds perhaps? My critics would at once decide that I was 'simply a Gnostic, one who knew nothing of the nitty-gritty of human reality'. So a scene from nature, for I do love nature. *After Christianity*, I should be told, 'the only possibility is a nature religion'. But there is some discussion of art history in the book; perhaps that could be illustrated? It is largely of the Florentine Renaissance, and Donatello seems to be my hero, so what of his Magdalene? I should immediately be told that I was 'quite unable to escape Christianity, try as I may'. So perhaps I could draw on the pre-Christian ancient world? *After Christianity* 'must be about a reversion to paganism'. The Enlightenment perhaps – with which I open the book? I should be told, as I have been before now, that I was 'hung up on the Enlightenment'. So something post-modern or avant-garde? I am sure that there would be cries that I had 'no understanding of the need for history and tradition'. Despairingly I thought that the cover would have to be just lettering. But then doubtless my religion would be said to be 'wholly cerebral, lacking any aesthetic sense'!

So back to the woman. Surveying pictures by men of women, I was struck as never before how almost invariably men paint what I have called in the book the male construct of woman: she is sexy, or demure. I moved to women painters. I love German art from the early years of this century. But if I chose Käthe Kollwitz I should be told I was 'angry'. Or if Paula Modersohn-Becker, the book would certainly 'be about earth mothers'. So what of Gabriele Münter? How interesting that she lived with Kandinsky for many years; years during which he wrote and published, in 1912, what became a classic: *Über das Geistige in der Kunst* ('On the Spiritual in Art'). I learn that Münter herself was deeply interested in theosophy. (And no – if I am not a pagan, a nature worshipper, a Gnostic or into earth mothers – nor am I a follower of theosophy.) Thus I came to choose a sumptuous picture depicting a woman – and people will say . . .? It seemed to me to embody the book.

Introduction:

A Shift of Paradigm

In a famous essay submitted for a competition, 'What is Enlightenment?', the great philosopher of the Enlightenment Immanuel Kant expressed himself as follows:

> Enlightenment is the exodus of human beings from their self-induced minority. Minority is the inability to make use of one's reason without calling on the leadership of another.[1]

Kant exhorts his readers: '*Sapere aude*!' (Dare to know).[2] 'Have the courage' – and Kant employs the familiar 'du' form – 'to use *your own* reason!' That, he says, 'is the motto of the Enlightenment'. It was 1784.

A hundred and sixty years later, in prison in Nazi Germany, a young pastor Dietrich Bonhoeffer, whose theology had been of a conservative disposition, picks up Kant's words. In the mid-twentieth century, the force of industrial society unleashed with terrifying power, Bonhoeffer concludes that the world has 'come of age'.[3] Humans no longer make recourse to that God in relation to whom they should understand themselves as minors.

Kant indeed seems to have had his sights set in large part on religion. (We may note that in his 'Strife of the Faculties' it is the conflict of philosophy with theology with which he is primarily concerned!) In his essay on 'Enlightenment' Kant continues:

> Laziness and cowardice are the reasons why such a large part of humanity, long after nature has pronounced them free of external leadership (they have come of age), nevertheless happily remain minors their whole life long; and why it is so easy for others to set themselves up as their guardians. It is so comfortable to be a minor. If I have a book which reasons for me, a pastor who has a conscience for me, a doctor who decides my diet for me, and so forth, then I don't need to take the trouble myself.[4]

Nine years after 'What is Enlightenment?', in his *Religion within the Limits of Reason Alone* (published in the form of articles to evade the Prussian censor), Kant was to lay out what was the first full 'demythologizing' of Western religion, proclaiming it to be, in picturesque form, a projection of human moral sensibilities.[5] Kant thus raised issues which have haunted theology ever since. Were there to be a God, of the kind which God had always been held to be, absolute and transcendent, the relationship to God would represent an ultimate heteronomy[6] on the part of human beings. For such a God – if God were to be God to the human – would necessarily have to be obeyed. Taking part in the academic procession which accompanied the installation of a new rector, Kant, upon reaching the church, would abscond.[7]

I do not believe that we can rescind this critique of Western religion. More conservative proponents of Christianity appear not to have reckoned with that. The Enlightenment has come to stay. Over the subsequent two hundred years human beings have come into their own. This represents a crisis for religion; for that religion, so I shall argue, is tied inexorably to the pre-Enlightenment paradigm. As long as religion is considered to be revealed – and Christianity is necessarily a religion of revelation – there must be a God who is other than the world, towards whom Christians will exercise a relationship which is in essence heteronomous. Christianity is not a religion which is simply grounded in human religious awareness; it must always have an external referent, to a God, a literature, or a revealed tradition, which takes a certain precedence.[8] From the belief in a transcendent God, there arises an ethical difficulty.

Furthermore (as Kant again saw), through claiming that truth consists in a particular revelation of God, Christianity clashes with modern knowledge. Liberal Christians have well understood the crisis. One might argue that they have spent two hundred years attempting to meet the challenge. German Protestant theology, which absorbed most profoundly the critique that the Enlightenment represented for Christianity, has tried every possible way out of the dilemma. Friedrich Schleiermacher – the first to respond in a serious way – founded religion in human experience, thus avoiding (initially at least) the particularity of Christianity. But how then should he also be Christian? By contrast the Dane Søren Kierkegaard declared Christianity to be incompatible with Enlightenment presuppositions, and consequently the 'truth' of Christianity to be of another order. In making such a move, Kierkegaard has been followed by much twentieth-century, so-called 'dialectical', theology. Such 'radical conservatism', as we may call it, counters the Enlightenment by declaring that Christianity cannot be accommodated. Present-day liberals evade the issue by reducing Christianity to a moral imperative, speaking simply in terms of praxis. But the question as to the truth of Christianity and its compatibility with what we otherwise know about the nature of the world is not to be avoided.

In the sphere of ethics, the Enlightenment paradigm of human equality has worked its way through, so that today it comprises what we consider a just society. In the eighteenth century, the Enlightenment led of course to the French and American revolutions, while in an earlier form it had already resulted in a less drastic constitutional revolution in the British Isles. These upheavals were grounded in a new understanding of the relation which should pertain between an individual and the society. (It does not follow that the eighteenth century necessarily lacked a societal sense; such a reading may well be of later provenance.) Society was now held to result from a contract between individuals rather than the earlier organic notion in which each person had their (God-ordained) place. The church had played no minor role in buttressing the earlier conception. Aristotelian notions of a right (and hierarchical) ordering had merged with a Christianity inherited from Constantine. God was hegemonic to the whole. In an Anselmian world, 'he' was the feudal Lord to whom ultimate allegiance was due. While at times finding itself in conflict with the emerging nation states, the medieval church in no way challenged the concept of a society in which each group had their allotted place. The court of heaven reflected the earthly realm. In particular women had a given place within such an order.

In the Enlightenment, such an organic conception of society was placed in question. Of course the revolution was far from complete. The forces of reaction consolidated themselves; revolutionary tendencies erupted in the constitutional revolutions of 1848; and again retrenchment set in. But the top was off the bottle and the new forces could not be suppressed. The late eighteenth and nineteenth centuries saw widespread granting of suffrage, first to white, propertied, males, and then to all males. Those women who argued that the 'rights of man' must be held to include the rights of woman (for women also were persons) fared badly. In vain Mary Wollstonecraft published, in 1792, her *A Vindication of the Rights of Woman;* while Olympe de Gouges, author of the pamphlet *Les Droits de la Femme et de la Citoyenne,* lost her head to the guillotine. By 1840 British and American women, present at the London World Anti-Slavery Convention (for many women were quick to see the connection between the abolitionist debate and their own predicament), were plotting in the gallery to which they had been confined.[9] In 1869 John Stuart Mill was to declare: 'We have had the morality of submission, and the morality of chivalry and generosity; the time is now come for the morality of justice.'[10] By the early twentieth century the movement for women's suffrage constituted, as H. G. Wells was to quip, a 'swarm of wildly exasperated human beings'.[11] Yet it was not until after the upheaval of the First World War that women, who had proved their mettle in the factories of the warring powers, were – in some major democracies at least – to win the vote. Gradually, but inexorably, the Enlightenment paradigm has worked its way through. In our generation, laws have been passed against discrimination on grounds of either race or sex, though notably the Equal Rights Amendment has yet to be ratified in the United States. We have started to speak of the rights of children, indeed of those of animals.

Well might it have been thought that 'God' would have had difficulty in surviving; an anachronism from another age. But the resilience of religion in the face of the onslaught of modernity has been remarkable; the forces of conservatism have been strong. The result, however, has inevitably been the siding of the church in large part with the forces of reaction. In his notorious *Syllabus of Errors* of 1864, Pius IX declared: 'If anyone says that the Roman Pontiff can, and ought to, reconcile himself to, and agree with, progress, liberalism and modern civilization, let him be anathema.'[12] Such an alignment on the part of the church has been in evidence in a row of Western European states. In France notably, throughout the nineteenth century and into the twentieth, the church sought to counter what the Revolution represented. It was a tussle fought out in every village in the Third Republic, the priest lined up against the school-master, the local representative of the state. With the breaking of the Dreyfus affair in 1898 the church, conservatism and antisemitism showed their true face. In Germany the Kirchentag, the national church assembly, held a day of thanksgiving for the defeat of the revolutionary stirrings of 1848.[13] In Britain religious bodies (together with coal mining!) are still today, uniquely, excluded from the provisions of the Sex Discrimination Act![14] Meanwhile the great atheists of the nineteenth and early twentieth centuries – Feuerbach, Marx, Nietzsche and Freud – have challenged humanity to abandon a God whom they held to be a projection of what man himself would be and to appropriate 'his' properties.

The import of the liberation of women, taking place within this wider scenario, has not always been reckoned with. Particularly is this the case in the sphere of religion, where its consequences are only just beginning to be felt. For within Western culture woman has represented that which is the 'other'. God has been conceived of as 'male'. Man has then been understood as in the image of God – witness Michelangelo's depiction of the creation, at the heart of Christendom, on the ceiling of the Sistine chapel. Yet at the same time man has placed himself in the 'female' position, humble, passive and obedient, in relation to the 'male' God. (Commensurately with this gendering of reality, it is a woman, the Virgin Mary, who has been held to epitomize, in herself and as representative of the church, what humanity should be in its relation to the 'male' God.) In relation to woman, however, man has constituted the upper term. Woman has thus been cast as the primordial 'other', in relation both to the male God and to men. Actual women have largely been left outside Western culture; present as its underside. When men took it upon themselves to become gods, to slay the father/monarch and, in the Enlightenment and what flowed from it, to constitute what has been called 'the regime of the brother',[15] they did not, as we have seen, admit women. In the nineteenth century, woman was, on the one hand, banished to be, as Engels dubbed her, 'the angel in the house'; on the other hand, the lowest rung in the hierarchy of a developing capitalist economy.

Western society has been hierarchical. In the case of the relation of men to women this has persisted into our age. Such an ordering of the world is, not least, built into our language. However, if feminism represents the self-realization of women and their recognition within society, so that woman ceases to perform the role of the 'other', then for the first time there will be no symbolic 'other'. When an ethic of equality reigns in theory, even if in practice much remains to be done, it becomes increasingly difficult to know what hold a God (conceived of as set hierarchically above humanity) can continue to have. The paradigm which gave rise to 'him', and which in turn 'he' consolidated, will have been overcome. For the very understanding of God which we have inherited was dependent upon an extrapolation of the human hierarchy into the realm of the divine. God was Lord, King, Judge, Father: a greater patriarch than the patriarchs at the top of human pyramids. Thus the loss of a primordial 'other', consequent upon the rise of feminism, represents the greatest unsettling of religion in four thousand years. If 'no bishop, no king', then we may say 'no patriarchy, no God'; or at least no God as God has been envisaged within Western society.

But of course Christianity has been canny. For it has not simply projected a transcendent God. Rather, it has spoken to a variety of male needs. Thus it postulates a revelation in which God becomes a man among human beings. Christianity is a religion of the Son and the Father, as Judaism was one of the sons in relation to their patriarchal God. It allows men to work through the son–father relation, so crucial, it would seem, to the male psyche. Indeed, through Christ, its representative, humanity is taken up to the Father. But women are again not fully included. For although women are theoretically part of that 'humanity' which is said to be taken on in the incarnation, this did not axiomatically result (and throughout the greater part of Christendom still has not resulted) in women being allowed to represent God to humanity. On the contrary, Christian culture has created the ideal of 'the feminine', as it appears through the male lens. The church – that in which men find themselves embraced in a greater whole – is held to be 'female'. Indeed God the Father has been conceived to be 'motherly'. This conceptual system, so I shall suggest, reflects male desire. We should note that within Christianity there is no symbolic place for articulate, self-actualizing woman, the equal of man.

We may conceptualize what is at stake in other words. In the jargon of the day, monotheism may be said to represent a totalization. God is supreme, one, transcendent, unified reality – all that Jacques Derrida denotes by talk of an attempt at absolute 'presence'. Such an exalted One must always create, in contradistinction to itself, that which is 'other' than itself. Bi-polarity is built into Western religion: humanity representing the 'other' and female pole in relation to the 'male' God. But men, while on the one hand casting themselves as the 'other', also aspire to be like or to join the One. Woman comes to be that which cannot be assimilated into oneness. Hence she has been held to represent that which belongs to the earth, or sexuality: all that is to be left behind in the bid to become spiritual and gain the likeness to God to which religion aspires. Thus monotheism itself may be said to have created the place which woman has occupied within Western religion. She is the 'supplement': that which is left outside, which cannot be incorporated. The only way forward is to break the paradigm open, so that its bi-polarity gives way to what we may call a heterogeneity, in which there is no longer that which is the One and consequently the 'other' to it.

Indeed, many feminists would claim that, although with the coming of the Enlightenment paradigm the particular hierarchy which the *ancien régime* represented was overcome, the Enlightenment does not itself express the heterogeneity which they desire. They would consider it no chance that woman has been so inadequately assimilated to the Enlightenment paradigm. While the *ancien régime* was vanquished, a system was perpetuated in which man was the norm and woman was other. It was the property of bourgeois males (before even the bodies of women) that was protected through the contractual society which arose out of Locke's notions of justice or Rousseau's proclamation of the general will. Far from being neutral – so much current feminist theory charges – the Enlightenment paradigm represented a contract between a narrow band of individuals with a view to protecting their interests.[16] Woman has until quite recently been considered in law to be part of male property! (The British government has just got round to changing income tax law so that married women are separately taxed!) The kernel of the Enlightenment paradigm was a particular conception of what it is to be a human self; that self was held to be self-contained and essentially aggressive, existing in competition with others. Such a depiction of the self, as placed in apposition to others, remains even in Hegel's insight that persons are constituted through their relations with others. His chosen example is that of the master/slave, wherein the two engage in a life-and-death struggle for recognition.[17]

Feminists are contending that this is a particular, and limited, way of understanding the individual. If we are selves through our relations – that insight passed into feminism through Simone de Beauvoir's application of Hegel's parable to man/woman relations – the current generation of feminists wish (as in some respects de Beauvoir did not)[18] a relational and not a monadic conception of the self. We must be clear, however, that the utopian society which feminists envisage, in which people are able to relate as whole persons, does not represent a going back behind the Enlightenment paradigm, but rather a progression beyond it. Women can ill afford to forego a rhetoric of rights: feminism is concerned for the full recognition of women as equally persons. But feminists hold that human beings must appropriate their affectivity, their concretion (which has been set aside in the disembodied male 'universalist' conception of justice and rights), then to enter into a world of equality as full persons. There is no longer to be an 'other', woman, who embodies the realm of the emotions, of the particular, set apart from the male world which represents the universal. Feminist women find themselves at the place where the world of egalitarianism and rights moves into something beyond modernism which allows of concretion and diversity. This shift from what modernism represents is equally apparent in the very different theoretical world of those feminists who, often against a background of 'object relations theory', believe that ethics involves a concern for particular others, rather than being cast exclusively in terms of an abstract justice.[19] We must needs bring together a recognition of the irreducible nature of what it is to be human and an appreciation of human diversity.

It would then be a misunderstanding to think that, in criticizing the Enlightenment paradigm, women are seeking to return to anything like the prior 'Aristotelian' notion of society. Women will never again be satisfied with a particular 'place' in a world which is normatively male. Yet (while women struggle to move beyond modernity), the church and Christianity are situated not at the interface of modernity and some kind of post-modernity, but rather at that between, on the one hand, the *ancien régime* with its 'Aristotelian' notion of society and, on the other, an Enlightened modernity. Thus, in Vatican II, the Catholic church finally thought it incumbent upon it to try to come to terms with the rights of women; well represented by the encyclical *Gaudium et Spes*. Yet that church still retains its rhetoric about the special place of

woman, revealed by the Creator. Woman is to be understood primarily
qua mother, while the Virgin is extolled. That is to say the church is still
playing with the male construct of 'woman', conforming to a male projection and satisfying male needs. While endorsing the struggle of
women for equal rights (what else can one do in the modern world?),
Paul VI in his encyclical *Octagesima Adveniens* warns against 'false
equality which would deny distinctions laid down by the Creator'.[20]
Protestantism, by and large, simply expects women to be men; or else,
equally, casts woman as wife and mother.

The epistemological basis upon which the organic, 'Aristotelian'/
Christian understanding of human relations was built was fatally undermined by the Enlightenment and the post-Enlightenment world.
Aristotle believed that an ordered, hierarchical society belonged to the
nature of things. Finite entities are held to be dependent upon the
infinite divine being, the world having a monarchical constitution, perceived in the hierarchical gradations of organic and inorganic, conscious
and inanimate beings. A notion of the good (or, within Christian
philosophy, God) forms the linchpin of the whole. In particular
Aristotle, notoriously, thought woman not another kind of (equal)
human being, but a misbegotten male. Within Christian thought, such
an understanding of the relation of woman to man was reinforced by a
literal reading of Genesis, taken up in the New Testament, according to
which woman was said to have been created from man and, subsequent
to the Fall, placed subordinate to him. One can imagine the shock – if
one believed such things – which the Darwinian discovery that women
and men alike are descended from the higher apes (in such a way that
neither could have preceded the other) represented. The reverberations
of the revolution in biology have still not fully worked their way
through at the level of theology.

Again, as we have said, Enlightenment epistemology ruled out the
kind of particularity upon which Christian doctrine rests. If history is a
causal nexus, then it becomes unthinkable that there could be any direct
intervention of God – other than in the form of 'miracle'. Moreover no
one age can be held to be closer to God than any other. By the
eighteenth century the cosmos had become too large for any such
particularity; hence the rise of deism with its abstract, impersonal God.
How should Christians continue to proclaim the uniqueness of Christ
in a world in which such uniqueness, according to the paradigm of
scientific understanding, had become impossible? Rather than God's
revelation being the apex of culture, christology becomes dislodged
from culture. Following Kierkegaard, Bonhoeffer (who at a later stage
in his career diagnosed a human coming-of-age), recognizing that
christology cannot be accommodated to the Enlightenment paradigm,

declared it to be true in the face of modern knowledge.[21] But for many people this disjuncture was to make christology simply untenable. As I shall argue, Christianity is left high and dry in an age in which the basic philosophical and scientific understandings upon which it was predicated and which are woven into it have departed.

Nor does the scientific advance beyond what we may call the Newtonian-Enlightenment paradigm which has taken place in the twentieth century aid Christian claims. Just as, in the realm of ethics, thinking has moved beyond (but not back behind) the Enlightenment, so also scientific understanding has moved forward, but essentially through (not back behind) the clockwork universe of Newtonian physics. Though there may be indeterminability at a sub-atomic level, quantum theory cannot be thought to allow gross violations of the causal nexus (such as a resurrection would represent) at the macro level. Again, a scenario in which time is understood as a dimension, moreover in which both space and time 'collapse' at the 'edge' of the universe, makes the idea of a God 'outside' space and 'before' time if anything less thinkable than in the Newtonian universe. Rather is it the case, both in nature subsequent to Darwin and within modern physics, that we have a paradigm which suggests the inter-relatedness of all. The static hierarchy of the ancient world within which Christianity came into being has been done away with. The anthropomorphic biblical God takes on the appearance of a fairy tale of primitive man. Meanwhile biblical criticism, developing amid the increasing sense of historicity present in the nineteenth century, enabled scholars to place the biblical texts within the social context of the ancient world. They must shed any absolutism.

Thus the question which confronts us is not whether we can revert to pre-Enlightenment sensibilities, recapturing the God of Christian history. That door, I suggest, is firmly shut. Rather, is it whether, on the far side of the Enlightenment and not ignoring it, there is a place for a concept of God in our modern or post-modern world. This is both an epistemological and an ethical question. Given an inter-related world of time and space and an expanding universe with 'boundaries' in black holes or ever-receding singularities,[22] how are we to envisage 'God'? If we are to speak of God, then God must surely be conceptualized as being part of the one whole. But that is a very novel notion of God; indeed it is to overthrow the notion of God as God has previously been conceived. Again, given that, since the Enlightenment, human beings have willed to come into their own and now women as well, indeed notably they, are speaking of self-actualization, there will be no place for a God in relation to whom humanity stands in a relation of heteronomy. God must be understood to complete what it is to be a human being and not be conceived as set over against humans. This again must make for a markedly different conception of 'God'.

The basis for theology (in an age in which the concept of a particular revelation is no longer viable) must surely be that experience of a dimension of reality which humans then name God. Human beings do seem to have a religious sensibility; indeed, women more so than men – there is reason to believe.[23] What are those experiences which, unaccountable for in any other way, constrain humans to speak of God? It is by no means necessary to conclude that, though the religious systems of the past may be untenable today, they did not represent an attempt to articulate an awareness of a dimension of reality of which we still feel compelled to speak. While Kant, in demythologizing Christian belief, concluded that it was a projection of human ethical intuitions, we should rather ask after the religious experience which human beings sought to convey. At the same time we must needs recognize that that experience was necessarily shaped by social paradigms which we no longer find acceptable. There is, we may think, no such thing as experience which is somehow pure and which humans as it were subsequently seek to put into words.

In this situation women have the advantage. At least feminist women are, relatively speaking, freer from the cultural norms whereby the male has priority and woman is cast as the 'other'. Women have less stake in the ancient myth. It is they who, through the development of feminist theory in recent decades, have moved in interesting ways beyond an 'Enlightenment' individuated notion of the self. Women may be thought more apt to understand human beings as relational selves. Again, it has been women who have recognized the importance of human self-realization, since this agenda is of personal moment in a world in which they have been seen as outsiders. Women will then wish to have an understanding of God which does not involve hierarchical presuppositions, so that God is not placed 'above' human beings – even metaphorically. A woman who has overthrown a heteronomous relation to the fathers will scarcely be of a mind to replace them with a 'father' God. Indeed, the very paradigms of inter-relationality which notably women are fostering may prove useful in the attempt to conceptualize what it is that God may be. God, so I believe, must be understood as a dimension of what is; moreover, as that through which we come to be most fully ourselves.

It may well be that we shall wish to move towards a new understanding of community. But that community can scarcely be held together by the hegemony of a Christian God, or a male order formed by those who see themselves as his vicars on earth. If we move away from the (false) individuality of the Enlightenment, it will not be, as

Alasdair MacIntyre would have it, through the coming of a new, Christian, Benedict.[24] Many women thinkers have applauded an 'Aristotelian' ethic of virtues, for it entails a concern for the character of the individual agent rather than simply rendering ethics in terms of impersonal universals. We shall, however, be obliged so to form our character in a context which lacks the overarching principle, called God, which Christendom took for granted. Reviewing MacIntyre, Martha Nussbaum writes:

> Pursuing the Aristotelian quest I have described without relying on piety is a difficult matter, but it was always likely that it would be, since human beings are on their own in a harsh and complex world. The difficulty, and the frequent loneliness, of such a search need not, and should not, cause us to long nostalgically for a unanimity that human life has never really had, or to sink for comfort into the embrace of an authority, whether religious or secular, that will give us order at the price of reason.[25]

It is within the heterogeneity of the modern world that we must pursue the spiritual quest, if such there is to be. No notion of God must be allowed to disrupt the centrality of human beings (understood together, one would hope, with the rest of the creation) to the picture. In this we cannot go back on the Enlightenment dethronement of God. Beyond autonomy (a falsely conceived autonomy which presupposes monadic selves) there must be a move to relationality and not back to a heteronomous relation to a Christian God.

It is in a setting no less radical than this that we must pursue the theological task. The old certainties are gone. Women are coming into their own. Scientific advances make old paradigms impossible. An ethic of equality reigns. But in such a world some of us would still give credence to a certain spirituality. We do not believe that all is lost, nor wish that the past could be retrieved. That past has profoundly harmed half the human race (and incidentally also the other half). Christianity has become untenable. But that does not necessarily entail a void. It may be that, free of the Christian myth, a new spirituality will flourish. Indeed, the very paradigms of relationality with which we are beginning to feel comfortable may allow us to capture something of that which is God. A religion based in human experience and in the will to conceive the world as having, at some profound level, sense and purpose, will precisely require for its conceptualization the kind of thinking in which feminists are engaged. It is with such a theological task that we must make a start.

I

Christian Particularity

At the outset of this book I shall, in this chapter, endeavour to explain what I mean when I say that Christianity cannot be true. The argument is that Christians must – by definition, if Christianity is to mean anything – claim that there has been a particularity in history; that is to say that there was a uniqueness present in the Christ event. However, at least since the eighteenth-century Enlightenment it has been known that there can be no such particularity. (I shall argue that modern physics does not make the Christian claim any more possible.) Thus Christian belief becomes a matter of faith. When, however, one considers what one is asked to have faith in as a Christian, it would be a rash person who would wager such faith – particularly in view of our understanding of the size of the universe today! I conclude, therefore, that Christian claims cannot stand.

My experience tells me that in the first instance I must clarify how I am employing the word 'particularity'. Let us call the way in which I intend the word in this chapter 'particularity' in the first sense of the word. I mean particularity as when one speaks of 'the scandal of particularity'; that is to say the claim that there has been a unique event, an interruption of the causal nexus of history and of nature. Since at least the Enlightenment we have been clear that there is a regularity to nature and to history. That is, in the first instance, to say that one event follows from another. Caesar crossed the Rubicon because he put one foot in front of the other; he did not suddenly find himself transported to the other side. History forms a causal nexus. Secondly, it is to say that events are one of a type. We can credit that Caesar crossed the Rubicon because crossing rivers is a category of things of which we know. Again, if we find a beetle, we take it for granted that this beetle is the offspring of its parents and that at least at this stage of the evolutionary process there will be other such beetles. One unique beetle does not appear from nowhere. Nature is a causal nexus.

To say that we know there to be a causal nexus (the question of what difference modern physics makes is a matter to which I shall come later)[1] is of course in no way to be a determinist. I mention this simply because in the past on occasion I have been misunderstood here.[2] For most people, even to raise this issue is presumably a red herring. Thus because Caesar had to put one foot in front of the other to cross the Rubicon, it in no way follows that he was not free to choose whether or not to do so! At least since the Enlightenment, as I have said, we have been clear that history and nature form a causal nexus. But the overwhelming majority of humankind have not in consequence been determinists! Personally I have yet to meet a determinist. That there is no particularity has nothing to do with determinism.

Now by definition Christians, I shall argue, must claim that there has been a particularity in history. Christians are those who believe that what we may call the Christ event is unique. Many Christians make such a claim in conjunction with the belief that there was a resurrection. But the claim that there has been an incarnation represents another possibility. Now to hold that there has been a physical resurrection is clearly to claim a particularity in the sense in which I am employing the term in this chapter. For there is, we may say, no class of things (resurrections) known to us of which this is simply another example. (Were we to change our minds and conclude that there have been many resurrections in history, then there would be nothing special about Jesus of Nazareth having been so raised, and the Christian claim that there was a unique occurrence at that point in history would fall.)

I shall have reason to discuss the question of miracles later in this book.[3] But let me already here, in order to clarify my point about particularity, discuss the implication for miracles. Thus if the Enlightenment understanding that there can be no intervention in the causal nexus is correct, it is impossible for water to be changed into wine. (Wine has carbon atoms and water does not, and carbon atoms do not appear from nowhere. Were it to be possible for the one liquid to become the other, then that must always be the case, whereupon we have no miracle.) On the other hand, to my mind there is no problem in claiming that Jesus was able to heal people, since I fully believe that 'miraculous' cures take place today. (That is to say there is no problem arising from a claim to particularity, as there are other examples: there may be a problem in understanding the relation between the mental and the physical such that spiritual healing is possible.) Indeed we may say that if it is the case that some persons who are deeply in tune with God have healing powers about them, then if one believes that Jesus was such a man, it is not surprising that he could heal. We may – as religious persons, for example – hold that much is possible that others do not credit. Indeed we may conclude that what 'Enlightenment man' has held to be possible has been excessively narrow. But whatever is possible must always and everywhere have been the case.

Before leaving this discussion of particularity, let me compare this use of the term with the more common use, in order once more to clarify the sense in which I am employing it in this chapter. Thus Christians will sometimes comment that what they value about their religion is its 'particularity', meaning by this that they value a religion which focusses on the life of this particular man, Jesus of Nazareth. They like the fact that his teaching was so concrete, that he told parables which relate to particular life situations; moreover that Christianity is involved with a particular history, that Jesus was crucified 'under Pontius Pilate'. These things are examples of particularity in what we may call a second sense. They in no way constitute a break in the causal nexus and do not involve a claim that a unique event has taken place in history. Now we may say this. If there has been a particularity in the first sense, i.e. the Christ event was unique (for example, there was a resurrection), then the religion to which such a unique event gives rise will also have about it a particularity in the second sense. People will look back to that particular segment of history, not only to the claimed resurrection, but also for example to the parables which this man told and the story of his life. It indeed causes problems for me, as a feminist, that Christianity has a particularity in this second sense: I shall consider that in the next chapter. But in naming this chapter 'Christian Particularity' I am wishing to consider the Christian claim to particularity in the first sense. I am considering questions of truth, not of ethics.[4]

It may well be the case that one appreciates particularity in this second sense in one's religion, while being unable to credit (as a post-Enlightenment person) that there could be a particularity in the first sense. Thus in the final chapter I consider the theme of 'attention'; to speak of attending to others as a spiritual locus is evidently to value particularity in the second sense. I by no means want an 'abstract' religion (as some people claim I do). Again, if at a Quaker meeting someone conjures up a particular image ('When we were in Africa a black woman who worked for us made a skirt which was a veritable patchwork quilt of all the spare pieces of material which came her way . . .'), it may be far more effective than were she to make some general statement about God. Particularity in this sense, as in the case of Jesus's teaching in his parables, may well be thought to be how we commonly make ethical and spiritual progress. But one can value particularity in this sense, while denying, as a post-Enlightenment person, that there could be particularity in the first sense.

Having, I trust, now clarified what I intend when I speak about the Christian claim to particularity in this chapter, I shall proceed to structure the rest of it as follows. In the first place I shall define what I mean by Christianity. I shall want to give as broad a definition as possible, while insisting that the term must actually connote something. In order to illustrate the breadth of my definition I shall consider the christologies of two theologians, Friedrich Schleiermacher and Rudolf Bultmann, who may be thought to have been the greatest liberal theologian of the nineteenth century and the greatest radical theologian of the twentieth century respectively. Both attempt to find ways of speaking of a uniqueness (or particularity) which, I shall have insisted, indeed belongs to the definition of Christianity. I shall argue that neither succeeds. Secondly, I shall turn to a detailed discussion of the fact that there can be no uniqueness of the kind that Christians must necessarily claim; and that consequently Christian claims must be a matter of faith. In conjunction with this discussion I shall expound Søren Kierkegaard's *Philosophical Fragments*. It was Kierkegaard who, in the wake of the Enlightenment, was the first to draw this conclusion. I shall argue that in this respect nothing has essentially changed with the advance of human knowledge since his day. Thirdly, to illustrate my theme further, I shall turn to the two extreme positions which Christian theologians have taken in the twentieth century in response to the predicament with which christology is faced. As my example of a radical conservative theology, I shall take Dietrich Bonhoeffer's christology lectures, and as my example of a minimalist christology the thought of some Anglo-Saxon, mostly British, Anglican, thinkers. Fourthly and finally I shall consider the question of historical evidence for a resurrection and so for particularity.

I commence then with the question of the bounds of what may legitimately be called Christian. I have already said that I want to give as broad a definition of Christianity as possible. Christians are surely those who believe 'the Christ event' to have been in some way unique. It should be noted that – unlike what some criticisms have claimed[5] – I have never said that Christians are those who believe *Jesus* to have been unique. To think Jesus unique would be to have a god. It would be equivalent to the claim that there was a single beetle. Christians have never made a claim to particularity in that sense, as though Jesus were a unique example of a species. Christian orthodoxy has always been that Jesus was a full human being like the rest of us. Classically (following the Chalcedonian definition of faith in 451), Christians have expressed the uniqueness in which they have believed by saying that the second 'person' of a triune God has both a full human and also a divine nature. These two natures are held to be conjoined in one 'person' or self-subsisting entity, the second 'person' of the Trinity. (The term 'person' here should not be confused with our use of the term meaning human being.)

It should be noted that I am not in any way restricting the definition of Christianity to Chalcedonian orthodoxy. It is clear that Christians have found that uniqueness to consist in different things and expressed it in different ways in one or another period of Christian history or tradition. Thus the earliest Christian statement of faith which we have is the use of the word ICHTHUS. The word is an acronym in Greek, compiled from the first letters of the Greek words for 'Jesus Christ God's Son Saviour', the word so created being – appropriately enough for those who understood themselves as 'fishers of men' – in Greek, 'fish'. Now those who made such a claim for Jesus (that he was God's Son and Saviour) scarcely made such a claim for any other! Again, since the Enlightenment, as the Chalcedonian, metaphysical way of expressing uniqueness (two natures in one 'person') has become suspect, Christian theologians have attempted to find other ways of speaking of uniqueness. We should note that (commensurately with my definition) they have in fact seen it as incumbent upon them to find some way of speaking of uniqueness if they were to be Christian. (That some recent theologians appear to depart from this is a matter I shall consider later.)

I emphasize these things because, despite the care which I thought I had taken in expressing myself, I have sometimes been thought to have a narrow or conservative definition of Christianity. (It is then said that, given that I have such a conservative definition of Christianity, no wonder I dismiss it as untrue!) Not a bit of it! I have always held that Christians are those who believe in a uniqueness, however that uniqueness may have been expressed. I am fully aware (and indeed say in *Theology and Feminism*) that that uniqueness has by no means always been expressed in terms of Chalcedonian orthodoxy.[6] (What I have sometimes said, which could be confusing, is that Christians are those who believe in the 'uniqueness of Jesus as the Christ'. Clearly such a definition is inadequate if 'the Christ' is understood simply to be equivalent to the original Jewish 'messiah', for the Jews did not think that the messiah who was to come would be unique in the sense in which we are discussing the Christian claim to particularity in this chapter. But such a definition of what it is to be Christian fails through not being restrictive enough, not through being too narrow! Since misunderstanding could arise on this score, I have more recently taken to saying that Christians are those who believe that there was a uniqueness in conjunction with 'the Christ event'.) Thus what I am ruling out, as not being a Christian position, is the belief that Jesus was a very fine man, deeply in tune with God, and no more than that.

Christians normally claim a uniqueness for the Christ event in conjunction with a claim about either an incarnation, a resurrection, or both. It is interesting that the focus of the claim has differed in different ages. During the patristic period the claim to uniqueness was based on a consideration of the nature of Christ's 'person', and thus involved incarnation. However, one would think that the most natural way for Christians to claim a uniqueness would be in conjunction with a resurrection. As we shall see, a theologian like Bultmann bases his thinking entirely on there having been a 'resurrection' (in his case we must put the word in inverted commas), avoiding all speculation as to the nature of Christ's 'person'. But other modern, post-Enlightenment christologies, as in the patristic period, have concentrated on the nature of Christ's 'person'; though it must be said that in the case of Schleiermacher and of much modern British christology which I shall be considering there has been an attempt to speak of the human Jesus's God-consciousness, thus avoiding metaphysical claims about the nature of his 'person'.

I shall therefore make a preliminary excursus into christology through a consideration of the positions of Schleiermacher and of Bultmann. I do this in the first place in order to underline the fact that I in no way hold a restrictive definition as to what is validly Christian, as though I were to restrict the definition to Chalcedonian orthodoxy. Moreover, I choose these two thinkers since, if it is possible to find a way to speak of the uniqueness of the Christ event in the modern world, one might think that one of these men would have succeeded. However, I must conclude that, ingenious as their respective attempts to speak of uniqueness in a way which is compatible with the modern world may be, they must each be judged to have failed. The question is then raised in the starkest form as to whether Christianity can be held to be possible, other than through making a leap of faith. (Indeed Bultmann's way of speaking in particular must necessarily involve faith.) The Christian claim cannot be made to fit with what, since the Enlightenment at least, we have known about the nature of the world.

Taking these two men in chronological order, I first consider Schleiermacher.[7] His was the first great attempt, after the Enlightenment and (pretty much) taking the modern world for granted, to find a way to be a Christian theologian. Schooled as he was in Enlightenment thinking and participating in the world of Romanticism in the early nineteenth century, Schleiermacher had largely gained a sense of what had become obscure in earlier ages: namely that Jesus was fully a human being like us. An indication of this is that Schleiermacher was one of the first to attempt to write a 'life' of Jesus. That Jesus was fully human is, of course, no more than simply Christian orthodoxy and should always have been recognized. There is, then, something of importance to note here; namely that at the beginning of modernity the sense of what it is to be a human being, with an individual subjectivity and consciousness, underwent a subtle change. It was this that caused the crisis for christology. It has always been a question for Christians how two natures, human and divine, could be conjoined in one 'person'. In the fourth century, Apollinarius had held that they could not, in consequence concluding that Jesus's human *nous* or mind was replaced by divinity – for which conclusion he was condemned as a heretic. Later there was a parallel controversy as to how two wills could exist side by side within one 'person'. Nevertheless, it was in the modern age, with the sense of what it is to be a human being which developed after the Enlightenment and Romanticism, that the crisis assumed new proportions. When people attained to a different sense of what it is to be a human person, it became difficult to conceive how this human could somehow be conjoined, in one 'person', with a second and divine nature.[8]

In attempting to find a way to speak of Christ's uniqueness – and so to have a christology – Schleiermacher avoided the earlier abstract and metaphysical statements as to the nature of Christ's 'person'. It is in this that his novelty lies. What interests Schleiermacher is the human Jesus's God-awareness or God-consciousness. (Indeed, as I shall discuss in Chapter VI, before he ever introduces the person of Christ, Schleiermacher's theology takes as its starting point the claim that there is a general human awareness of God.) Schleiermacher was living at a time when biblical criticism was in its infancy. He believed (and it is important to realize this in forming an estimate of his christology) that the middle chapters of John's Gospel, in which Jesus speaks of his relation to his 'Father', came pretty much verbatim from the lips of the human Jesus. Thus those chapters, he thought, tell us of Jesus's consciousness of the 'Father'. We now of course know that it is quite unlikely that the Fourth Gospel was written by the beloved disciple, but was of a much later date. We have, then, no such immediate access as Schleiermacher assumed to Jesus's consciousness.[9]

Schleiermacher's starting point is (as I have said) a claim that there is a general human awareness, or intuition, of that which he names God. But Schleiermacher knows full well that if he is to write a Christian theology, he must find a way of speaking of the Christ event as unique or, in his vocabulary, of our redemption being through Christ. Given such a general human awareness of God and the understanding of Jesus as a full human being, how then is Schleiermacher to speak of the uniqueness of Jesus as the Christ?[10] What he says – and it is an ingenious attempt at a christology – is that Jesus has an *Urbildlichkeit* and a *Vorbildlichkeit*; that is to say, respectively, an 'arche-typicality' and 'exemplarity'.[11] Jesus, for Schleiermacher, is a kind of 'second Adam', an ideal man who instantiates what we also could be, thus providing an example for us. But we are forced to ask: is there or is there not a uniqueness here? Schleiermacher blurs that issue. He tacks close to the wind, trying to speak of uniqueness while yet retaining Christ's full humanity. Thus he says of Jesus that he had an unclouded awareness of God. But is Christ's God-consciousness different *in kind* from ours or not? It would seem that human beings, – if they are fully and simply human – do not have an unclouded God-awareness!

The issue as to whether Schleiermacher's attempt at a christology succeeds is not straightforward. For traditionally it has been held that it cannot pertain to the *definition* of a human being that human beings sin – in Schleiermacher's terms, that humans have a clouded God-consciousness. Christians have always maintained that the fact that Jesus was (so they held) sinless did not of itself make him other than fully human. This, for example, was the Cappadocians' argument against Apollinarius' belief that in Christ's case divinity had been substituted for a human mind so that he might be sinless. As the New Testament would have it of Christ, he was 'tempted like as we are, yet without sin'.[12] Again, were it the case that human beings necessarily sin, then we could not be held responsible for sinning. Nevertheless we must surely maintain that it is not in the nature of human beings as we know them to have an unopaque God-consciousness. We may not allow Schleiermacher both to have his cake and eat it.

I turn next to Bultmann's very different, but equally post-Enlightenment, attempt at a christology.[13] Bultmann's endeavour is so impressive precisely because he in no way compromises the fact that, as he knows full well, nature and history are a causal nexus, an interconnected whole, and there are no unique examples or interventions. Bultmann is a modern man. It would appear that it is axiomatic for him that there could be no physical resurrection of a type which would break the laws of nature, a one-off event, unique of its kind. Certainly he never adduces any such thing. Nor, as I have mentioned, does he become embroiled in metaphysical speculation about the nature of Christ's 'person', which one suspects would be uncongenial to him both as a New Testament scholar and as an existentialist.

How, then, is Bultmann to find a way of attributing uniqueness to the Christ event? He, too, is quite clear that he must do this if he is to remain within the bounds of Christianity. What Bultmann does – and if I am none too clear here it is because Bultmann himself is none too clear – is to postulate that there are two spheres to reality, two kinds of 'history'. These he names *Historie* and *Geschichte*. By *Historie* Bultmann intends the normal causal sequence of events (such that there could be no one-off, unique, events). And by *Geschichte* he means – what? A kind of supra-history; or perhaps a realm of meaning. Given these definitions, Bultmann can then argue as follows. The cross of Jesus was of course a normal historical event in the realm of *Historie*.

(Crucifixion was a way in which the Romans killed their victims.) But a resurrection cannot be a historical event in the sense of being part of *Historie* (there is no class of things in our world called 'resurrections'). The resurrection, so Bultmann maintains, belongs to another realm, that of *Geschichte*. If we can swallow this, we acquire the necessary uniqueness. For the resurrection can then be said to be the resurrection of *this* particular man who died on the cross, lending a uniqueness to him in the realm of *Historie*.

The problem, of course, lies in the interface between the realm of *Historie* and that of *Geschichte*. There can clearly be no continuity between them. *Historie* is the normal historical sequence of events (which does not allow of resurrections). Bultmann thus speaks of the resurrection as being of another realm, an 'eschatological' event which breaks into our world. It is not of our world (it cannot be part of *Historie*) and yet somehow it takes place in our world (whatever that could mean). It follows that the resurrection could never be proved and the relation to it must be one of faith. But the fact that it requires faith, it must be realized, makes the resurrection what it is for Bultmann. Were it simply to be an event in our world, one of a class of things, resurrections, there would be nothing remarkable about it. It is because it belongs to the realm of *Geschichte* and breaks into our world that it is what it is, world-shattering. Christians who ask whether Bultmann 'really believes' the resurrection, meaning by this a grossly physical event which is part of *Historie*, are asking not only for an event which Bultmann well realizes could not exist, but for one which could not have the significance that the resurrection has for him.

One may well question, however, as I should wish to: why should one credit the existence of this other realm, *Geschichte*? Of course there is a realm of meaning and interpretation in our world. Again, there is no problem in saying that the earliest Christians clearly believed that whatever it was that they called the 'resurrection' was revolutionary. But if it is the case that they believed that something had happened which was other than a normal historical event (in the realm of *Historie*), then I for one should simply want to say that they were mistaken. There can be – so I should want to maintain – nothing other than what Bultmann names *Historie*. Nor do I find, as Bultmann believes, that 'the preaching about the death and resurrection of Jesus of Nazareth' has the effect of delivering me into authentic living. But then, as Bultmann says, the relation to the resurrection is necessarily one of faith, not knowledge. We could only be speaking of knowledge had we to do with something in the realm of *Historie*. I do not, then, think Bultmann to have found a way, compatible with all else that we know about the nature of the world, of speaking of the Christ event as unique.

I return once more and by way of summary to the question as to the bounds of what may legitimately be called Christian. Christians are those who, in whatever way they may speak of uniqueness (and they have done so in various ways), find themselves compelled to speak of the Christ event as having had such a uniqueness. Other than define Christianity more narrowly (for example, by limiting the definition to Chalcedonian orthodoxy), which I find no reason to do, it seems to me that this is the only definition of Christianity which there could be. What cannot (as I have said) be held to be a Christian position, if one is not to muddle terms, is the belief (simply) that Jesus was a very fine person who was deeply in tune with God. To hold that Jesus was deeply in tune with God is indeed a theistic position, but if no more than that is being said, it is not a Christian position. The belief that Jesus was a great teacher and that is the end of it is not even a theistic position. An atheist might well hold this. It is also, as a matter of historical fact, the case that until very recently Christians have taken it for granted that, however they might express it, to be true to their faith they must claim a uniqueness in conjunction with the Christ-event.

Thus far I have given a definition of what I believe to be the bounds of Christianity. Furthermore, I have suggested that two modern (post-Enlightenment) attempts to find a way of speaking of that necessary uniqueness which Christians must claim in fact fail. Moreover, I chose to consider Schleiermacher and Bultmann because – as the greatest liberal theologian of the nineteenth century and radical theologian of the twentieth century respectively – they might have been thought to have made the most promising attempts. If, however, readers are to be convinced that every avenue has been explored, it will be necessary to consider theoretically, on an *a priori* basis, why such attempts must fail. I shall therefore proceed to expound Kierkegaard's consideration of the situation in which Christianity is placed in the post-Enlightenment age. Kierkegaard concludes that the 'truth' of Christianity which Christians acknowledge can in no way be made to fit with the knowledge that we possess. Consequently the relation to Christian claims must be one of faith. In the course of my discussion I shall also raise and consider issues which have come on the scene since Kierkegaard wrote; this is, of course, necessary if one wishes, as I do, to maintain that nothing has changed in regard to the rightness of Kierkegaard's conclusion.

Kierkegaard's *Philosophical Fragments*,[14] written in the wake of the Enlightenment and more immediately in response to Hegel's attempt to synthesize the claims of Christianity with modern knowledge, is, I think, the clearest exposition which there has been of why Christian claims cannot be made to fit with human knowledge and cannot be arrived at through reason. Kierkegaard recognizes what the Enlightenment means for Christianity. He responds, not as had Schleiermacher by attempting to find a way of speaking of uniqueness which is compatible with that which otherwise human beings know to be the case, but by drawing attention to the clash. The acknowledgment of the 'truth' of Christianity becomes a matter of faith and is not to be attained to through reason. Kierkegaard's claim that the 'truth' of Christianity must be related to in faith is, moreover, important because it forms the background to much twentieth-century theology, whether that of Barth, Bultmann or Bonhoeffer (which, in the case of the latter two, I consider in this chapter).

In his book Kierkegaard sets up 'Socrates' against Hegel (the enemy who finds no mention by name). For 'Socrates' we can simply read knowledge as it is accessible to humans; the way the world is apart from any talk of revelation. 'Socrates' here stands for the Enlightenment, or for modern knowledge (other, that is, than the Hegelian attempt, through the mechanism of the unfolding of *Geist*, spirit or mind, in history, to synthesize Christian claims with all else that is the case, which Kierkegaard is disputing). That Kierkegaard chooses Socrates as a figure to set against Hegel may not, in the event, be wholly helpful if it has the effect of obscuring the fact that what is being said is that Christianity cannot fit into modern knowledge. For 'Socratic truth' is commonly held to be simply that truth which can be elicited (as in Plato's discussion in the *Meno*, where Socrates demonstrates that the slave boy knows innately the truths of geometry); whereas much modern knowledge has of course been acquired by empirical observation. Moreover, as has become patently obvious since Darwin, but was only beginning to be apparent in 1844 when Kierkegaard published his book, that in which the causal nexus of nature consists at any one point unfolds over time. Kierkegaard speaks neither of what is empirically the case, nor of the fact that the causal nexus is slowly changing over time. However, there is no problem in what Kierkegaard calls truth 'A', Socratic truth, encompassing these things. 'A' is all that is the case apart from the claims of Christianity. 'A' is truth which, potentially at least, is available to all people in all times and places. It is truth which is intrinsic to the world, given with all that is.

Having thus described the nature of human knowledge under 'A', Kierkegaard proceeds to pose the question on which his book hinges. How would things have to be for them to be otherwise; for that paradigm of truth which he has named 'A' to be escaped?[15] The answer will be readily apparent. There would have to be a revelation; something, that is to say, would have to be 'given' to humanity which was not intrinsic in the nature of things, capable, potentially at least, of being discovered. He names the concept of such a truth 'B'. (Kierkegaard does not, in *Philosophical Fragments*, commit himself to the existence of such a truth; he is simply considering theoretically what would have to be the case.) It follows, furthermore, that there would have to be a moment at which this knowledge was given to humankind; so that whereas previously humanity was devoid of it, now it was present. Indeed Kierkegaard says – and I think that his logic is not fully watertight in taking this additional step – that if we are not to be speaking of a truth which is intrinsic to the nature of things (and so are not to be drawn back into 'A'), then we must say of truth 'B' that it cannot simply be that a person brings this truth to humanity (as though that truth could be one among others), but that that person must be, in himself, 'the Truth'. Truth 'B' is thus not to be had apart from the teacher (or should we write Teacher?) who *is* the Truth; unlike the truth as to the sum of the angles of a triangle which exists as truth quite apart from Socrates. To be separated from this Teacher is then to be in sin, whereas, in the case of 'A', not to know the truth is mere ignorance.

Now Kierkegaard (who has in mind the Chalcedonian definition of faith and thus orthodox Christianity) knows full well that it is not that Christians hold that Jesus was a god walking around on earth, so that on meeting him one would immediately be aware that something strange was afoot. It is no part of the Christian claim that the causal nexus is broken in the sense of there being one unique example of what appears to be a human being but is actually a god. (As Kierkegaard elsewhere remarks – commenting on those who suppose that it is in such a belief that Christian claims consist – as though God were to appear as a 'large green bird'.[16]) For God to appear as a peculiar man (a god), or a large green bird, would be paganism: it would be for one item in the world to be God, or a god. Jesus, however, as Christians indeed hold, was a human among humans.

How then should this man, a human being like others, alert his contemporaries to his uniqueness, that is to say, in Chalcedonian terms, that conjoined in one 'person' he has a second and divine nature? (For, says Kierkegaard, we cannot think that God should have such contempt for humans that he should come among them without divulging the truth of the matter.) What he will do, says Kierkegaard, is to perform some signs or miracles. A miracle can of course *prove* nothing; a miracle is not part of the causal nexus, so that something could be deduced from it. (The human temptation, as Kierkegaard comments, is to ask the conjurer to do the trick again; that is to say, people wish to understand how what has happened is part of the causal nexus, so to dismiss it as a miracle.) I think it important to remark here that Kierkegaard was living before the full onslaught of biblical criticism, so that he did not cast doubt on the historical veracity of the miracles, as we might well wish to. But then this book is simply a theoretical consideration as to what must necessarily be. Thus, irrespective of biblical scholarship, one may, in an act of faith, credit miracles; indeed Kierkegaard's point is precisely that this is the only way in which one could credit a miracle. Once he is alerted by the miracle, it is up to the individual whether he will 'believe' that this man is (also) God. Faith must always be such a leap. By the very nature of the case, that this human being has a second and divine nature is not something which could be proved. It is a claim to uniqueness: human beings as we know them are not conjoined in one 'person' with a second and divine nature.

Christianity, then, is advancing a claim which can in no way be part of the knowledge that we otherwise have (and which therefore, we may say, does not disrupt that knowledge). The Christian claim sits uneasily alongside human knowledge, incapable of being assimilated. Nor has faith anything to do with reason. The Christian claim relates to a revelation as to what is the case: a revelation for which human knowledge cannot prepare us. Thus in concluding his book, Kierkegaard gives us a 'Moral' in which he sums it up. To purport to make an 'advance' upon Socrates while remaining within the Socratic system (truth 'A') – that is to say to take the Enlightenment system (human knowledge) and then to try to expand it to allow for Christianity (as Hegel has done) – that at least is 'not Socratic'. (Better to stay with Socrates/ the Enlightenment/ human knowledge without distorting its nature.) The only way in which one could make an 'advance' upon Socrates/ the Enlightenment/ human knowledge is to claim something quite other, in a different sphere. Such is the claim of Christianity, which cannot be made to fit with what is otherwise the case. The Christian truth is not simply another datum which could somehow be absorbed into all else that is.

Indeed Kierkegaard thinks that the truth which Christianity proclaims flies in the face of reason, for that this is the God in time is a contradiction in terms. Hence Kierkegaard refers to this Truth, truth 'B', as the Paradox. We may put it in this way. God is not a human and a human is not God, or so one would think, for God is eternal and the human is in time. To say of this one 'person' or entity that he is both fully human and fully divine must be a paradox (at least as far as human reason is concerned). (That Kierkegaard may judge this paradox to become more 'comprehensible' to faith is an issue in Kierkegaard scholarship with which we need not concern ourselves here.) Whether such a claim must in fact constitute a paradox, as Kierkegaard supposes, is a matter on which I shall have some further remarks to make. But even if one concludes that it does not, it must be pointed out that this in no way affects Kierkegaard's argument. For in any case it is a truth which does not form part of knowledge and cannot be assimilated to it. It can only be related to in faith.

I shall now proceed to consider what I have found to be common misconstruals of what has been said. I shall also consider other objections which may be made, arising out of circumstances which have come about since Kierkegaard wrote, and which, I shall argue, are equally invalid. What I wish to maintain is the correctness of Kierkegaard's point as to the incommensurability of Christian claims, so-called Christian 'truth', with the rest of human knowledge or truth. (Incidentally this may be as good a point as any to respond to Christians who, coming out of what they call a post-structuralist context, remark that there is 'no such thing as truth', and thus that Kierkegaard's argument falls. If there is 'no such thing as truth', then neither does the Christian claim that Christ is 'the truth', or 'the Logos', hold! There can be no uniqueness.)

First, then, people will sometimes say (as they think, by way of objection) that much that is the case remains to be discovered. They think that this objection counters the claim that all human truth (apart, that is, from the claims of Christianity) is encompassed by what Kierkegaard has called 'A'. But that not everything which is the case has yet been discovered is, of course, quite beside the point. In previous ages human beings did not know of sub-atomic particles, let alone quantum effects. But there were always sub-atomic particles, and quantum theory, if true, describes what always was. No claim is being made that the whole of what is comprised by 'A' is known to human beings at any one time. The claim is simply that whatever is the case must be the case always and everywhere, even though it should have taken until the twentieth century (or beyond) for it to be discovered. This is quite different from the supposed 'truth' of Christianity, which, had there been no revelation, could never have been discovered. The Christian 'truth', if such it is, is not intrinsic in the nature of things waiting to be discovered, but must be given to humankind. To say then, as though this were an objection, that 'things keep on being discovered', or indeed that what is the case is quite different from what was at one time thought, constitutes a misunderstanding.

Secondly, it will be said that what I have called 'the causal nexus' is fundamentally open, so that new things can arise. Again this is, of course, the case; but it is mistaken to think that the fact that this is so helps Christian claims. To make such a comment is again to misunderstand what is being claimed to be the nature of 'A'. Let us put it this way. At one point dinosaurs roamed the earth. At that point in history there was consequently no problem in another dinosaur appearing, the offspring of its parents. What would not be possible would be for one, unique, dinosaur to appear on the earth today. As I have said, things exist within a causal nexus and are one of a type. For a single dinosaur to exist would be equivalent to the appearance of a large green bird (or a god who walked around on earth, or indeed a resurrection). No suggestion is being made that the causal nexus is in any way closed. On the contrary, since Darwin we have known that it is fundamentally open, fluid and developing all the time. Indeed, chaos theory suggests that we can in no way predict the path which a pendulum released between two magnets will follow, while the flap of a butterfly's wings may lead to a storm the other side of the earth. But that these things are the case does not allow us to think that there could be a one-off example of something (like a resurrection).

Thirdly, though, what of the fact that, as we now think, there is a randomness and indeterminacy at the sub-atomic level? Does not this perhaps make a resurrection conceivable? For some years now I have taken opportunities as they presented themselves to question scientists and philosophers of religion on this count. I am told that, incredible as it may seem, it is *conceivable* that the computer at which I write could be transported so that it was to be found outside in the hall; however, this would represent a quantum event of such magnitude as to make it realistically not worth considering. Now for there to be a resurrection would, equally, be an event of such a magnitude. It is not then that, in predicating my argument upon Kierkegaard's consideration, I have failed to take account of what we now think to be an indeterminacy built into nature. One can be perfectly cognizant of the fact that, as we think we have discovered to be the case, there is a randomness at the sub-atomic level, while insisting that this does not make a resurrection possible. (The fact that there is such an indeterminacy does not, of course, in itself constitute a rebuttal of the Enlightenment insight that nature remains constant: if there is indeterminacy at the sub-atomic level, then there always has been indeterminacy at the sub-atomic level.) Moreover, the randomness which we think to exist at the sub-atomic level normally equalizes out statistically at the macro level at which we live (and at which any resurrection would have to take place). But furthermore, in the case of a claim for a resurrection, there are additional problems. We cannot imagine what a resurrection would be. There are no such things as resurrections in our world. The idea of a resurrection constitutes a claim to particularity in quite a different sense from the movement of my computer through a quantum effect. If I so wished, I could perfectly well transport my computer into the hall. But in the case of a resurrection (understood in a physical sense as a coming back from the dead) we have no other examples: it would be a biological claim without precedent.

A further and fourth misunderstanding which I have already touched upon should also be countered here. It will be said by some that there are many things which we do not fully understand, for example extra-sensory perception. It will then further be claimed – as though this constituted an objection to my argument – that any 'narrow Enlightenment understanding' as to what is the case may well be quite inadequate. Indeed people before now have asked me how it is that I can believe that healing is possible through prayer and then proceed *a priori* to deny that there could be a resurrection. But the point is not – as I have discussed already – that we have fully determined what is possible. It may be that all kinds of things are possible which typically 'Enlightenment' thinking, or Bultmann, or many modern people, have failed to credit. All that is being claimed is that whatever is the case must be the case always and everywhere. What is being denied is that there could be a resurrection, or that a human could be conjoined in one 'person' with a second and divine nature, either of which would constitute a unique example, one which would not be one of a type.

Let me then summarize once more what is being claimed and what is not. It is not being claimed that we in any way know all that there is to be known; moreover that nature and history are not, as a causal nexus, constantly changing and unfolding; moreover that, at least at the sub-atomic level, there is not an indeterminacy (though this appears to balance out statistically at the macro level at which we live); nor, finally, that there is not much which may well be the case which we have thus far failed to explain. But that these things may be the case would not seem to help the proponents of a uniqueness such as that which Christians must necessarily claim. As I have said, for there to have been a resurrection, there would have to be a class of things, resurrections, of which this was an example. (And if there were such a class, then the resurrection of Jesus would not be unique and nothing could be deduced from it as to his uniqueness, the claim on which Christianity depends.) Of course it is not the case that Christians hold that Jesus *qua* human was unique. But there is no reason to think that this human being, and he alone, had a second and divine nature conjoined in one 'person' with his human nature; nor that he, and he alone, had a perfect God-consciousness (or however else one might wish to express a claim to uniqueness). I think we must hold that the Christian claim to uniqueness is incommensurate with what we know the world to be. Christian claims must rest on faith.

It may also, finally, be important to draw attention to the fact that it is not relevant to say (as I have heard it said) that Kierkegaard's depiction of Christianity is a farce. Christians, so it is said, look to the whole life of Christ and not simply to some intervention; besides which, the

claim that there has been a particularity in Christ is only to be understood within the whole context of the history of God's dealing with the
Jews. In the discussion in *Philosophical Fragments* which I have eluci-
dated, Kierkegaard is drawing attention to a single point, namely the
incompatibility of an incarnation with what otherwise we know to be
the case about the world. Whether he sufficiently describes the life of
Christ elsewhere in his writing is another issue; I would think it difficult
to argue that he does not. Again, it does not actually help a Christian
attempt to make Christianity commensurate with the rest of knowledge
to claim that incarnation can only be understood within the whole
context of salvation history. Either there has been a uniqueness such
as Christians claim or there has not. Whether the claim that God was
related to the Jewish people in a unique way can be said to constitute a
claim to uniqueness – such as that which Christians must necessarily
claim – is unclear. (I have suggested that it would be easier as a
Christian to stake one's claim to uniqueness on there having been a
resurrection than on God having had a unique relationship to the Jewish
people.) Such a claim would not constitute a breaking of the laws of
nature (as would a resurrection), nor could it be considered to be a
uniqueness such as that man and he alone had had a second and divine
nature. However, it is in some sense a claim that there has been a
uniqueness, in that the proposition is being denied that God is equally
related to and known through all of human history. (Inasmuch as in this
sense a claim to uniqueness is being made, it must be ruled out as impossible.) Nor can one arrive at a claim to uniqueness by as it were making
a run at it; as though the revelation of God was somehow concentrated
in this segment of history, and then supremely focussed in Christ.
Kierkegaard himself discusses this in another work. One can indeed
have a great and a yet greater man, so that, judging at least by his effect
on world history, Napoleon was an extraordinarily great man. But
to claim of a man that he has another and divine nature is to make a
qualitatively different claim.[17]

  I move on. There is, however, a different kind of claim which can be
made, which does not (as in the case of the previous objections) arise
out of a misunderstanding as to how the world is, such that Christian
claims are incompatible with it. It could be held – this is essentially
Kierkegaard's claim as to what truth 'B' would have to consist in – that
there is a breaking in of Truth. A Christian might then believe that the
incarnation is in some way to be compared to the creation of the
universe (though it should be noted that such a parallel need not be
drawn, it would be possible simply to hold that there had been a breaking in of a truth of a different order in the midst of history). Such a
Christian might claim that, in the incarnation, a 'new creation' is

present, in some way parallel to 'the Big Bang'. Indeed, fascinatingly, Kierkegaard himself in an 'Interlude' in *Philosophical Fragments* – how good that he places it in an 'Interlude' and does not suggest that the incarnation need of necessity parallel anything else – considers the case of the star 'coming into being'. In an age which did not know that energy can be converted into matter, this way of putting it forms a kind of parallel to that qualitative change in which an incarnation must consist. This is in any case – as Kierkegaard recognized – quite different from a claim that there could be a transmutation *within* the course of history, so that something qualitatively different, the God in time, could come into being (what Kierkegaard thinks to be the Hegelian claim).

Let me give some examples of Christians who argue in this way (and thus who are not necessarily confused about what is possible within history – other than in the case of such a claim). We should note that such a belief must necessarily be held *a priori*; it could not be held, of such an incarnation, that it is part and parcel of all else that is the case. The most that can be said is that it is not logically impossible that, if God could create the 'Big Bang', then there could be a second 'creation', or however the incarnation (or I suppose resurrection) is to be understood. Here are some examples of such an approach. Janet Martin Soskice writes:

> That God as Creator, eternally present to creation, might raise a man from the dead . . . does not seem to me to be an impossibility. It would not be 'intervention' because it would be of a piece with God's creative activity. We might not be able to comprehend how God could so act, but this does not eliminate the possibility. We cannot comprehend how something (the universe) could arise from nothing, literally nothing, at the Big Bang and yet most astrophysicists believe . . . that the universe did have such an origin.[18]

Again, and in parallel, Cardinal Newman asks, of miracles, whether they are really 'unlikely, supposing that there is a Power, external to the world, who can bring them about; supposing they are the only means by which He can reveal himself to those who need a revelation; supposing that He is likely to reveal himself; and He has a great end in doing so'.[19] Again, here is James Packer: 'Denial of the Resurrection can be made to seem reasonable only on *a priori* grounds – that is, by assuming, as rationalist-positivist historians do assume, that only parallel cases, real or imagined, within the system constitute explanation, and by ruling out in advance creative acts of God in his world.'[20] And again Michael Green comments: 'If we are reduced to a God who is supposed to be the source of our world but is too effete to become involved in it personally . . .'[21] and so forth.

Unlike the various escape routes which I have considered and blocked in the course of my argument, this line of reasoning of course holds water. If one's understanding of God (as mine is not) is that God created the universe and exists somehow apart from it, then it is not illogical to hold that, in what would constitute a unique intervention, God came to earth in the person of Jesus Christ. Before considering this claim, we should note what is being said and I am sure rightly. An incarnation, or a resurrection (in any case a unique event), is a happening of this kind of magnitude. It is incommensurate with nature and history as the causal nexus which we otherwise know. What does not make sense is to speak of the incarnation and resurrection as though they were rather remarkable events, but essentially on a continuum with all else that we know about the nature of the world. If there were to be an incarnation or a resurrection, then someone like me (who holds that all that there can possibly be is what Kierkegaard calls 'A') is simply wrong. It is not that a truth of type 'B', an incarnation or resurrection, could somehow be 'added' to the things which are possible under 'A'. As my teacher Arthur McGill rightly used to claim, either Christ is world-shattering or he is nothing.

So let us consider the claim that there has been a unique event, of the order which Christians must claim if Christianity were to be true. As we now know, the earth is not at the centre of the universe, as was thought at one time. Our sun is a star, one among millions, in fact part way out within one arm of a galaxy which we call the Milky Way. And as we are now discovering, galaxies themselves form clusters. Consider, then, the claim. We are being asked to believe, are we, to put it crudely, that God put in an appearance on planet earth? The mind boggles. Of course the so-called 'scandal of particularity' has been with us since at least the eighteenth century. Indeed, one might go much further back and comment that Christian claims were held by the Greeks to be 'foolishness',[22] though that was presumably quite as much on account of the fact that one who was a Galilean carpenter and had met with crucifixion could be believed to be the Son of God as on account of the fact that any human being could be held to have such significance. Nothing, it might be said, has essentially changed since the eighteenth century (or indeed since the early church).

That may be granted. It is indeed the case that, with our discovery as to what is now estimated to be the size of the universe, nothing, qualitatively, has altered. Nevertheless, it would seem reasonable to think that there comes a point when a change in our knowledge of the scale of things causes us to pass through a threshold. The sheer difference in size from what humans had always supposed to be the case has as a corollary that we must make a jump to another degree of improbability. Thus when human beings thought that Jerusalem was at the centre of the world – as the map which was found in Hereford Cathedral depicts – and that the world in turn stood at the centre of the universe, not surprisingly their mind-set allowed them to credit the uniqueness of the events which Christianity claims. By the end of the eighteenth century, a geocentric universe having given way to a heliocentric universe, it seemed unlikely. Hence the advent of talk of a 'scandal of particularity'. But to hold to the truth of Christianity in view of our present knowledge is to make a yet more far-fetched claim (in the sense that to hold the same thing in a different age is essentially to hold something different).

Moreover one must raise questions about the nature of the parallel which is being drawn, such that proponents of this way of thinking say that if God 'caused' the Big Bang, then 'he' could bring about a resurrection. This suggests that there was an event, the Big Bang, which God somehow caused. However, the Big Bang is scarcely the name for an event – in some way parallel to an incarnation or resurrection. The Big Bang is the name we give to a singularity which we cannot reach but must always approach. It is difficult to know what, then, it could mean to speak as though God somehow existed 'outside' the universe or 'before' the Big Bang – and so brought it about. Surely, as I shall suggest later, God must be understood as a dimension of the one reality which is? If a Christian really thinks that God could be spoken of as 'outside' and 'before', then there is a difference of theology (a difference in understanding as to what the term God could imply) between that person and myself which in turn leads to a different esti-mate as to whether christology is conceivable. But it may be that those who attempt to draw a parallel between the Big Bang and such unique events as a purported incarnation or resurrection are aware of the limitation of such a comparison?

What one must wish, however, is that those who have simply assumed that a unique event (such as an incarnation or resurrection must be) can somehow fit with the rest of reality would recognize that this is not the case. That is, one wishes that they would follow Kierkegaard's argument. One hopes that, upon recognizing what kind of an event such an incarnation or resurrection must be, considering its sheer unlikelihood, they would abandon their belief in it. Thus they would recognize that everything is (as I believe we must claim after the Enlightenment) one inter-related whole: what Kierkegaard names 'A'. One must conclude that Christianity cannot be true.

What, however, of the fact that some eminent scientists apparently think Christianity and modern science not incompatible? The eminent scientist most commonly mentioned in Britain in this connection is John

Polkinghorne, the former Cambridge professor of mathematical physics
turned priest and author of many books on science and religion. I shall
therefore consider Polkinghorne's position as well as I may in a short
compass. I shall also look at the work of Keith Ward, a philosopher of
religion much interested in the interface of science and theology. Now a
scientist (or a philosopher of religion) has as much right as anyone else
to take a leap of faith. In other words, one like Polkinghorne can say
that 'given the belief in this kind of a God' certain things might follow.
But what we must be looking for (and what I do not find) is a proof
that a resurrection or incarnation is not incompatible with how we
otherwise find the world to be. I have never seen such an argument
emanating from one who is informed about modern science.

I shall take two examples from Polkinghorne's writing, one relating
to resurrection and one to incarnation. Take, first, resurrection. In a
consideration of Christ's uniqueness, and thus precisely pertinent to our
present concern, Polkinghorne writes:

> Christianity claims that God was in Christ in a unique way. If that is
> true it is to be expected that unprecedented events might occur, for
> Jesus represents the presence of a new regime in the world. I believe
> that it is possible to form a coherent picture of God's activity in the
> world that embraces both the fact that in our experience dead men
> stay dead and also that God raised Jesus on Easter Day.[23]

This exactly illustrates my point. Polkinghorne argues from faith. Given
that God was in Christ in a unique way, it is hardly surprising that
unprecedented events might occur. Consequently he believes God's
activity in the world to be twofold: a uniformity (dead men stay dead)
and the possibility of a particular event (Jesus was raised). However, so
far this is not to have shown that the peculiar event fits with the world
as we know it.

So then we continue. Can an argument be produced which allows
such an extraordinary event as a resurrection to be commensurate with
what we otherwise know? Leading up to the quotation which I give,
Polkinghorne has attempted this. When – so he tells us – certain metals
are cooled below a critical temperature, they are found to enter a
different and unexpected state: they become superconductors. Polkinghorne comments:

> When we change from one regime to another (from conduction
> to superconductivity) radically different results can follow (the
> resistance vanishes). Changing circumstance can lead to totally
> unexpected effects.[24]

Fair enough. But it can hardly be said that this helps us in the case of a resurrection! When a certain metal is cooled to this temperature it behaves in an unexpected way. But presumably it always does so when cooled to this temperature. The experiment can be repeated: it is one of the facts of our universe. However, we have no class of things, resurrections, which happen time and again under certain circumstances. Moreover it must be said that, although the fact that metals become superconductors might not have been expected (what is the case is more complex than we had imagined), there is no sense in which this discovery is discontinuous with all else that we know. But for a dead man to rise would be biologically unthinkable.

Consider, secondly, a discussion of incarnation in recent writing of Polkinghorne's. He writes:

> No one can deny that human solidarity in Christ and true divine presence in the man Jesus are extremely difficult and mysterious concepts which run counter to contemporary habits of thought. Yet, we have learnt from science that common sense is not the measure of everything. The unpicturable quantum world can only be understood if we are willing to accept the counterintuitive concepts which correspond to its actual nature. It would scarcely be surprising if encounter with divine reality turned out to demand its own conceptual framework also.[25]

Look again at the structure of this argument. If there is a 'divine reality' of the type that Polkinghorne surmises (that is to say, starting 'from above', from faith) then it would be 'scarcely surprising' if it turned out to demand its own conceptual framework. In other words Polkinghorne does not, thus far, attempt to argue 'from below' that these unexpected events are commensurate with what we otherwise know. So then what is his argument 'from below'? The idea of God being present in Christ is extremely mysterious; the quantum world is likewise 'counter-intuitive'. But to suggest that these two are somehow parallel, that quantum physics is parallel to the idea of a unique incarnation of God in one person, is nonsense. Quantum physics, however counter-intuitive, is something about which scientists have become convinced, through many experiments which can be repeated. It has practical effects in our world. Again, the quantum world has some kind of an interface with the world of Newtonian physics, however far we still are from being able to bring these two together. No parallel exists. Nothing has been said which would allow the uniqueness which Christians must claim.

I turn next to the argument of the philosopher of religion Keith Ward in a recent work *Religion and Revelation*.[26] Ward tells us that 'if there are no other factors affecting a closed physical system, then its constituents will act in accordance with regular patterns of energy-interaction, which enable the universe to exist as a stable and predictable system'. Yes, clearly. He continues:

> But such patterns are modifiable in various ways when other physical factors, such as change of motion or gravitational field, interact with the system. Why should it not be the case that mental factors also modify the behaviour of energy-systems, in accordance with intelligible factors that are at present unknown to us?

And, in a footnote, Ward cites Polkinghorne, who remarks that 'the physical world participates in a wider noetic world'.[27] Again, I personally have no quarrel with this: in Chapter VI I consider the fact that I believe prayer to be powerful. But now Ward makes a quite different kind of move. He writes:

> One can plausibly conceive of God's intentions as modifying the patterns of behaviour that obtain in the physical universe. This will presumably not happen at random or in arbitrary ways. God will modify causal patterns only for a good reason . . . The whole system, including the patterns of regularity which normally obtain within it, depends at every moment for its existence upon God . . .[28]

Look what kind of an argument this is. It exactly parallels Polkinghorne's. As Ward says, given the kind of God which he believes to exist, God could plausibly modify the patterns of behaviour which otherwise exist! But this is scarcely an argument 'from below'. It does not show us that an event such as a resurrection or incarnation is commensurate with what we know about the nature of the world. We have already considered the fact both that quantum theory would not seem to allow of a resurrection and that a resurrection would not simply represent a large quantum effect.[29] Christianity is a matter of faith.

I must finally add what may be considered to be in the nature of a footnote to the foregoing discussion. In recent years effort has been expended by Christians in refuting the claim that it is a *logical contradiction* to hold that, in Christ, there was both a human and a divine nature.[30] I agree that it is an open question whether an incarnation would be a logical contradiction; and it forms no part of my argument that it does. My argument is that there could not be the *particularity* which an incarnation would constitute. On the question whether it would be a logical contradiction, the following brief comment may be made. The Dominican Herbert McCabe is surely correct in maintaining that it is not a contradiction in the sense that it would be a contradiction to say, of a certain animal, that it was both a human and a sheep; for a human and a sheep are two incompatible kinds of animal, whereas God is not one of a class of things of which a human is a mutually exclusive example.[31] Nevertheless it could still be argued (as Kierkegaard supposes and as Maurice Wiles responds to McCabe) that a contradiction is present, for (according to normal Christian definitions) God is uncreated, whereas a human is created and exists in time.[32] McCabe's point then only scores if one's definition of God allows that being God is not incompatible with what it is to be human; and it is precisely the possibility of that which is at issue.

My conclusion, then, is that the claim of particularity which Christians necessarily make cannot be allowed to stand. What I wish now to do, in order to clarify the argument of this chapter further, is to consider some twentieth-century christologies. I shall consider the two extremes of a 'high' and a 'low' christology. As an example of a 'high' christology, I shall take the work which I think the most impressive example, Dietrich Bonhoeffer's *Christology*.[33] The book which we have was compiled from his students' notes of lectures given in 1933 and published after his death. Bonhoeffer looks back to Kierkegaard and then gives a twist to Kierkegaard's position. In considering 'low' christology, I shall take some examples of modern British (basically Anglican) thought. One could well argue that since the Enlightenment Christians have been looking (in vain, as I think) for a way out of the impasse created for them by the modern recognition that there is no particularity. Schleiermacher and Kierkegaard represent the two alternative logical moves which one might make in the face of this dilemma. I am unclear that more recent christologies have made any significantly new suggestion as to a way forward, other than perhaps Bultmann's, which I have already discussed.

I commence with Bonhoeffer. Following Kierkegaard, Bonhoeffer postulates two kinds of truth. He calls his two truths (Kierkegaard's 'A' and 'B') the human 'Logos' and the 'Anti-Logos' who is Christ. As Kierkegaard also points out, though Bonhoeffer underlines it, the human Logos (the human mind) must fight against the possibility of a Logos which is Christ (which, as we have said, cannot possibly fit with all else that is). For Bonhoeffer, as also for Kierkegaard, before Christ one can only give way in faith. Nevertheless, there is a different emphasis in Bonhoeffer as compared with Kierkegaard. Kierkegaard prefaces his *Philosophical Fragments* with a quotation from Shakespeare, 'Better well hung than ill wed': that is to say, Christianity and human truth (Socrates) must be kept separate, not wed in an illicit union (Hegel's position as Kierkegaard conceives it). By contrast Bonhoeffer's lectures open with a quotation from Kierkegaard: 'Be silent, for that is the absolute'. That is to say, before the Truth which is

Christ, the human Logos can only be silent, having nothing to say.
Kierkegaard is an Enlightenment intellectual who always, I should want
to argue, gives human reason its due. At least at this stage of his career
and in this respect, Bonhoeffer is very much a 'dialectical' theologian
who holds revelation to have priority and humanity to be flawed.

To a greater extent even than is the case with most theology,
Bonhoeffer's christology lectures are not to be comprehended apart
from the circumstances in which they were given. As a young woman
undertaking a doctoral thesis on the Third Reich, I well remember
coming across an entry in an index of Hitler's papers in the Bundes-
archiv in Koblenz: 'Kirchliche Angelegenheiten: Evangelische Kirche'
(Church Affairs: Protestant Church). I ordered up the file. The second
or third item (subsequent to Hitler's advent to power at the end of
January 1933) was a letter from a chaplain and lecturer at the
University of Berlin, one Dietrich Bonhoeffer. He had written straight
to the Reichskanzlei (the Reich Chancellery) to complain about the
nuisance caused by Nazi students molesting other students in the
quadrangle. (Bonhoeffer would have been just on twenty-seven.) Soon
he was to be standing in solidarity with his friend Pastor Franz
Hildebrandt, who was under threat of dismissal from the increasingly
Nazified Protestant Church on account of being Jewish. In 1933
Bonhoeffer (who had spent a year in the Anglo-Saxon world at Union
Theological Seminary in New York) was almost alone among German
pastors in being that quick off the mark on what was a matter of
conscience. He was to lose his life.

It was against the backdrop of these circumstances that Bonhoeffer
gave the lectures of which we have the substance. The text may well be
read as a powerful theological response to National Socialism on the
part of one who had grasped its essence. Bonhoeffer takes up the
Zeitgeist – and reverses what is to be said. Instead of an absolute faith
in and allegiance to Hitler, he speaks of an absolute faith in and
allegiance to Christ. But note that there is the same (as I would think
dangerous and unjustified) jettisoning of all that the Enlightenment
represents – human reason, the liberal standards of university culture –
before allegiance (to Christ or Hitler) in an act of faith. Bonhoeffer
declares that, coming from outside, that Logos which is Christ seeks to
be at the centre (thereby disrupting human truth). Christ is thus the
secret, unacknowledged, centre of the universe. Confronted with this
claim, the human reason must either must deny him; or else give way in
a stance which resembles Thomas's 'My Lord and my God'.

Moving away from the particular historical context in which these
lectures were delivered, what should we say? Bonhoeffer's point is
surely correct. A revelation that Christ is God cannot peacefully co-exist

with human reason, neither disturbing the other, as though each truth could be placed in its own box, labelled respectively 'faith' and 'reason'. If there is a particularity, such as that 'Christ is the Truth' would represent, this must disrupt all that we thought we knew. Since the Enlightenment, or perhaps since the ancient Greeks, humans have pretended (if Bonhoeffer is right) that the human Logos was the measure of all things. Humans had thought that they had gained a certain control over their world; that knowledge was secure. If truth is a man, is this revelation, this Logos, then human truth must, as Bonhoeffer says, resist it, be cast in doubt, or give way in worship and discipleship. If Christians are correct, then the 'Enlightenment' presupposition that all that there is is what Kierkegaard names 'A' is profoundly mistaken. Such a particularity (if true) cannot represent just one more fact about the world. It takes the ground on which we thought we stood from under us. But for this very reason I should want to hold that such a claim to revelation cannot possibly be true.

What is interesting is that for me this is not simply an epistemological matter (I cannot credit that there could be anything other than that which Kierkegaard names 'A') but an ethical stance. I wish to stay – if one can put it in that way – with the dignity of human beings and the possibility of their attaining to truth. Any concept of God which I may wish to hold will need to be commensurate with the rest of truth. That is to say, I may hold a broader or deeper understanding of what is the case than whatever 'Enlightenment man' (whoever that mythical figure may be) has commonly thought. But I cannot conceive of a truth which should disrupt or deny what we know. In Kierkegaardian terms, God will be commensurate with and a deepening of what Kierkegaard names 'A'. Whatever I may mean by God, God must be everywhere and always available. There can be no particular revelation, no Truth 'outside' myself, or other than the world of which humans are a part. Were such a Truth to exist, as Bonhoeffer indeed says, one would have to orientate oneself towards it. Such a Truth must necessarily require a heteronomous relation to it on the part of the human. Christ disrupts my human Logos with the claim that he is 'the Truth' (in Bonhoeffer's terminology the Anti-Logos). In his later *The Cost of Discipleship* (in German *Nachfolge,* the one word connoting both 'discipleship' and 'consequences' – a title which Bonhoeffer took from the entry on Kierkegaard in an edition of the encyclopaedia *Die Religion in Geschichte und Gegenwart*[34]), Bonhoeffer considers what it means to cling to Christ. As a feminist I wish to remain centred in myself; or for humanity to remain centred in itself.

Furthermore, while hardly wishing to disparage the perspicacity and extraordinary courage of this young man (who was to die at a much younger age than mine now), I believe a Bonhoefferian theological stance politically mistaken. Of course I am clear as to why, in the circumstances of the Third Reich and given the lack of any viable liberal tradition in Germany, it seemed to Germans in the church who wished to mount some kind of resistance to the regime that they should do so on the ground of an allegiance to God. During the years of the so-called church struggle, Protestant Christians got to their feet to say the creed (as had not earlier been the custom). In a totalitarian state in which others are confessing their allegiance to Hitler, to declare 'I believe in God, the Father Almighty' is a political statement. Moreover I have to recognize that, in the German case, it was not the great universities, the liberal newspapers, the left-wing trade unions, or indeed the liberal Christians, who mounted any kind of resistance to the National Socialist creed when the chips were down. It was the conservative, Barthian, Confessing Church which did so, and that on theological grounds. Nevertheless, I should want to maintain that human rights can ultimately only be safeguarded through belief in human beings and in the liberal values which are a corollary of this belief. I do not wish to conform to a mind-set which only allows of a choice between allegiance to one Lord or to another, to God or to the devil. I have more faith in humanity's ability to stand on its own feet than such a stance represents. I am a feminist. I wish an ethical position in which I do not give over my being to any person or to any God who lies outside myself. Hence it is not simply that I do not believe there could be any truth other than Kierkegaard's 'A'. I also hope that there is none such.

I move on to what must be the other extreme in twentieth-century christology. A number of the most senior British scholars, mainly Anglican, have in recent years propounded christologies which one might call minimalist. I am thinking here of the work, notably, of John Robinson,[35] Geoffrey Lampe, John Hick, Maurice Wiles and John Macquarrie. None of these men could be said in the first instance to be 'liberation theologians'. It is not Jesus's message, Jesus's 'opting for the poor', which interests them. Rather, the concern which drives them is the need for an understanding of the nature of Christ which on the one hand can be held to be Christian and on the other is thinkable by modern men and women. That is to say, these theologians are concerned with precisely the question which interests us: whether a christology can be found which 'fits' all else that we know to be the case in a modern, post-Enlightenment age. A further – and more recent – concern is that Christians should take the claims of other world religions seriously. The extreme position towards which a member of this 'school' might veer would then be to hold that being a Christian entailed no more than standing within a certain tradition, any claim that the Christ-event had a uniqueness about it being dropped.

The theologians whom I mention may thus be said to stand within a tradition which emanates from Schleiermacher (whether they are familiar with his work or not). As I have suggested, it would seem that Kierkegaard represents one possible approach to christology in the face of modernity (and Bonhoeffer looks back to him), and Schleiermacher the opposite one. Schleiermacher, we recall, spoke of the God-consciousness of the human Jesus; it is this consciousness which singles him out. In similar fashion Geoffrey Lampe speaks of Jesus' perfection in terms of 'the completeness and unbrokenness of the communion' which he enjoyed with God. Lampe comments:

> In Jesus the incarnate presence of God evoked a full and constant response of the human spirit. This was not a different divine presence, but the same God the Spirit who moved and inspired other men, such as the prophets. It was not a different kind of human response, but it was total instead of partial.[36]

Here, likewise, is John Hick (a Presbyterian):

> So what I myself see when I try to peer back through the New Testament documents to the person who lies at a distance of some two generations behind them is a man, Jesus, whose immensely powerful God-consciousness made God, and God's demanding but liberating claim upon men and women, intensely and startlingly real . . . He was so transparently open to the divine presence that his life and teaching have a universal significance which can still help to guide our lives today.[37]

Jesus, we may say, made the perfect human response to the one whom he called 'Father'; he had an unopaque God-consciousness. Thus he attained to the highest to which a human can attain and forms an example for us.

But is this a christology? We return to the question which we considered in conjunction with Schleiermacher's position. Human beings are capable of responding to God (or so one may maintain as a theist). They may lead moral lives, indeed provide an example for others in their conduct and through their spirituality. How is Jesus of Nazareth to be differentiated from all other such good people: prophets, seers and saints? Is to hold such a 'christology' simply to maintain that, within the Christian tradition, Jesus of Nazareth is the one to whom we look as having been such a person? I repeat: how is this a christology? Further, one might make the following comment. Are we not back with a Jesus who reflects the culture of the men who write about him – the phenomenon to which Albert Schweitzer so pertinently drew attention at the beginning of this century?[38] Within such a christology we hear little of the prophet who disrupted the world around him, overturning the money-changers' tables!

It is not of course the case that these theologians are unaware of the implications of their position or the difficulties which it entails. Here, for example, is a consideration of the matter by John Macquarrie. Macquarrie comments: 'In Jesus Christ a new level of humanity has been reached.' He wishes to say that 'the difference between Christ and other human beings is one of degree, rather than of kind'. His Jesus is one who reaches up to God, and in whom God is present to humanity: 'In Jesus Christ we are confronted with both the deification of a man and the inhumanization (Incarnation) of God.' Jesus represents the vision of a humanity to which we are all capable of attaining: 'From where we are, we do not yet know what humanity is to be, but Christian faith points to Jesus Christ as the revelation of the fulfilment for which humanity is destined.'[39] What are we to say? Is this Jesus fully a human being or is he not? If he is (which is Christian orthodoxy), then what could it mean that 'a new level' of humanity has been reached? Does Macquarrie intend simply a quantitative difference? Are we simply speaking of God dwelling in Jesus, in the sense in which God dwells in each of us, though we may be more, or less, perfect? If so, why look to him in particular? But if Macquarrie intends a qualitative difference, then how is it that this man remains one of us? Humans are not perfect.

Part of the drive behind the desire for a 'low' christology (though, other than in the case of Hick and to some extent Macquarrie, it is not particularly noticeable in the authors whom I have mentioned thus far) is, as I have said, the impact which the presence of other world religions has made on this generation of theologians. If one is involved in ecumenical discussions, or simply lives in a First World inner city where today other religions are much in evidence, what is one to think of the Christian claim to particularity? Does one hold Jesus to be united in one 'person' with a second and divine nature, or in some other way to be distinguished from the founders of other world religions? It is this issue which exercises many of those who, for example, contributed to John Hick's *The Myth of Christian Uniqueness*.[40]

Here is the eminent Canadian professor of comparative religion, a Presbyterian in his background and a student of Islam, Wilfred Cantwell Smith, contributing to that volume.

No one . . . has ever argued that all religious forms are always equally effective; that God is equally successful every day in all His/Her/Its attempts to bring human beings into salvific relationship to

Himself/Herself/Itself . . . [The question is not] whether the figure of Christ has served as a form in which God has entered history and been active within it . . . Our concern is with whether this has been and is one form among others.

And Cantwell Smith concludes: 'I myself . . . am not able to think of any reason that one might reasonably have for denying that God has played in human history a role in and through the Qur'an, in the Muslim case, comparable to the role in the Christian case in and through Christ.' Thus he speaks of 'God's . . . activities over the course of human history'.[41] Such a stance must – one would have thought – cause fearful theodicy problems, as I shall later consider.[42] (How come that 'God's activities over the course of human history' have not included doing something for women? How come that all his prophets have apparently been men?) To stick with our present concern, however, if a reasonable definition of Christianity is that Christians believe the Christ event to have been unique, however that uniqueness may be expressed, there is presumably no way in which Cantwell Smith's position as here represented could be called a christology.[43]

The question as to what form christology can take if it is to be compatible with modern thought is one to which the Anglican patristic scholar Maurice Wiles has devoted much attention. Wiles asks whether there is any element in Christianity which, were it to be interpreted mythologically, would result in the religion ceasing to be Christianity. In a well-known article 'In What Sense is Christianity a "Historical" Religion?', Wiles concludes that there are no supposedly historical facts which, were they to be shown not actually to have taken place, would entail the jettisoning of Christianity. (Other than, presumably, were Jesus to be shown not to have lived?). Wiles writes as follows:

> Of course Christianity derives from certain past events. And the record of those events in scripture . . . continues to be of central importance to the religious life of the Christian church. But the precise way in which it has been understood to be important has changed down the ages . . .

Thus he concludes:

> Ought we not . . . to be saying something like this? 'Our faith emerges from and continues to relate itself to such and such a historical heritage. As Christians we should seek to understand that heritage as fully as we can. One of those forms of understanding is assessing what was the nature of the happenings through which Christianity came to birth, in so far as the evidence enables us to form a responsible historical judgement about them. What we discover by such

means is part of the raw material in the light of which our faith judgements have to be made.'[44]

In a further essay, contributed to the collection *The Myth of God Incarnate,* Wiles concludes that Christianity is not tied to an incarnation in anything other than a mythological sense.[45]

In response I must insist that if Christianity is called a 'historical' religion simply in the sense that Christians are part of a continuous history which reaches back to Jesus of Nazareth (a quite different sense from that in which I employ the term in the next chapter),[46] as though being Christian consisted in nothing more than siting oneself within a certain tradition, something essential has been lost. The decisive point about Christianity has always been (and surely always must be) that Christians believe there to have been a revelation in Christ. That in different ages Christians have spoken in different terms of the uniqueness which is the implication of such a revelation is certainly the case. But Christianity is not just 'historical' in the sense that historically it had its origin in the life, death and teaching of one particular man. Being Christian cannot be held to mean no more than being part of a particular community, like being English.

To continue. If one were to hold to Wiles' position, would one not be able to take whatever one wished from the Christian tradition, looking elsewhere for other insights? Wiles, I assume, would respond to such a suggestion as follows – and I quote him in an earlier essay:

'Why *this* story?' . . . It would be pertinent to point to the directness of the relation of Jesus to God in contrast to the mediatorial role of the person of Jesus himself in Augustine's and Francis' own understandings of their relationship with God. In other words the story of Jesus is not an arbitrarily chosen story; from a Christian standpoint, it is the story of that historical happening which did in fact create a new and effective realization of divine redemption at work in the lives of men, and which has remained the inspirational centre of the community of faith to which we belong from that day until now.[47]

Clearly this is a most interesting response. Nevertheless it begs the question. Is one saying – as it were bringing in a claim of particularity through the back door – that the reason why Jesus was confident in his unmediated relation to God, whereas others within the tradition have spoken of a relation mediated by Christ, is that Jesus of Nazareth was indeed the Son of God, in a sense in which this is not true of others; in other words that he was unique? We are back with the questions which Lampe's or indeed Schleiermacher's position raises: is the claim being made that Jesus of Nazareth was, in whatever way, qualitatively different from other human beings?

Suppose, however, that someone does not wish to hold to the ambiguous position which this quotation from Wiles represents, but simply wishes to say that her Christianity consists in the fact that she stands within a tradition the fount and source of which is Jesus Christ. That is to say – in a phrase which I find useful – she sees God through a 'Christ-shaped window', as opposed to one shaped, for example, by the Buddha. That is not, I must maintain, in itself a Christian position. A person who is not a Christian, while yet a theist, might wish to say that too! There is no reason why he should not acknowledge that, given that he grew up within the Western tradition, the shaping of what he understands God to be has to a considerable extent been influenced by Jesus of Nazareth's conception of God. It may well be contended that, simply as a matter of historical fact, within the Western tradition a new era in our understanding as to how God should be conceived of dates from Jesus. But holding that to be the case does not in itself make one a Christian.

I think, then, that one must round on the suggestion that what is rightly to be called a christology could fail to make any claim to there having been a uniqueness. In the first place that is not congruent with what Christians have always believed. From the earliest days Christians have not simply proclaimed Jesus' message, but a *kerygma*, a message, about Jesus. To repeat what I said earlier: either the Christ event is shattering, or it is nothing. If it is nothing – that is to say, Jesus was just a rather fine human being and that is the end of the matter – then one can take or leave him as one will. No one who is Christian could possibly assent to such a proposition! Christianity is a religion for which people have died as martyrs – not inconsistently if it is true.

Not least there is a question of integrity here. What can it mean to belong to a church which recites the Creed week by week if one has decided that it is pure myth? If one does think that it is simply a myth, a religious symbol system, then I should have expected that one would be under an absolute moral obligation to think out whether it is a 'true myth'. That is to say, is it true to what is the case? Thus, when we examine whether the Christian myth is indeed a 'true symbol', we must conclude that this is far from being the case. For example, we now know that human beings are formed from an equal number of chromosomes from the male and the female parent. By contrast, the Judaeo-Christian myth (in one of the two creation stories) depicts the woman as formed from the man, indeed created to be his helper and on account of the 'Fall' subordinated to him. Again, the Christian and indeed the Jewish religion concern, respectively, the relation between a (symbolic) 'Father' and a 'Son' and a (presumed 'male') God and his sons. Is such a symbol system 'true' to anything other than the lineaments of the patriarchy which we have known? Does it reflect our ideals? If one holds that the Christian story is a religious myth and nothing more, then one is faced with the question as to whether it is a suitable vehicle for human faith.

Yet in the writings of liberal theologians such as those whom I have just been considering we commonly find no hint of a suggestion that Christianity has ever been anything other than beneficial to humankind. Christianity – as I shall hope to show in Chapters IV and V of this book – is not, however, some harmless myth. It has been that ideology which has been central to Western culture and which has served to legitimate patriarchy in the West. Let us put the matter like this. If someone believes that Jesus is the Son of God (or however else he chooses to express his belief in Christ's uniqueness), then one's only ethical response can be to comment that, if it was God's 'intention' to 'send' Christ, it is odd that 'he' did not foresee the consequences of so doing. But if Christianity is simply a myth, then for heaven's sake let us depart from it forthwith. To continue to propound a patriarchal story which is not even mythically true to what we know to be the case or commensurate with our ideals is, to say the least, ethically dubious.

Nor, on the other hand, should one be impressed by a liberation theology which, evading a consideration of the 'person' of Jesus, looks to his message. Black, Latin American and indeed feminist theologians have sometimes wished to dispense with traditional issues of christology in this way. In the absence of a christology in which Jesus is held to be in some manner unique, we are left with what is not yet a christology: the story of a man who is a revolutionary prophet and disturber of the social order. As in the case with the 'low' christology which the British theologians propound, one must ask: why, if Jesus is not uniquely related to God, should one look to his teaching? Might one not equally well look to the message of Karl Marx or Ché Guevara? Nor is it necessary to be a religious person to espouse a radical political vision. Alternatively, one could adopt a social message which in part took its inspiration from Jesus (as Gandhi notably did), without being a Christian. If one is not a Christian and one does not have a christology, then one can look to Jesus' teaching in so far as one judges it useful and otherwise ignore it (a matter which I shall consider in the course of the next chapter).

Fourthly and finally in considering the issue of the truth of Christian claims, there is one remaining question which readers will certainly wish me to address. What of the so-called 'historical evidence' that there was a resurrection so that (contrary to all expectation, one might say) Christian claims to particularity are justified? Should not such 'evidence' be allowed to overrule all other considerations? I shall consider this question here.

In the first place it must be said that there can be no such thing as 'historical evidence' for so peculiar an event as a resurrection. A (secular) historian must take for granted that there is a certain constancy to nature; precisely the constancy which I have assumed and which leads me to say that Christian claims cannot be allowed to stand. As I commented earlier, it is through the fact that rivers are crossed today that one can credit that Caesar crossed the Rubicon. But there are no examples of resurrections as a category to which a purported resurrection could belong. A resurrection then is not something which can be caught in a (secular) historian's net.

The eminent philosopher of history F.H.Bradley, responding to those who doubt the uniformity of nature, makes precisely this point:

> 'Uniformity', we shall be told, 'is an empty phrase; similar causes are doubtless followed by similar effects, but in the varied field of history there are causes unlike those which present themselves in our present experience, and which consequently imply the presence of unfamiliar results.' . . . Our difficulty is this – we are asked to affirm the existence in history of causes such as we can find nothing analogous to now in our present experience. On the other hand, it is only from our knowledge of what is that we can conclude to that which has been; and, this being so, how can we first infer from the world to the existence of historical evidence within the world, and then, starting from that, proceed out of the world, when all the time we are unable to stand except upon the basis of the world?[48]

Thus the only way in which it would seem to be possible to arrive at a Christian theology which is predicated upon belief in a unique resurrection is to commence with that resurrection as an article of faith. But then we have a circular argument: we are assuming what one would have thought we were setting out to prove!

With such a consideration in mind, I turn to the work of the outstanding twentieth-century theologian who has made belief in a historical resurrection the central plank of his theology: the German Protestant theologian Wolfhart Pannenberg. Here I shall consider the argument of his major work *Jesus – God and Man*.[49] Pannenberg would have us understand that he wishes to undertake a theology 'from below'. He belongs to the generation of those who, turning on the dialectical theologians who wished in their christology to commence from revelation (a theology 'from above'), and more particularly denying Bultmann's distinction between *Historie* and *Geschichte*, argued that theology must be grounded in history.

Now there is (apparently) only one passage in the Christian scriptures which is of a sufficiently early date to merit serious consideration as 'evidence' for a resurrection: I Cor. 15.3–8.[50] This is the passage in which Paul tells us that Jesus first appeared to Peter, then to the twelve, then to five hundred persons some of whom were still alive (so that presumably they could be questioned), and last of all to himself as to one born out of time. What are we to say of this text? In speaking of the appearance to himself, Paul presumably has in mind his experience on the Damascus road. However, what we learn of that experience in Acts 22 is that, whatever it was that Paul supposedly saw and heard, it was not evident to his travelling companions. It would seem, then, that we are scarcely speaking of some experience which has the objectivity of hard historical fact. Now there is nothing in the Corinthians passage to suggest that Paul intended that his experience was to be differentiated from the other appearances which he mentions. Presumably, then, we are not concerned here with grossly physical appearances, of a type which must be held to break the laws of nature. Rather, we are in the interior realm of meaning and interpretation.

Thus Pannenberg, who has purportedly set out to write a theology 'from below' – and for whom therefore this passage in 1 Cor. 15 is crucial – at the end of the day wheels in other 'evidence' to support his case, thereby making his theology – one might well think – a theology 'from above'. Pannenberg (who is here somewhat of a Hegelian, or perhaps a disciple of Augustine) tells us that history must have a meaning. ('Why so?', we may ask.) Our lives, he says, can only be thought to have meaning if there is the promise of eternal life. (Again, why?) Such considerations are then advanced as 'proof' of the resurrection. The argument proceeds thus. The resurrection must be interpreted within the framework of thought of the first century. At that time there was no concept of an individual resurrection, but such a resurrection could only be proleptic of a future general resurrection of all. The resurrection of Christ must therefore be an 'eschatological event' from 'beyond': one which breaks into history, allowing us to hope that we too shall be 'raised', so giving meaning to our lives. We must conclude that Pannenberg – the very theologian who has told us that he will ground theology in history – would seem first to lack sufficient hard evidence to be able to do so, and secondly to need to adduce other considerations in the attempt to make his case.

If this is the best case that can be mustered, it would seem to be a weak argument for a resurrection of a physical nature, one which contravenes the uniformity of nature. Other arguments put forward (I think of C.F.D. Moule's fine book *The Origin of Christology*[51]) take as their point of departure that, other than postulating a resurrection, there is no way in which the christological claims made for Jesus by the earliest Christians can be understood. But that is no argument for an event which breaks the laws of nature. Thought by some to have been the shroud in which Christ was buried and to show physical signs that something peculiar had happened, the Turin Shroud has been carbon dated and found to be medieval. (I can sleep quietly at night.) Thus I find there to be no historical 'evidence' to lead me to change my (*a priori*) belief that there could have been no such thing as a resurrection.

Finally we may note that some of those who speak of a 'resurrection' admit that they are not speaking of something without parallel. Thus John Macquarrie comments: 'We are not confined to those visionary experiences recorded in the New Testament. Throughout the history of Christendom, men and women have claimed to have encounters with the living Christ, especially in a eucharistic context.'[52] Such 'encounters' scarcely entail hard historical evidence. Again, the Swiss Catholic theologian Hans Küng seems to deny that he is speaking of a unique historical event. He writes: 'The raising of Jesus is not a miracle violating the laws of nature, . . . not a supernatural intervention which can be located and dated in space and time.'[53] If this is all there is to be said, then no particularity (in the sense of a break in the causal nexus) is entailed!

Yet surely there can be no better ground than that of a purported resurrection on which Christians might wish to base an argument that God intervened in the process of nature and history. Are we not driven to the conclusion that Jesus was a singularly good man, a Galilean prophet who had a profound awareness of one whom he called his 'Father'? But – as I have argued – that is not a Christian position. As one who is not a Christian, I myself have no difficulty in holding this. Of course one could speak of a resurrection in a weak form meaning simply that the disciples had a sense that Jesus was still with them. But then people do sometimes have a strong sense of the presence of someone who has just died; I remember I had such a sense when my father died. Again, if what we are talking about were to be a near-death experience, then there would be other examples. In either case there would be no uniqueness, and Christian claims that there had been a unique occurrence in history must fall.

An interesting question arises. If resurrections – and any other claims to particular interventions – do not fit a modern world order (so that we must deny them), could it be that, in the context of the ancient world, what was being claimed at that time was not thought to contravene how the world is? My question is this. Were these purported occurrences, which must seem so remarkable to us, and on which, as revelations of God, Christianity has been based, not unthinkable in the ancient world in the way in which they are today? If people in the ancient world were never claiming that what they experienced broke the causal network of history and of nature (and in any case did not have our post-Enlightenment recognition that there is such a causal nexus), then we lack any uniqueness on which to base Christianity. I am no expert in the history of antiquity, but it is a question worth asking. I note, for example, that Augustine, living in North Africa in the early fifth century, apparently thought that two men of whom he knew had come back from the dead![54] Again, one of the earliest Christian apologists, Origen, living in the third century, argued for the virgin birth of Christ by pointing to other examples of virgin births![55]

My point is well made by Leslie Houlden:

> The isolation of incarnation and resurrection for treatment as prime and crucial instances of direct divine action, while it may seem a concession to modernity, effectively falsifies the role they formerly played. Once peaks in a landscape full of hills, all seen as such instances, they now stand out like naked pillars of rock in a plain.[56]

Indeed Bultmann's obstinate refusal to let go of the concept of 'resurrection' (which forms the pivot of his theology), while otherwise denying all miracles and interventions, essentially gives the concept of resurrection a very different status from that it would have had in a world in which 'miracles' were common. To say the same thing in a different age is to say something different! Given a world in which such things were conceivable in exceptional circumstances, it becomes more explicable that belief in the virgin birth or resurrection of Christ should have gained currency.

In this connection we should recognize that the idea of resurrection was common currency in the Jewish world in which it came to be believed by the early Christians that Jesus had been raised from the dead.[57] Indeed we read in the Christian scriptures of the dispute between Pharisees and Sadducees over the issue. The idea of an eschaton, of a general resurrection of the dead and of the messiah were inextricably linked in Jewish visionary thinking, so that if people believed that Jesus was the messiah it is scarcely surprising that they were open to the idea that he had been raised. It was not, of course, thought that there would be a single resurrection of one person – consequently we find Paul expecting that the end was nigh. Pannenberg tells us that Jesus' resurrection must be interpreted within the context of the understanding of resurrection present in the first century. Is it not rather the case that we should place the fact that Jesus was believed to have been raised within the context of the fact that the thought-world of the time included the idea of a resurrection?

Should we not then explain the belief of earlier ages in things that we now know not to be possible exactly as did Bultmann? That is to say, people expressed what they witnessed in terms of their current world outlook or *Weltanschauung*. Thus Jesus healed people: this, as I have said, I think we need not doubt – remarkable healings also take place today. By way of an explanation of the fact that a mad man was apparently cured, people said that a devil had gone out of him and into a herd of pigs: not quite what we should be most likely to say today. Furthermore, people 'externalized' what were changes in understanding (or a heightened meaning or perception) in their lives, projecting these changes as though they were actual historical happenings. Thus they arrived at a new insight that death could not actually overcome life (was that the insight they reached?) and expressed this in terms of resurrection. In Bultmann's terminology, they translated *Jenseits* (that which is beyond, the realm of meaning), into *Diesseits* (that which is 'this side', everyday occurrences which they could understand). In that world people had no other terms in which to express themselves. Moreover they did not differentiate sharply between myth and history as we do. They were ill-informed as to what is possible and what is not.

In the case of virgin birth how the belief grew up would seem to be obvious. The Hebrew behind the Greek (Septuagint) version of Isaiah 7.14 simply implies a young girl; whereas the Greek translation has the specific connotations of a virgin. The author of Matthew's Gospel, keen as ever to show that in Jesus prophecies have been fulfilled, picks up this verse and applies it to Jesus.[58] We should note moreover that the passage in Matthew is a late and unreliable strand. St Paul evidently knew nothing of such a remarkable occurrence as a virgin birth, for he never mentions any such thing – which he surely would have had it been part of his faith.

But whatever may be the explanation as to how such beliefs as virgin birth and resurrection grew up, I do not think that we can credit them. What we must now do is to move beyond Christianity, that myth through which religious consciousness has been captured and articulated over two thousand years. In the Introduction to this book I suggested that since the eighteenth century a new ethic has come into being which demands human equality. Again, modernity brought with it a new paradigm for understanding the laws of the natural world. Christianity has been placed in crisis. Either Christians must continue with the former, pre-scientific, understanding of the world, such that their theology remains divorced from the rest of human knowledge. Or else – as has increasingly happened – they must make a move sideways, holding that the Christian story, though not 'actually' true, represents a 'true myth'. But what if this myth is not 'true', if it is not a helpful story?

What if our ethics clashes with the 'truth' which this myth is supposed to convey?

The connection between the scientific understanding of the world which we now possess and the question of ethics is this. So long as people consider that what they think to be a myth is somehow ethical, they are under no real obligation to discard it. Only in this way can one understand the reluctance to leave behind the myth which male scholars in particular (for most theologians and churchmen have been male) have shown. They cling to it like an empty shell, a building which they can no longer inhabit, not knowing where to turn. (Meanwhile, what it is to be a spiritual person comes to mean assenting to this unlikely story, rather than living a certain kind of life; a matter which I shall consider in Chapter VII.) By contrast, when one has no motive for wishing to credit the truth of the myth – and a feminist surely has no reason for wishing to retain it – then one can see it for what it is. Why anyone who calls herself (or himself) a feminist, who believes in human equality, should wish to hold to a patriarchal myth such as Christianity must remain a matter for bafflement.

II

Continuity and Discontinuity

As we have said in the previous chapter, Christians are those who claim that there has been a particular revelation in history. Belief in such a revelation entails, as a corollary, that Christianity is a 'historical' religion in a quite different sense from other creeds and beliefs. Christian theology must function differently from other arts or science subjects. It is this with which I shall be concerned in this chapter. For I believe that human religion should be historical in the sense, and only in the sense, in which other subjects and human endeavours are historical. In that case (unlike in Christianity), we shall have the freedom to draw on the past as we will and to discard what we will. That is to say I believe that, in the matter of continuity and discontinuity with the past, religion should function like all other disciplines. By contrast Christianity, in that it is a 'historical' religion in this unique sense, is tied to the past in a way in which other disciplines are not. I have argued before[1] and shall argue again here that this makes Christianity sexist.

I shall divide this chapter roughly into three parts. In the first place I shall consider what I have just mentioned, which I have previously discussed in *Theology and Feminism*, that Christianity is a 'historical' religion in a unique sense. In the course of examining this I shall look at misunderstandings of what I am saying which have arisen and I shall refute critics. Secondly, I shall consider the implication of the fact that Christianity is 'historical' in this sense, namely that Christianity is necessarily sexist. In particular I shall consider whether liberal or radical versions of Christianity (which according to the definition I give in the last chapter I might think hardly Christian) avoid this sexism. I shall suggest that it is by no means averted. Furthermore, I shall consider whether, as is sometimes suggested, it would help to look to the stories of women in the Bible. Again I shall conclude that this may serve only to compound the problem. Thirdly and lastly I shall come to what may be considered the heart of the matter. Women today have a very different subjectivity from that which they had in previous ages. It is this which causes such difficulty when, as in the case of Christianity, a religion is 'historical' and necessarily has one foot in the past. Thus I shall conclude that in religion, as in all other fields, we should

commence from the present, drawing on the past as we wish and looking to the future. We should discard a myth which is no longer valid and
which does not reflect the relations between women and men that we
would have.

I commence, then, by considering the implications of the fact that, as
we have seen in the last chapter, Christians believe there to have been a
unique revelation of God in a past period of human history. The result
of this belief in particularity (what, in the previous chapter, I named
particularity the first sense of the word) is that Christianity also has
about it a particularity in the second sense which I delineated.[2] Because
Christians believe that there was a unique revelation in a past period of
history and supremely in Jesus of Nazareth, the particular circumstances
which pertained in that society (for example the particular parables
which Jesus told) come to be central to the religion. It is not that
Christianity simply commences with some philosophical notion of God,
or with human religious experience in general, or with a natural theology which purports to find God in the beauty and order of the world
(as well a religion might). Christians look to quite specific stories and a
quite specific history. These stories and this history are retained in
literature which has the status of scripture. It is constantly recited in
religious services and informs the minds of Christians.

Let me repeat: Christianity is 'historical' in a sense in which this is not
true of other arts and science disciplines and which need not be true of
religion. I find that this is frequently misunderstood. People will remark,
'But is it not the case that all human endeavours are historical?' No
human thought, so they say, arises outside history, devoid of the colour-
ing of the era in which it arose. Moreover, they continue, we exist and
must necessarily exist in some sort of continuity with the past. Now all
this is, of course, the case: no one is disputing that. The difference lies
in the fact that Christianity is not simply historical in the sense in which
other disciplines or ideas are historical (they arose in a certain period of
history), as though Christianity simply consisted in an idea or an ethic
(as does for example Marxism, which bears the marks of the nineteenth
century). Christianity is not simply an idea which happened to arise at
a certain period in history. Christians believe (unlike those who practise
any other discipline) that there was a particular revelation, that truth
was in some sense given to humankind at a certain point in history.
Therefore they must look back to the literature of that time (which is
held to be inspired), or to the words of the one whom they consider to
have been a revelation, in a way which is not the case in any other
discipline.

Let us spell this out yet again by means of some examples. Take the
case of music. Even as abstract a discipline as music is clearly practised

within a tradition and has historical continuity. Consider Beethoven. He is unthinkable apart from the tradition of Haydn and Mozart which he inherited, that is to say outside the context of something as specific as the Vienna of the late eighteenth century. Yet Beethoven is extra-ordinarily innovative. He can both take from the past as he will, standing within a tradition, and yet break free from the past where he will. There is no norm against which he must measure what he would do. Then take the other extreme of human disciplines, that of the hard sciences. There has been much talk in recent years to the effect that science is conducted within a certain tradition, or paradigm. Every so often the gap between what are perceived to be the experimental results and the paradigm within which scientific interpretation takes place becomes too wide, so that a jump is made to a new paradigm. That is to say that there is no norm against which scientists must measure what is the case; if the disparity becomes too great, a jump is made. There is no revealed truth of the kind that the church tried to enforce in the time of Galileo which forms a benchmark against which scientists must measure what they would say. And so it is in all human disciplines other than Christian theology.

In the case of Christianity, however, by definition this cannot be so. For Christianity does not simply propound the truths which Kierke-gaard named 'A', truths which are constantly available or which are inherent in the way things are. Christians believe that there was a particular revelation in history. Therefore, as I have said, they must constantly refer back to that history. A service of worship which made mention of God, but in which no reference was made to Jesus or to the Christian revelation, might well be called theistic. But it could not rightly be called Christian. In Christian worship, reference will be made to what Christians believe to have been the revelation of God in a particular history. Indeed, this is central. The parables with their con-crete imagery and the history of that time will then be retold in the present. I discussed this in detail in *Theology and Feminism*.

I have discovered it to be necessary at this point immediately to counter certain misunderstandings of what has been said in declaring Christianity to be in this sense a 'historical' religion. Thus to my con-siderable astonishment I am held to have a 'fundamentalist' view of Christianity. Nothing could be further from the case. (In fact when I counted myself a Christian I was deeply liberal in my presuppositions and I have retained that sense of what Christianity can be.) Thus to say that Christians must necessarily refer to a past period in history and to literature which arose at that time is not to adjudicate on the issue of what status should be accorded to that history and literature. Christians hold very different perspectives on this issue. For some, the very words of the Bible are inspired and everything that Jesus did and said was an act of God which must stand for all time. But others hold it to be incumbent upon us to think out the implications of biblical teaching for the circumstances which pertain today; indeed to jettison certain things which Jesus is purported to have said in the light of either deeper biblical truths or present-day circumstances. Nor am I fundamentalist in the sense of thinking that there is only one way in which scripture can be interpreted. As Luther well remarked: 'The scriptures have a wax nose.' Thus in no way would I deny that Christian feminists may not legitimately find all kinds of new things in scripture, or interpret the scripture in a different sense from in the past.

However, as I shall argue in this chapter, all this is quite beside the point. For whether the scriptures are given the status of being infallible, or whether they are held to reflect the outlook of a particular time so that it is legitimate to modify biblical teaching, it is still these particular scriptures, with their concrete imagery and history, which are read in church or synagogue. Again, however the scriptures are interpreted, it is still these scriptures, telling of these events, with the portrayal of men and women present in this literature, which is interpreted. What I wish to argue, then, is that it is what is conveyed at a sub-conscious level that is crucial. Precisely because it is at a subconscious level that certain presuppositions are conveyed (for example as to the natural relation of women to men), the effect is much less amenable to being countered.

Thus people will say that we find a certain message in the scriptures and that this can be applied to new circumstances. Now this is of course true. In this vein it is often held today that Christianity demands the equality of women and men; that although it has not been recognized for two thousand years, this is the message implicit in Christianity. The case of women is then further compared to that of slaves. For eighteen hundred years people did not recognize that Christianity was incompatible with keeping slaves. But now we have. Likewise, so it is supposed, the question of the equality of women can be solved. But that is not the case. For Christianity does not simply consist in a message (e.g. that all persons should be treated with dignity); it is also a belief that there has been a revelation in history. Christians have, as central to their faith and religious practice, a particular literature. Whatever may be the principles to which people hold on a conscious level, that literature conveys at a sub-conscious level that women are subordinate to men and lesser persons.

Secondly, it is frequently pointed out to me that Christians do not just look to the Bible. There is much else in the tradition. Thus a philosophical theology, derived quite as much from ancient Greece as from

Palestine, has been a major influence more particularly in the Anglican and the Catholic traditions. Likewise, Christians have frequently held to a natural theology, finding God present either in the beauty or the order of the natural world. Moreover, talk of religious experience is by no means foreign to Christianity. As is the case with regard to biblical interpretation, Christians have evidently held very varied views as to where knowledge of God is to be found. Those of a more Barthian disposition have wished as far as possible to exclude any idea of a wider or more general revelation. Others have willingly acknowledged the presence of God in other world religions, or thought that knowledge of God could be attained through human reason. It is sometimes supposed that I have simply failed to recognize these things.

Not a bit of it. I do not doubt that Christians draw on many sources. All I have insisted upon is that, whatever else Christians may look to, they must always look (and in fact always do look) to the revelation which they believe to have occurred in ancient Palestine. Christianity cannot discard belief in that revelation and remain Christianity. The fact that Christianity is a 'historical' religion in the sense in which I have described it does not preclude Christians from finding intimations of God elsewhere if they so wish. But they cannot lose an anchor in one particular history. In fact what impresses me about Christians is that no sooner is some contentious issue mentioned, such as whether women should be ordained, the status of homosexuals, whether divorce should be allowed, or the rightness or not of pacifism, than they launch into a discussion of what the Bible allows or what Jesus said. It is axiomatic to Christians (and this, I should contend, is simply a function of the fact that Christianity is a 'historical' religion) that they must pay some attention to a past period of human history. This is the case even if it is only to say that what was believed at that time was pertinent to that society and needs in some way to be translated to fit modern conditions.

Thirdly, it is often said that all human religions are historical, as though it were axiomatically the case that religion must be historical. This again is a confusion. It may or may not be that most world religions are more, or less, 'historical' in the sense in which Christianity is 'historical'. That is an interesting question. Thus it would seem that Western religions are perhaps historical in a sense that is not, by and large, true of Eastern religions. Within Western religions it is believed that in some sense there has been a revelation of God/YHWH/Allah in history. The ways in which Judaism, Christianity and Islam differently relate to history would make an interesting study. Neither Islam nor Judaism quite believe that there has been an interruption in the causal nexus as do Christians, or that there has been a human being who, in a second nature in one 'person', is God. Nevertheless, both religions look back to a particular history and literature. Perhaps all the major religions that we know, Eastern as well as Western, revere a founder, who of course lived in a particular era. They may bear the marks of the era of their foundation. It would seem, however, that Eastern religions are not 'historical' in the particular sense in which this is true of Christianity.[3]

Yet again, this discussion, interesting though it may be, is quite beside the point. For it is clearly not necessary for a religious position or a spirituality to be 'historical' in the sense in which this is true of Christianity. Even if there should have been no example of a religion which is not 'historical', in the particular sense in which Christianity and possibly other religions are 'historical', it is perfectly possible for our spirituality not to be 'historical' in this sense. Take a religious position in which the understanding of God is based on human spiritual experience. One may well contend, as I should wish to, that in all ages humans have been aware of that dimension of reality which is God. People may then be held, in different ages, to have conceptualized that which is God in different ways. Thus one may think that in ancient Palestine, people attempted to capture their awareness of God in the story which later became the Judaeo-Christian myth. But in a religion based on human experience, in which there was no belief that there had been a particular revelation of God, it would not be necessary to regard this myth as anything other than a sacred story which we can now discard. In our day and age we may find other symbols for expressing that which is God to be more appropriate. Again, were one to hold that the concept of God is arrived at through human reason, then presumably such a proof of the existence of God would have been available to human beings in all times and places, even though it might be that people were better able to formulate it in one particular age. Again, even though there may have been no religion which did not arise through the life of a founder, there is no intrinsic reason why human beings should not come to develop a spirituality which did not originate with any particular person. Christianity is 'historical' in a way in which religion clearly need not necessarily be.

Fourthly and finally, in what is a complete misunderstanding, people will say that I wish to promote an ahistorical religion. Indeed, I have been accused of having 'a view from nowhere'. It is then said that, on the contrary, we necessarily cannot jump outside our past but must stand in continuity with it. But no one has spoken of jumping outside our past. I am fully aware that my own religious position will stand in some continuity, even a strong continuity, with the way in which people have formulated their experience of God in the Western tradition. (In fact I think that the experience is not easily to be separated from its formulation.) Indeed I have had singularly little interest in, for example, becoming a Buddhist. As I am well aware, in my whole orientation I am Western. To say that one does not believe that there could be a particular revelation in history of the kind that Christians claim is not to become ahistorical, nor is it to fail to live within a tradition. It is simply to believe that religion must be historical in that sense, and in that sense alone, in which all human disciplines are historical. One will both draw on the past and move forward.

It follows that it is also a complete misunderstanding to accuse someone who holds the position which I am advocating of being inconsistent when they find something of value in the past. People have sometimes noticed that I suddenly refer to Julian of Norwich or to Schleiermacher and have concluded that this was inconsistent of me! But if we live in some way within a tradition, as surely we must, then we shall find nuggets of gold in the past which inspire us. What it is never necessary to do, given the religious position which I espouse, is to measure what one would say against some benchmark in history. For I am denying that there has been any particular revelation in history with which one should compare what one wishes to think. Nor, obviously, is it the case that those who stand within the Western tradition, but who are not Christians, will necessarily wish to draw on the same aspects of the past. Nor, as a feminist, will one only, or perhaps even primarily, wish to look to women in the past. (It has been men who have been the theologians and who have been allowed to have the ideas.) Nor need one deny that one may well be influenced by the Western tradition in ways which one scarcely recognizes and which one would be quite unable to discard. Nevertheless, it makes all the difference in the world (as will become apparent in Chapter VI, when I explore my own theological position) if, in thinking out how it is that God had best be conceptualized, one is not tied to the past.

I have thus previously named my position post-Christian. I intended this terminology very exactly. That is to say, the position which I am espousing is *post*-Christian, in that it does not adhere to a belief in the truth of the Christian revelation. It is therefore not Christian. On the other hand, I am aware that for all the world I am post-*Christian*, born and bred within Western Christendom. The disadvantage of this term – as I discover – is that the term post-Christian is often equated with being an atheist! It is surely highly significant that in our society, if one is not a Christian (or an adherent of some other world religion), one is taken to be an atheist. It is apparently inconceivable that if one adheres to a Western form of religion (and is not Jewish or Muslim) one could be anything other than Christian. However, there would appear to be every evidence, at least in British society, that increasingly many people are coming to have a spirituality which in some way stands in continuity with the past while discarding the Christian myth.

Discussion of an example of a misreading of my work will further serve to clarify the position that I am advocating. The example which I choose is a review article by Susan Dowell of my *Theology and Feminism* for a feminist periodical.[4] Dowell's critique draws heavily on the work of Rosemary Ruether in another review article of *Theology and Feminism*, published in the *Scottish Journal of Theology*, to which I shall also refer.[5] I choose Dowell's work because she holds a British, left-wing, feminist perspective which has been profoundly influenced by liberation theology (and indeed specifically by Ruether). It is a perspective commonly found among British feminists who remain Christian and within the church. I turn to Dowell's writing because I have frequently heard this kind of a critique of my work. Politically I might dissent little from what she has to say. (I am much closer than I think she suspects.) But that is beside the point.

Ruether and Dowell alike think that both in the Hebrew scriptures and in the Christian gospel there is a prophetic stance and a social teaching which our world sorely needs. On the basis of such a stand, Dowell castigates me for (apparently) failing to appreciate the radical social critique which is present in the Judaeo-Christian tradition. Thus she asks whether it is not the case that 'there are countervailing trends within [a Christian culture's] scriptural and traditional sources which are grounds for fundamental change in its patriarchal patterns'? She thinks that there are 'deep parallels between Old Testament and Marxist analyses of and impulses towards justice'. The Gospel's ' "preferential option for the poor" ' is, she claims, 'normative and central to the tradition'. Furthermore, both Ruether and Dowell following her take issue with the fact that I have said that Christianity is a 'historical' religion, commenting that it is not primarily a historical religion but a vision of the future. 'It is this redemptive future, not past events,' writes Ruether, 'which is ultimately normative.'[6]

Now this critique is tangential to my work. I have not primarily written about the call for social justice inherent in the Christian message (other than, interestingly, when I was still within the church and arguing for the ordination of women). However, I am quite clear that Christianity and Judaism may well have a radical social message. Certainly I have never denied that this is the case in any of the writing which I have undertaken since I left the church and Christianity behind me. What, however, I am insisting on is that Christianity cannot be defined simply as a social message. As I have said, one could be an atheist and adopt the social message of Christianity. Now the Christian social message may be admirable (while in other respects problematical

– that is another discussion). But that does not affect the fact that, as adherents of a religion of revelation, Christians necessarily make reference to a past period in human history. Again, it is not to be denied that a vision of the future may well be the benchmark against which Christian social teaching should be measured. But even if that is the case, Christians must also and necessarily look back to a past period in history in which they believe a revelation to have occurred.

Furthermore, Dowell complains of my insistence on a 'discontinuity which makes even a vision of a Christian-faith-wrought transformation inaccessible' to me. But no; that is not the case. There is nothing about my position as I explained it in *Theology and Feminism* which makes the Christian vision unavailable to me. As a matter of fact I do not doubt that in some respects the Christian vision has been beneficial to humankind. I should not even doubt that it may have been useful to those who wished to promote the equality of women (though I think the way in which Christian imagery has served to legitimize sexism out-weighs the good which a message of social justice may have done). Nor have I ever doubted, as seems to be supposed, that Christianity is any-thing other than a living tradition which can change and adapt. Thus it is not necessary to inform me that Christianity has 'always understood itself as a living community with a present and a future'; that it has 'reinterpreted its scriptural sources in response to new circumstances', and so forth. Clearly these things are the case. However, none of this affects the question as to whether Christianity could possibly be true. Personally I cannot credit that God, whatever God may be, could stand in a different relationship to one human being, Jesus of Nazareth, from the way in which God is at least potentially related to all people in all times. I cannot credit the particularity which Christianity proclaims. Therefore I am not a Christian. Moreover it does not make the slightest sense for Dowell to comment: 'I have no wish to argue with Hampson's rejection of Christianity as untrue: if it is for her, so be it.' Either there has been a particularity, a uniqueness, in history such as Christians claim, or there has not.

Continuing further, Dowell proclaims that 'Hebrew thought, from which Christianity arose, did not believe that god could be conceived of apart from god's work in Creation'. Declaring the world to be 'full of shit, war and corruption', Dowell asserts that 'the god which sustains [her] being in such a world is a Just God'. Now I have no reason to doubt that Hebrew thought does not conceive of God apart from God's work in creation. Again, if there is a God (that is to say a God who is a kind of anthropomorphic agent and who acts in the world, as has been the dominant conception within the Judaeo-Christian tradition), one would certainly hope that God is just. But this does not address the question as to whether such a God exists. I mention this because, in Ruether's work at least, I can find no evidence that she actually believes in God (however understood). Ruether constantly tells us, as does Dowell here, that the people of Israel believed such and such about God. Maybe. But as far as I can see Ruether never affirms that she too believes God to act in history.[7] (I myself do not believe that God is what I have called an anthropomorphic agent who could in this manner act in history; though I do think that that which is God is effective. I shall discuss this in Chapter VI.)

Ruether – and Dowell likewise, as would appear from these passages – seems to have transmuted Christianity into a social message without remainder. If one does not think Christianity to be true, would it not be preferable to adopt its social message (if one believes that to be right), while openly stating that one is not oneself a Christian? Or is it a question of pragmatics, given that the Christian church holds the power which it does, particularly in North America but also in Britain? One can attempt to use it to bring about change, while disguising from others (and perhaps from oneself?) that one does not actually believe Christian claims. I do not intend to be overly sarcastic. To place oneself outside Christianity may appear to render one powerless, while there is much in this world which needs changing and the Christian church might be an effective agent of change. In actuality, however, I must believe that it is the truth which is ultimately powerful. If Christianity is not true (as I think it not to be), to remain within the Christian church can only be a short-term gain.

Moreover, to adopt such a pragmatic policy, if this is what it is, is not without its problems. It is worth saying this because I suppose (from what I hear) that many people who remain within the Christian church, not simply Christian feminists, increasingly doubt that Christian claims are 'literally' true. When in former ages Christians were fired by the Christian eschatological vision, they presumably conceived that God would actually bring such a utopia into effect. However, it is questionable that it can carry the same compulsion if one believes it to be simply a myth. Presumably the point of proclaiming the myth (if that is what one thinks it to be) is to encourage *human beings* to bring about social justice. But then Christianity has simply become a humanism and Christian belief superfluous. This is not a very honest state of affairs. Thus I remember being present at a consultation of the World Council of Churches at which all sorts of radical politics was being propounded, duly backed up by the citation of biblical verses. It impressed me that it was not acceptable to question (in like radical manner) the truth of the Christian myth which lay behind the biblical verses. Moreover it was apparently unacceptable to propound the radical political views without backing them up with biblical verses: an interesting testimony to the fact that Christians feel it incumbent upon them to make constant reference to the past revelation. All this is not very satisfactory.

Furthermore, in proclaiming a myth which they no longer believe in 'literally', liberal Christians (among them Christian feminists) may well be playing with fire. For the repetition of the myth may have the effect of consolidating belief in it on the part of other (often less educated) Christians. This applies, not least, to talk of the eschaton. Thus I have not forgotten, at the height of the Cold War in the early 1980s, being driven away from an American Air Force headquarters in Colorado (where I had been shown a chapel with stained glass windows depicting fighter planes – to such an extent were the Christian myth and reality enmeshed), and my host telling me that God would bring in the end of the world some time and she did not mind if it was in her generation.

I wish to move on. In the central section of this chapter I shall again consider, as I did in *Theology and Feminism*, why it follows from the fact that Christianity is a 'historical' religion (in the sense in which I have defined it as such) that it is necessarily sexist. I shall not, however, consider in any detail the sexism embedded, for example, in the parables or in what we know of Jesus's outlook, as I did in my earlier book, and must refer readers to that.[8] What I shall do is to turn my attention to two matters which continue to be hurled at me. First I am told that the sexism of scripture can be circumvented through a liberal reading. Secondly, it is constantly said – as though it would help – that one can look to the stories of women

The reason for believing Christianity necessarily to be sexist is, as I have said, this. Since Christianity is a 'historical' religion, in that it is believed that there has been a particular revelation in history, Christians must constantly refer back to a past period in human history. Now that past history (this is notably true of ancient Israel) is the history of a profoundly patriarchal, indeed frequently misogynist, society. Through the recital of that past history or, for example, of the teaching of Jesus, the norms and presuppositions of that society, not least concerning the respective roles of women and of men, will be carried into the present. That will have the effect of consolidating past social arrangements and more particularly a certain view of women. To read such stories to our children as sacred literature may be thought not to be a morally neutral act of no account.

Now it is often said that people are fully capable of distinguishing between (for example) past roles given to women and our present society. Thus it does not follow from the fact that in biblical society women were by and large financially dependent on men that they

should not be bank managers in our present world. Moreover, it is said
that this discrepancy will always be present, unless we simply discard
the whole of past literature, which is our heritage. Thus it does
not follow from the fact that, as we may think, the portrayal of the
character of Shylock in Shakespeare's *The Merchant of Venice* is antisemitic, that we need be antisemitic today. There are different issues to
be unravelled here. In the first place, I do not think one should be so
sanguine about the effects of reading patriarchal (or antisemitic, or
racist) literature, biblical or otherwise. But secondly, even were it not
the case that the recital of biblical literature tended to promote the con-
tinuation of past social relations, I personally should find it profoundly
offensive that stories in which women played a secondary role to men
were recited in a place of worship. By contrast, one is not attempting to
use Shakespeare as a vehicle for one's spirituality (or so I assume).

But thirdly, as I have already said, it is not so much what is conveyed
to the conscious mind that is problematic. Hearing a story in which
women play secondary roles, a Christian feminist may well be able to
dismiss this aspect of the story or to adjust her thoughts (though it
may annoy her, and other people may well not make such an adjust-
ment). Rather, it is what is conveyed at a subconscious level that is
so pernicious and so powerful. For if one reads literature which contains
presuppositions that one has not clearly articulated to oneself as being
simply that – presuppositions which need not be the case – one cannot
begin to counter them. What these presuppositions may be is a matter
to which I shall draw particular attention in Chapter V, where I consider the projection of woman that is present in biblical and later
Christian writings. Moreover biblical literature is in a crucial respect
different from other literature. For biblical literature is held to be
sacred; it is read in a sacred setting in church or synagogue and thought
to be in some sense the word of God. This gives that literature an
authority which other literature lacks. We convey biblical imagery to
our children in schools and Sunday schools at the tenderest age. It
would be difficult to argue that it does not have a most powerful effect.
Every crib present in a shop window at Christmas shows one woman
present, *qua* mother, while the story is centred on the birth of a baby
boy and all the other figures present (fulfilling various roles and representing several occupations) are men.

It should also be noted that, as I have already mentioned, when one
is considering the sub-conscious level, it makes very little difference
whether one has to do with a conservative or a liberal Christianity.
However the text is being interpreted, it still concerns a group of
characters who are men, who hold the reigns of power, and women,
who do not. A parable in which only male characters are represented

may be read in any number of ways; it still revolves around the activities of some men. At a subconscious level this is what is conveyed; indeed it may have all the more effect for the fact that the concentration of the listener is focussed on some quite other aspect of the story which has nothing to do with gender. Moreover, what may be conveyed at a sub-conscious level may be subtle indeed. Thus in recent years feminists have illuminated the way in which the narrator of a biblical story, for example, depicts women as treacherous or as schemers, while failing to draw attention to the fact that in a society in which women are denied power such underhand manoeuvres may be the only way in which they can influence events.[9] Again, the impact which a story of rape or male voyeurism (such as the David and Bathsheba story) may have on those who hear it may be disguised by the fact that it is heard as a 'sacred' story. It may also be that it is received very differently by the women who hear it than by the men.[10]

I shall next take some examples of more liberal or radical readings of scripture in order to consider whether, from a feminist perspective, the problems which one would think to be present in a conservative reading are mitigated. Let us commence with a consideration of the work of some liberal British theologians, among them those whose christological position I considered in the last chapter. I mentioned there the work of Maurice Wiles, who considers that being a Christian may consist in no more than belonging to a certain tradition. Moreover, he regards the incarnation as mythological. From a feminist perspective something needs to be said about each of these propositions. In regard to the first, it is very unclear how it helps women for the emphasis to be placed on the unfolding tradition. Women have been second-class citizens in that tradition. For example, there is an almost total lack of role models, either in the biblical literature or in the later tradition, to which women who are Christians could look. A sense of being part of a continuing tradition, which may seem axiomatic to one who is a natural son of the fathers, will essentially be unavailable to one who is paradigmatically an outsider. Women must necessarily have a very different relationship to a tradition which has singularly failed to honour them as equals. As for holding the incarnation to be mythological, it must be said that it is still the story of a God (conceived of as 'male') coming to be incarnate in a male human being.

But furthermore, it is far from being the case that a diminishing of the claims being made for Jesus necessarily aids women. For the emphasis to be placed on the human Jesus (who was male) rather than on the incarnation of divinity does not serve to make him more inclusive. On the contrary, it might well be said that if it is held that God in Christ took on humanity, then women equally form a part of that humanity.

Thus in the patristic period, in which christological propositions were worked out against a (Platonic) background of real universals, God was said to have taken on what it is to be human, in which we are all included. With the loss of this philosophical context, the tendency is to deify one particular instance of humanity (as the fathers would have called it), the man Jesus of Nazareth.[11] If Jesus is spoken of as the Christ, then women may be said to bear the same relationship to him as do men. If the emphasis is on the human Jesus, then women are quite clearly of the opposite sex.

Consider the following liberal re-writing of a well known biblical passage (Hebrews 11) in which, with other world religions in view, John Macquarrie attempts to make the text more inclusive. Thus the litany of faith:

> Jesus and the other saviour figures [were] all of them seeking to realize the highest possibilities inherent in being a human person. In their several ways, they pursued justice, righteousness, love, compassion, peace and whatever else belongs to the well-being of the race. In them there is concentrated for us the greatest spiritual striving and aspirations that have been known on earth. They are figures of faith and hope who must not be forgotten. . . All of these saviour figures were mediators of grace. We have seen what this means in the case of Jesus Christ, yet these others too were emissaries of holy Being. They too had given themselves up to the service of a divine reality, who might work in them and through them for the lifting up of all creatures upon earth. . . These saviour figures then were human beings, as Jesus Christ too assuredly was. . . I mentioned that in Hebrews the procession of the men and women of faith begins before Abraham. . .
>
> By faith Moses, when he came of age, refused to be called the son of Pharaoh's daughter. . .
>
> By faith Mohammed. . .
>
> By faith Gautama Buddha. . .
>
> By faith Krishna. . .
>
> By faith Confucius. . .
>
> And what more shall I say? For the time would not be sufficient to tell of Gideon and of Barak, of Zoraster and of Lao-tzu and of Nanak and of others who through faith subdued kingdoms, worked righteousness, obtained promises, quelled aggressors.[12]

Does such a re-writing help women?

Let us take the traditional rendering of the text first. How do women fare? There is at least a mention of two women; albeit one of them, Sarah, owes her inclusion to the fact that she became the mother of a (male) child after the menopause, while the other, Rahab, is a prostitute! Pharaoh's daughter – who might well be thought to have exemplified great faith in saving the life of a child – is not recorded. So let us turn to the men of faith. Not only do I find that, as Macquarrie reiterates, they subdued kingdoms and quelled aggressors, but they stopped the mouths of lions, waxed valiant in fight, turned to flight the armies of aliens; indeed they were stoned, sawn asunder, slain with the sword, wandered about in sheep skins – and so forth. They strike me as singularly masculine heroes. How, I must ask, should they edify me? I may find myself somewhat bored by their exploits. They are not my kind of heroes. It is unlikely, then, that they will mediate 'faith'. In so far as they mediate anything, it would seem to be faith in the wrong kind of things! (Yet I do not doubt that all this is still recited in churches.)

But if Hebrews 11 does not come out of the wash too well, Macquarrie's re-writing caps it. His is an unmitigated male lineage. 'Let us now praise famous men and our fathers who begat us.' Yet Macquarrie has no solution. For women have not been the founders of the world's religions. It has been male thought schemes which have governed humankind.[13] Nor, as I have already indicated, is it necessarily helpful that Jesus is reduced to being simply one religious leader among others, a man among men and women.

What we need to do is precisely what Macquarrie fails to do: namely to take a far more radical step. We should – men and women alike – face what this litany, in either form, represents. Half of humanity, throughout the ages and in all cultures, has effectively been prevented from expressing its spiritual aspirations or its understanding of that which is God. Culture and religion have been male; formed by men with – as we shall see – a 'place' for woman. It does not do to patch up the past. We need revolution. Only when men can be prized free from their ancestry, can we, women and men together, begin to create something new. Moreover there is another interesting question to be asked in this connection, a good example of the way in which male pre-suppositions have been written into the religion we have known. Is it likely that, in supporting what they wished to say in a religious text, women would give a recital of ancestors? Would they not be more likely to refer to their own religious understandings in the present?

Let us turn, however, to a consideration of one of those few biblical tales which primarily concerns women and their world. I take the book of Ruth, for it is the obvious example. If we consider such a story, will the problems of which I have been speaking be overcome? The answer to this question needs to be unpacked. But I have to conclude that to focus on the stories of women may actually do more harm than good.

I quote in the first place from the writing of one who has had a major concern for a liberal hermeneutic, Dennis Nineham.

> A modern Christian who reads the Book of Ruth cannot hope fully to fathom, let alone adopt towards anyone today, the attitude of a young Moabite widow in the eleventh century B.C. towards her widowed mother-in-law; yet reading about Ruth's loyalty to Naomi may well give the reader a salutary jolt in connection with his insensitive attitude toward some elderly relative or even toward old people in general.[14]

What shall we say?

Since the modern Christian here is of the male sex, let us first consider 'him'. Will he perhaps be given such a jolt; is this how he will read? Maybe. However, given that the story is about a woman caring for her mother-in-law, is it not more likely that the message which he takes from it will be along the following lines? 'How good women are at looking after one another! What close bonds they have! Indeed, how splendid that my wife looks after my mother as she does!' But suppose (though this seems unlikely) our male reader indeed applies the story to his present circumstances, so that he devotes more time to caring for an elderly relative. We are still a world away from his becoming politically conscientized, so that he questions why, in today's world as also in ancient Israel, it is overwhelmingly women who bear the burden of looking after the sick, the frail and children (often losing their chance of a career as a result).

Now consider a female hearer of this story. What will it convey to her? Of course it is not to be denied that many a woman may delight in the tale; may see in the friendship between Naomi and Ruth a pattern of female relationships which she much admires and which reflect her own. It is undeniable that the two women show courage and resourcefulness; that they are outgoing and imaginative in their dealings with men and in fending for themselves. But there is nothing about the story which suggests that prevailing social arrangements should be upset. In the case of Ruth and Naomi, circumstances may work out well for the women. However, as I have said, the story's obvious message is that women are doing precisely the right thing when they set their own ambitions aside and care for someone else. The story extols a woman who is selfless, not one who decides to realize her own potential.

Here I must consider an interesting article by a colleague of mine on the book of Ruth, from which I have learned much. Richard Bauckham argues that that book contains two strands, a male perspective and a female perspective. Thus while it is the case that the legal process is conducted by the men at the gate of the city, it is the women's perspective which is crucial. 'The women manage the continuity of the generations, not in legal but in practical and affective terms.' Moreover, despite their patriarchal form, such social arrangements as patrilineal descent and inheritance 'can operate in practice as structures for women just as much as for men'. The narrative shows the legal provision, for example the law of gleaning, 'operating for the benefit of Naomi and Ruth'. Indeed, Bauckham claims, the 'female voice' of the narrative exposes as 'pitifully inadequate' the male voice which is concerned with tracing a male line of descent.[15]

This is all very fine. Such readings, whether by women (such as those quoted by Bauckham) or by men, may well enable those who remain within the tradition to view it differently. Nevertheless, to call such a reading feminist, whether carried out by women or by men, or to suggest that it meets feminist concerns, must be a long way short of the mark. For feminists have commonly wanted to undermine and do away with 'complementary' worlds for women and men. They believe that, in a world of 'complementarity', what is designated 'feminine' will always tend to 'complement' what is male and not vice versa. Look at this text. It may well be that the law of gleaning makes it possible for Naomi and Ruth to eat while Boaz is generous. But which sex is represented as needing to glean and which as bountiful? Bauckham tells me that it would normally have fallen to a son to support his mother in her old age. But only, surely, in the sense of economically providing for her, something which men had the means to do. I cannot believe that it would be sons rather than daughters who undertook the day-to-day work of feeding, cleaning and caring for elderly relatives in their sickness. The story, I repeat, does nothing to suggest that gender should not be determinative as to the role a person has in the society. As Bauckham himself comments, the story 'certainly presupposes social and economic structures which make it very difficult for a woman to survive without a male provider'. What the book of Ruth depicts is two women determined to provide for their future security in the only way open to them: through Ruth coming to have a male child.

Let us not, then, be under any illusion that the problem of the sexism of scripture is solved by the device of looking at passages which concern women or which reflect a 'female perspective'. The most that such passages show us is what the perspective of women was in a past, patriarchal society. Such a perspective may indeed serve to relativize the otherwise overwhelmingly androcentric perspective of the scriptures. But given a feminist stance there are insuperable problems. In the first place a feminist woman may well not recognize herself in women from the past, so profoundly are women changing. Secondly, it cannot be said that the scriptures convey any sense of what equality between women

After Christianity

and men, or the overcoming of gender roles, would mean. Thirdly, a feminist woman may well, as a feminist, have a different value system: she may wish that men, too, would abandon a concern for patriarchal genealogies, not simply that women should provide another perspective.

The extent to which women today have come to have a profoundly different sense of themselves, so that they find themselves to have little in common with the women of past generations, is a matter to which I shall come in due course. We simply are not going to find, in the biblical literature, women in whom this generation of women see their reflection. Career women, women who are feminists, who are articulate agents in their own right, and particularly the younger generation of women who are beginning to take an equality with men for granted, in a very real sense have no ancestry. There has not previously been a generation of women like the present. This is something which Christians have not begun to tackle; for there is little that they can do. Some well-meaning men seem to have no inkling of the gap. This past Christmas, supposing that I should approve, a Catholic priest told me that this year in his church he had a shepherdess in his crib scene (worshipping, I am sure, the baby boy), as well as, of course, 'our Lady'.

But why, one wonders, are men (as not infrequently happens) telling women that there is 'a place' for them in Christianity, given for example that Jesus seems to have associated with women and to have had good relations with them? Are men supposed to find themselves in Simon Peter, or John the beloved disciple? They do not commonly suggest that they should. One will hear it said that Jesus was open to women; no doubt that is the case, in so far as he treated each individual with respect. Again, it will be pointed out that women were the first to discover the empty tomb. Let us momentarily reverse the scenario. Suppose that, for over two thousand years, we had had a religion which revolved around Goddess sending her daughter to earth. (Would she, one wonders, ever have been absent herself from the earth? But that is another story.) And some men who, in the late twentieth century, were questioning the relevance of this to them were to be told, 'But she was awfully nice to men, even allowing men to keep her company'. We see how crazy it is! Indeed what is notable about the story of the women discovering the empty tomb is that they were to go and tell Simon Peter and the disciples. Why? Because, in that society, women were not even given the dignity of being allowed to give valid testimony – as witnesses in a court of law.

Minimally, feminism must surely involve the equality of women and men. But the Bible is simply not concerned for such equality. It will not give us a picture of what we seek. Biblical people could have had no inkling of what we might mean by such equality. Judith Ochshorn has suggested that ancient Israel was much more deeply gendered than the surrounding polytheistic societies.[16] There is nothing in Jesus' message about the breaking down of gender roles. He has no social analysis of patriarchy. Not one of his parables turns on the idea that women should, for example, be admitted to the courts of the temple to which only men were admitted; or that the obligations of prayer laid on men in that society should equally be incumbent on women. The women in his parables perform wholly conventional roles performed by women in that society. Moreover there are almost no women in the parables. His focus is virtually exclusively on men, who have any number of careers and occupations. Most women are referred to as wives, sisters and daughters – usually their names are not even given.[17] Considering the desperate plight of women in his society, this apparent lack of any awareness that the lot of women needed to be changed must strike us.[18]

But – it will be said – Jesus was a man of his time. If Jesus is simply considered to be a rabbi who was in many respects a fine ethical teacher, one who lived two thousand years ago, then indeed the matter could be allowed to rest there. (Though when we look at the case of women it might well be necessary to mitigate the sentiments sometimes heard that Jesus was far ahead of his time.) What is problematical is to be looking to Jesus for guidance on any number of ethical issues today, as do Christians. How could the views of such a man possibly be definitive on such questions as pacifism or homosexuality? He knew nothing of the evil which twentieth-century totalitarian states could wreak. He did not have the sensibilities which we have come to have – even in the last decade – about sexual preference. In the case of relations between women and men, he could not have begun to envisage the insights we have now arrived at. If one is not a Christian, one can learn from Jesus' teaching if one finds it perceptive; but one can also look elsewhere, probably to sages in our own time or to one's own consciences. One can without further ado judge Jesus' teaching irrelevant or mistaken. Such a stance is the only possible one for a mature human being with moral responsibility. It is what women who are feminists must demand.

But what of the idea, which seems to have been fundamental to Christian feminism in recent years, that one should look to women in the past? More particularly in the Catholic church – where women have no hope of being admitted to the hierarchy or of being ordained – many women have wished to form a semi-separatist movement within the greater body of the church, commonly known as 'womanchurch'. Such women understand themselves as being part of a long line of women, stretching from the past to the present and into the future. Elisabeth Schüssler Fiorenza, the German biblical exegete who has spent many years in the United States, is particularly associated with this line of thought. But it has been widely influential and adhered to. Thus Susan Dowell castigates me for, apparently, 'rejecting the value of any kind of solidarity – politically or symbolically realized – with other women across time and space'.[19] In conversation Schüssler Fiorenza has challenged me in like manner. This has compelled me to think out where I stand on this matter and why it is that I hold such a very different position from others.

In the first place I must say that – when I come to think of it – it does not seem to me that I reject the value of 'any kind of solidarity – politically or symbolically' with other women. Upon leaving the church, my first act (given that I should have so much free time now that I was no longer working day and night for the cause of women's ordination) was to join 'Chile Committee for Human Rights'. That was in 1981, at the height of the Pinochet regime. It was a symbolic move on my part. I wanted to stand in solidarity with women who had been yet more profoundly hurt by patriarchy than I had myself. And I worked for years, unstintingly, writing letters to Chilean generals (on headed writing paper with all my degrees which as a feminist I should never otherwise use!) to let them know that someone was watching the fate of Marcela or Arinda. I smuggled food and medicine and warm clothes into that prison; one year even a Christmas cake! Out of the prison came letters, hidden in books when their relatives visited the prisoners, with poetry, appreciation and messages which other people were so kind as to translate from the Spanish for me. The women had been brutally tortured but they kept the flame of life alive. This involvement was one of the most dramatic episodes of my life, profoundly affecting me. I remember that what I was doing raced across my mind when Schüssler Fiorenza charged me as she did. In my silence I needed to take the charge seriously and to think out where I was. For it was true that I did not think that we should be paying the slightest attention to biblical women.

Why not? Because biblical women are dead and gone. We can know almost nothing of them. Moreover we can do nothing whatever to help them. The Chilean women – as I discovered to my huge astonishment and delight – were radical feminists. They and other women put together and circulated a feminist news sheet. They had shown courage beyond my imagining and they needed my help. Across the gulf, we had much in common. Marcela had been a university student when she was picked up by the secret police on the street one day. Arinda was employed as some kind of a research bio-chemist. These were the women with whom it made sense to stand in solidarity. They changed my life; opening doors for me and allowing me to see the world differently. Arinda wrote poetry; the sky for her was in diamonds, cut by the wire of the perimeter fence. I told her that in my life I had no time to see the sky! We in our privileged existence in the West had lost something. During those years I got my first personal computer and explained it to her. She was fascinated. And all this in correspondence smuggled in and out of a Chilean prison. She lives. The women were set free. Patriarchy, at its worst, did not win!

But what of the call to show solidarity with biblical women? Let me try to take that seriously. Where does it come from? What motivates it? It is not necessarily the case that one like Schüssler Fiorenza or indeed Phyllis Trible[20] wishes us to look to the hopeful stories of women in the past, as the book of Ruth might be thought to be. It is quite as much the case that they wish us to show 'solidarity' with women in the past in their suffering. The sense then is that women have been oppressed in every age. Trible compares the story of the dismemberment of a woman in the Hebrew scriptures with a newspaper report of the dismembered body of a woman being found in a New York trash can.[21] In an effective discussion which must cause one to think, Schüssler Fiorenza argues that a people need a history if they are to enjoy self-identity. She points to the way in which, astonishingly, blacks in the States in recent years have wanted to 'own' the history of slavery and back behind that their African ancestry, exemplified by Alex Haley's book *Roots*. A people's history, Schüssler Fiorenza believes, can lend them transformative power. She writes: 'The enslavement and colonialization of people becomes total when their history is destroyed because solidarity with the faith and suffering of the dead is made impossible.'[22] More than once she cites the words of the feminist artist Judy Chicago who, through her painting, has attempted to rescue the lives of women of the past from oblivion. Chicago comments: 'Our heritage is our power.'[23]

The first comment that I should like to make on this agenda is that I find it significant that it should be associated particularly with one who is German, living in the United States, and Catholic. In the first place, German. I remember Schüssler Fiorenza saying something about her life in Germany after the war and about her family having earlier had some connection with the church resistance. If one's past was the immediate German past (as I have found in the case of German friends of my generation born in or immediately after the Third Reich), naturally if one is to have a self-identity one is going to look for an alternative past which one can honour. One needs to find some kind of ancestry which one can claim. But secondly, the quest is extraordinarily American. It never ceases to amaze British people, who may live a mere train ride from the place from which their family came, that Americans cross the Atlantic to make a pilgrimage in search of their 'roots', while they never themselves even make the train ride. Is it perhaps the very lack of roots in North American society which drives people to look for them? And

thirdly, this agenda is profoundly Catholic. If one belongs to a church
in which the men find an identity by conceiving of themselves as living
within a succession which goes back to the apostles, it is hardly
surprising that women should in like manner wish to situate themselves
within a heritage. I lack these sensibilities because I do not have these
needs.

But there are other issues here which have nothing to do with one's
personal situatedness. I cannot see the point of the quest. As I have
previously indicated, it fails to confront issues which, at the end of the
day, it is not possible to evade.[24] Thus one must presume that Schüssler
Fiorenza and others wish to focus on the women around Jesus because
it is somewhat problematic for feminists (particularly for those who
sense a solidarity with their 'foresisters') constantly to look to a male
Christ. Consequently Schüssler Fiorenza shifts the focus of attention
from the texts to the earliest Christian community, a community of
women and men. She has indeed shown – one may think – that women
played a more vital role in that community than male scholars have
been wont to recognize: that is an interesting historical observation. But
if one is working not simply as a historian but as a Christian and a
theologian, as she claims to be, then presumably the reason why one is
looking to those women is that they acknowledged Jesus as the Christ.
Otherwise one might as well look to the women of Greenham Common,
or Chile, for inspiration. One cannot, then, evade issues of christology.
Could it possibly be that Jesus was the Christ; that he was unique?
Indeed, is it possible – as some Christian feminists have phrased their
dilemma – for women to be content with a male saviour? I have never
seen Schüssler Fiorenza, any more than Rosemary Ruether, acknowledging the truth of Christianity.[25] Nor indeed, I think, consider its
viability for feminists.

There is, moreover, another question which must necessarily be
faced. What kind of an identity can we sense with people in the past?
Can we put ourselves in their shoes? I agree that one may sometimes
be brought up against an astonishing sense of the constancy of the
human condition. Sitting on a train which has unaccountably stopped
late at night, with nothing to read but a copy of Plato's *Symposium*,
I can find myself giggling, so that the other passengers must think I
am reading a racy novel. But I am not being asked to express *solidarity*
with these characters. How should I sense solidarity with women,
largely unknown, whose social circumstances were quite other than
mine, living in the first century? It seems to me a travesty of history
to suggest (as Phyllis Trible seems prone to do) that the suffering
of women is simply a constant. I have civil rights of which women
could not have dreamt two millennia ago. We should not underestimate

what women have achieved. How then should the lives of women in the ancient world be relevant to me?

And there is yet a further issue which must concern us here. Is it politically adept of women to stress their solidarity with (and by implication their similarity to) women in the first century? Precisely our problem is that many men fail to comprehend that women today are in a very different place, with a wholly different sense of themselves. Many a man is only too willing to believe that there is an 'essential essence' to 'woman', so that nothing much is needed by way of a change in attitude towards women, whether within the church or outside it. Do we not fuel such an outlook through this strategy of solidarity with past women? Furthermore, it is necessarily a solidarity with women in their disadvantage, in that women in the past did not have the rights or opportunities which at least Western women enjoy today. Moreover, it may well be that the attempt to sense oneself as part of a 'sisterhood' with such women (while unable to help them) can only serve to induce in women an inferiority complex which, precisely, they need to overcome. What women should do is to have the courage to claim equal rights and be fully adult members of our society. May it not be much more politically effective that I should confront men with my equality with them, denying that any model for relations between men and women is to be found in the past?

However, Schüssler Fiorenza believes that we inevitably lie within what she calls the 'trajectory' of the Christian religion. Since it is this past with which we have to live, we must transform it. Biblical texts – so she tells us – 'affect all women in western society'.[26] Do they? And if they do, what should one do about it? I have myself suggested that, through the reading of biblical texts, particularly within a sacred setting, the long arm of the past reaches into the present. But it does not follow that one should attempt to reinterpret these stories. Are they re-interpretable? Even a story like Ruth, as we have seen, does not portray the *equality* of men and women. It is one thing to re-read these stories because one is a Christian on other grounds (for example, one finds oneself forced to confess that Jesus is the Son of God), so that willy-nilly one finds oneself an insider to Christianity and then as a feminist one wants to do the best with these stories that one can. But Schüssler Fiorenza singularly fails to state that she has any such christological belief. Had one then not best leave these stories alone? It must be a counsel of despair to suggest that, unable to step outside the biblical trajectory, we can only reinterpret texts.

Nevertheless, let us consider the argument that it could be useful to women that these stories are re-read. In this connection I cannot but remember a story which Susan Brooks Thistlethwaite gives us (presumably from the slums of Chicago) and which remains heart-rending. In a shelter for battered women and considering her plight, a woman commented (with reference to Eve): 'God punished women more'.[27] What an indictment of biblical religion! Faced with this woman what should I do? Even in this eventuality I cannot think that I should do anything other than gently to suggest that we know these days that it is not that God created Adam and Eve, but that we are descended from the higher apes. There can then be no reason for women to play into the hands of those who suggest that the Bible must contain some kind of 'truth', even if only in a mythological sense, so that all that we can do is to reinterpret. Besides which, in the case of the woman in the shelter it would not be honest to go along with her interpretation, when it is neither historically accurate nor morally plausible to believe that God 'punished' women. Schüssler Fiorenza will sometimes draw attention to the work of the Costa Rican biblical exegete Elsa Tamez and she herself is clearly much concerned for the situation in central America. But it cannot be said that, even in Latin America, women have no option but to be Christian, so that one should show solidarity with them in this. My own experience suggests quite otherwise. The women whom I supported never gave the slightest indication of being Christian. It would be hard to say that their struggle was thereby the less effective.

It may be that part of what is at stake is something quite other: namely the difference in the academy in Britain as compared with the United States and perhaps also continental Europe and elsewhere. There is also a profound difference in regard to the society as compared with the United States. Thus in Britain today there is no reason why I need to be a Christian in order to work as a theologian (although I am unusual). All universities are state-funded and academic tenure (such as it is) allows freedom of conscience. Ancient universities have divinity faculties. I am not forced to work in religious studies, which is not my interest. An incident which took place in relation to Harvard Divinity School was illuminating for me in this regard. An alumnus myself, I submitted and had accepted a piece for the bulletin sent out to alumni. Suddenly and inexplicably I was told that it could not be published; when I pressed further, I was told that it 'did not conform to the mission policy of the school'! If even Harvard (presumably because it is dependent on financial gifts) cannot allow academic freedom, where are we? It must be much more difficult in the American climate to work outside Christianity.

However, I am far from wanting to suggest that we should not study biblical literature within the academy. There may be a strong case for subjecting to scrutiny documents which are so central to our heritage. But this cannot be because we wish to find solidarity with biblical characters or to emulate their understanding of relations between women and men. Effective work is being carried out in biblical studies which illuminates what is wrong with our inheritance. It may show, among other things, that male brutality towards women has been long-standing; or that male pornography has remained in essence the same. I think for example of the work of Cheryl Exum, an American biblical scholar now living in Britain, who is illustrating in a striking manner how problematic the Hebrew scriptures are.[28] It may also be that we have something to learn for our society (though not, one suspects, in the realm of the treatment of women). Seated next to a (male) professor of the Hebrew scriptures at a dinner party not long ago and discovering him to be an atheist, I asked why this was his chosen occupation. He replied: 'Because the Bible is a dangerous and powerful book.' It is important for that to be recognized. Schüssler Fiorenza asks: 'How can a feminist biblical hermeneutics situate its readings of the Bible in such a way that they do not reinscribe the patriarchal discourse of sub-ordination and obedience?'[29] The answer might be: by pointing to the pervasive sexism and misogyny of this text which has been fundamental to Western culture.

In the third part of this chapter I wish to focus on something which we come up against once and again, namely the question of women's changed subjectivity and its implications for women's relation to Christianity. It may also be that men sense themselves differently from the way they did in the past, but this difference is presumably not quite as great as is true in the case of women. Furthermore, and connected with this, there is the question as to whether feminists have not, concertedly and knowingly, wished to gain a new sense of self, one which I shall suggest fits ill with Christian presuppositions. Changing subjectivity must, by the nature of the case, be something which is difficult to pin down. Nevertheless, not to attempt such a discussion would be to fail to point to the gap between where many women find themselves today and the presuppositions of a theology which has come from the past. It is central to the whole issue of the compatibility of feminism with Christianity.

Let me commence by pointing to an article in which Luce Irigaray responds to Elisabeth Schüssler Fiorenza (since we have been consider-ing her work). An eminent feminist theorist in the French tradition, Irigaray is in fact greatly interested in questions of spirituality. While she is by no means unappreciative of Schüssler Fiorenza's endeavour, it is nevertheless where Irigaray places a question mark against it that she is of interest for our present purposes. In order to appreciate the import of her query, it is important to know something of Irigaray's own work. Irigaray conceives that women, if they are ever to come into their own,

will need to acquire a 'transcendental' in which they can find themselves
reflected; just as, we may say, men have had, more particularly in the
Judaeo-Christian tradition, and more generally in Western philosophy.
Irigaray does not think that any real change can come about without a
change in women's subjectivity.

It is from such a perspective that Irigaray approaches Schüssler
Fiorenza's enterprise. While the work may be interesting historically,
she finds that it leaves wider and deeper questions unaddressed.
Schüssler Fiorenza, so Irigaray comments, 'describes what already
exists without inventing a new subjectivity'. Though, she says, 'social
strategies' may be useful, 'they lack subjective dimensions'. Moreover –
evidently wishing to find a discussion of women's spirituality – she
writes: 'Sociology quickly bores me when I'm expecting the divine.'
In Christianity, Irigaray writes, man 'furnishes the parameters of
individual, social, and cultural identity. But for women that model is
inadequate. . . It does not furnish them certain needed representations
of themselves, of their genealogy, and of their relation to the universe or
to others.' Thus she continues: 'Can a claim to equality be acceptable
without a fundamental respect for the subjective rights of both sexes,
including the right to a divine identity?' [30] Irigaray's own agenda is not
something which I can discuss further here. What I find important is the
raising of the question of women's subjectivity and whether that can be
satisfied within Christianity.

In the next chapter I shall therefore need to consider the shift in self-
understanding which has come about for many women through
feminism. Without such a consideration one cannot begin to understand
the strained relationship which women have to Christianity. However,
let me here give the following vignette, which exemplifies well what is
at stake. At the time that, as president of the European Society of
Women in Theological Research, I was considering the struggles of
women on the Continent to be accepted in academic faculties, I heard
the following story. A Dutch woman known to me, upon being appointed to a position in a theology faculty, went to pay the obligatory visit to
the local bishop. The following conversation ensued. Was she married?
(Would a man, one wonders, have been confronted with such an opening gambit?) No. Did she live at home? (Again, would a man have been
so questioned?) No. What did she think of Jesus Christ? She had, she
said, some problems with him. What were they? Well, for example, he
had said 'Follow me', whereas she did not think that one should follow
anyone! The story may cause a quiet smile. I want to suggest that, far
from being flippant, her comment encapsulates a profound change in
women's consciousness. What one must question is: why was such a
woman still trying to find a place within the Christian church?

It is difficult to see how Christianity can survive in this climate. Fundamental to feminism has been the overcoming of what one might call deference to members of the opposite sex, or more generally (in the peace movement, for example) to powers and authority. This does not of course mean that women do not wish to have good relations with members of what I prefer to call the neighbouring sex. They may well think that it is only as they are granted equality and so are enabled to be fully themselves that such good relations can ensue. Now when we juxtapose such an outlook with Christianity there is a basic clash. For, as we have said, by its very nature Christianity entails the possibility of heteronomy. Christians understand God as transcendent and as 'other' than the self. Moreover they believe there to have been a revelation in history, so that Christians must find an authority in that revelation or in the literature which tells of it. If one were simply to retain that authority within oneself, at that moment one would not be allowing God to be God to one. But as the Dutch woman said, she did not think she should be following anyone else.

We should notice that the problem with which we are confronted has nothing to do *per se* with the fact that Jesus was male. It has to do with a change in self-understanding. Through the women's movement, women have learnt to put themselves at the centre of the picture. This is not to be 'selfish' or 'self-centred'; that would represent a profound misunderstanding. Women are saying, 'I want to be at the centre of "my" world', not 'at the centre of "the" world' – as men have not infrequently thought themselves to be. This is an ethical stance. It represents an understanding of the nature of human maturity and moral responsibility. (One suspects that those feminist women who believe this more keenly have left Christianity behind long ago.) It is not necessarily an atheistic stance: it may be compatible with a profound spirituality. But that spirituality (or understanding of God) will need to be predicated upon the self (in a manner which I discuss in Chapter VI). What are profoundly incompatible with such a stance is, for example, the attitudes of worship or obedience which, we note, are fundamental to Western religion, whether Judaism, Christianity or Islam.

Thus it may be of the essence of feminism that a feminist cannot call anyone else 'Lord'. Of course a Christian will say that whereas it would indeed be blasphemy and idolatry to have such a relationship to any other human being, the whole point is that one is not worshipping a human being but the second person of a triune God. This solves nothing. For I should not want to worship God. If one has cast such attitudes aside on ethical grounds, it is fundamentally impossible to import them into one's religion again. It may of course be profoundly problematic that Christians, women and men alike, have seen as their

'Lord' one who was a member of what has been the dominant sex. It is
doubly impossible to have to worship someone of the opposite sex. But
I am suggesting that more fundamental than either of these is the
problem for a feminist of worshipping *per se*. (Thus what we lack in the
image of Jesus which has been handed down to us is the sense that he
needed to listen to and to learn from anyone else, let alone a woman.)

At this point it is liable to be said by a patronizing male (for so he
must be named), 'But haven't women benefited from Christianity? Isn't
it precisely because the West has been Christian that the rights of individuals have been respected and women have come into their own?' I
find such comments so offensive that I almost do not know where to
start. Christianity has been that ideology which, intricately interwoven
with Western culture, has served for two millennia to justify the subordination of women. Of course other patriarchal ideologies may have
functioned similarly in other cultures. It may also be that, at its best,
Christianity entails the integrity of each individual. But the issue of
women's equality is not, as I have said, comparable with that, for
example, of the freeing of slaves (to which Christianity is often held to
have led), in that there is nothing about its symbolism which supports
slavery (unless it should be held that Jesus was 'white', which he was
not). However, the symbol system of Christianity is against women.

It must, then, be said that it is quite unclear that Christianity has
served the cause of women, or indeed that of human rights more
generally. In his *The Idea of Holiness and the Humane Response*, John
Armstrong argues eloquently that it has been in periods which have
been less influenced by the Judaeo-Christian tradition that progress in
honouring the integrity of individuals has come to the fore: ancient
Athens, the Enlightenment, and the secular twentieth century.[31] It is by
no means self-evident that Christianity has 'helped' women. (At one
point – in a society saturated with Christianity, in late medieval and
early modern Europe – women were burnt to death in considerable
numbers.) But whatever may be the case in regard to the alleged benefits
of Christianity, it must be said that women no longer need to look to
Christianity for their self-integrity. Even if Christianity helped to give
rise to feminism, feminism has now outgrown its progenitor. Women
are turning on the Judaeo-Christian tradition and levelling the charge
that it privileges the male.

Nor can it rightly be said that feminist women are demanding a
religion 'which suits them', as though Christianity were somehow
ideologically neutral. As I shall hope to show in Chapters IV and V,
men have adhered to a religion which for two thousand, if not four
thousand, years has been profoundly bound up with male subjective
needs. There is nothing 'objective' about Christianity. Indeed, one

would think that it fits badly with what we know about the world scientifically in the modern age. That school of Christianity which has been the most adamant about the 'objectivity' of revelation in recent years may be thought to have been the more deeply moulded by the male psyche. In an analysis of the vocabulary in a section of Karl Barth's *Church Dogmatics*, a former (German) student of mine showed it to be packed with hierarchical, authoritarian, indeed militaristic vocabulary. Far from women demanding a religion which 'suits them', it is a certain kind of feminist theology (such as I shall advocate), which is free from the Christian myth and conceptualizes God non-anthropomorphically, that opens up the possibility of a theology in which neither sex is privileged over the other.

What it is interesting to note is that, whereas separatism may be an understandable response on the part of those women who remain within the Christian church, if one could exist in an idyllic realm in which men had left behind their allegiance to a past symbolic structure, no such separatism would be necessary. (Or at least separatism on account of the religion would not be necessary; it would still be important in a religious gathering, as in any other, that men should not dominate women.) It may then well be that, by remaining within Christianity, women in effect continue to shore up a sexist religion in which God is seen as one, singular, 'other', and in the male image. Thus, interestingly, Irigaray comments:

> Personally I prefer to try everything in an effort to preserve the dimension of a sexual mix because that difference seems to me to safeguard those human limitations that allow room for a notion of the divine not defined as the result of narcissistic and imperialistic inflation of sameness [the term she commonly uses for the nature of male thought, in which essentially there is only one sex]. What's more, both sexes need to form an alliance based on mutual respect; this is still far from happening.[32]

The trouble with the reduction of Christianity to either a social message or a particular kind of community is that such a conception fails to grasp the whole symbol structure of the religion with its deleterious effects. If, by contrast, women come to formulate how they want to understand God, the male God and religion will be relativized. It will be seen to be a social construction.

If we are to have a living spirituality, it will need to be commensurate with our self-identity. What I have suggested is that many women have a radically different sense of themselves, certainly from that of women in the ancient world, but different also from that of the majority of women until quite recently. What counts here is our ideals. If one's ideal is the equality of women and men – that in one's personal relations one should treat men as equals and oneself be treated as an equal – it will be this, rather than the less than perfect world in which one lives, that is operative in relation to one's spirituality. One's spirituality and one's ethical ideals must necessarily cohere. It is not enough for feminist theology simply to talk of liberation, as though one could speak of a 'solidarity with the poor' and, in parallel, of a 'solidarity with women' (which presupposes women's disadvantage). A spirituality which women will be able to integrate with the persons that they are must take account of their subjectivity. Thus a religion which in its symbol system fails to reflect the new-found sense of themselves which women have come to enjoy (in the Western world at least) will be judged irrelevant.

Here I shall doubtless be told that it is not possible to construct, in independence of a social setting, a discourse of rights by which our religion is subsequently to be judged. 'All truth' – so we are told, by those influenced by a certain kind of (basically North American) 'post-modernism' and relativism (if I may call it that) – 'is socially con-ditioned'. I believe any such comment to rest on a confusion. Of course – as we have become aware in our generation as never before – it is no doubt the case that paradigms for social relationships arise within a certain social setting and bear the stamp of that age. This is true not least of the expression of human rights which came to the fore in the Enlightenment. Of course it is also the case that those ideals have frequently not been translated into practice (particularly in their appli-cation to women). Nevertheless, I believe it to be a profound mistake to fail to recognize that such a conception of justice is deeply embedded in our culture. These ideals are now enshrined in law in our societies. We cannot advocate a religion which somehow falls short of them with-out there being a glaring anomaly. It is precisely because the Christian religion and church have lagged behind the implementation of these ideals in our society that they are now under fire. The question is whether Christianity, tied as it is in its symbol system to a past ordering of society, can possibly serve us in the future.

And yet there is something else to be said. It may be the case that, in a sense which is very new in human history, in our society we are more influenced by the anticipated future than by any strong sense of continuity with the past. In this respect I am intrigued by remarks, made over twenty years ago now, by Anthony Dyson concerning the impor-tance of such a sensibility for theology. In his Hensley Henson lectures delivered in 1973, The *Immortality of the Past*,[33] Dyson considers the conjecture that there has been a profound shift of consciousness in this regard. He quotes remarks of the historian J. H. Plumb in 1968 lectures published as *The Death of the Past*. Plumb, arguing that 'we are witnessing the dissolution of the conditions which tied man to his past', comments: 'The strength of the past in all aspects of life is far, far weaker than it was a generation ago. . . Wherever we look, in all areas of social and personal life, the hold of the past is weakening.' Thus Dyson, speaking of the past as being in 'galloping dissolution', ponders the idea that it may now be something else which is 'decisive in shaping human consciousness'. He continues:

> I refer to the discovery of the future. I have in mind, not the many utopias and schemes of universal history which abound in human thought, but rather the way in which the relatively close, this-worldly future has begun to exercise a determinative influence over the present. This is not simply an extension of man's awareness that he belongs to an evolutionary process. For that awareness defines him as a product of the past. On the contrary, the discovery of the future implies a power of human creativity in and over against the present. For some decades, more and more human beings have become aware that mankind now possesses the possibility of radically different futures, each of which is in some measure causally dependent upon contemporary choices in thought, values and planning. Moreover, this pull from the future is not only intellectual in character. It gains psychological roots from the sense of urgency it imposes about the decisions which must be made. . . So, because on the one hand rapid change and discovery have broken man's sense of intimate and organic relationship with the past, and because on the other hand the shaping of the future will more and more affect the way in which the present is justified, we can envisage an increasing tendency to understand the present not so much in relation to a known past, not only in its own terms, but from the constraints of alternative futures.[34]

Dyson considers what the implications for theology may be. 'Such a shift,' he writes, 'threatens to throw into disarray the traditional functions of, and relationships between, history and theology.' He asks: 'May the shift become so decisive that the practice of Christian theology must change, not only in style and emphasis, but in its entire self-understanding? Will there remain a significant social function for the historian which can serve the theologian's cause?' And he judges that: 'If theology is sensitively to anticipate changing cultural consciousness and thoughtfully to measure its response to such changes, such questions may not be brushed aside.'[35]

What has decisively come on to the scene since Dyson wrote is the women's movement. That has caused us radically to rethink the ethics of the relationship between men and women. It may represent a more fundamental revolution in human affairs than we have experienced for

four thousand years. Obviously it will have untold implications for
something as symbolic and as vital to human beings as their religion.
This much at least we can say. It is very unlikely that in future women
will be able to fit themselves into the box to which men have assigned
them in the religion of the past. (What shape that box has had I shall
come to consider in Chapter V.) Thus where one must question Dyson's
analysis, written before the women's movement had made any substantial impact, is in simply assuming that it is the 'Christian religion' which
must change. For Christian theology is, as I have argued, of its very
nature tied to a past ordering of human relations.

Should our churches then be turned into museums? This poignant
question was addressed to me in a letter from a woman who, fundamentally in agreement with what I had said, found herself perplexed
as to its implications. Her description of her village church brought
vividly to my mind that church which has stood for almost a thousand
years in the Sussex village in which my mother lived for a quarter of a
century, and in which, at a younger age, I used to worship. Here each
generation has left its mark. To say that our churches can become
concert halls, though true, seems trite. We should not, however, hide
from ourselves the fact that these days such churches are only visited by
a small minority of the population. In one generation it has become
almost impossible to maintain church choirs; the younger generation
has simply fallen away. Nor, more seriously, should we fail to recognize
that the Christian religion propounded there has been inimical to the
interests of women. We are necessarily to some extent at sea as to how,
in future, we should express our spirituality. The disruption in their
spirituality which feminist women like myself have been through is not
to be underestimated. But it is no answer to think that through a
nostalgia for the security of the past we can retrace our steps. We have
become different persons.

To say this is not of course to be indifferent to the past. That would
be a very different matter. We may love our heritage. Personally I have
a keen sense of the history of my country and more widely of the
European past. As a small child I learnt to date the architectural styles
of churches and cathedrals and as an adult (to the astonishment of
others when I am spot on) date everything around me! It is no chance
that for many years I studied and then taught history. There is, of
course, no reason why we should lose our love for the past. Indeed we
may come to value it if anything even more deeply in our shifting world.
But that is a very different proposition from the contention that we
should find ourselves in relation to the past, more particularly in our
religion. In our thought, we must have a dialectical relationship to what
has been. Without our intellectual heritage we could not think. More-

over, we shall find elements in the past that we can appropriate for the future. But there is also much that we must jettison if we are to be true to our present-day values.

Now such a relationship to past human religion is open to us precisely if we envisage religion as functioning like any other discipline in relationship to the past. The problem with Christianity is that Christians hold that there has been a revelation in history, so that the past becomes a necessary point of reference. That is heteronomous. It is not how we think today. We need to take responsibility for our ethical stance and, equally, for our spirituality. Particularly in the matter of the relationship which should pertain between women and men we shall not find adequate models in the past. Our ethical sensibilities and our overcoming of hierarchical relations must, in turn, affect our understanding of God. It is not somehow ahistorical to abandon a primitive religious myth. That it will seem like a disruption is only because our religion has lagged so far behind our understanding in other spheres. If we fail to move on, we may well be left without any kind of viable spirituality. Discontinuity, never comfortable, would look to be a necessity. For it is unlikely that the way in which men formulated their understanding of God in an ancient Near Eastern culture will be relevant to us today.

Western religion has served many functions. It has mediated to other generations some explanation of the universe and the place of humanity within it. Christianity and notably Judaism (for better or for worse) have provided societies with a moral code. But if one is a theist, one need not doubt that, whatever else religion may have been, it has also represented a response to that dimension of reality which is God. As in our age, so in every age, people have been aware of that which we name God. We may well come to conceptualize God otherwise; that is another matter, which I shall discuss presently. But whatever God is – a force or power which enables love, insight and healing – God has always been. The whole complexity of the interweaving of religious sensibilities with other needs and desires is something which I shall attempt in part to elucidate in Chapters IV and V. But before we turn to such an analysis of the thought-forms of Christianity it will be useful to probe the nature of feminism further. Only then shall we have a grid through which to read the past and a measure of that with which any future conception of God must be compatible.

III

Feminist Ethics

In his book *Towards Deep Subjectivity*, Roger Poole contends that different systems of thought occupy what he terms different conceptual spaces. Poole writes:

> Every age has its characteristic conceptual space . . . Every thinker brings a space into being which he establishes as peculiarly his own . . . Just how one wins through to a space one can think in involves a very interesting series of conceptual transformations . . . The thinker shapes himself as he thinks. He excludes or includes, he modifies the shape of his world. Philosophical space is thus the space of choice. The thinker has to decide not only what is right and wrong but also what he wants to *become* by deciding the matter this way rather than that way. In deciding what he wants to become, he decides indirectly what he wants his world to become. All thinking is legislative. The vital moment in this process of transformation is when the *alternatives* offered in a preceding system have to be *rejected*.[1]

The magnitude of the revolution which feminism represents could well be characterized by saying that, in these terms, it occupies a new conceptual space. In this chapter I shall in particular be concerned with the feminist understanding of the self. In thinking about the self, feminists may well be held precisely to have rejected the previous alternatives. Feminism is, moreover, legislative. Not only do feminists critique the past from a feminist perspective, but that perspective itself constitutes a vision.

The idea of this chapter is to provide the necessary background to the remainder of this book. My thesis is that feminists (for all their differences) have a radically different understanding of the self-in-relation from that which has been built into Western theology. It is from the perspective of this different understanding that feminists critique the theology that we have known. In the two chapters which follow I shall be attempting such a reading and critique. But it is also this differing conception of the self-in-relation which I think to be crucial as we consider what theology and spirituality should be. The penultimate chapter will then be dedicated to the question of how we should conceptualize God in relation to the self. In the final chapter I attempt to describe the practices which may enable such a spirituality.

In calling this chapter 'feminist ethics', I am employing the word ethics as shorthand for a life-style, a value system, and a way of conceiving of the self. I have avoided the word theory (as in 'feminist theory'), for that word has come to have specifically 'French', post-structuralist connotations. A considerable part of the chapter will concern writers who have come out of an Anglo-Saxon, in particular 'object relations', psychoanalytic tradition. However, there are no clear lines of demarcation, for many American feminist theorists in recent years have been profoundly influenced by the French tradition. I shall also have something to say about the French tradition, which I shall then take up again in particular in Chapter V. I shall assume no familiarity with the writing I discuss. Readers who know their way around the field may wonder whether I am glossing over the profound differences which exist. What I am attempting to do here, however, is to show the commonalities of assumptions rather than the different theoretical ways in which feminists have worked. For I believe that feminists hold in common a profoundly different understanding of the self from that upon which Western theology has been predicated.

It has been difficult to know how to give some sense of a wide and varied field of writing without swamping the reader with names and tendencies, disputes and differences. I have tried to introduce a few salient writers. I begin the chapter by giving a vivid illustration (my own) from the field of art history, a field in which the impact of a feminist analysis is immediately apparent. I then turn to insights in social psychology and to post-Freudian psychoanalytic thought, basically in the Anglo-Saxon tradition, though I shall also mention French Lacanian thought. Taking these insights, I shall illustrate how feminists have used them to analyse political philosophy from the early modern period. I think that such an exercise shows well what might, in parallel, be accomplished in theology. In the second half of the chapter I switch my attention from the feminist analysis of male thought (and art) to the question as to how feminists themselves wish to think about the self in relation. I attempt not to carry on this discussion in a theoretical vacuum but to provide pointers to the fact that such thinking has been forged in the furnace of women's experience in the women's movement over the last twenty-five years. It is because theory and praxis have mutually informed one another that the feminist revolution has been secured.

I commence, then, with my illustration drawn from the history of Western art. The visual expression of culture allows us to grasp in dramatic form the charge being made by feminists. Feminism has given us a new perspective from which to analyse the past; and once one's eyes have been opened, one can never restore one's former blindness.[2] My illustration is that well-known square in the centre of Florence, the Piazza della Signoria, and the sculpture displayed in it. I hope that some of my readers at least will be able to follow me around the square in their imagination. It is a square not without historical significance. It might well be contended that here, if anywhere, the cradle of modern Europe is to be found. A square (and notably this one) is a public space in which a civilization represents itself. Against the backdrop of this space people over generations carried on their daily lives; sold their sheep and cattle; entertained themselves; and performed civil and ecclesiastical ceremonies. As the Renaissance art historian Martin Kemp has it, the Piazza della Signoria was 'the place where the theatre of civic life was conducted'.[3]

Consider now the sculpture present in that square. It was statuary placed there for the populace to see, indeed in some cases to induce political conformity. We do not have here an art gallery but a public square. Moving clockwise from the point of entry into the square from Piazza del Duomo, first we have the equestrian statue of Duke Cosimo I de' Medici, representative of the family whose fortunes were bound up with that of Florence at the height of its power, his sword slung at his side. Then we have the Neptune fountain: innocent enough, we might think, though in fact it was built to celebrate Florence's acquisition of a navy. Then next the Marzocco, a heraldic lion taking its name from Mars, the god of war, protector of Florence. Then Donatello's Judith and Holofernes; this time, she has a weapon in her hand. Then a copy of Michelangelo's David: man displayed at twice his natural size, with sling and stone. As we pass to the loggia, 'holding up the dripping head of Medusa, while her revolting trunk lies at his feet',[4] stands Cellini's portrayal of Perseus slaying the Medusa. 'In the gesture with which he [Perseus] holds out the severed head from him, in the look of secret delight that is already half remorseful for all that dead beauty, in the heroic grace with which he stands there after the murder, the dead body marvellously fallen at his feet, Cellini has proved himself the greatest sculptor of his time.'[5] Beyond him, we have the 'splendidly composed'[6] Rape of the Sabines. Then the Rape of Polissena; beyond that Hercules fighting the Centaur.

What may we learn? In the first place woman portrayed as an agent is absent (with the exception of the Donatello, to which matter I shall come). The square tells us of the doings of men. But woman is also present: as beheaded, or carried off in terror to satisfy men's lust. The extent of the incipient violence must strike us as extraordinary. Every major statue portrays a murder or rape, a weapon is at the ready, or the statue was constructed in celebration of war. Perhaps violence and sexuality are closely allied in the male imagination? In the centre of the square actual violence is commemorated with the plaque which marks the spot where, in 1498, Savonarola was burnt at the stake. And it has seemed perfectly natural that these should be the scenes upon which the gaze of generations has fallen. Neither the guide books nor the volumes of art history apparently find it remarkable. Today the tourists descend from their buses, click their cameras and think nothing of it. It is just the normal panorama of Western culture, depicting, we should note, almost equally scenes from the Bible and from ancient mythology. Suppose for a moment, however, that the square had displayed the activities of women. Suppose it had shown women torturing men's genitals and preparing for battle. And suppose that, over the generations, women had gone about their daily business against such a back-drop. We see the absurdity of it! So now what of the Donatello, the work of a man, himself clearly homosexual, who seems to have had a unique capacity to depict women in their strength, the equals of men?[7] At one point – so our guide book tells us – his Judith was wheeled out of the square. Why? Because it was not thought fitting to show a woman murdering a man![8]

Feminism represents that different conceptual space from which one can see. Feminist discourse has given us a stance from which to 'read' the past. What appeared unremarkable is now seen as culturally specific: the product of a system called patriarchy. The world is shown to be gendered. There is a construction of masculinity, and equally of femininity. Violence is perfectly normal, whether directed against other men or against women. But perhaps there is something exceptional about the square which I have chosen; it may be atypical. Before we come to any such conclusion, let us progress to the neighbouring, ecclesiastical, square, the Piazza del Duomo. There again we find famous sculpture: baptistery doors. And what was the scene chosen for the competition for the commission for those doors in 1400? Abraham's near-slaughter of Isaac on Mount Moriah. What an odd choice, one might think, of a scene for a competition for baptistery doors! That is, until one recognizes, first, that baptism is the ceremony which marks the entry into the world of the male religion, displacing as it does the natural birth from a woman,[9] and furthermore, that the story of Abraham and Isaac may well mark the securing of patriarchy in a (male) God-father-son genealogy.[10] Knowingly or not, the scene they chose was exactly pertinent! Feminism is the interpretative perspective which we have lacked. It takes a journey with a feminist friend[11] to gain it.

The point is that Western culture has been sufficiently hegemonic that there was no questioning of the whole until the rise of feminism. Susan Bordo writes of the Western intellectual tradition:

> The tradition, we should remember, reigned for thousands of years and was able to produce powerful works of philosophy, literature, art, and religion before its hegemony began to be dismantled, under great protest. Located at the very centre of power, at the intersection of three separate axes of privilege – race, class and gender – that tradition had little stake in the recognition of difference (other than to construct it as inferior or threatening Other). This is not to say that this tradition is univocal. Rather, my point is that it produced no self-generated practice of self-interrogation and critique of its racial, class and gender biases – because they were largely invisible to it.[12]

Feminism represents such an interrogation. True, an individual – as perhaps Donatello – may in the past have traversed the norms, half-knowing that what he did was subversive. But feminists are the first to attempt consciously to stand outside this whole cultural production. They wield as an instrument of analysis a well thought-out theory about its inadequacy and relativity. Feminists have an agenda: they want to change the world. What is remarkable is that feminism represents a shift of considerable proportions which has taken place among large numbers of women in the space of little more than twenty years.

Consider next the field of theology. It, too, is a cultural production. Of course that does not mean that there may not be complex and multiple reasons for that construction, among them that there is a dimension of reality which we may call God and which humans have endeavoured to express. Nevertheless, the particular shape which Christian theology has taken has been forged within patriarchy. How could it have been otherwise, given that patriarchy has been the cultural milieu within which creativity has been conceived? The biblical literature is not exempt from this. The Bible represents the understanding of God of men living under patriarchy. The question is whether the paradigms for God and humanity which have been conceived under patriarchy are further viable. I am suggesting that they are not. For when humanity comes to an ethical divide of the magnitude represented by feminism, anything which does not conform to our new ethical awareness needs to be cast aside. It will be judged and found wanting. Ethics and religion correlate closely, so that it must be impossible in the long run to hold to a religious position which embodies paradigms that we cannot consider ethical. For God is supposed to be good, and religion to speak to our highest aspirations. Hence the challenge to Christianity.

It becomes evident that an interrogation of theology is far from being

a side-issue in this our secular age. For theology has undergirded and
legitimized Western culture. The society's conception of God has been
integral to that culture's self-understanding. Biblical stories and scenes
are fundamental to our heritage (as our tour around the Piazza della
Signoria made evident). Theology *par excellence* has been the screen on
to which ultimate values have been projected. A transcendent monotheism and a God conceived as 'male' have, I shall argue, had the effect
of consolidating a certain construal of gender and of relations between
the sexes. Particular gender arrangements are given an ultimate sanc-
tion: they are thought to conform to the way in which things ought to
be, decreed from on high. In his theology man has given his imagination
scope. Woven into that theology in particular is man's understanding of
his sexuality, his fears and his desires. This is hardly surprising if, as we
may suppose, our sexuality and our spirituality are at the core of our
being. Now the male conception of sexuality has been in large part
culturally formed within the matrix of the patriarchal family. Hence the
importance of studying gender relations within the family if that projection which is Christian theology is to be understood. To this I shall
now progress.

What it is important to convey here is the development in psychoanalytic thought which has taken place since Freud. Two interconnected
emphases of Freud's in particular have come to be challenged. First,
Freud took the development of the boy child as his norm (despite the fact
that so many of his famous patients were women!). Indeed he proclaimed that he did not understand women; hence his oft-quoted remark
'*Was will das Weib*?' – What does woman want? Freud thought the
development of woman problematic, believing that she failed sufficiently
to free herself from the mother (which is of course in itself a value judgment). On the other hand he viewed the boy as emerging from the
Oedipus conflict relatively unscathed: that is to say, free of his mother
and modelling himself on his father. Secondly – and this is not discon-
nected – Freud paid little attention to the pre-Oedipal relation on the
part of either boy or girl with the mother. By contrast, second-generation
Freudian thought saw the relation with the mother as crucial. This is true
notably of British 'object relations theory', as it came to be known, of the
1940s and 1950s. Moreover it has become very apparent that, far from
traversing with ease the distance between the near-symbiotic relation
with the mother to being an independent self modelled on the father, the
male finds this passage fraught with difficulty, retaining a much more
ambivalent relation to the woman than Freud had recognized. Furthermore, feminist theorists have a different estimate of what it is to be a self.
Thus they evaluate the whole question of independence and relationality
otherwise. I shall now endeavour to illustrate these issues.

I commence with some discussion of 'object relations theory', more especially as it has been developed in the United States and particularly by women. Object relations theory is so called because the other (in the first place the mother) is understood to become an internalized 'object'. That is to say, the self is understood as profoundly relational. The aim of therapy is to resolve the internal constellation of relations to others so that it is non-conflictual. As Nancy Chodorow, to whose work I shall turn shortly, comments (paraphrasing Freud's 'where id was, there shall ego be'): 'Where fragmented internal objects were, there shall harmoniously related objects be; and where false, reactive self was, there shall true, agentic self be, with its relationally based capacity both to be alone and to participate in the transitional space between self and other self that creates play, intimacy, and culture.'[13] Such a statement immediately draws us into what ontologically Chodorow (in common with many other women in different ways) wishes there to be: namely what in her vocabulary she calls a 'transitional space' between self and other – that is to say, 'held' space within which creativity can blossom. (Chodorow's talk of 'play' is presumably a reference to the work of the well-known British object relations theorist D.W. Winnicott.)

Chodorow has been the most influential of American feminist object relations theorists. Her *The Reproduction of Mothering*, published in 1979,[14] was a landmark in providing an explanatory hypothesis as to the genesis of sexism. Chodorow points to the fact that in all known societies the task of 'mothering', that is to say tending to the needs of young children, is overwhelmingly the work of women. Boys and girls are thus placed in an asymmetrical situation. For the boy, the issue of being a separate person becomes entangled with that of being of the opposite sex to the basic carer. As in all Freudian theory, he is understood to model himself on the father to gain the necessary individuation. However, the pull of the mother is far greater than Freud had recognized. The boy then tends to utilize the mother as an object over against which he defines himself, denying her her own subjectivity. In the attempt to find himself (which is so difficult) he commonly comes to 'put down' everything he associates with femininity. 'Learning what it is to be masculine comes to mean learning to be not-feminine.'[15] Boys develop what Ruth Brunswick (quoted by Chodorow) calls 'what we have come to consider the normal masculine contempt of women'.[16]

The little girl is very differently situated. She can much more easily experiment with both individuation and symbiosis. Being herself is not associated in the same way with seeing the two sexes as opposites. Hence girls develop what Chodorow names 'permeable' ego boundaries, as compared with the more 'rigid' ego boundaries found in boys. It is such permeable ego boundaries which Chodorow seeks to commend. As she says: 'Selfhood does not depend . . . on the strength and impermeability of ego boundaries.'[17] Thus from Chodorow's perspective, it is male, not female, development that is problematic. Object relations theorists speak of the 'split' internal image of the mother which so frequently occurs in boys. She is on the one hand idealized and desired, on the other denigrated and feared. Of boys Chodorow remarks:

> They come to emphasize differences, not commonalties or con-tinuities, between themselves and women, especially in situations that evoke anxiety, because these commonalties and continuities threaten to challenge gender difference . . . Male heterosexuality is embedded in Oedipal devaluation, fear and contempt of women as well as a fear of the overwhelmingness of mother and of acknowledging emotional demands and needs. Male dominance on a psychological level is a masculine defence and a major psychic cost to men, built on fears and insecurity; it is not straightforward power.[18]

Researchers have in fact found men to differentiate on the basis of gender more than women (for example, giving small children different toys to play with according to whether they believe the child to be male or female).[19]

It will also be useful to mention the work of Robert Stoller (which has not least influenced Chodorow) here. Stoller, a Californian psycho-analyst, has worked extensively in the field of gender identity. In an article published in English in 1974, 'Facts and Fancies: An Examina-tion of Freud's Concept of Bisexuality',[20] Stoller challenges Freud's analysis of human development. He writes:

> [Freud missed] the full significance of the symbiosis with mother and its tidal pull . . . to *being the same as mother*, which would be the destruction of masculinity . . . [He] never questioned that the male's relationship with his mother was fundamentally heterosexual. Freud therefore makes what I consider two errors. The first was that he assumed as a biological given that maleness was the firmer, more natural state . . . The second was that he said the male is off to a healthier start because his relationship with his mother is by definition heterosexual.[21]

In regard to the first of these (Freud's assumption that biologically male-ness is the firmer and more natural state), Stoller points out that, as we now know, every foetus is in the first place female and remains so but for the presence of the male chromosome. (Stoller's own understanding of the development of gender identity is, however, cultural rather than biological.)

In regard to the second (Freud's belief that the male is off to a healthier start), Stoller maintains that, on the contrary, the opposite is the case. For the boy:

> Heterosexuality comes only after a massive piece of work . . . The little boy must break from the original, primal symbiosis in which he and his mother are at first merged . . . [Thus] not only are [females] probably the stronger, not to say the primary sex, but their very 'homosexuality' may give them an advantage . . . I am suggesting that the sense of maleness and the later development, masculinity, are a bit less firmly established in males than the sense of femaleness and femininity in females . . . Within even the fortunate little boy's sense of maleness is buried more primitive merging with mother's identity. The same merging in the little girl only strengthens her sense of femaleness . . . Deep within . . . the pull toward merging again into mother's femaleness terrifies and enthrals men.[22]

It is this, Stoller believes, that explains 'the roots . . . of much of what is called masculinity – preoccupation with being strong, independent, untender, cruel, polygamous, misogynous, perverse'.[23] An analysis such as he has given would again fit well, as he points out, with the fact that, as he and others have established, the fear of homosexuality is much more marked in men than in women.

Moving momentarily to the field of French, Lacanian, psychoanalytic theory, let us, for all its differences, note the following similarity. Lacan, too, conceives the tidal pull of the mother to be far stronger and the task of separating from her much more difficult of accomplishment than Freud had recognized. Lacan believes gender to be discursively constructed; that is to say, it is something we learn as we enter into language and culture. The subject must align him- or herself on one side of the gender divide. But at the same time, for Lacan the self (whether the subject is aware of this or not) is in no way integrated. Of the boy one must say – and Lacan considers development from the perspective of the male! – that he yearns for the wholeness which he thinks the woman can give him. As the American feminist theorist Nancy Fraser remarks: 'The Lacanian ego is an imaginary projection, deluded about its own stability and self-possession, hooked on an impossible desire for unity and self-completion.'[24] (It is fascinating to note that, for all his difference from Lacan, Sartre had a similar view of woman as somehow *en soi*.) Lacan reads as though at least the male of the species is left for ever unsatisfied, mourning and desiring what he has lost.

We may also remark on the fact that the son may wish to cast himself as weak or sinful (perhaps as 'feminine') in relation to the father. The British object relations theorist Ronald Fairbairn analyses this in religious terms. Fairbairn thinks that the concept of the good father and his law is created by sons (and daughters?) in the mental act of internalization. The individual takes badness on himself in order that his belief in the goodness of authority may be maintained. Fairbairn writes:

> Framed in religious terms . . . it is better to be a sinner in a world ruled by God than to live in a world ruled by the Devil. A sinner in a world ruled by God may be bad; but there is always a certain sense of security to be derived from the fact that the world around is good – 'God's in His heaven – All's right with the world!'; and in any case there is always a hope of redemption. In a world ruled by the Devil the individual may escape the badness of being a sinner; but he is bad because the world around him is bad. Further, he can have no sense of security and no hope of redemption. The only prospect is one of death and destruction.[25]

This mechanism will find its resonance in theology, as we shall see.

However, I now progress to work in social psychology, in particular that of Carol Gilligan. Gilligan's work comes out of a different setting from that of Chodorow, namely in the first place the observation that girls do not fit the criteria for the development of moral maturity which had been suggested by the social psychologist and ethicist Lawrence Kohlberg. But some of her conclusions as to the conception of the self typically found in males and females are similar to Chodorow's. Gilligan's *In a Different Voice* (1982)[26] has been extraordinarily influential. (One may comment that it is a problem of some magnitude, an astute indicator of the fact that men are the dominant sex, that even the founding texts of feminist theory which have now been absorbed by a whole generation of women have often not been read by men who would consider themselves well educated.) Gilligan's work, as also Chodorow's early work, has come in for much flak in recent years. I am not sure that this is well founded. In the first place, Gilligan's work is held to be too impressionistic (in response to which one might well comment that it would appear to have rung bells with a great many women), and too selective (which Gilligan denies, though the sample has indeed been American). In the second place it is held to polarize male and female development – perhaps inevitably, when such work seeks to delineate types. Gilligan in fact specifically states at the beginning of her book that she is seeking to depict two modes of moral reasoning, which she finds present in the voices of men and of women respectively, though they are not necessarily or always aligned that way.[27] In the third place, in recent years both Chodorow's and Gilligan's work has been held to be 'essentialist' – the most damning judgment among the current generation of feminist theorists! This is an odd comment, given that they suggest that gender formation takes place within the context of family society and is not in any way biological. When this work first appeared the point was well grasped.[28]

I shall give a brief description of Gilligan's work here which will serve our purposes. In the course of carrying out certain empirical tests with boys and girls, men and women, Gilligan has come to the conclusion that the two sexes delineate the self in its relationships strikingly differently. The male self is commonly constituted by 'difference' and 'separation'. Asked to describe themselves, men situate themselves in the centre of the picture, seeing the world in relation to them. 'Individual achievement rivets the male imagination.'[29] Involvement with others is held to be a 'qualification of identity', rather than 'leading to its realization'. Men tend to break out of situations which they characterize as smothering and they fear intimacy. In one experiment, in which people were given pictures and asked to write stories to go with them, a high percentage of men responded to a picture showing two people sitting side by side on a park bench by a river over which there was a low bridge by writing stories which ended in murder or rape.[30] By contrast women, Gilligan concludes, understand the self as constituted by 'connection' and they fear isolation. Asked to describe themselves, women speak of their relations with significant others. Gilligan quotes David McClelland who writes that ' "women are more concerned than men with both sides of an interdependent relationship" and are "quicker to recognize their own interdependence" '.[31] In the same experiment there is overall less violence in women's stories. But the picture in response to which women wrote stories which involved violence showed a man standing by himself in the lighted window of a high-rise office block, the only picture which showed a person on his own. It would seem, then, that women believe aggression to result from 'the isolation of the self and . . . the hierarchical construction of human relationships'.[32] Gilligan writes: 'It appears that men and women may experience attachment and separation in different ways and that each sex perceives a danger which the other does not see – men in connection, women in separation.'[33] Her diagnosis is that men and women have diametrically opposed tasks. Whereas men need to learn to be a self-*in-relation;* women need to come into their own, to be a *self*-in-relation.

From her perspective Gilligan, too, is critical of male psychoanalysts (and specifically Freud) who write their presuppositions as to what the self should be into their work. She makes this charge against Freud:

This disengagement of self from the world outside . . . initiates not only the process of differentiation but also the search for autonomy, the wish to gain control over the sources and objects of pleasure . . . Thus connection – associated by Freud with 'infantile helplessness' and 'limitless narcissism' . . . gives way to separation. Consequently, assertion, linked to aggression, becomes the basis for relationships.

Freud speaks of the 'primary mutual hostility of human beings' and the 'aggressiveness' that 'forms the basis of every relation of affection and love among people'. The single exception to this is located in women's experience: 'the mother's relation to her male child'. But this love is not to be shared by the son who would 'make himself dependent in a most dangerous way on a portion of the external world'.[34] Feminists start from a very different perspective, leading to a radically different estimation.

We have been considering the fact that the passage which the boy undergoes in separating from the mother may well be fraught and remain incomplete. But the relation with the father is not easy either. Within patriarchy, father-son relations, indeed male-male relations more widely, have been hierarchically ordered and deeply competitive. Freud himself commented:

Even in our middle-class families fathers are as a rule inclined to refuse their sons independence and the means necessary to secure it and thus to foster the growth of the germ of hostility which is inherent in their relation. A physician will often be in a position to notice how a son's grief at the loss of his father cannot suppress his satisfaction at having at length won his freedom.[35]

One wonders how much has changed. Reviewing a recent collection of essays, *Fathers and Sons*,[36] Mary Beard compares the attitudes which are revealed with the attitudes present in a similar collection by women writing on their fathers. The male authors 'cast themselves in the mould of the New Man'. 'But amid the tears even the New Man, it seems, defines his masculinity against the decaying remains of his father. "Perhaps it is only then" writes Hoyland [a contributor] "when the father grows frail, that we finally become men in our own eyes." ' The men construct the father 'as a clearly defined foil, over whom they themselves, as sons, must in the end triumph'. By contrast the daughters' view of their father appears to be multifaceted: 'There is no place in the daughters' view for that unitary vision of "fatherhood" (distinguished only as good or bad fathers) that stalks the men's writing.' This is a fascinating observation, pertinent to theology.

The evidence surely points to the fact that the son-father relation is both of extraordinary importance and, equally, difficult of resolution for the male. Not for nothing do the two primary myths of our culture, the Oedipus myth and Christianity, both concern the relationship of a son to a father.[37] The son tests his masculinity in relation to the father, desiring both to identify with him and to slay him in order to come into his own. The basic context which gives rise to such a dynamic is clearly that of the patriarchal family. The father is a distant figure, while the mother is the one who is close at hand, with whom the son can develop an intimate relationship. The father becomes a competitor for the love of the mother. At the same time there is no possibility of a close relationship with the father which would allow the development of 'permeable' ego boundaries. The son's relation to the father becomes problematic in a way which finds no parallel in the daughter's relation to the father and which indeed is not mirrored by the daughter's relationship to the mother. Chodorow's suggested cure for the ill which she describes is therefore that men should take an active part in parenting. (Indeed we may think that this is increasingly happening, and if the analysis is correct, may in time generate a profound change in men's psychology.)

We have little cultural material which reflects women's relations with their mothers or with other women. Since they have not been the concern of men, women/women relationships find scant reflection in the world of art and literature. But the thinking which in recent years has derived from a feminist context is fascinating. It is not only descriptive of what is found to be the case, but is also legislative, advocating the possibility of a very different understanding of the self-in-relation. Each person retains her own individuality, while bound by deep ties to the other. The other is like the self, while also a distinct person. Hence self-definition is not understood to be formed through conflict with another. Much of the practice of the women's movement has clearly tried to bring about the possibility of such relationships. To what extent women may be hindered in coming to be themselves through too close a relation to the mother is of course an interesting question. Freudian theory has assumed that the girl, too, needs the father as the third term to allow her to differentiate herself from the mother. Some writers (Gilligan, for example) have suggested that women are afraid of going too far out on the web of human relationships.

I have already mentioned some Anglo-Saxon writing on the girl's relationship to the mother. Here is the French psychoanalyst and feminist theorist Luce Irigaray, in a passage in which she contrasts the play of girls with Freud's observation of the famous '*fort/da* game. Freud watched a small boy playing with a cotton reel on a piece of string, casting it from him and drawing it back again, announcing as he did so '*fort!*' (away) and '*da!*' (there again). He concluded that the game reflected a playing out of the absence and renewed presence of the mother, thus learning to cope with it. [38] By contrast with the '*fort/ da* game, in which the mother is viewed as an external object over which the small boy, in his play, gains control, Irigaray describes the girl.

> She dances, thereby constructing for herself a vital subjective space, space which is open to the cosmic maternal world . . . This dance is also a way of creating for herself her own territory in relation to the mother.
>
> And does she speak? If she speaks, it is mostly in a playful way, without giving special importance to syllabic or phonemic oppositions. It may be bisyllabic, or like a litany, and rather singsong, modulated tonally. This language corresponds to a rhythm and also to a melody . . . Sometimes it takes the form of silence.
>
> Women's relation to the 'same' between them, and the girl's relation to the mother, are not to be mastered by the *fort-da*. The mother always remains too familiar and too close. The girl has the mother, in some sense, in her skin . . . Furthermore, the sexual movement fundamental to the feminine is much closer to gyration than to the gesture like little Ernst's of throwing away and drawing closer. The girl tries to reproduce around her or inside herself a movement whose energy is circular . . . both inviting and refusing access to the territory thus inscribed . . . Little girls . . . describe a space around themselves and do not move a substitute object around . . . Woman always speaks *with* the mother; man speaks in her absence.
>
> The girl-subject does not master anything . . . [Girls] do not want to master the other, but to create themselves. They only control the other . . . if they fail to create their axis, fail to be free to create themselves. They . . . need to be born to themselves and to gain their autonomy themselves, . . . to stand centred about their own axis, an axis which passes microcosmically from their feet to the top of their head, macrocosmically from the centre of the earth to the centre of the sky. [39]

Thus Irigaray – not unlike Chodorow, as we have seen – depicts woman as growing within the subjective space created through her relationship to the other, space in which she both feels safe yet also has individuality.

I turn next to a consideration of the way in which insights gained in the fields of psychoanalysis and social psychology have been employed by women in the field of political philosophy. I have already said that I find this work suggestive of what may also be possible in analysing the paradigms present in Christian theology. Political theory and

systematic theology are not unalike in relevant respects. Integral to both
is a structure of thought, a consideration of the self in relation, and
ethics and values. Both political theory and Christian theology are
imaginative, having a projection of the human in the state of nature and
equally of a utopian ideal or eschaton. Thus both subjects display a
canvas on which those who have created them (men) have told us about
their desires and wishes, their fears and hopes. In analysing classic texts
of political theory, feminists have shown how certain presuppositions
about the nature of the self in relation to others and a certain construal
of gender is written into the text. I believe in like manner that there is
much to be learnt about the male psyche from theology (as I shall
attempt to show in the next two chapters).

In this work in political science there has been a considerable concentration on texts from the early modern period, and it is this which I
shall consider. The readings are in one sense predictable. Yet the extent
to which the texts conform to type and are shown to reflect a certain set
of presuppositions is fascinating. I shall suggest that the analysis of the
paradigms of Christian theology is even more interesting, for it may be
that desire and sexuality have more tendency to be sublimated in the
realm of religion than in political theory. In the texts of early modern
man the norm for humanity is very evidently taken to be the single male,
who is portrayed as isolated and competitive. Women and children are
largely absent from the scene. None the less, there is present what
we may call a construct of the feminine, which is related to nature or
viewed as that from which the male protagonists have escaped. I give
some examples from the work of a number of feminist theorists.

Seyla Benhabib quotes Hobbes: ' "Let us consider men . . . as if but
even now sprung out of the earth, and suddenly, like mushrooms, come
to full maturity, without all kind of engagement to each other." ' She
comments: 'This vision of men as mushrooms is an ultimate picture of
autonomy.'[40] (The word 'autonomy', of course, here connotes independence and isolation.) In this quotation the earth takes the place of
woman! Jane Flax likewise comments, with reference to Rousseau: 'Just
like a small child, Rousseau's natural man seems to have only two
choices: isolation or total engulfment . . . Reciprocity, in the sense of
mutual interdependence and independence is not possible.'[41] Descartes'
view of the self, exemplified by his famous *cogito ergo sum*, naturally
comes in for much comment. Of Descartes, Flax remarks: 'Social relations are not necessary for the development of the self . . . It appears to
come into the world whole and complete.' In an extraordinary analysis
in her book *Speculum* (which plays on the idea of woman as a mirror
through which man achieves self-identity), taking off from Descartes'
work on optics, Irigaray makes this charge:

Representation here is auto-affective, auto-affecting solipsism. It embroiders its dream of potentiality alone in its chamber . . . But now, by a stroke of almost incredible boldness, it is the singular subject who is charged with giving birth to the universe all over again, after he has brought himself back into the world in a way that avoids the precariousness of existence as it is usually understood . . . In a speculative act of denial and negation that serves to affirm his autonomy.[42]

As Benhabib remarks, the message conveyed by the texts of early modern man is 'simple and profound: . . . in the beginning man was alone'.[43]

And what of woman? She is inevitably cast as 'mother'. On Descartes Flax comments:

The longings for symbiosis with the mother are not resolved. Therefore, one's own wishes, body, woman and anything like them (nature) must be partially objectified, depersonalized and rigidly separated from the core self in order to be controlled.

Meanwhile Rousseau's natural man has an intense dislike and fear of dependence on another, a situation which is thought to lead inevitably to servitude.[44] 'Woman' is the opposite of what man himself represents. Benhabib comments:

Woman is simply what men are not; namely, they are not autonomous, independent, but by the same token, nonaggressive but nurturant, not competitive but giving, not public but private. The world of the female is constituted by a series of negations. She is simply what he happens not to be. Her identity becomes defined by a lack – the lack of autonomy, the lack of independence, the lack of the phallus.[45] The narcissistic male takes her to be just like himself, only his opposite.[46]

Woman is cast as that from which man must differentiate himself. She represents a connectedness which he must deny.

Lacking a relation with a woman as an equal other and needing to escape from the mother, man meanwhile sets up 'the father' as the one in relation to whom he shall constitute himself. The realm of the father comes to be represented by the abstract sense of 'law'. Of Descartes, Susan Bordo writes:

Reunion with the (mother) world is, however, impossible for Descartes and for the Cartesian era . . . It is striking that only God the father can provide the reassurance Descartes needs. In the absence of a sense of connectedness with the natural world – and that includes, for Descartes, a sense of connectedness with one's own body – only a guarantee 'from above' can alleviate epistemological anxiety. [It] may also be described in terms of separation from the maternal – the immanent realms of earth, nature, the authority of the body – and a compensatory turning toward the paternal for legitimation through external regulation, transcendent values, and the authority of law.[47]

This analysis is at one with the way in which God 'the father' has often comprehended in himself the maternal, something which we shall consider later.[48] Benhabib likewise finds that, for early modern man, the law replaces the absent father.

[These individuals] have to re-establish the authority of the father in the image of the law. The early bourgeois individual not only has no mother but no father as well; rather, he strives to reconstitute the father in his own self-image . . . Now ego boundaries are clearly defined. The law reduces insecurity, the fear of being engulfed by the other, by defining mine and thine.[49]

The analysis of the role of the law here may also be pertinent in relation to a consideration of Judaism, as we shall see.[50]

This may be a suitable point to draw attention to the question of the nature of ethics which runs through this work. Gilligan finds that boys think about ethical dilemmas in terms of abstract rules and justice, while girls by contrast give thought to the particular needs of all those who are involved, themselves included. Confronted with the famous case as to whether Heinz should steal a drug from the pharmacist to save his wife's life, girls subvert the question as posed by the researcher, trying to find a way in which the human relationships between all participants may be maintained for the future. Further, Gilligan finds that boys will spend hours considering the rules of the games they play. By contrast, in the case of a dispute girls will either allow the rules to be broken with impunity, or even stop the game rather than exclude someone.[51] It is a charge frequently levelled in the feminist analysis of male texts of political philosophy that what is thought to be ethical is to hold 'a view from nowhere' (Thomas Nagel). Ethics is either Kantian or perhaps utilitarian; that is to say, equality before an (abstract) law rules. In this respect Benhabib distinguishes between what she calls the 'generalized' and the 'concrete' other. Thus for example the present-day Kantian deontological ethicist John Rawls believes in a 'substitutionalist' ethic in which an issue should be decided under a 'veil of ignorance' (i. e. one does not know who is occupying which position when the matter at hand is decided). In this way the other is 'generalized'. Benhabib contrasts this with an ethic which takes note of the particular circumstances of a 'concrete' other. Such a construal of the ethical is deeply consonant with an 'ethic of attention', which has been developed by women in particular and which I shall consider in the final chapter.[52]

The discussion of feminist work in political science may well be summed up in noting a distinction which Caroline Whitbeck draws between what she calls a 'self-other *relation* and a 'self-other *opposition* . In a self-other *opposition*, which is held to be a typically male way of construing the self, the fact that the other is distinct from the self is translated into the conception that the other is a threat. The self is defined over against the other. By contrast, in a self-other *relation*, which is held to be typical of women, the self still defines itself with reference to the other, but in this case there is the possibility of mutual self-realization. Self-interest is understood to be something which cannot neatly be separated from the interests of others (hence also an ethic in which someone takes into account the needs of all, including herself). In the history of modern European thought it was of course Hegel who first articulated the insight that the self is formed in relation to another. And he, notably, cast this relationship in terms of a con-flictual relationship, the outcome of which was the hierarchy of master and slave. Of his two protagonists, Hegel tells us that they are *ungleich* (unalike) and *entgegengesetzt* (set in opposition to one another),[53] though he sought an eventual outcome other than conflict and hierarchy. This leads Whitbeck to remark that: 'If a mother saw the emerging person who is her child in the way that Hegel describes, human beings would not exist.'[54] Benhabib, likewise, names Hegel's position 'trans-', as opposed to 'inter-', subjective.[55]

Even from the sketch of feminist work in political philosophy that I have been able to give, it will be clear that insights may be gleaned by using psychoanalytic findings as a tool of analysis. In the chapters which immediately follow, as I have said, I shall in part attempt to do some-thing similar in relation to theology. It is perhaps important here to make what may be a necessary distinction between the *analysis* of cultural constructs (whether the writings of political philosophers or the paradigms of Christian theology) and any *causal relationship* between the male unconscious and cultural forms. The question as to why patriarchy came about is not one which I can enter into, if indeed there is light to be thrown on that tangled subject. The most that could be said is that the structure of the patriarchal family (for example) would seem to be a site in which a particular outlook is engendered which may then find its reflection in cultural forms. Even here, as I shall further consider, one must take care not to underestimate the complexity of the

material. However, the question of the genesis and continued maintenance of patriarchy (could it be answered) is not without import
for the further question of how it might be dismantled. Thus Nancy
Chodorow who, as I have mentioned, advocates dual parenting as a
mechanism which may engineer change, stops far short of suggesting
that this on its own will bring about the demise of patriarchy. Others,
such as the American postmodern thinker Iris Marion Young, have
warned against any such simplistic suggestion.[56] Indeed, it is said that
too great a concentration on the level of personal relationships within
the family might well have the effect of diverting attention from the
urgent matter of the power relationships which pertain within society.
In the realm of theology, we not only need to confront the way in
which, for example, the understanding of God as father may serve to
legitimize abuse of power within the patriarchal family (a matter which
I shall consider later).[57] We should also not forget that religious institutions such as churches and the public recognition given to the Christian
religion serve to consolidate male hegemony in our societies.

   In the second half of this chapter, I shall turn to the question as to
how feminists themselves wish to conceptualize the self and consequently also their ideals for society. What I think we find is that
feminist thinking does not fit the previous schema. Feminists want the
lines to be drawn differently from the way they have been drawn
within male thought. As Poole comments, 'the *alternatives* offered in a
preceding system have to be rejected'. Thus I shall suggest that feminist
women overwhelmingly think in terms of a 'self-in-relation': integration
and relationality not standing in contradiction to one another, but
rather enabling one another. Again, feminists wish to find ways to conceptualize agency and responsibility without these concepts entailing the
isolated model of the self with which they have been associated in male
discourse. Feminists do indeed have in mind a differently delineated
subjectivity and consequently also a different ordering of society. They
will, then, need to shape old words differently or to forge new concepts
to express their meaning. The feminist revolution reaches to that depth.

   A good place to commence on this investigation will be to look at
the ambivalence present in feminist thinking about male modernity.
Modernity, in the Enlightenment and what flowed from it, brought with
it a discourse of rights and justice. Now it is clear that women too may
benefit from the fall-out. Generations of women campaigned for women
to have the vote. In the 1990s in Western democracies we still have not
achieved anything like equal salaries and terms of employment. Yet
there is a profound suspicion that the discourse of modernity, in the
form in which we have known it, is inadequate. This must be fuelled by
the lack of results. It must strike us as a significant statistic that, two

hundred years after the advent of a rhetoric of rights and justice, according to the United Nations women own 1% of the world's property while they put in two thirds of the world's working hours. We must then question whether it may be no chance that women have not fared better. The rhetoric of modernity arose within a particular historical context. It was created by white, bourgeois males and it reflected their needs. Law, for example, has been about the defence of (male) property rights and a securing of the private rights of individuals (so that until very recently rape was apparently not rape if it was conducted within marriage). Significantly, it took until this century for women simply to gain the vote.

Feminist women widely believe, then, that, far from all that is required being that women should have access to the same male public world, we must transform the relation between the public and the private. Indeed, the public world which we have known has only been possible because men consigned the personal, the affective and the emotional to the world of women. It is assumed that the male, in his public role, is 'unencumbered' by, for example, the need to look after children. The public world that has governed us has been predicated upon what its members held in common: being male, white, middle class, and (outwardly at least) heterosexual. Specificity, embodiment and needs have all had to be put aside. As Flax says: 'Enlightenment discourse was not meant to include women, and its coherence depends partially on our continuing exclusion.'[58] What we must aspire to, however, is a public realm in which human beings, in all their diversity, can be themselves. Thus a feminist like Young, believing that modernism has failed women, argues that what we should advocate is not 'universalism', but what she calls 'heterogeneity'. There must, she says be 'an openness to unassimilated otherness' and a 'politics of difference'.[59] This represents a very different kind of 'individualism' from that of the isolated self which political theory has thus far reflected!

Nor is it the case that the discourse of 'rights' that we have known is adequate to the 'rights' which women need to be protected and the relationships which they would think to be functional. Again Flax writes:

The political problems intrinsic to both pluralism and pragmatism include how to resolve conflict among competing voices; how to assure that everyone has a chance to speak; how to ensure that each voice counts equally; how to assess whether equality or participation is necessary in all cases or in which cases; . . . how to instil and guarantee a preference for speaking over the use of force; and how to compensate for the political consequences of an unequal distribution and control of resources.[60]

As she rightly says, the absence of these considerations in male texts is significant, reflecting as they do the culture of those who have felt no need to be worried by such 'details'. Simple majorities (one man, one vote) may well be used to quash the vital needs and interests of others. Hence the preference in much of the women's movement for 'consensus' decision-making. But consensus decision-making requires skills and practices – the ability to listen imaginatively to others and to find common ground with them – which are not to the fore within the culture of competitive individualism.

Let us take an example of the need to fashion concepts differently, women's relationship to the (male) concept of 'autonomy'. Now autonomy, etymologically, means being *auto-nomos*, giving the law to oneself, i. e. taking responsibility. Its opposite is heteronomy, other law, i.e. acting in obedience to another's will, thereby letting that person take responsibility from one. In this pure sense of the word 'autonomy', the women's movement may precisely be said to have been about women achieving an autonomous status. Yet situated as it has been within the context of male thought and Enlightenment discourse, the word autonomy has come to connote an individualistic, substantive and non-relational notion of the self. It is this which women wish to subvert (while yet finding ways to speak of effective agency and of individual responsibility). It will therefore be necessary to recast the meaning of the term, if indeed it can be retrieved, to convey what a woman like me intends. (Although I explain myself carefully in using this word, I note that I am constantly misunderstood.) It is significant that even a feminist like the British philosopher Jean Grimshaw, whom one might well place at the opposite end of the scale from a post-structuralist outlook, believes that the concept of autonomy will have to be differently nuanced.[61] Perhaps the term 'inter-dependent autonomy' may serve us?

In relation to this discussion about the nature of the self, what strikes me as significant is that even those women who have been the more concerned to get away from any kind of 'essentialist' notion are wary of theories which would deny a centredness. Take, for example, Flax, who may be a good indicator, standing as she does at a juncture between object relations thought and French theory, both of which have profoundly influenced her. Flax writes:

> Only when a core self begins to cohere can one enter into or use the transitional space in which the differences and boundaries between self and other, inner and outer, and reality and illusion are bracketed or elided.[62]

And again:

I am deeply suspicious of the motives of those who would counsel
. . . a [postmodernist] position at the same time as women have just
begun to re-member their selves and to claim an agentic subjectivity
available always before only to a few privileged white men.[63]

One who has been a therapist working with women as well as, in her
case, being a political theorist could hardly deny the critical importance
for women of coming to have a sense of self.

The discussion which I have pursued so far should not be taken to
imply that there are no significant differences between feminist theorists.
That is far from being the case. As I have already suggested, there
have been profound divergences, for example, in the debate about
'modernity'.[64] The cleavage lies in large part along the 'French' (post-
structuralist) versus 'Anglo-Saxon' divide, although that statement is
too simplistic in that the divide is a jagged one. Inasmuch as it follows
Lacan, French theory must think that gender is constructed within the
discourse which is language and culture. The American psychoanalyst
and feminist theorist Jessica Benjamin puts the importance of this well:
'[It] defines gender as a less mutable, symbolic structure; it becomes
constitutive of the psyche, rather than a function of historically constructed relationships.'[65] French theory may then appear overly deter-
ministic. As Fraser comments: 'Any number of trappings of male
dominance now appear as invariable features of the human condition.'[66]
Fraser, therefore, is among those who want a more pragmatic approach.
Transgressive practices, she argues, may give rise to discursive innova-
tion and this in turn lead to actual change. That would certainly seem
to have been the case in regard to the many gains which the women's
movement has brought about.

Now these debates are not without consequence for theology. If the
issue is the controlling nature of symbolic structures and language
versus the possibility of transgressive practices bringing about shifts in
understanding, its import may readily be seen. For my argument in the
chapters which follow is that the Western concept of deity has pre-
eminently been that symbolic structure which has reinforced a certain
ordering of society. The question, then, is this. Is it the case that the
theological imagination will have to shift (the question indeed being
how it can, or whether it will simply perpetuate itself) before women
can come into their own, either in the sphere of religion or indeed more
widely, in so far as Western (male) monotheism is a controlling symbol
in our culture? Or can transgressive practices (possibly even – within the
realm of the church – ordaining women) themselves bring about a
theological and indeed also a social shift? Certainly the coming of
women into their own makes the masculinist bias of Western theology

look decidedly odd, while in ethical terms placing a question-mark against its further existence. It may well be that, as I suggest, these changes will destabilize the religion.[67] It may also be that a shift in the understanding of the spiritual will, in turn, promote a reordering of gender within the society.

I come now to focus more specifically on feminist discussion of the nature of the self. I shall begin by defining my own understanding, using the vocabulary which I have adopted. I like to speak of the self as being 'centred in relation'. In using such a phrase I wish to capture the sense that the self is both 'centred' and 'relational'; moreover that it is not that there is conflict between the two. Thus we are able to acquire centredness because we are in relation. Since Hegel at least we have recognized that it is through our relationality to others that we form a subjectivity. A many-faceted self comes to be itself through the interplay with others. But it is also the case, I would maintain, that it is only as we have a certain centredness that we are able to be present to others. Of course in using the expression 'present to others' I am not meaning to imply that we are ever fully 'present' to ourselves, in the sense of wholly knowing ourselves. We are constantly, we may think, in flux, having no 'essential' nature or 'substantial self'. Nevertheless it is not until we have a certain integration, a certain centredness, as I have called it, that we can be sufficiently free of ourselves to be present to another.

I deny, then, that centredness is something that is acquired through rigid ego boundaries. Rather, the self with rigid ego boundaries is liable to be a weak self, threatened and spending its energies defending itself against others. Such a self (as the existentialists well knew) will misuse others as tools (as *vorhanden*, available) in order constantly to prop up what is an inadequate sense of self. Or, equally, unable to maintain its sense of self, the person will attempt to lose himself or herself in another. It could well be contended that women have all too often been on the receiving end of both these tendencies present in a male self which was less than secure in itself. Men have dominated women, wishing women to boost their ego; or alternatively, they have wished to 'lose' themselves in woman. What we have here is a self (if we can call it that) which swings between having rigid ego boundaries and (because this is unbearable), wishing to dissolve all sense of self. By contrast, the model which I and other feminists are advocating is one in which the self is centred in relation, i.e. a self which, while having a certain integrity and agency, finds itself through deep connections with others. We may think that this is the only adequate understanding of what it is to be a human being. I shall, then, proceed to look at the work of a number of other women who express something similar.

I commence with the work of Jessica Benjamin. A psychoanalyst and feminist theorist, as I have mentioned earlier, Benjamin has a background in the object relations tradition. She speaks of what she calls 'inter-subjective space' between persons. She writes: 'Intersubjective theory sees the relationship between self and other, with its tension between sameness and difference, as a continual exchange of influence.'[68] The question then is why such a tension between self and other through which each recognizes the other and each acquires a subjectivity should need to break down. For Hegel this is clear: because every tension carries within it the seeds of its own destruction, leading, for him, to domination of one by the other. 'If we wish to argue that tension can be sustained,' writes Benjamin, 'it behooves us to show how this is possible.'[69] Benjamin perceives here a fear that dependency on the other amounts to a loss of independence, as though recognition of the other would compromise the self. Domination begins with the attempt to deny dependency; as though (as both Hegel and Freud surmise) dependency were the equivalent of surrender!

Benjamin is particularly interested in the phenomenon of 'splitting': namely 'any breakdown of the whole, in which parts of self or other are split off and projected elsewhere . . . [such that] opposites – especially good and bad – can no longer be integrated; in which one side is devalued, the other idealized, and each is projected onto different objects'.[70] Thus (as we have seen) it frequently happens that the boy 'splits' in relation to the mother.

> The mother stands as the prototype of the undifferentiated object. She serves men as their other, their counterpart, the side of themselves they repress. The view of mother as object resounds throughout our culture. In general psychoanalytic discourse, the child relates to the mother as to an object of his drives, and correspondingly devalues her independent subjectivity.

But the corollary of this has only too often been a woman's lack of a sense of her own subjectivity; 'her willingness to offer recognition without expecting it in return'.[71]

Benjamin's thinking as to what could change is fascinating. Noting that both Erik Erikson[72] and Winnicott designate women's 'inner space' as passive, by contrast – using the term 'space' metaphorically and picking up language derived from Winnicott as to the possibility of holding oneself and bearing one's feelings without losing or fragmenting oneself – she wishes to suggest that women should use space creatively to gain a sense of authorship in their lives. Benjamin thus seeks to challenge a British psychoanalyst and feminist writer influenced by French theory, Juliet Mitchell (author of an early and influential work on *Psychoanalysis and Feminism*[73]). She argues that we do not have to rest content with 'the phallus' as the only object of desire (that is to say, the way in which sexuality has been delineated in a patriarchal world is not our only possibility). Benjamin believes that what women 'desire' is 'the exchange of gestures conveying attunement'. She writes: 'Women make use of the space in-between that is created by shared feeling and discovery. The dance of mutual recognition, the meeting of separate selves, is the context for their desire.' Nor does she think that this is foreign to men. 'We should consider the intersubjective mode where two subjects meet, where not only man but also woman can be subject.'[74] I find this work fascinating.

I turn, however, to work in a different field which has equally made an impression on me: that of Seyla Benhabib, to whose readings of classic works in political philosophy I have already drawn attention. Benhabib, a political scientist, comes basically out of the (Frankfurt) school of Critical Theory and carries on a running dialogue with Habermas as well as with Hegel, Marx and Freud. But as is so often the case among feminist theorists she has been eclectic in what she has absorbed and wants to bring together. She is also influenced by both the work of Gilligan and French feminism, allowing these to interact in what is a fertile matrix. Here is Benhabib on the self-in-relation:

> We seek to comprehend the needs of the other, his or her motivations, what s/he searches for, and what s/he desires. Our relation to the other is governed by the norms of *equity* and *complementary reciprocity*: each is entitled to expect and to assume from the other forms of behaviour through which the other feels recognized and confirmed as a concrete, individual being with specific needs, talents and capacities . . . In treating you in accordance with the norms of friendship, love and care, I confirm not only your *humanity* but your human *individuality*. The moral categories that accompany such interactions are those of responsibility, bonding and sharing. The corresponding moral feelings are those of love, care and sympathy and solidarity.[75]

And again, on what it means to be a self and to respect other selves:

> The grammatical logic of the word 'I' reveals the unique structure of ego identity: every subject who uses this concept in relation to herself knows that all other subjects are likewise 'I's. In this respect the self only becomes an I in a community of other selves who are also 'I's. Every act of self-reference expresses simultaneously the uniqueness and difference of the self as well as the commonality among selves. Discourses about needs and motives unfold in this space created by commonality and uniqueness, generally shared socialization, and the

contingency of individual life-histories.[76]

It is such a vision of the self in relation to others which many women have fleetingly glimpsed within the feminist community.

Naturally women whose background is that of a divinity school, or who are simply interested in questions of spirituality and ethics, have not been immune from these developments in other disciplines. Indeed divinity schools have often been at the forefront of developing feminist ideas. More widely, one may say that the feminist movement, in the form, for example, of the peace movement of the 1980s, has had about it a profound spirituality. The movement attracts those who want to change the world, who care for the earth, or who work (for example in counselling) in enabling women to live more creatively. I have already mentioned the work of Caroline Whitbeck. Whitbeck is a member of the Society of Friends (Quakers) and also writes within a Quaker setting. I shall speak here of the work of two other women, Anne Klein and Eleanor Haney, both of whom have had a more specifically theological formation. All three of these women are known to me personally, so I am able the better to place their work in context.

Anne Klein, an American and a specialist in Tibetan Buddhism, seeks to bring insights from Buddhism into feminist discourse. We need, she suggests, 'an expanded vocabulary of subjective states'.[77] Klein's interest, again, is that women shall come to themselves, while having a relational understanding of the self. She writes: 'Many women seek a style of identity that is powerful, yet favours the relational over the individual.' Buddhism, Klein claims, offers 'a positive view of an interdependently understood identity'. Feminists seek 'groundedness', 'clarity', a sense of 'self-esteem' and 'internal cohesiveness'. French feminists, Klein comments, have focused on an 'almost paradoxical' – I should want to suggest it is only paradoxical in terms of our old vocabulary – 'vision of an identity that is both self-contained and non-exclusive'. What Klein wants is a 'way of thinking of a strong self whose power does not depend on its ability to oppose, project, or conceive itself as radically separate'. The Buddhist notion of a (self)-observing presence is useful here. For women, who often have had only too little sense of themselves, to hold up before themselves a model of perfection has been profoundly unhelpful: the paradigm of 'struggle against self . . . has built-in dangers for women'. By contrast, 'awareness is a non-oppositional mental posture that is at the same time self-empowering'.[78]

Secondly, I wish to draw attention to the work of Eleanor Haney. Haney comes from a background in Christian ethics, having taken her doctorate at Yale with H. Richard Niebuhr. While remaining in some way in contact with Christianity, she has moved to a post-Christian women's spirituality and she is part of a lively group of women who are creating an alternative religious milieu. I mention here a fine article of hers which I have found never fails to meet with acclaim and call forth reverberations when I have used it in speaking to groups of women. I find that significant. Under the title 'What is Feminist Ethics?'[79] Haney asks after the nature of friendship. Within Christianity, love has basically been understood as *agape:* that self-giving love which does not count the cost. Haney suggests that the feminist understanding of friendship rather conforms to what should rightly be called *philia:* a love between centred selves who are essentially equals. Of the notion of friendship she writes:

> To make friendship central is both to transform the power relations that most often hold between individuals, groups, and people and the earth, and to be a participant in that transformation. Friendship is a relation of mutuality, respect, fidelity, confidence, and affection. It is impossible in, and therefore a rejection of, most competitive patterns, adversarial patterns, exploitive patterns, authoritarian patterns, and paternalistic patterns of relating. To begin to make friendship a reality is to begin acting as a friend. That is, to demonstrate in one's speech and behaviour that one is not superior or inferior and that one will no longer countenance being related to in those ways.

And further:

> In the effort to name that way of being that is both independent and responsible and yet related and interdependent, I and some other feminists use the term *centring.* That seems to come closest to describing a way of being that is neither autonomous [viz. in the 'male' sense of independent] nor dependent, nor, somehow, both, but a finding and living out of the still point, the axis, the centre of one's own life. The centring self lives on her own terms, out of her own roots, in tune with the reasons of her heart and head, competent and capable of shaping, in concert with others, our individual and corporate lives.

She continues:

> I wish to [suggest] that a feminist ethic is first of all appropriately related to traditional Christian ethics as a critique and an alternative. The concept of centring . . . is on the one hand a critique of, and indeed a contradiction to, the emphasis on self-sacrifice and centring in God characteristic of Christian ethics because it places the self in a position of importance and authority. From that perspective, centring

in one's self smacks of egotism, greed and all the ills the flesh is heir to. Yet, on the other hand, self-centring is precisely that movement of one's personal existence that brings women into an at-homeness with the universe. It is one pole of a graceful relationship with all that is, it is one extremely important step in a process of coming into congruence with others, of becoming whole.[80]

I am sure that I have been profoundly influenced by this text, which comes as close as could be to describing what is also my ideal for what it is to be a human being.

In attempting to articulate the understanding of the self-in-relation held by many feminist women, I think it is important – if the notion is to be rightly comprehended – for the discussion to be contextualized. Women's sense of self clearly bears some relationship to the practices in which women have been engaged over generations. Thus the kinds of work which, for better or worse, have been the lot of women – caring for young children, teaching, social work, tending the sick and the dying – have involved them in what Whitbeck has called 'self-other relations' as opposed to 'self-other oppositions'.[81] Discussing this, Whitbeck wants to speak of practices which promote a 'mutual realization' of persons and the 'skills and virtues necessary for eliciting the strengths of others'. She writes:

> If the other is another person, to be mutually created and transformed, relationships between people are understood as developing through identification and differentiation, through listening and speaking, with *each other*, rather than through struggles to dominate or annihilate the other. That the images associated with transformation are non-violent should not be taken to suggest that the transformations are less profound, or more gradual, or easy, but only that the process of change is more complex than that which can be represented in terms of successive dualistic oppositions.[82]

This represents what Whitbeck calls a different ontology: a different understanding of the self from that of a self engaged in 'successive dualistic oppositions'. Furthermore, some women have suggested that women's different skills, pre-eminently those acquired for example through 'mothering', are exactly those of which the otherwise 'male' world of politics is most in need.[83] To argue thus is of course not necessarily to hold that women have different intrinsic possibilities *qua* women (which would be an 'essentialist' position). It is a discussion of practices which have been learnt within the particular contexts in which people's lives have been set.

As I have already suggested, in discussing feminist theory it is crucial

As I have already suggested, in discussing feminist theory it is crucial that we recognize that feminists have not come to the conclusions which they have simply through reading books of theory. These ideas have been grounded in the women's movement, although the vision has often been less than fully realized. The ambience of that movement has been extraordinarily important in allowing women to achieve a new self-recognition and to become skilled in ways of working which are other than those of the 'male' public world. It may well be that women have traditionally maintained decidedly equal and non-hierarchical relationships between themselves. What has changed with the women's movement is that women have come to feel comfortable with adopting those ways of acting and being within the context of large groups (mostly in a separatist, women's only setting, for it has been found that men so quickly disrupt non-hierarchical ways of working). Women have experimented with forms of shared leadership (or no obvious leadership) and consensus decision-making. Nor have such ways of working been confined to middle class, feminist women. Through the miners' strike in Britain for example, many so-called 'working-class' women found that they could work together and that they possessed a strength of which they had never dreamt.[84] The fact that some women today earn salaries which are the equal of men's, or that (not least within working-class society) the woman is the breadwinner, has of course also profoundly changed women's sense of who they are.

If they are to be full participants in society, it is essential that women heal and come into their own. For women have clearly been damaged through being the other to men, who have been held to be the norm for humanity. Women have not known how to take themselves seriously. It has been around the needs of others that their lives have revolved. The problem is that women have so frequently lacked either the power base from which to establish their rights or sufficient sense of themselves to be able to do so. They have been socialized to put themselves second and enjoined to be gentle, patient and forgiving. In a lecture I heard on 'Anger, Stress and Human Illness', Ernest Johnson reported that, according to his research, suppressed anger was a major cause of illness and that it was overwhelmingly women who suffered from this.[85] (It is perhaps not insignificant that Johnson, who has grasped these things, is black.) Women have been only too inclined to think that they are the ones who are at fault, or to punish themselves. Thus in Britain one in six women who is confined in prison injures herself, as compared with only one in a hundred men.[86] In recent years it has emerged that women who have been abused as children, as indeed also women who suffer abuse at the hands of their husbands, frequently believe at some deep and unspecified level that they themselves have brought this about. A woman psychologist commented to me, significantly, that in counselling women it was important (as it was not in relation to men) to ask 'What are your needs?'. For women to come to envision themselves as competent, self-legislating adults, who have rights and who may accomplish their wishes, would represent a transformation of our society.

Hence the intense interest, in the early days of the women's movement and still today, in women's therapy, in groups which promote self-actualization and in 'consciousness' raising. Jean Baker Miller, whose *Toward a New Psychology of Women*, published in 1976, was a bestseller, well captures the needs of women in this respect. Baker Miller writes:

> Personal creativity is a factor of supreme importance . . . [It consists in] a continuous process of bringing forth a changing vision of oneself, and of oneself-in-relation to the world . . . Especially important [is] the right to participate in creating one's own personhood . . . In fact, there are women today who are outstanding in their ability to act on the basis of their own perceptions and evaluations . . . Such women have a strong conviction of their own worth and of their own right to self-development and authenticity . . . For women to act and react out of their own being is to fly in the face of their appointed definition and their prescribed way of living. To move toward authenticity, then, also involves creation, in an immediate and pressing personal way. The whole fabric of one's life begins to change, and one sees it in a new light.[87]

As Baker Miller comments, what women desire is 'feeling effective and free along with feeling intense connections with other people'.[88]

Before bringing this chapter to an end, I wish to make some further more general remarks and finally to draw some conclusions. We should be clear that what I have attempted to describe constitutes what we may well call a paradigm shift in thought. Moreover, what is important is that women have learnt in practice what it means to conceive of themselves differently, so that they will be unable to undo the revolution which has been accomplished and to return to their previous self-understanding. Yet – as is often so in the case with paradigm shifts – the measure of the feminist revolution as to what it means to be a self may not recognized for what it is. Whitbeck (who is a physicist by training as well as a philosopher) reminds us that paradigm shifts tend to be interpreted in terms of the previous understanding, since people lack the vocabulary or the conceptual apparatus which they must acquire before they can grasp the change. This is certainly so in the case of feminism! Men (and those women who have not participated in the women's movement) have lacked the practical experience to understand what is afoot. Hence they may completely mistake what women are saying, underestimating the rift between the old and the new.

This becomes most evident when women speak of self-actualization or self-realization. In my experience this is frequently heard as though one were promoting some kind of Fichtean egoism! It is simply not comprehended that one is speaking of coming to oneself-in-relationship; able, through having come into one's own, to be present in a new way to others. It is taken for granted that such a concentration on self must be at the expense of others. Male egoism has indeed frequently been at the expense of women, as men have seen women only in relation to themselves and not as having their own subjectivity and independence. It is this that feminist women have come to find so impossible. What men (and non-feminist women) need to grasp is that in constructing a discourse about assertiveness, rights and autonomy, women are starting from a different place from that which privileged men have occupied. Self-deprecation is still the lot of most women, including women who to all appearances have outwardly achieved in a 'male' world. It is within such a context that women's talk of empowerment should be understood. It should not be confused with 'power over' or exploitation of others.

Not least, it is imperative that women should come into their own if they are to be able to engage in relationships of equality with men. The self-assertive virtues of courage, audacity and the ability to be forthright need not involve domination of others. They will make for a clarity in relationships which previously we have lacked as women have either simply allowed men to take the lead, or (in a world in which women had no power) got back at men in underhand ways. The training which many women have had within the women's movement and the personal relationships to which they have become accustomed in their dealings with other women need to be brought to the relationships between women and men. As many women come to earn salaries and wages which are the equal of men's (something which we are still far from achieving), the shift may well become axiomatic. Ideology has a material substructure; that at least Marxism has taught us.

Meanwhile, women who have for the past many years participated in the women's movement or read feminist literature must look at much about the male world askance. It often appears that so little has changed. Men simply have not had the experience, for example, of consensus decision-making within the context of a large group or a work situation. Rather than attempting a meeting of minds, committee meetings will be carried on at the level of the externalities of rules and procedures. Petty hierarchies will be maintained. Voting, as I have already commented, will be used as a crude mechanism which circumvents the need to find a way in which the vital concerns of others can be met. In his essay 'What is Enlightenment?', with which I began this book, Kant avers that 'the step to adulthood is held to be dangerous by the far greater portion of mankind (and by the entire fair sex)'.[89] On the contrary, it may well be today that women are the sex which is less likely to be ruled by convention, the less inclined to be obsequious in the face of authority. For it is women who have had to risk jobs or respectability through sticking up either for themselves or for those principles in which they believe. Women who have come under the sway of feminist ideas will be unwilling to bow to heteronomous relationships, demanding a rightly defined autonomy.

Again, despite the image of the 'new man', it must seem to many women that the relationships which pertain between men often bear the marks of being much as ever they were. They appear, to women, so external. Men's talk is of cars, sport or computers. Judith Viorst is probably right when she says that 'What most men I know describe as a "very close male friend" is – by most women's standards – a mere acquaintance.'[90] Men seem to have no easy intercourse with others across boundaries, in the way that most women take for granted. The sole close relationship which most men have seems to be with their partner. Male relationships tend to be competitive and concerned with honour. Men wish not to become entangled and not to let down the mask themselves. Male hierarchy gives the impression of being an attempt to keep others at bay; to control them so that they are not a threat and do not come too close. As we have seen, Carol Gilligan claims that in describing themselves women will tell of relations with significant others, in a way that men tend not to.[91] Hence also the interesting thesis of Audrey McCollum's in her book *The Trauma of Moving*.[92] McCollum shows how drastic it is for many women to uproot themselves, thus losing their network of friends; a trauma neither under-stood nor taken into account by their male partner, who will willingly take a promotion in a distant town.

I conclude, then, that in wishing to promote an understanding of the self as centred-in-relation, women are advocating something which does not easily fit male categories. The old vocabulary will not quite do, in that it tends to see self-fulfilment and relationality as mutually exclusive. The self which feminists are advocating is neither on the one hand enclosed within itself, nor on the other hand does it sacrifice self in the service of others. It does not know isolated pride, but equally wishes to avoid self-deprecation. There is a certain stability to a self which has become observant about itself, in the sense that the person is present to him- or herself, yet also open to others. We have overcome the instability which consists in veering between self-enclosure on the one hand, and self-loss on the other. Rigid ego boundaries are, as we have said, the mark of a fragile, not of an integrated self. It is only through the kind of flexibility which many women have had to learn through the many demands made upon them, living as they do in the midst of a network of friends and relationships, that one can be centred in relation.

Though they have been the dominant sex (perhaps because they have been the dominant sex) men, it must often seem, lack a centredness (in the right sense of that term) in themselves. Hence women come to be for them – as Virginia Woolf notably put it – those who reflect their self-image back to them.[93] Woman is then placed in the role of supposedly 'complementing' a man. Such a man may feel that he is the master. Yet, as Penelope Deutscher well remarks: 'Insofar as masculine identity is dependent on the feminine as its "negative *alter ego*", masculinity can be interpreted as peculiarly fragile.'[94] Indeed, such men seem to view themselves as curiously incomplete – referring to 'their' woman as their 'better half'. Ever since Aristophanes delighted the guests (at the dinner party which Plato conjures up in his *Symposium*) by suggesting that we are each halves of a whole and must spend our lives looking for our other half,[95] men (if heterosexual) have looked to women to give them a completion which they found themselves to lack. Hence man's construal of 'woman' as a being on to whom he can project all those qualities which seem to him unmanly. As Flax has it: 'Patriarchal society depends upon the proper engendering of persons, since gender is one of the bases of social organization.'[96] Woman under patriarchy has been forced into the role of holding for humanity those attributes which man finds himself unable to appropriate.

Feminism represents woman's non-conformity to the place which she has occupied in patriarchal society. That this is the case is not insolence on the part of women. It is simply that women are coming into their own as equal citizens of the world. But if equality does not mean joining the male world as 'equal men', then the whole will shift slightly as woman is no longer prepared to be either man's opposite or his complement. Women desire a self-integrity, from which they can, not least, reach out to men. As Irigaray remarks, in terms which take up the thought of Emmanuel Levinas – but which bear comparison with Benjamin, Benhabib, Flax, Haney, Klein, Whitbeck and indeed myself: 'I love you . . . I neither make you submit to me, nor do I consume you. I respect you (as irreducible).'[97] That is a different kind of love from what has often passed as love. What we have known should rather be described as either exploitation of others or an unwarranted sacrifice of self on their behalf.

In setting himself up as the subject, man has cast woman as his other, indeed using her as the scapegoat who takes the brunt of his inadequate sense of self. But – as Marilyn Massey remarks – if in coming into their own women can resist the need for such a scapegoat and can refuse to project evil on to men or any other group, then we shall have 'a new and finally mature human'. It will, she comments, be a world which will 'allow for difference without domination'.[98] At its best, feminism is about an eclecticism and a diversity held within relationships of equality. In such a world, what will become of God?

Appendix

Some readers will undoubtedly ask after the import of the biological differences between men and women. There are a number of respects in which it would seem that there is a small but possibly significant difference. We should, however, remember that we have no neutral testing ground: all tests are, necessarily, carried out within our present, patriarchal, society.

(a) *Brain symmetry* (cf. Jeanette McGlone, 'Sex Differences in Brain Asymmetry', *Behavioural and Brain Sciences*, Vol. 3, 1980, 215–63. For a summary of recent research, which would seem to confirm McGlone, see Michael Rugg, 'La différence vive', *Nature,* Vol. 373, 16 February 1995, 561). There appears to be slightly greater brain lateralization in men than in women, i. e. more marked assignment of functions to each side of the brain. (This is tested through, for example, the ability of the non-impaired side of the brain to cope with all functions after an accident. There is a relative lack of language disability in women with a left brain lesion.)

(b) *Numeracy/literary skills.* It is well established that boys show greater visual/spatial and mathematical ability, whereas girls show greater verbal ability. However, these differences do not show up until the ages of twelve to thirteen, which must raise questions as to how far they result from socialization.

(c) *Field dependency* (cf. for example E. E. Maccoby and C. N. Jacklin, *The Psychology of Sex Differences*, Stanford, CA: Stanford University Press 1974, 97–105, and especially the evaluation on pp. 129–32). Field independence is 'the ability to separate a target element, such as a hidden figure, from its complex background'. Boys are better at these tasks than girls. Fascinatingly, cultural factors appear to be of paramount importance here. People show more field dependence in cultures where there is an emphasis on conformity, reliance on authority and restriction of the autonomy of the individual. Comparisons between African cultural groups have shown that adult males obtain higher scores on spatial tests in the cultures where young children are allowed more autonomy. Among Eskimos, where children of both sexes are allowed considerable independence, there is no sex difference. This suggests that the gender difference in our society may well be socially induced.

(d) *Empathetic distress in the newborn* (cf. A. Sagi and M. Hoffman, 'Empathetic Distress in the Newborn', *Developmental Psychology*, Vol. 12, no. 2, 1976, 175–6). Research which has so far been conducted has suggested that, in response to the recorded cry of a newborn girl, newborn girls cry more than do boys. The non-constant is that a cry of a newborn girl was invariably used. Tests have been conducted thirty-four hours after birth, so the results would seem to be relatively free of cultural conditioning.

Feminists have fought shy of this kind of evidence; understandably so in view of the fact that it can quickly be used to suggest that women are 'more suited' to certain tasks. It should be remembered that humans are culture-creating creatures and thus that in any case, whatever we may conclude, we do not need to conform to biology. In the present state of the evidence, it would appear that the perceived differences result overwhelmingly from cultural conditioning. But it is interesting that if the tests show anything, they would seem to suggest that women's brains are more integrated and that women have a greater sense of relationality! Perhaps feminists have nothing to fear!

IV

Christian Idolatry

In this chapter I shall consider the structure of Christian theology. I shall suggest that it is partial: hence the title 'Christian idolatry'. That is to say, I want to consider the proposition that the paradigms of Christian theology reflect the hopes and aspirations, the needs and the fears of men. Its modes conform to structures typical of the male psyche. In Western culture women have been excluded from conceptualizing ultimate reality. Meanwhile the concept of woman is given a particular place by men within what is their religion. It is to this that we shall turn our attention in the next chapter.

I am aware of the pitfalls in such a venture. Referring to Julia Kristeva's readings of Christian thought and of Renaissance painting, the feminist theorist and philosopher Nancy Fraser warns us against treating historical material 'as reflexes of autonomous, ahistorical, psychological imperatives like "castration anxiety" and "female paranoia" '.[1] Obviously there is no simple way in which one can place something as complex as Christian thought, which has developed over two thousand years in widely different cultures and contains very different traditions, on a grid called male psychology. Nevertheless, the only alternative to attempting such a study is to fail to open up these questions. I do believe that much about the structure of Christian thought is illuminated by considering what we may learn about the concerns of the male psyche. In particular a consideration of the place which the boy and consequently also the man have had within the patriarchal family can cast light on theology.

In carrying out such a study, I shall therefore as far as possible take care not to reduce the complexity of the material. Certain motifs within Christian thought have been to the fore in one or another Christian tradition. They may be thought to correspond to different characteristic traits of men under patriarchy. Some may seem to be in tension with one another, but that should not surprise us. I am certainly not in any way suggesting that everything that I consider in this chapter and the next is true of all Christian theology in all traditions at all times. I also hesitate at points to draw direct lines of inference between what I have considered in the previous chapter and what I seek to elucidate here. It is for the reader to judge what links are valid. What I wish to do is no more than to place some question-marks against Christian thought, though they are fairly major question-marks.

I shall take major themes of Christian theology. I shall also necessarily have something to say about Judaism, in that obviously the paradigms and motifs which were present in Judaism were in large part translated into Christian thought or adapted to the new schema. In the first place I shall consider the theme of a transcendent monotheism, common to Judaism and Christianity (and also Islam, though as my concern is basically the Christian religion, I shall have little to say of Islam). Secondly, I shall consider a corollary of the postulation of a transcendent God, namely the question of the negotiation of the space or distance between God and humanity. This takes various forms within Judaism and Christianity: the idea of covenant, of sacrifice as appeasement, and, in Christianity, the incarnation of the Son of God. Finally I shall consider a theme exclusively present in Christianity, that of God understood as Trinity. In each case I shall, by implication, suggest that it is somehow very unlikely that women would have given religion these basic forms.

The question which presses upon us here is whether this is a cultural or a biological analysis. It is dogma among feminist theorists (at least of the current generation) that perceived differences between men and women are due entirely to the different formation which the two sexes receive within culture. I have no particular reason to quarrel with the idea that the differences are a cultural creation. In the previous chapter I pointed to the different positions which the small girl and the small boy occupy within the patriarchal family. But I should be reluctant to state categorically that there is no biological basis to cultural forms. Rather is it that the response of human beings to their material nature is mediated through culture. When it comes to the doctrine of the Trinity in particular it seems to me that there is every evidence that men's and women's different genitality leads to their conceiving the nature of love differently.

What is the relationship of this study to previous (largely reductionist) work by men undertaken in the nineteenth and twentieth centuries? Both Feuerbach and Freud, notably, have suggested that human religion is a projection. In his *The Essence of Christianity* of 1841, Ludwig Feuerbach gave an intricate reading of Christian theology.[2] Freud, in what was a long-standing interest in religion, analysed it in various writings as, for example, an attempt to solve the father/son relationship.[3] But both Feuerbach and Freud were men, living before the rise of feminist theory. What I think is now open to us, as was not open to them, is to relativize Christian theology and to pronounce it masculinist. Feuerbach is interested in the dynamics of the Trinity (indeed he regrets the absence of a female element), but he does not begin to say that this doctrine reflects the way in which men have understood their sexuality. Again, Freud really does not consider how differently women might wish to think about ultimate reality.

I am, then, suggesting that feminists will be able to bring light to bear on the forms which Western theology has taken in a parallel way to the exploration of political theory, to which I drew attention in the last chapter. The presuppositions woven into the structure of belief are peculiarly masculinist. Of course work has already been accomplished by both Jewish and Christian women. I intend to bring this together and to make some suggestions of my own. There is much work on monotheism (notably, fine work by Jewish women) but as yet little on the understanding of God as Trinity. Perhaps that strikes too close to the heart of Christian theology. However, I shall suggest that women who remain Christians may in fact construe the Christian God in a subtly different way from men. Many women have been appalled by the theme of sacrifice, while we may have reason to think that women would not have construed the relationship between God and humanity through the legal (and hierarchical) device of covenant.

Before commencing on my analysis I wish to draw attention to the importance of such a study in the realm of religion. Religion is hegemonic to human culture, knitting together human relationships and giving a society its *raison d'être*. Their conception of God is a large canvas on to which human beings can project their understanding of reality. Religion has an ultimacy about it. It both reflects the culture and, we may think, in turn legitimizes the societal structure. To speak of religion as a construct in this way does not of course preclude the possibility that there is a reason why humans should have created such a figurative projection. For myself, I am a theist. It is, however, to contend that the particular forms which religion has taken, its motifs and dogmas, its doctrines and paradigms, reflect the society, and more particularly what has been the male reality.

Of course male scholars have not be unaware of the way in which religion performs this hegemonic function. John Bowker, the noted sociologist of religion and student of its forms, writes:

> Religions are the basic systemic means through which individuals and communities have organized and protected their own continuity and survival, and have identified the worth and value of being human. Religions are the basic and primordial cultural achievements, through which gene replication is secured, enhanced and protected. *But also* religions have been validated to their adherents and participants, not

simply because they create stable contexts for breeding and nurture, but because they have in any case identified (and continued to make available to others in later generations) particular achievements and opportunities in the exercise of this particular human energy.[4]

Such an analysis makes clear the centrality of religion to human culture. What has been less recognized, or not recognized at all until recently, has been the way in which theology has kept in place the respective positions of men and women within society. There may well be a growing awareness among men of this (and some discomfort about it). In a book dedicated to male responses to feminism in religion, James Mackey, the systematic theologian, writes: 'People do use religious beliefs to prop up power and its unequal distribution in human societies, and they will always do so.'[5]

However, we must go much further than that. We need to show that Christian theology, as indeed more widely human culture, has been a male creation. It is French feminist thought, influenced as it is by Lacan, which is coming to raise serious questions as to whether human culture is not almost exclusively a male construct. (This does not mean that it does not have an understanding of woman, the male view of 'woman', written into it. In the next chapter I shall suggest that, far from being a side-issue, the 'place' of woman is pivotal to the whole creation.) This raises the extraordinary thought – which is probably true – that at least in Western culture women have had no way in which they could begin to think out how it is that they would conceptualize God. The most that they could do has been to use the structure of thought which men have provided as a vehicle for their consciousness of God. Since we must think that consciousness of God cannot be separated from its construal in language and concepts, this amounts to saying that women have been largely assimilated, or have assimilated themselves, into the male religion. Hence the power of religion: the male construction has been the construction to which we have all adhered.

The relativization of male religion, showing it to be just that, is then a crucial first step. Once women recognize this, they may in time be better enabled to think out how they would conceive of God. It is upon such a quest that I embark in the final two chapters of this book. It is clear that this quest is not easy. One may wish to draw on something of the male past. Again it must be said that women will think very differently here. Men, too, may wish to move beyond the religion which we have known. If (as I have contended) Christianity is simply untrue, then quite apart from the question of the morality of our espousing a religion which is so heavily geared towards the solution of male needs and the expression of male ambitions, men too should wish to move on.

Such a reading of religion as I undertake in this chapter and the next is thus a necessary preliminary to being able to discard Christian paradigms. We must show them up for what they are. It is feminist theory which, as never before, allows us to do this.

I commence, then, with a consideration of monotheism, that theme which is the most basic of all to Western religion. By monotheism here I intend not simply the understanding of God as one, as opposed to polytheism, but the particular form which monotheism has taken within Western culture. God has been conceived to be hierarchically placed above humankind. God's oneness involves 'his' self-sufficiency. God exists before the creation and is responsible for the creation. 'He' is envisaged as having absolute power and knowledge. There may be something to be learnt here from feminist experimentation in recent years, in the United States in particular, but also in Europe, with the idea of the Goddess. Not only has this shown us the extent to which we take it for granted that the Western God is male, but it has placed before our eyes a very different way of conceiving of God/Goddess. For the Goddess is commonly understood as not absolute and certainly as not separated from humanity. This throws into relief the nature of the male God.

By way of illustration of the common conceptualization of the monotheistic God, I shall repeat some definitions of monotheism here. (I shall consider the understanding of God as Trinity later.) Again, let me draw attention to the fact that I have said that different emphases within Christian theology correspond to different aspects of patriarchy or the male reality. The scene is complex. The way in which I describe God here, through descriptions which I give, may well be a product in particular of the absorption of an Aristotelianism into the theology of the West. Such definitions are then more likely to emanate from Catholic, or Anglican, strands of the tradition. Nevertheless those who are unhappy with these definitions should note that the concept of God as monotheistic and as transcendent is nothing if not central to the Hebrew scriptures. Indeed one of the sources which I cite derives from Judaism. What I am suggesting is that such a God represents self-enclosure, autonomy (in the sense of independence) and power, understood as power over that which is not itself.

Here, then, are the definitions given under 'monotheism' and also for monotheism under 'polytheism' in the *New Dictionary of Christian Theology*.[6] The entry for monotheism was contributed by Ronald Clements. He writes that monotheism 'has conceived of its object as a single personal supreme being'. In contrasting polytheism with monotheism, the article on polytheism, contributed by Aylward Shorter, tells us that monotheism is 'the notion of God as self-subsisting being or pure act'; 'divine reality as a personal and as a free autonomous power at work in human history'. Such a definition of course reflects the Aristotelian-Thomistic heritage of Christian theology. Thomas Aquinas believes that God is that being which is self-subsisting being or pure act, needing nothing else to fulfil it.[7] But I cite equally a statement coming from the Jewish tradition. At the outset of lectures on monotheism, held under the auspices of a Jewish foundation, Lenn Evan Goodman writes as follows: 'The concept of God is that of a being of absolute or infinite perfection.'[8] I am reminded also of what I once heard a leading liberal Anglican churchman remark at a conference (and made a note of it): 'When God created he did not have to take into account anything else whatsoever.'

Here are some further examples. The Oxford philosopher of religion Richard Swinburne informs us: 'By a theist, I understand a man who believes that there is a God.' And by a 'God' Swinburne understands something like a 'person without a body (i. e. a spirit) who is eternal, free, able to do anything, knows everything, is perfectly good, is the proper object of human worship and obedience, the creator and sustainer of the universe.'[9] In like manner, the philosopher of religion Richard Gale writes that God is 'an infinite being who freely bestows his grace upon people according to no discernible law or rule when he causes them to have a direct perception of him'.[10] In an entry for 'theism' in the *Encyclopaedia of Religion and Ethics,* A. E. Taylor gives what has apparently become a classical definition:

> We shall probably not depart far from the implications of current language if we agree to define theism as the doctrine that the ultimate ground of things is a single supreme reality which is the source of everything other than itself and has the character of being (*a*) intrinsically complete or perfect and (*b*), as a consequence, an adequate object of unqualified adoration or worship.[11]

Certainly not all theologians would be happy with these definitions.[12] Nevertheless, it cannot be denied that such an understanding of God has been fundamental to Western theology and that it largely represents the public perception as to what God is.

Reading from a feminist perspective, let us now consider what it is that has been suggested. I quote. God is conceptualized as 'free', 'able to do anything', 'autonomous', as acting 'according to no discernible rule or law', 'the source of everything other than itself', not needing to 'take into account anything else whatsoever', an 'object of unqualified adoration or worship'. What a nightmare! God would seem to be the reflection of the male's wildest dreams. Even more interesting perhaps than that 'he' is powerful (we might think that this somehow belonged to the definition of a God who is monotheistic and transcendent) is that God is self-sufficient, alone, not in any way constrained, and not needing to take into account what is other than 'himself'. Indeed classically God has been held to have aseity, that is to be *a se*, complete in God's self. What kind of fears of entanglement have been projected? Why, indeed, should such a situatedness be thought necessary for the exercise of power (if by power we simply mean the ability to bring about change)? The evidence speaks for itself.

From the fact that this has been the projected model of God, it does not follow that men have simply seen themselves in God's image or God in theirs. God represents some kind of understanding as to what perfection would entail. It may well be that 'he' reflects what – with part of himself – many a man would like his circumstances to be! But it is also the case that men have placed themselves at the opposite pole to such a God, in what has been a bi-polar construal of reality. God then represents that which is perfect and powerful, while humanity is by contrast construed as weak and sinful. Consequently humanity, as we shall have reason to consider, is often conceptualized as 'female', in relation to a God for whom male metaphors are employed. Monotheism is thus instrumental in consolidating a gendered conception of reality.

The point to note here is that a transcendent monotheism, by its very nature, creates that which is 'other' than itself. Monotheism makes for hierarchical structures, in which what is God and what is not God are understood by contrast with what the other is. There comes to be what Rosemary Ruether has named 'a model of domination and dependency'.[13] A particularly fine statement of what is entailed is given by Rita Gross, the Jewish thinker and student of Eastern religions. Gross writes:

> Monotheistic thought does tend toward dualism. The One is distinguished from all other phenomena and valued and exalted above them as supreme. The One and all else are not only distinct but separate and, more important, there is a gulf between them. The One is on high and all else is of lesser reality and value, under its control, whether that control be loving or tyrannical. Those who consider themselves to be in relationship with that One repeat these patterns, creating separations between themselves and those outside the community, as well as within it. Awareness of variety and distinctiveness usually finds expression in relationships of hierarchy and power over, both in monotheistic thought and its social spillovers. The moral vision becomes one of sameness, of becoming like the One or on the side of the One insofar as this is possible. When sameness is not desired, possible, or allowed, hierarchical

dualism is the only remaining solution. 'You shall be separate from those.' The attractions of finding the One or being the One are deep but profoundly dangerous.[14]

Monotheism creates insiders (who are like) and outsiders (who are other).

It is fascinating to note that Gross (a Jew who has converted to Buddhism) believes that there are motifs present in Eastern religion which are very different from those found within monotheism. They may be much more acceptable to feminists; indeed they cohere closely with ways in which feminists wish to structure the understanding of the self in its relations. Thus Gross suggests that some systems of Eastern thought 'provide models for thinking about distinctiveness, separation and relationality . . . that should be utilized by anyone interested in these issues'. What attracts her is that (as she perceives it in Eastern thought) 'multiplicity can be handled without absolutizing hierarchy' and 'the interplay of separation and relationality can be affirmed and explored'. Gross concludes that 'distinctiveness need not entail a hierarchy of value, as it so often does in crude monotheism'.[15] Many feminists have precisely been interested in finding ways of speaking about multiplicity and heterogeneity. It is significant here that some feminists have suggested that it may well be that polytheism is less inimical to the values which they would espouse.[16]

Is there then any direct evidence that a monotheistic conception of God makes for human hierarchy? Are non-Western societies, some will ask, any less hierarchical? This is not a question which I have either space or competence to explore. There are, however, a number of things which should be said. In the first place the fact that, say, Eastern societies have also treated women abominably does not invalidate the fact that, in the West, monotheism may have been a cultural construct which has led to the subordination of women. I should think it undoubtedly the case that, in the case of Western societies, a monotheism which has been conceived using male imagery has played a role in keeping male hegemony and hierarchy in place. This applies to the society at large. Within Christianity it has been said by many until recently that it would be unsuitable that women should be ordained (and this relates to the understanding of God, not simply of Christ), while it is surely no chance that within orthodox Judaism rabbis must be male.

The question of the correlation between the understanding of the ultimate and the social relations pertaining in a society which subscribes to a given understanding is an interesting one. I am no social anthropologist; nevertheless a few remarks are in order.[17] There is apparently some correlation between African societies which have adopted Islam and a hierarchical ordering of the society, as compared with those societies which have retained a traditional African religion.[18] Whether a certain society has been attracted to Islam because of its (patriarchal) structure or whether Islam caused the social structure to become what it did is, of course, a wider question. In a fascinating study *Society and Cosmos,* the social anthropologist Signe Howell shows how the Chewong people, a remote tribe in the Malay peninsula, reflect in an intricate depiction of the cosmos a society which is almost free of competitive and conflictual relationships and in which the chief sin is to eat on one's own – a veritable feminist panacea![19] Turning to the ancient world, the feminist thinker and historian Judith Ochshorn, herself a Jew, puts forward the thesis that there is a correlation between the fact that ancient Israel was monotheistic and that gender as a cultural construction was marked in that society (so that women could not be priestesses and there were strong taboos against women's biological functions), as compared with the surrounding polytheistic societies, in which there was less construal of gender.[20] All this certainly seems to support our thesis as to the social consequences of monotheism.

Indeed in this context it may be significant that in recent years biblical scholars have come to the conclusion that in ancient Israel monotheism was much more difficult to establish and under greater threat than had at one time been recognized. In particular women marrying into the society seem to have brought their polytheistic religious sensibilities with them.[21] In any case it is surely no chance that the God of monotheism was designated by names which suggested superior males in that society: King, Lord, Judge. (I shall consider later how this God was sometimes understood to have 'motherly' qualities.)[22] Woman has, of course, frequently been coupled with 'nature'. Both society and nature are then designated 'female' in relation to the 'male' God, who is seen to transcend nature. The French feminist theorist Simone de Beauvoir writes: 'To glorify the mother is to accept birth, life and death under their animal and humanly social forms at once, it is to proclaim the harmony of nature and society.'[23] And Eric Mascall, the high church Anglican philosopher of religion, in the context of arguing that women cannot be priests, points to the fact that all theistic religions in which God or Gods transcend the created order and stand behind nature and history have male priesthoods.[24]

Clearly we should in no way underestimate the fundamental impact which monotheism has had on the ordering of Western society. Subsequent to a visit to China, when she was perhaps particularly alerted to these things, the French semiotician and psychoanalyst Julia Kristeva wrote as follows:

One betrays . . . one's naiveté if one considers our modern societies
to be simply patrilinear . . . or capitalist-monopolist, and ignores the
fact that they are at the same time . . . governed by . . . monotheism
whose essence is best expressed in the Bible: the paternal Word . . .[25]

Likewise the major French philosopher and thinker Jacques Derrida
responds thus to the contention of Jean-Luc Marion that a theandric
hierarchy does not necessarily result in a political hierarchy:

No doubt, but what it is also *necessary to see* is the historic,
essential, undeniable, and irreducible possibility of the afore-
mentioned perversity which is perhaps only considerable by first
having been observable, as one says, 'in fact' . . . How is it possible
that . . . the distance between the two hierarchies [Marion's con-
tention] can have let itself be overstepped or 'traversed' . . .?[26]

Monotheism has been hegemonic to Western patriarchal culture.

Perhaps not surprisingly it was the German philosopher Friedrich
Nietzsche who in the nineteenth century drew attention to the way in
which monotheism has confined and curtailed human beings. Contrasting monotheism here with an ancient paganism, Nietzsche averred:

But above and outside, in some distant overworld, one was permitted
to behold a plurality of norms; one god was not considered a denial
of another god, nor blasphemy against him. It was here that the
luxury of the individual was first permitted; it was here that one first
honoured the rights of individuals . . . Monotheism, on the other
hand, this rigid consequence of the doctrine of one normal human
type – the faith in one normal god beside whom there are only
pseudo-gods – was perhaps the greatest danger that has yet
confronted humanity . . . In polytheism the free-spiriting and many-
spiriting of man attained its first preliminary form . . .[27]

That Western society can return to polytheism would seem to be doubtful! It is certainly not something which I should advocate. (My own
understanding of God, as will become clear, in some way exemplifies a
wholeness; though it may be more 'dispersed' than a classical monotheism.)[28] Nevertheless I believe it to be important that we keep in mind
this critique of monotheism as we consider what kind of religion is commensurate with the human relationships which we would have.

It would, then, seem to be the case that a transcendent monotheism
comports ill with the society which feminists seek to create. 'He' is
singularly undemocratic. He is one and alone, separate from the rest of
reality. Moreover, as we have seen, the male God appears to reflect
something about the male psyche. He is self-sufficient. He allows no

competition. (Pseudo-gods are named idols.) He has the first word and the last. Everything is ultimately under 'his' control. By contrast feminists are interested in relationality, heterogeneity, multiplicity and a lack of control. They believe in a fundamental equality in which each is valued and allowed to come into his or her own. To say the very least (even if it should be disputed that monotheism has in some sense caused and served to legitimate the society which we have known), the monotheistic God scarcely conforms to feminist values! He is fundamentally inimical to relations of interchange and reciprocity. It says much about Western culture, so we may think, and also about women and men, that it is inconceivable that the Western God could have been primarily conceptualized through female metaphors.

Nor can Christians be allowed to get off the hook by saying that the conception of God and of the divine/human relationship which is depicted in the 'New' Testament is somehow wholly other than that in the Hebrew scriptures. It may be that a different metaphor comes to the fore, in that God is now primarily understood as Father. But the God of Judaism can be merciful, while the God of the Christian gospel may be wrathful. The nature of the human relationship to God is still hierarchical. Consider, for example, that prayer, the so-called 'Lord's' Prayer, reputed to have come from the lips of Jesus. It may bring us as close as it is possible to get to an understanding of Jesus's conception of his relationship to 'him' whom he called his 'father'. Moreover it is the biblical passage which, before any other, has governed the conception of the human relationship to God held within Christendom.

The prayer opens by addressing God as 'father'; the term used is that by which the head of the family was designated in what was a deeply patriarchal society. Our mind is directed not to ourselves but to God. 'He' is conceived to be 'in heaven', a reality both other than ours and which transcends ours. 'He' is addressed as one would address a sovereign: 'Hallowed be thy name'. Christians pray that 'his' kingdom come, 'his' will be done; not that their will should be realized. Earth is to reflect the pattern of heaven – 'on earth as it is in heaven'. What is in effect a feudal relationship of absolute dependence is then envisaged: 'Give us this day our daily bread.' The phrase recalls the time in the wilderness when the children of Israel were dependent on the manna given by God one day at a time. Christians ask for forgiveness for their sins; furthermore that they should not to be led into temptation but delivered from evil. In the form in which the prayer is normally recited, it ends by again lauding God: 'For thine is the kingdom, the power and the glory.' This is to be the case 'for ever and ever'. And the one who prays adds 'Amen': so be it.

It is important that I am not misunderstood here. There is something noble about this prayer. We must be able to direct our minds to a reality greater than ourselves. It is evidently important that at times we should ask for forgiveness and that we should forgive others. We have to live a day at a time if we are to do so with any sanity. And so forth. Nevertheless the particular framing of these things, good in themselves, should be noted. Moreover what the prayer lacks is significant. Thus nothing is said of any intrinsic human goodness. There is no talk of coming again to be centred in oneself. There is no recognition of a necessary self-assertiveness, so important for those who lack sufficient sense of self to learn. Given the form in which it is cast, it could hardly be said that this prayer reflects anything other than a patriarchal and hierarchical order, an order which it aims to cleanse and to re-establish. What else, we may say, should we expect to come from the lips of a first century Jew? But it is far from a feminist ordering of reality. Thus feminist re-writings of the Lord's Prayer which I have seen do not simply refer to God as Mother (or perhaps Spirit); they embody a different ethos. 'Forgive us our trespasses as we forgive those who trespass against us' may be recast as 'may I learn to have compassion for myself and others'.[29] There has been a subtle but all-important shift in sensibility.

In view of these considerations we may turn momentarily to a study conducted in the United States of the way in which boys and girls respectively envisage God. It is highly suggestive and one must think that one might well achieve the same results in other Western cultures; it would be most interesting for further work to be undertaken. David Heller had children draw pictures and listened to what they said about them.[30] Thus a twelve-year-old boy draws a God with a beard, fierce-looking, his hands placed nonchalantly on his hips, looking down on the viewer of the picture. Heller concludes that the boys in the study describe a God who is profoundly rational, a thinking and knowledgeable God, who is omniscient and who guides people. One boy commented: 'God communicates as if he is talking long distance'. Another describes a deity who lives in a desert, away from people. Heller writes: 'The children describe this distance with an undercurrent of frustration and helplessness.' He questions whether this God may not reflect 'unmet paternal needs'. He notes, moreover, the anxiety which the boys manifested when the researcher suggested that the deity might be female.

By contrast, the understanding of God which the girls in the study portray is fascinating. A seven-year-old girl draws a picture of a very evidently female God, wearing a large hat, with a smile on 'her' face and a flower sprouting beside her. The girls, Heller concludes, speak of a God who has aesthetic appeal, associating the idea of God with art, dance and music. One girl connects religious feelings with drawing: 'Because making pictures and being creative makes me feel so good.' Another shows pleasure as she thinks of how 'God made my blue eyes just like God made the sky'. The God whom the girls depict shows emotional intimacy, and they often stress physical closeness. The girl who drew the picture of God wearing a hat commented: 'God is smiling like when you feel his presence beside you.' Significantly, some girls show fear that their androgynous understandings of God may meet with criticism. Yet if these young women are in any way representative, their conception of God has clearly not been drowned out by patriarchy! (At what age do they learn to conform, or will this generation not conform?)

It is clearly not possible to generalize from one study like this. Nevertheless it is worth remarking on its exemplification of some of the differences to which Carol Gilligan draws attention. In particular it would seem to suggest male fear of intimacy, in contrast to what is natural to females.[31] Certainly the language of much theology is a world away from what one might think women would want to use (and certainly from feminist values). There is a certain vocabulary for God and for God's relation with humans, which is somehow taken for granted as axiomatic, and which pervades the language of sermons, prayers, liturgies and hymns. This is not least noticeable in the Presbyterian culture which surrounds me in Scotland. The Reformed tradition has always majored on the majesty of God on the one hand and the depravity of humans on the other. Hence it must seem only natural to envisage a hierarchical relationship between God and humanity and consequently also to employ a language of worship and obedience for the human relationship to God.

Consider the vocabulary present in the following extract, which is in no way untypical. It is taken from William Storrar's *Scottish Identity: A Christian Vision*. I place in italics words to which, in the context of the present consideration, one might wish to draw attention.

For seven hundred years, from the fourteenth to the twentieth centuries, this one theological vision of Scotland has *dominated* the imagination of Scottish Christians in their thinking about our nationhood. It is the vision of God as the *Almighty, judge* and *ruler* over the *destiny* of the nations. It is the glorious vision centred on Christ as the *ascended Lord, victorious* in heaven and through the advance of his *Kingdom* on earth, *conquering* the nations in *power and glory*. It is a *triumphant* vision of the *conquest* of Scottish national life by the Christian Church, Faith and Ethic. Whether held by medieval churchmen, seventeenth century covenanters, or Victorian moral reformers,

this vision looked at Scotland through the eyes of a *triumphant* Christ
in *glory, looking down* upon the nations of the earth from the *judge-
ment* throne of heaven.[32]

And so on. I surmise that this rhetoric would strike the majority of
leaders of the kirk as in no way remarkable. But – if this is the world of
God-language – a conceptualization of God as female would be extraordinary. The only female figure of whom such language could be
predicated is that male construct of the 'feminine' which Britannia
or Athena represent!) Indeed it is not many years since the General
Assembly of the church threw out, without debate and amid considerable uproar, a report which suggested that more 'feminine' language for
God might be acceptable in prayer.[33]

At this point it may be objected that the powerful God of whom the
scriptures speak acts to overturn the hierarchies of this world. 'He'
'casts down the mighty from their seat' and 'exalts the humble and
weak'.[34] It is significantly into the mouth of a woman, Mary in the
Magnificat, that the evangelist places such words. This is of course an
interesting observation. It has precisely been within the Reformed
tradition, which has such a sense of God's almightiness, that this understanding has been to the fore. God is to be worshipped and 'he' alone.
God comes in judgment, condemning the *hubris* (the overweening pride)
of humans and showing up the powers of this world for the idols
that they are. It was such a theology, articulated notably by Karl
Barth, which fired the Confessing Church in their opposition to the
totalitarianism of Nazi Germany. Again, in South Africa in the days
of apartheid, the Bible was interpreted in this light by those in the
Reformed tradition who wished to mount a critique of the regime. More
widely, it is perhaps not surprising that much 'liberation' theology,
Protestant and Catholic alike, has been strongly biblical, turning in
particular to the Hebrew scriptures.

What should we say? Should not women, those who have been at the
bottom of the heap, think that they stand to gain much? God is
portrayed as overturning the unjust structures of society and coming
with strong arm to save. There is surely a dilemma here. It is not for me
(for I am not in their situation) to gainsay that it may be that women in
the Third World, or indeed who belong to the so-called Fourth World
in our midst, could find motifs which are useful here. We saw that
liberation theologians like Rosemary Ruether and Susan Dowell are not
averse to such language,[35] though the way in which any particular
theologian employed it would need to be studied in detail. Meanwhile
David Nicholls, in a study *Deity and Domination* which lacks any
particular consideration of the situation of women, is ambivalent as to

the political efficacy of such theology.[36] In employing this rhetoric, women would be turning conceptions which 'male' theology has put into their hands against the patriarchal world. But on the same count it must be pointed out that the reiteration of such themes and the perpetuation of the conception of God upon which they are predicated fails to allow a more basic shift to another conception of spirituality and of God to come about. We may well question with Audre Lorde whether the master's house can ever be dismantled while employing the master's tools.[37]

Before leaving the discussion of monotheism, it is appropriate that we should at least briefly consider that school of theology which, finding it to be problematic, has in recent years wished to qualify a monotheism such as that which is envisaged in the original definitions that I gave, namely process theology. Utilizing the thought of Alfred North Whitehead, a British philosopher who spent much of his career in the United States, 'process' theologians have contended that the common understanding of God as absolute is misguided. By contrast, in process theology God is said to respond to the world, taking up the particular circumstances which pertain and bringing new possibilities into being. Thus there is held to be some kind of reciprocity between God and humankind. Unlike the God of classical Western theism, the God of process theology allows 'himself' to be affected; he is, in oft-quoted words of Whitehead's, 'the fellow-sufferer who understands'.[38] It is not surprising to find that, particularly in the United States, a number of feminist theologians have found process thought attractive.[39]

I myself am much more sceptical. Consider the following quotation, as an example of process thought. It comes from John Cobb, a well-known American process theologian, writing an article on the major American process thinker, Charles Hartshorne. The God of Aristotle, Cobb has commented, is unaffected by the world. And he continues:

> More consistently and vigorously than any other philosopher, Hartshorne has attacked this prejudice. True human excellence does not involve insensitivity or indifference to others but rather empathy with them. Alongside acting for the benefit of others, it includes feeling their feelings with them. This is especially important when others are suffering. In the human case this excellence is attained only very partially at best. But the divine perfection means that God perfectly receives all that happens in the world and perfectly responds to it. Far from being unaffected by our suffering and our joy, God suffers fully with us and rejoices fully with us.

It may be thought that such a statement well represents what those attracted to process thought think to be its potentiality. Comparing the structure of process thought favourably with that of other theological schools, Cobb continues:

> Especially in recent years Thomists have re-emphasized that the *esse* of Thomas is to be understood not as being-in-general but as the act of being, that act by virtue of which beings receive their being. Barthians have recently stressed that their emphasis on the sovereign freedom of the divine will is a radical denial that God is static. Indeed there have been arguments that the Thomistic and Barthian views of God avoid the image of a static God *more* successfully than does Hartshorne. These arguments . . . do not fully respond to Hartshorne's point . . . However dynamic God's activity in the world may be, if it is not responsive to the changing situation in the world, it cannot be the perfect form of action Hartshorne attributes to God.[40]

The God of process thought is in dialogue with the world.

But how should this essentially help women in regard to the alienation from classical theism which they feel? One should notice the depth of the anthropomorphism present in process thought, exemplified in the quotations which I have given. The God of process theology, though a kindly father, is still very much in charge. Indeed there is something about process thought which is profoundly paternalistic, while the depiction of the human being may strike us as reflecting the lives of privileged males. Listening to (male) process theologians speak, I have more than once been struck by these things. On one occasion I took notes. God was said to have 'supreme freedom', while we have 'various degrees of freedom'. God 'offers us alternative possibilities', respecting our 'limited autonomy'. He allows us 'freedom' as 'self-determining creatures'. We should see God 'as seeking to influence by luring us or by persuasion'. The speaker spoke of the 'initiatives God is constantly introducing'. God 'seeks to maximize the possibilities present in a situation'. A woman sitting next to me had evidently come to similar conclusions. She remarked: 'It sounds like the kindergarten'. According to this understanding of reality the man sees himself as being in a wide open space with multiple choices. When he makes a mess of things God deals him another hand. But women have not normally enjoyed a social situatedness like that which this theology reflects. Rather, finding themselves placed within limited and restricted circumstances, women have tried to enhance their own and others' lives. It is perhaps worth remarking on the fact that if feminist women wish to actualize themselves and to allow the mutual self-realization of persons, then (of the three options with which Cobb presents us) it would seem that the Thomistic-Aristotelian option might best serve them. God is seen as working through and empowering the whole creation.

In the central section of this chapter I turn to a cluster of motifs central to the Judaeo-Christian tradition. They are alike a corollary of transcendent monotheism. If God is understood to be other than humanity, moreover if God is conceived to be good and humanity sinful, then that difference between God and humanity (whether ontologically or morally conceived) must needs be traversed. I shall consider three motifs: first, covenant; secondly, incarnation (or the theme of the father/son relation); and thirdly, sacrifice, which is intertwined with the other two and which I shall therefore consider together with them. It is clear that one matter which we shall have to consider in conjunction with these themes (given, again, that God is on high and other than humanity) is that of the heteronomy present in the human relationship to God. Covenant I shall discuss primarily in the context of Judaism, though Christianity, notably the Reformed tradition, also employs the language of covenant. Incarnation is a Christian theme, though the father/son relation is common to both religions. A consideration of sacrifice is apposite in relation to both Judaism and Christianity.

I commence with covenant. Within the Jewish scriptures (which became the Christian 'Old Testament'), covenant is the fundamental motif which allows a bridging of the difference between YHWH and his chosen people. Moreover an understanding of the relationship as covenantal is closely inter-related with the understanding of law, or Torah. For an elucidation of the theme of covenant, I turn to recent work of the American Jewish scholar Jon Levenson. What Levenson shows is that covenant had very precise connotations in the society in which it was used as a metaphor for the relationship between YHWH and Israel. (We may note in passing that Levenson automatically refers to YHWH as 'he' and Israel as 'she'!). Covenant describes the relationship existing between two kings. The powerful sovereign would offer a relation of suzerainty (a covenant) to the other, at the same time threatening that if a voluntary submission was not forthcoming, war would ensue. Levenson writes:

> The obedience YHWH requires of Israel is not the conformity of an automaton with its computer programmed by God, but the obedience of an ancient Near Eastern vassal, that is, a king loyal to a greater king . . . The re-presentation of that moment of choice keeps alive the element of human autonomy in the dialectic of divine suzerainty. This is the element that distinguishes covenantal theonomy from theocratic tyranny . . . [Nevertheless] for all the language of choice that characterizes covenant texts, the Hebrew Bible never regards the choice of decline of covenant as legitimate

... The language of free choice notwithstanding, to decline ... would be an unpardonable act of ingratitude.

In choosing to be obedient, Israel in effect has no choice.

Covenant, then, is not to be understood – as it would be within the context of liberalism – as a contract freely undertaken between those who have an essential equality. The understanding of law as Torah is of the same nature. Quoting David Novak, Levenson remarks: 'The laws of the Torah "are nothing but decrees" and must be practised whether we deem them humane or not.' Thus Levenson speaks of the 'paradox' of 'this curious dialectic of autonomy and heteronomy'. On the Jews he comments: 'Chosen for service, they must choose to serve.' Furthermore, covenant, so Levenson argues, is closely related to the concept of God as creator. Unlike its polytheistic neighbours, the Hebrew tradition lifted the deity out of the rest of creation. The essence of the relationship of such a God to humanity is captured within the Hebrew Bible by the word 'mastery'. Levenson speaks of 'the need for a *continual* surrender of autonomy, which is prominent in biblical thought and results in a crucial daily obligation in Rabbinic practice'.[41] Such an explanation is illuminative! This is a masculinist hierarchy if ever there was one. It is not feminism. It is not even a free association of (bourgeois) equals.

Covenant is, of course, a legal notion of the relation existing between God and humanity. The relationship is conceived in terms of justice, rules and laws. There are rights and duties. The metaphor of covenant is thus different from (I am not adjudicating as to whether it is preferable to or more problematic than) the familial relationship suggested by the metaphor of Father and Son. Perhaps it is significant that Calvin, the architect of the Reformed tradition, was a lawyer by training! But the fact that the Hebrew scriptures are given such a central place in the Reformed tradition is surely the reason for the prominence given to the motif of covenant. Or perhaps the Hebrew scriptures are given this centrality because they appealed to Calvin? (I shall have reason later to mention the way in which, standing within that tradition, Karl Barth draws out the covenantal theme in allotting their respective places to man and woman.[42]) In a covenantal theology, questions of obedience and disobedience are to the fore (as indeed they would seem to have been both within the Hebrew scriptures and within the Reformed tradition). Indeed, it may well be thought that monotheism leads in a straight line to the concept of ethics as a decalogue, handed down from on high. The resultant ethos is one of uniformity and conformity. While it may be unwarranted to make categorical generalizations, it would seem unlikely that women would have conceived of the relationship to God in terms of law and covenant.[43]

The context of covenant is a suitable place at which to consider the story of the testing of Abraham's readiness to sacrifice his son in obedience to YHWH.[44] It was to Abraham that the covenant was granted, and through this son that it was to be fulfilled. The tale has been described as 'central to the nervous system of Judaism and Christianity'.[45] Carol Delaney, a social anthropologist, believes that it may mark the point in history at which patriarchy was being established; indeed, specifically, the shift from a previous belief that the father had a role in conception to the conjecture that his was the primary role. By establishing the authority of the paternal God, the story functions to establish patriarchal authority. Delaney comments: 'The authority becomes omnipresent but invisible. This, more than anything, *legitimates* the patriarchal way of life.' Descending from father to son, paternity is taken back to primeval history, so that the story becomes a 'metaphorical framework' which legitimates it. The idea of seed is that of the transmission of the essence of the father to the son from one generation to another.[46]

Within Christianity, the story has served to illustrate the absolute obedience which God requires. Most famously, it is taken up by Kierkegaard in his *Fear and Trembling*.[47] Kierkegaard spells out what is no more than the logical corollary of a transcendent monotheism. If the ethical relationship to others (the law which says thou shalt not kill) were to be countermanded by a direct command from God, that ethical relationship would have to be suspended. Kierkegaard calls such an eventuality a 'teleological' suspension of the ethical; that is to say, a suspension in favour of that higher *telos*, or goal, which is God's command. We should note that the fact that this state of affairs can potentially arise is a direct consequence of conceiving of God as other than the creation, and then allowing that God should be God. If God is not simply to be subsumed under the ethical, so that to obey God becomes, without remainder, to conform to the ethical, then there must always be the possibility that the will of God will contravene what human beings perceive to be right. If God is one with the ethical, then God is of no consequence. Within the Judaeo-Christian tradition, in which God is other than the creation, the relationship to God is at least potentially heteronomous, such that the human must be obedient to what he or she conceives to be God's will, rather than obeying his or her own conscience.

Thus from the human perspective the conception of God comes to have a certain arbitrariness.[48] We are reminded of what Levenson tells us of Torah: that it is to be obeyed absolutely, whether or not it is understood. Such an arbitrariness is parallel to that found in the book of Job. It is not that God gives Job an answer. The 'answer' is that God's ways are past finding out and that Job is to be content with contemplating the mystery and wonder of the universe. Within the Western tradition, worship and obedience are, as we have said, the hallmark of the relationship to God. The human is at peace as he acknowledges that God is God. Not for nothing does the word 'Islam' mean both 'peace' and 'submission'. Within medieval Christendom, that icon for God which is a single eye looked down on the worshippers from high on the chancel wall with an uncanny authoritarianism. Feminism would disrupt such an order.

It is, then, hardly surprising that the story of Abraham's preparedness to sacrifice Isaac should have called forth feminist derision. As the British Jewish scholar Naomi Segal comments: 'Both son and father dazzle by their appalling submissiveness.'[49] In an analysis which draws on Gilligan's depiction of the differing ethical sensibilities of men and of women, Nel Noddings castigates an Abraham who puts absolute obedience to an absolute God before the natural relationship of a parent to his child. Noddings writes:

> Abraham's obedience fled for protection under the skirts of an unseeable God. Under the gaze of an abstract and untouchable God, he would destroy *this* touchable child whose real eyes were turned upon him in trust, and love, and fear. I suspect no woman could have written either *Genesis* or *Fear and Trembling* . . . The one-caring [her expression], male or female, does not seek security in abstractions cast either as principles or entities. She remains responsible here and now for this cared-for and this situation and for the foreseeable futures projected by herself and the cared-for.[50]

That is to say Noddings advocates an ethic of care for the concrete particular; an ethic such as I have already considered in my discussion of Gilligan, or I shall elucidate further in a discussion of the ethics of attention.[51]

And what are we to think of the following feminist midrash on Genesis 22? It was written by my friend Marion McNaughton (a member of the Society of Friends [Quakers] who has worked for many years as a feminist facilitator and peace activist) after witnessing the medieval mystery plays performed in York which re-enact biblical scenes. McNaughton weaves together a critique of any heteronomous relationship to a transcendent God, an abhorrence of sacrifice and blood-letting, and a feminist vision of a different future.

> And with heavy heart Abraham went to his wife Sarah and said, God has told me to take our son Isaac, whom we love, and sacrifice him as a burnt offering.

And Sarah said, A shrewd move. This God is no fool. This is Her way of testing you. What did you say to Her? And Abraham replied, I said nothing. I want God to know I will obey Him without question. I will do as He commands.

And Sarah threw up her hands in despair and said, Abraham you are a bone-headed fool. What kind of a God do you think you are dealing with? What kind of a God would want you to kill your own son to prove how religious you are? Don't be so stupid! She's trying to teach you something; that you must challenge even the highest authority on questions of right and wrong. Argue with Her, wrestle with Her! But Sarah's words smacked to Abraham of blasphemy, and he went into the mountains with his son Isaac.

And Sarah said to God, Sister, you are playing with fire. He is too stupid to understand what you are up to. He won't listen to me and he won't challenge you; if you don't stop him, he will kill our precious son. Is that what you want? And God said, Sarah, they have a long journey to the mountains; I'm hoping one of them will see sense. And Sarah said, Like father like son. You'll have to send an angel.

And it came to pass as Sarah foretold, and the angel of the Lord spoke to Abraham the first time and told him not to kill his son. And Abraham sacrificed a ram as a burnt offering. And the angel of the Lord spoke to Abraham a second time and told him his offspring would be as numerous as stars in the heaven and would possess the gates of their enemies.

And the angel of the Lord spoke to Abraham a third time and said, Because you were ready to kill your own son in the name of your God you will be known as a great patriarch and millions will follow your example. And they will believe that He is indeed a jealous and a demanding God, and they will willingly sacrifice their sons in His name and to His glory. And there will be bloodshed and slaughter in all the corners of the earth.

And Abraham returned to his wife Sarah and said, God is well pleased with me for I am to be a mighty patriarch. And Sarah said nothing. But she took the garments of Abraham and Isaac that were stained with the blood of the ram, and she carried them to the river to be washed. And the river ran red with the blood of generations to come, and Sarah wept bitterly.

And God came to Sarah at the water's edge and said, My sister Sarah, do not weep. You were right, it will take time. Meanwhile hold firm to what you know of me and speak it boldly. I am as you know me to be. Many generations will pass and a new understanding will come to the children of Abraham, but before then I shall be misheard and misrepresented except by a few. You must keep my truth alive.

And Sarah dried her eyes and said, As if I didn't have enough to do.[52]

It is in the story's re-telling that we recognize the depth of the patriarchal assumptions embedded in it. Moreover we are brought up against the diametrically opposed nature of these assumptions and feminist ideals.

Commensurately with the conception of God which we have been considering, the primary understanding of sin within the Judaeo-Christian tradition has been that it consists in pride and, related to that, idolatry. By pride is to be understood here an unjustified pride or *hubris:* a setting up of the self in the place of God – hence the connection with idolatry. (Consider for example the passage in Romans 1 where Paul speaks of those who, becoming vain in their imagination, failed to glorify the creator, and consequently set up idols in 'his' place.) Pride is the attempt of a creature, who as creature should rightly be dependent on the creator, to refuse to acknowledge that dependence. (Sin is – we may well say – on this view, to challenge the father.) A classic exploration of pride as *hubris* within Christian theology is that given by Reinhold Niebuhr in Gifford lectures of 1939–1940, in which he effectively brought such an analysis to bear on the totalitarian ambitions of Nazi Germany.[53] Niebuhr recalls the ancient Babylonian myth which finds its echo in Isaiah, in which Lucifer (that is to say the 'light bearer', Venus, the morning star) commits the 'sin' of attempting to fly higher than God, in consequence of which he is cast down into hell (becoming the devil).[54] In this conception of the divine/ human relation, what is absolutely prohibited is that humanity should apostasize and worship other 'gods'. For as the Hebrew scriptures proclaim, 'The Lord thy God is a jealous God.'[55] Other 'gods' are idols. The true God will allow no competitors; unlike the heathen gods, 'he' is not one among many. We are at the antipodes from ideas of eclecticism and multifariousness.

Having considered these themes to do with the father/son relationship, patriarchy, and the transcendent God, we may note a feminist critique of this whole structure of thought. Through her persistent questioning and her posing of an alternative, Luce Irigaray's interrogation of the French Jewish thinker Emmanuel Levinas throws into relief the paradigms present in the tradition. Irigaray levels the charge that Levinas has simply translated what is the Jewish paradigm into secular mode. According to this paradigm male identity is constituted through the relationship between man and the absent God; or, in terms of

Levinas' thought, that between the father and the son. Woman becomes the 'other', for Levinas the beloved, rather than the one in a relationship of reciprocity with whom man comes to find his self-identity. Furthermore, the God of patriarchy, who speaks in his absence to humankind, is a profoundly authoritarian image.[56] Irigaray directs our attention by contrast to the Song of Songs, which she believes to come from an earlier period and to reflect a sacred marriage.[57] It is within such a carnal representation of the relationship between male and female that Irigaray herself wants to locate what she conceives to be 'the divine'.[58]

Thus Irigaray writes:

> What radical difference distinguishes the God who makes his presence known in the law from the one who gives himself, through his presence, as nourishment, including nourishment of the senses? How does it come about that the God of the writing of the law cannot be looked upon? . . . For God, in this period of theophany, does not share, he dictates [*il impose*]. He separates himself, when he gives Moses the inscription of the law . . . The law creates invisibility, so that God (in his glory?) cannot be looked upon . . . Why, at this period of the covenant, does God suspend the link between the two most spiritual of the senses, thereby depriving men of the carnal representation of the covenant? Is this not a gesture that breaks with the more feminine cultures?[59]

Such a critique and the opposing of an alternative structure relativizes the male paradigm.

With the story of Abraham's near slaughter of Isaac in view, I turn to consider the theme of sacrifice. Alienation from the concept of sacrifice would seem to be near-universal among women, those who remain within 'patriarchal' religions as well as those who have left. Carol Delaney asks:

> Why is the theme of child sacrifice *the* theme chosen by Biblical writers to express devotion to God? Why is Abraham's willingness to kill Isaac seen as an expression of great piety? Why is Sarah's point of view noticeably absent? Does the story have the same meaning for women, or is it a symptom of masculine culture?[60]

And we may again cite Luce Irigaray, here interrogating René Girard, whose work on the nature of sacrifice is well known.[61] Girard suggests that, through the direction of aggression towards another who becomes a scapegoat, sacrificial religious rites serve to mediate relations between men. Irigaray retorts:

Why did speech fail? What was missing? Why kill, cut up and eat as a sign of the covenant? And isn't it possible to analyse why speech was so inadequate that such an act became necessary? Was it, for instance, because of a lack of harmony between words, acts and bodies? Are cultures sacrificial if they manage to unite acts, words, microcosmic and macrocosmic nature and the gods?[62]

Women may well ask such questions. In teaching Kierkegaard's *Fear and Trembling* it has often occurred to me to wonder what kind of a God those who – over generations – have recited the story of Abraham and Isaac can possibly have believed in, that 'he' should have demanded any such thing? How could 'he' play with humans in this manner, to test absolute loyalty to 'him'? Why indeed, considering the theme of sacrifice more generally, should God need to be appeased? And why sacrifice in order to appease?

This brings me directly to the third motif which I shall consider under the rubric of the crossing of the distance between God and humanity, that of God as Son and thus also incarnation. I shall again be interested in the particular way in which this motif is cashed out; that is to say I shall analyse the understanding of incarnation in terms of *kenosis*, of self-emptying. Moreover in conjunction also with this motif I shall consider the motif of sacrifice, now in its Christian context. But before I begin, let me be allowed – as one who is not a Christian – to pose naive questions of a type I am sometimes tempted to ask. In incarnation, so it is said, one who is co-equally God as the Father is God comes to humanity. Comes from where? Indeed, why the blasphemy of ever suggesting that God was 'absent'? As Karl Barth will have it (alluding to the parable of the prodigal son), the incarnation is the journey of the Son of God to the 'far country'.[63] (Humanity is a 'far country'.) In much of Christian theology it is the presumption of human sin in the Fall which necessitated the incarnation.[64] What Fall?

In commencing our consideration of the Christian theme of Sonship and so also of incarnation we should again notice that it is predicated upon the presupposition that there is a problem: that there is a distance to be traversed between God and humanity. This gap is, as we have said, conceived in both ontological and in moral terms. The Son may then be held to be a mediator; this is notably so within the Reformed tradition (whether in Calvin or indeed in Schleiermacher). Christ is not, of course, an intermediary being: in Christian orthodoxy he is understood to be both fully God and fully human – though it may well be thought that in practice Christians have been much less clear about this. However, the Son is what we may call a 'transitional' figure: facing two ways, corresponding to his two natures. As the second 'person' of a triune

God, the Son is God with us; while the human Jesus, who is conjoined without division in one 'person' with a second and divine nature, takes humanity into the Godhead. Thus for example in the second century Irenaeus writes that Christ 'was made a human among humans, that he might join . . . humanity to God'.[65] Or again, in the fourth, Athanasius likewise holds that the Word 'was made a human in order that we might be made divine'.[66] Thus also the priest, who within Catholic Christendom stands *in loco Christi*, at the altar traditionally faces God, representing humanity to God, and faces humanity representing Christ as God to the people. Christ, or the priest, pleads with God 'the Father' on behalf of his brethren, while Christ, or the priest on his behalf, can grant God's forgiveness. It may be noted that the Virgin Mary has also often performed the role of a transitional figure; but in her case, significantly, she can only represent humanity in relation to God. Indeed she is often a transitional figure between humanity and her son, pleading with him on its behalf![67]

Let us turn next to a consideration of the manner of Christ's coming to humanity. The incarnation in human form of one who in 'himself' was God has been interpreted in Christian history as a divestment of power and privilege. Taking up the verse in Philippians 2, in which Paul comments that 'though he was in the form of God', he 'did not count equality with God a thing to be grasped, but emptied himself [in Greek, a form of the word *kenosis*] taking the form of a servant', Christians have developed a kenotic christology. Nor is such a notion anything other than all of a piece with wider themes in Christianity. It would be mistaken to think that Christians have only been concerned for dominative power (the authority of God the Father). The theme of love as a giving up of self is deeply embedded in Christianity. This may be held to have been exemplified by Christ on the cross. But equally it is present in, for example, the exposition of love as *agape,* that love of which Paul tells us in I Corinthians 13 which, not counting the cost, seeks not its own, bearing and enduring all things.[68]

If we are to critique the theme of *kenosis*, as I shall wish to, it is important to understand its power and its centrality to Christianity. I quote here the words of one who was my teacher in systematic theology, Arthur McGill. Though he died before he had written all that he should have done, McGill's imaginative work was nevertheless an inspiration to his students. The quotation comes from a book intended to bring an understanding of the wealth of Christianity to a more general audience. McGill discusses here the implications of the fourth century debate between the Arian position and what, through the councils of Nicaea (325) and Constantinople (381), became Christian orthodoxy.

We must now ask: *What is God like in his relations to men?* There can be only one answer. God exercises his power in relation to men through self-giving love and service . . . For [the heretic] Arius, God's complete self-sufficiency means that within the world he appears in the form of absolute domination. As God depends on nothing, everything else depends on him. As he is completely rich, everything else is completely poor. As he is completely powerful, everything else is completely weak, and is called to revere his power . . . According to the Trinitarian theologians, nothing could be more contrary to the power of God that men encounter in Jesus Christ than this Arian picture. Far from being a vessel of dominating mastery, Jesus is just the opposite. He does not come on clouds of glory. He does not stand over his followers, ordering them hither and yon to do his bidding and vindicating his authority by unopposed acts of self-assertion . . . God's divinity does not consist in his ability to push things around, to make and break, to impose his will from the security of some heavenly remoteness, and to sit in grandeur while all the world does his bidding. Far from staying above the world, he sends his own glory into it. Far from imposing, he invites and persuades. Far from demanding service from men in order to enhance himself, he gives his life in service to men for their enhancement. But God acts toward the world in this way because within himself he is a life of self-giving [the doctrine of the Trinity].[69]

Such an understanding, many Christians will think, represents that for which Christianity stands.

But from a feminist perspective what should one say? Consider first the apparent popularity of kenotic theology in the nineteenth century. Kierkegaard gives us the parable of the king who clads himself in rough garments that he might win the love of the lowly maiden.[70] The one who divests himself of his kingly attributes is of course designated male; humanity, whose love is sought in the incarnation, is a lowly maiden. In the late nineteenth century, kenotic theology was prominent in the thinking of a group of highly privileged Anglican bishops and church leaders.[71] They were the generation who 'condescended' to work among the poor, for example building settlements in the East End of London. The theology exactly fitted that divestment of privilege which, as Christians, they saw to be incumbent upon them. We should by no means disparage their good intentions or their efforts. My question, however, is this: is the theme of *kenosis* useful to women? It would not appear necessarily to imply a restructuring of society but rather a mitigation of its ills.

What feminists await, however, is a paradigm shift. Thus the commendation of a kenotic theology to women, saying that it represents 'the undoing of the power and privilege of patriarchy', does not really meet the point. Feminist women are not looking for condescension on the part of men. They want equality. Such rhetoric has then failed to grasp the feminist ideal. Thus I should want to argue that, at the end of day, it is not useful to women that (instead of dominating them) men should, in self-effacing manner, serve them. What women must wish is for men to come in themselves to be 'centred' persons; a very different conception of what is needed than that of self-abnegation. As centred selves, men will cease to dominate others while at the same time allowing women, in their strength, to become centred selves in relation to them. We need a much more radical shift, and a different shift, than that which *kenosis* represents, still presupposing as it does a world of privilege and its divestment.[72] Again, love had perhaps better be seen as an exchange between two parties (as *philia*), rather than as the self-giving in which *agape* consists.

It is of course peculiarly problematic that, in sermons without number and over generations, the Christian ideal of self-sacrifice and humility should have been preached (by men) to women. For women were the last people who should have been the recipients of such an exhortation. If such a model of the Christian life is held up before those who are inclined to suffer from low self-esteem, it can only serve to undermine any fragile sense they may possess of the need to stick up for their rights. Women have had difficulty precisely in gaining sufficient sense of self-integrity. In our society they have been taught to look up to men in innumerable and subtle ways. I well recall in my twenties, when a man whom I dearly loved was treating me appallingly, reading over and over Paul's depiction of *agape* in I Corinthians 13: love bears all, love never fails. Had I only had the guts to challenge him about his behaviour it would have helped me to reconstitute my sense of myself. Indeed, in the case of some women, the theme of self-sacrifice may be thought to reinforce what is clearly self-destructive behaviour. By contrast what we need if we are to have fully functioning relations between women and men is for women to come into their own. That is to say, we require a sense of the way in which people can empower one another – something that has notably been present in the women's movement.

Nevertheless, Christian feminist theologians have sometimes thought the theme of *kenosis* useful. Rosemary Ruether in particular has spoken of a *kenosis*, or undoing, of patriarchal values through the motif of the incarnation.[73] (I have even heard it suggested that God was incarnate as a man because it is men who need redemption!) However, I turn to what I think to be a striking piece of writing, in which Karen Bloomquist relates the theme to what has been the situation of some women.

Jesus is not a model for women to imitate, in some kind of scapegoat, self-sacrificing role. To identify with him in that sense would only increase our victimization and mutilation. We are not to give ourselves up to be crucified for anyone's sake but are [and she quotes Carter Heyward] 'to struggle together against the injustice of all human sacrifice, including our own'.

And she continues:

The cross reveals to us intimations of the God who identifies with us in the cruciform sufferings that are already a part of our lives as women . . . One of our students describes in powerfully moving terms her experience of being raped, and as she lay there on the ground fearing that she would be killed, what flashed before her was a vision of Christ – of Christ as a woman – 'because only a woman would understand'.[74]

What should we say?

As a Christian feminist, Bloomquist advances the thesis that there can be a reading of Christianity which 'depatriarchalizes' God. I can see that this writing is powerful. Why, however, am I not convinced? From my own perspective, I must first comment that such a reinterpretation of the theme of incarnation evades the question as to whether we could possibly believe that there could be any such thing as an incarnation of God. But secondly, even in regard to the symbolism, it is apparently not quite apposite. Thus Bloomquist is forced to twist what might be thought to be the obvious interpretation: it is not that we should identify with Christ in his suffering but that we should resist suffering. Indeed, we are told that what the woman who was raped needed in that extremity was a female saviour with whom to identify.

But more fundamentally, I am in no way attracted to that theme which seems to have been prominent in Christian thinking following Bonhoeffer's articulation of it, and more especially since Jürgen Moltmann's *The Crucified God*: that (in Bonhoeffer's words) 'only the suffering God can help'.[75] I do not have the least desire that God should take on our condition. To speak biographically for a moment, the idea that Jesus was God was not present in my background and I did not in fact learn until my late teens (at an age after I wanted to be ordained) that some people thought this. Thus with my very different understanding of God (which I shall spell out in detail in Chapter VI), I wish rather to conceive of God as a power and a love which lifts us out of suffering and which heals us. In the meantime I often see very little evidence that those who take the Christian imagery upon themselves actually wish to speak of the concrete effects of that which is God, present in the world.

I shall proceed next to consider how it is that Christianity speaks to the father-son relationship and, in conjunction with this discussion, I shall return to the theme of sacrifice. Judging by the Western myth or considering psychoanalytic enquiry, we may think the father–son relationship to be both momentous and frequently problematic for the male. For an analysis of what may be afoot in the religious symbolism I turn to Paul Ricoeur's thought-provoking article 'Fatherhood: From Phantasm to Symbol'.[76] Ricoeur juxtaposes Freud's delineation of the Oedipus complex and the dynamics present within Christianity. With reference to the Oedipus complex he writes:

> What I shall retain from it for what follows is this: the critical point of the Oedipus complex is to be sought for in the initial constitution of desire, namely, its megalomania, its infantile omnipotence. From this proceeds the phantasm of a father who would retain the privileges which the son must seize if he is to be himself.

And he comments:

> The stake involved in the dissolution of the Oedipus complex is the replacement of an identification with the father which is literally mortal – and even doubly mortal, since it kills the father by murder and the son by remorse – by a mutual recognition, where the difference is compatible with similarity.[77]

In coming through the Oedipus complex, the boy learns that he does not need to kill the father (which would 'kill' him, too, through guilt). He can identify with the father, learning that the fact that they are of the same sex is something with which he can live peaceably, in that it allows of difference.

But what of Christianity? As far as Freud is concerned, the following must be said:

> As to Christianity, it invents a religion of the Son in which the Son plays a double role: on the one hand, he expiates, for us all, the crime of having killed God; but, at the same time, by taking over the guilt, he becomes God at the side of the father and thus replaces the father, providing an outlet for the resentment against the father. Freud concludes: Christianity, offspring of a religion of the father, becomes a religion of the son.[78]

Ricoeur thinks that if Freud is correct in holding that the 'murder' of the prophets, first Moses and then every prophet who plays the role of Moses, is a reiteration of the murder of the father, it follows that the Suffering Servant theme is that of the death of the father.

To interrupt the exposition of Ricoeur momentarily: where, we may ask, are women in this? If it is not the case that women have repressed a desire to murder the father, then neither is it meaningful that the son should replace the father as the one towards whom aggression is directed. Nor, in turn, will it help them that Christ should be seen as having expiated the resultant guilt. It may well be that, as far as men are concerned, Christianity brilliantly represents a symbolic solution to Oedipal rivalry, transmuting the relation with the father from one of fear to one of love. But if women do not know an Oedipal rivalry with the father, resulting in the desire to kill him, if they do not experience the guilt which this induces in the male, then the whole resolution of this scenario, present in Christian symbolism, is not particularly apposite to their situation.

But to continue. Ricoeur finds that, at its best, Christianity replaces the theme of the sacrifice of the Son with an understanding in which the Son voluntarily lays down his life as a gift.

> The Just One is killed, certainly, and thereby the aggressive impulse against the father is satisfied by means of the offspring of the archaic paternal image; but at the same time, and this is the essential point, the meaning of the death is reversed: by becoming 'dead for another', the death of the Just One achieves the metamorphosis of the paternal image in the direction of a figure of kindness and compassion. The death of Christ stands at the end of this development: it is as an oblation that the Epistle to the Philippians celebrates it in its liturgical hymn: 'He humbled himself, . . . obedient unto death' (Phil. 2.8).
>
> Here is completed the conversion of death as murder into death as offering. Now this meaning is so much beyond the expectation of natural man that the history of theology abounds in purely punitive and penal interpretations of the sacrifice of Christ which make Freud entirely right, so tenacious is the phantasm of the murder of the father and the punishment of the son. For my part, I would believe that the only truly evangelical Christology is one that would take entirely seriously the word of the Johannine Christ: 'No one takes my life. I give it.'

In this case:

> That death would be at the same time a murder on the level of the phantasm and of the return of the repressed, and a supreme abandonment, a supreme dispossession of self, on the level of the most advanced symbol.[79]

Murder is replaced by self-sacrifice.

Ricoeur is thus suggesting that two themes are interwoven in

Christianity: that of sacrifice and that of self-giving. Indeed, we may say that Christ's 'sacrifice' on the cross has often been interpreted in terms of a total self-giving, a pouring out of self, for others. It is the opposite of a self-sufficient pride. But again the question must be raised as to the relevance of such symbolism to women. Thus a recent Church of England report seems to take seriously what has been a feminist critique here.

> In a society seeking to be sensitive to the place of women [sic] we have to take seriously the use to which concepts of sin have been put in the past and might be put in the present . . . The statement that God in Christ responded to human violence, to hatred and the abuse of power, by absorbing on the cross the worst that humanity could do raises this question in acute form. Was Christ responding to, and absorbing, primarily the sins of men? . . . And if the self-sacrifice of a man is indeed a healing and saving response of a saving God to the sins of men, what would be the response of a saving God to sins of collusion and of failure to act with an appropriate self-assertiveness and responsibility?[80]

But the authors have no answer to their rhetorical question. Christianity, and Judaism before it, have grown within a masculinist framework.

That brings me to the theme of sacrifice, in its Christian context. The concept of sacrifice has of course been central to the Christian tradition. It has been suggested, notably by Girard, as we have seen, that sacrifice is a way of mediating between those who are at enmity by the use of a scapegoat. Sacrifice is the mechanism through which God's wrath is held to be turned into forgiveness. We should note that, of the various soteriological themes present in Christian theology,[81] it has been the so-called 'Anselmian' or 'Latin' understanding that has been the most persistent.[82] That interpretation of soteriology has provided the framework for the mass found within the Catholic tradition. Meanwhile the idea of Christ's death as a substitutionary atonement has been the central theme within much of Protestantism.

For Anselm the Son is what I have called a 'transitional' figure. *Qua* human, the Son lays down his life/ is sacrificed to God the Father; for it is humanity which has sinned and must pay the debt. But since, in a second nature, the Son is God, the grace which is released through his sacrifice is superabundant. Because he is sinless and not himself in need of it, that grace may be made available to his brethren. The social context within which the action is played out is that of feudalism; it employs the language of dues and rights within a hierarchical setting. Christ pays the feudal due, a recompense for sin, to the overlord. We

may think this an extraordinarily legalistic understanding of relationships. Law, order and obedience rule, while a relationship is re-instated
through sacrifice. It may strike us as unsurprising that, living as he
did in the late eleventh and early twelfth centuries, Anselm should
have construed soteriology in these terms. What is of interest is that this
sociological explanation should apparently have been found so powerful that it has been retained down to the present day. It would seem that
something fundamental to the (male) psyche is being enacted. There is
a fear of chaos. Indeed, maintenance of a just social order and an interpretation of the relationship to God in legal terms has, as we have seen,
been fundamental to the tradition from the Hebrew scriptures forwards.

Women – as I have already remarked – appear almost universally to
dislike the theme of sacrifice. Here is the comment of two women, both
Anglican priests, in an article on the sadomasochistic tendencies present
within Christianity. Beverly Harrison and Carter Heyward write:

> This spiritual paradigm of Christian pain as virtue and as pleasure
> was also developed theologically. The Christian drama of salvation
> has been staged historically as a transaction between an almighty
> God and a powerless humanity. As the lower relational entity,
> humanity has been cast as a 'fallen' partner, able to be 'saved' or
> 'redeemed' into right relation only insofar as human beings know
> ourselves to be unworthy of anything but punishment from God. Into
> our unworthy lives comes Jesus, the Christ, to bear our sins and to
> submit, on our behalf, to the Father God's Will. Thus, standing in for
> us (as only the elder obedient Son is worthy to do in this patriarchal
> scheme), Jesus is humiliated and killed, becoming thereby a perfect
> sacrifice to the Father. As the classical portrait of the punitive
> character of this divine-human transaction, Anselm of Canterbury's
> doctrine of the atonement . . . probably represents the sado-
> masochism of Christian teaching at its most transparent.[83]

May it not be that Christian women will come rather to value, as a
soteriological theme, the Irenaean understanding of salvation as healing
(conforming to the etymological derivation of the word)?

But it is not only women who find the theme of sacrifice alienating. I
quote the words of a former Catholic priest, looking at the familiar with
new eyes. Tony Bartlett writes:

> Shortly after resigning the clerical priesthood I was staring at a
> crucifix in a Catholic church in North-West London. Suddenly I was
> no longer looking at the theological axis of Christianity connecting
> together guilt, death, expiation, forgiveness, salvation and everlasting
> life. Neither did I see the traditional icon of devotion. Here was a

naked man, six foot and more, suspended on a vertical machine of slow torture, blood oozing from living flesh, in a large viewing place open to the public. What sort of unsavoury organization could be centred upon such an exhibit? . . . At the core of these [reactionary themes] is a violent God who can never be satisfied with the human project . . . The key apparatus and conceptual grip of this God is ritual sacrifice involving an innocent victim, something . . . deeply embedded in our thinking . . . [I]n the sphere of Christian religion [we] have actually integrated it into the very message that should have abolished it. It never seemed plausible to me that a God of love should demand the savage death of any human being, let alone his son, because he needed to avenge his burning wrath at wrongdoing . . . True, the Reformation took the figure of Christ off the cross, but evangelical preaching still rehearses obsessively for the ear what it removes from sight; one event in scripture obliterates in significance all other events: the Crucifixion. The rite of the Catholic mass is actually called a sacrifice which is a ceaseless enactment of Calvary viewed as a victim offering for sin.[84]

Arguing that this is not the message of the gospel, Bartlett comments on the significance of the fact that (given that this is the case), the theme of sacrifice has been retained and reiterated within the Christian church.

Some feminists have wished to point to the negative impression which must be made on children by such images and stories. Thus the feminist theologian Rita Nakashima Brock comments:

Christology is often based in implicit elements of child abuse. Jesus, in his human aspect, is sacrificed as the one perfect child. His sacrifice upholds the righteousness of the father who otherwise would require obedience from his incapable, sinful children.[85]

That such an interpretation has some basis in the tradition is suggested by what Levenson tells us of the connection between the Pauline interpretation of sacrifice and that found in the Hebrew scriptures. Levenson believes that there is a strong parallel between the theme of the sacrifice of the firstborn son (often metaphorical) within Judaism and the interpretation of the death of Christ within Christianity, where the Father allows his Son to be killed. It is this Jewish context, Levenson argues, which Paul has in mind when he writes in Romans 8: 'What then shall we say to this? He who did not spare his own Son . . .'.[86] He comments: 'As Jesus supplants Isaac in Paul's theology, and the Church, the Jews, so does God supplant Abraham in the role of the father who did not withhold his own son from death itself.'[87] God is now the father who, in this case, allows his son actually to die.

Sheila Redmond likewise draws attention to the profoundly problematic nature of some of the paradigms found within Christianity.

> Religious values such as suffering, martyrdom, the role of the female, the role of the child, attitudes toward sexuality and marriage are all prescribed and proscribed in certain ways within the Christian religious structure. Children learn five virtues: (1) the value of suffering; (2) the virtue of forgiveness; (3) the necessity of remaining sexually pure (especially for little girls);[88] (4) the fact that they are in need of redemption; and, most important, (5) the value that is placed on their obedience to authority figures.[89]

She continues:

> [The] Gospel of John plays an enormous role in the minds of most Christians. This Gospel emphasizes Jesus' self-knowledge and his willingness to go to the cross to die, uncomplaining. John's Jesus teaches that one must accept willingly whatever the father does, for whatever the father does is right, justifiable, and must be obeyed. What made the crucifixion right and unquestionable is that the end (salvation of the human race because of its need for redemption) justified the means (pedocide). The father is the exemplar on earth of the image of the father god in heaven . . . This kind of religious symbolism tolerates violence in family life and justifies, in particular, violence against children by fathers and other authority figures.[90]

Christian teaching can clearly be pernicious when it is so interpreted.

Of course not all Christianity has been like this. (It was quite absent from my background.) But much has been. Feminists have naturally wanted to level the charge that such a thought structure is profoundly patriarchal. Nakashima Brock writes:

> The doctrinal dependence upon patriarchal gender systems becomes clear when god as mother is substituted for father. The doctrines are not only virtually incomprehensible, the very suggestion of such substitutions raises enormous negative emotional reactions.[91]

Suppose a 'mother' were to allow her 'daughter' to be sacrificed. The very idea strikes us as absurd! Moreover, what kind of a picture of God is conveyed, both through the Abraham/Isaac story, which we have considered, or through such an interpretation of the death of Christ? Is it not that of a parent who alternately blows hot and cold, first giving Abraham a son in his old age, next demanding his sacrifice; one moment loving his Son, the next moment allowing him to die? Particularly through the writings of the feminist child psychiatrist Alice Miller, we have been alerted to the fact that one of the most devastating circumstances for a child is to be caught up in a relationship with a parent who one moment conveys love, and the next behaves punitively.

It may then be that any naming of God as 'father' can carry a potential danger if a connection is made (as inevitably it will be) between human fathers and the heavenly 'father'. Talk of God as 'male' and as rightly in control can have the effect of augmenting patriarchal authority in situations in which exactly the opposite is called for. Bloomquist writes:

> Exclusively male imagery and language for God continues to legitimize patriarchy and the paradigm of male 'control over' that undergirds the violence-laden situation we find ourselves in today . . . The hostile reactions that female references to God continue to arouse in many church-related and secular audiences are indicative of the deep symbolic and emotional hold that patriarchy still has on most people. Rationally we *know* God is not male, but 'he' still provides the security and order that many seek, thereby justifying the use of violence to maintain that order.[92]

As we know full well today, in cases of violence perpetrated against women and children, what is needed is not subservience to patriarchal authority (often taken for granted by all parties) but rather resistance.

However, some male theologians have wanted to deny that God can be understood as the reflection of human fatherhood. Christianity, it is claimed, represents not patriarchy, but its overcoming. Thus the first General Secretary of the World Council of Churches, a Dutchman from a Reformed background, W. A. Visser 't Hooft (a man of wide experience and deep humanity), wrote in his old age a book on *The Fatherhood of God in an Age of Emancipation*.[93] Enumerating the various ways in which patriarchal relations had been overcome in the political and social spheres during his lifetime, Visser 't Hooft nevertheless argues for a retention of the concept of the 'fatherhood' of God. So too does Karl Barth (to whom, indeed, Henrietta Visser 't Hooft – at a date earlier than her husband's writing – had addressed spirited letters on the topic of the supposed 'subordination' of women[94]), arguing that divine fatherhood is the measure of human fatherhood and not vice versa. Basing himself on Ephesians 3.14–15 ('For this reason I bow my knees before the Father, from whom every family in heaven and on earth is named'), Barth writes: 'From [the] Fatherhood of God what we know as fatherhood among us men is derived. The divine Fatherhood is the primal source of all natural fatherhood.'[95] More recently the Scottish (Barthian) theologian T. F. Torrance has stated that:

> The fact that 'God is Spirit' (John 4.24) and 'the Father of spirits'

(Heb. 12.9) means that we must think of the Fatherhood of God and the relation of human fatherhood to it in an altogether *spiritual* and *imageless* way, and thus without ever reading back descriptively into God the creaturely content or finite imagery of human father-hood.[96]

Meanwhile Robert Hamerton-Kelly, who has made a special study of the use of the term 'father' in the Christian scriptures, draws attention to a distinction which is Ricoeur's. 'Ricoeur,' he writes, 'describes the contrast between Freud's unresolved Oedipal father-god and the Bible's resolved Oedipal father-god as that between phantasm and symbol.'[97] Hamerton-Kelly believes:

> The biblical symbol 'Father' shows no Oedipal content. His children are bound to him by the free choice called 'faith' rather than the enslaving sexual bondage that Freud finds in all modern relationships between parents and children . . . The intimacy and accessibility of Almighty God is the essence of Jesus' 'good news'. God is not distant, aloof, not anti-human, not angry, sullen and withdrawn; God draws near, very near; God is with us.[98]

God is the good father: the one who is accessible.

It is hardly for me to respond on behalf of Christian women. Nevertheless I do wonder whether all this effort on the part of male scholars, devoted to showing that God's is an acceptable 'fatherhood', can be of any avail. Are those women who, still finding themselves able to use a parental term for God, but who in consequence of their feminist disposition have adopted 'mother' or perhaps 'mother/father God', prepared to revert to the term father now that they have heard the 'correct' interpretation? One suspects not. 'Father' is a powerful symbol which cannot but carry certain connotations. One should not be so naive as to how images function. Nor can one write off the historical legacy which the term father must needs brings with it.

But secondly – and here I speak as one who is not a Christian – those who argue for the acceptability of the term 'father' (or indeed, perhaps, to a lesser extent 'mother', in that that word has different connotations) have not grasped the more fundamental revolution which feminism represents. Inasmuch as human beings have come to have full moral agency, why should they employ parental images for God? As I have already commented, women who are feminists and have struggled to overcome heteronomous relationships to others (in particular to men) are unlikely to be prepared to rescind their moral autonomy in a relationship to a transcendent God. This is the case whether or not this God is symbolized as 'male'. All anthropomorphic language for God becomes peculiarly inappropriate, and language which is 'male' and in any way authoritarian the most inappropriate of all.

I come now to the third and final theme which I shall consider in this chapter, that of God conceptualized as Trinity. It has been the central symbol for God in Christian culture. If a transcendent monotheism manifests a hierarchical conception of relationships and reflects an understanding of the self as self-enclosed, then God conceived of as Trinity might well be held to exemplify exactly the opposite. For the Trinity is said to show the nature of God as being, within 'himself', an internal dynamism of love. Does it not then manifest a deeply relational notion of the self? How fascinating, we might say, that men have been the ones who have wished to capture the ultimate in such a symbol. As in the case of the theme of *kenosis*, and again in the theme of crucifixion understood of an outpouring of self, so in the doctrine of the Trinity the nature of that love is said to consist in a self-giving.

A helpful unpacking of what is involved in the doctrine of the Trinity is again to be found in the work of McGill's from which I have already quoted. At the Council of Nicaea the Son was said to be 'of one substance' *(homoousios)* with the Father; that is to say, he is as equally God as is the Father. During the controversy which subsequently broke out, Athanasius, the leader of the Nicene party, made a further crucial move. For he held that:

> The divine power met in Jesus – what is called the 'Son' of God – is generated from God the Father. After the analogy of human generation, the Son derives his reality from the very being of the Father.

By contrast:

> Arius was convinced that divinity . . . *cannot be communicated*. It cannot be passed from one being to another; it cannot be generated or begotten or produced. For divinity, he says, by its very nature, is *wholly self-contained*, is fully *complete in itself*. It has no need for change, no need to extend itself or communicate itself or generate itself.

The decisive mark of God (according to Christian orthodoxy) is not power but love:

> Between the Father and the Son there exists a relationship of *total and mutual self-giving*. The Father and the Son are not just entities who contain within themselves a divine level of reality, and who tenaciously hold onto what they have, in the fashion of Arius' God. The Father and the Son have divine reality in *a state of action*, in the

action of total self-communication. In fact, Athanasius' point is that this state of action, this act of self-giving is the *essential mark of God s divinity*. The Father and the Son do not have their identity in terms of the reality that they possess and hold onto within themselves, but in terms of their giving this reality to the other. If God's reality in himself is the relation between Father and Son, then God is this staggering dynamism of mutual self-communication. Because the Father holds nothing back but gives all his glory to the Son, and because the Son holds nothing back but offers all that he has to glorify the Father, God within himself is supreme in the order of love . . . Always there was the Father generating the Son, and the Son glorifying the Father . . . More interestingly, Athanasius points out that any God with the kind of monadic unity and self-sufficient absoluteness that Arius celebrates must be, within himself, an *agonos theos,* a sterile God. Such a God is not generative, not fecund; in short, he must be a dead God. He must be a light that does not shine, a fountain that has gone dry, a barren thing. And if within himself he is such an inert and barren unitarian monad, asks Athanasius, then where does he get the creative power to produce the world? . . . Throughout all eternity the Father is communicating his reality to the Son; and throughout all eternity the Son is giving all glory to the Father. These are not acts which cause changes in God; they are eternal processes which make up God's essential aliveness.[99]

Thus the relation between the Father and the Son. In the 370s attention turned to the Spirit who was deemed likewise to be God, this being confirmed at Constantinople, so that thenceforth Christendom had its triune God.

The understanding of God as profoundly relational, which the doctrine of the Trinity seems to imply, has been latched on to by recent Christian writers. Those who wish to propound this contrast such an understanding with the self-enclosed, monadic conception of the self, which they believe to derive from the Western Enlightenment. The Eastern orthodox theologian John Zizioulas in his book *Being as Communion* writes in this vein.[100] More recently, the British nonconformist theologian Colin Gunton has taken up this theme in his *The Promise of Trinitarian Theology*.[101] Trinitarianism might well be held to represent an undoing of a 'masculinist' enclosed self, and it is evidently in this that its appeal to some men lies.

I shall shortly come to a discussion of the precise nature of the relationality which is involved. There are, however, some preliminary remarks to be made. It is not necessarily the case that God need be patterned upon the human; as though it were the case that, if we are to conceive of the self as relational, then God must be understood as exemplifying in God's self the kind of relations which men and women should have. There are ways of conceiving of God which are not the transcendent monism of what appears to be a discrete entity, yet are not trinitarian either. Furthermore, it is likewise the case that a conception of God as Trinity is not the only 'relational' way of conceiving of God. Thus the conception of God which I shall advocate in Chapter VI of this book is profoundly 'relational', in that God is immediately related to that which we ourselves are. But it is not trinitarian. Nor yet is it a transcendent monotheism (and it is not pantheism).

Furthermore, one might well remark on the following. The understanding of the relationship between the Father and the Son within the Trinity as one of equality may be said effectively to overturn the Arian and Greek presupposition that that which is dependent is less perfect than that which is not; for the Son, though coming forth from the Father, is equally God. But it can hardly be said that it has followed that the relationship between God and humanity has been conceived to have such an equality. There has indeed been a strand of Eastern thought (which I cited), manifested in the first place in Irenaeus and taken up in the so-called 'Athanasian' creed, which holds that through being assumed in the incarnation of the second 'person' of the Trinity, humanity undergoes a certain divinization.[102] Thus, as a recent liturgical rendering of the 'Athanasian' creed would have it: 'Divinity is bound to human nature and manhood taken up to God.'[103] But in most Western theology, following Augustine (and markedly within Protestantism), the divide between God on the one hand and humanity on the other has been far too great for trinitarian thinking to have had much effect in this respect. Thus Gunton himself tells us: 'There is, of course, a relationship of authority, for God is creator and Lord'; and again: 'It is one thing to be God, another to be the world.'[104]

I come now to a consideration of the relationality exemplified in trinitarian theology. Does it model that relationality which feminists seek in construing the self as relational? Provisionally, I may say the following. Given the vocabulary which men employ to describe it, it seems to be a model of self-giving, of outpouring of self (which is still concerned with self rather than necessarily focused on the other). It would not appear to consist in that centredness in self and presence to another, a model of a reciprocity between two, which so much feminist theory describes. Now self-giving, as we have said in our discussion of *kenosis*, may not in itself be a particularly apt model for women to emulate. Indeed, may it not rather appear to be a male response to the male dilemma of being caught up in a self with over rigid ego boundaries? Given more 'permeable' ego boundaries, there can, by contrast, be an interplay between the two, each of whom remains centred in herself.

What, then, does this model of love as an outpouring of self reflect? In the form of trinitarian thought, it appears to have been meaningful to men, as we shall see, across all times and cultures. Why should men (for let us be clear that it has been men) have constructed the model for God as Trinity in the first place? I have already suggested that there has been something about the social situatedness of men (not least within the patriarchal family) which may have resulted in their becoming isolated and individuated, and consequently needing to break through the barrier between self and other.[105] It is also of course the case that if that one wishes to say that 'the Son' and 'the Spirit' are equally God as is 'the Father', and if one does not wish to have three gods (a tritheism), then one will need to find some way of speaking of one-in-three and three-in-one. Nevertheless, the particular language which men employ for trinitarian love and the depth of emotion which they invest in it has led me to the conviction (held over many years now) that the Trinity is a reflection of how men experience love in the sexual act.

Since it is unfashionable among feminists to allow that the different thought forms which men and women employ might owe anything to what Erik Erikson terms 'genital morphology',[106] I must explain myself carefully. I in no way wish to deny that it is within culture that we construct our sense of identity and indeed interpret our physicality. It is clear that it is the social structure of what is a patriarchal society that has led many men to become rather isolated selves. For want of other adequate channels (such as female conversation), their sexuality may become the way in which men can 'break through' to another. If men are singularly inarticulate about their personal feelings, they will need such an expression. As we have said, many men seem only to relate to the world in any kind of intimate way through their partner, otherwise lacking meaningful personal relations in a way which seems strange to many women. It is not then a matter for criticism that men should employ erotic language in their construction of the idea of God. However, in view of the evidence which I shall adduce, I find myself unable to think that male sexuality in no way affects the particular shaping which the doctrine of the Trinity has had.

What is a matter for criticism, as we have seen in the case of Irigaray's critique of Levinas, is that men should so often have had a love affair with the divine, substituting a relationship with God for an equal relationship with another human being. As I have mentioned, Feuerbach did not fail to notice this, writing:

The Christians . . . substituted for the natural love and unity immanent in man a purely religious love and unity; they rejected the real life of the family, the intimate bond of love which is naturally moral, as an undivine, unheavenly, i.e., in truth, a worthless thing. But in compensation they had a Father and Son in God, who embraced each other with heartfelt love, with that intense love which natural relationship alone inspires. On this account the mystery of the Trinity was to the ancient Christians an object of unbounded wonder, enthusiasm, and rapture, because here the satisfaction of those profoundest human wants which in reality, in life, they denied, became to them an object of contemplation in God.[107]

Woman is the one who is renounced in loving such a God. This is something which I shall need to consider further in the next chapter.

In the present context let us note – given the title of this chapter, 'Christian Idolatry' – how problematical it is that men should have absolutized their particular way of conceptualizing God, as though it and it alone was appropriate for both sexes. The Italian feminist theorist Rosi Braidotti who, working in the Netherlands, belongs to the Continental school of feminist thought, writes as follows: 'Although philosophical thought depends on the male sexed body, the male embodied subject is precisely that great non-said of Western philosophy.'[108] It is in the lack of recognition of the partiality which is present that the problem lies. Thus in considering the Trinity, what should hold our attention is not simply that the model for ultimate love has been constructed as the love between two poles, Father and Son, both of whom are cast in male terms; though that in itself is problematic enough. It is the fact that the whole conception of God as Trinity may reflect what has been the experience of only one sex and that this has gone unrecognized. As the feminist thinker Starhawk comments, in another context: 'The erotic is the realm in which the spiritual, the political and the personal come together.'[109] How men experience their sexuality has come to be externalized in a symbol which then becomes a basic datum of theology for the whole of humanity.

The first question which arises in this connection is obviously that as to whether the doctrine of the Trinity is a manifestation of homoeroticism. That it is has sometimes been a feminist charge. We have an unanswerable question here. It is well-known that many Christian priests have been homosexual. But many more are not and are equally trinitarian Christians. The Christian understanding of ultimate reality as consisting in a relationship between a 'father' and a 'son' must be said in the first instance to have come about on account of what was believed about Jesus; who was male and who would seem to have referred to God as 'father'. The magnification of this relationship within Christian

thought may owe quite as much to its potential resolution of the father/
son relationship (which I have considered) as to any desire to exclude
women. That these things are the case must not, however, be allowed to
obscure the fact that the lack of a female pole in the symbol for ultimate
reality may be thought to have been profoundly harmful to women.
Relations between women and men might have been very different had
God been understood as a relationship of love between two, one of
which was symbolized as 'male', the other 'female'.

Secondly, I turn to a consideration of the particular expression of that
love which is said to be the love manifested in intra-trinitarian relations.
This leads me to think that the Trinity is in some way an expression of
men's experience of their sexuality within that social context which is
patriarchy. Most obviously, we should note the cashing out which there
has been of the technical term used for that inter-relationality of the
three persons: in Greek *perichoresis,* in Latin *circumincessio.*
Etymologically the term in Greek signifies a cyclical motion, suggesting
an encircling of the three persons around one another. Hence its
rendering in Latin by *circumincessio* (from *incedere,* to 'permeate' or
'encompass'), so that it is often glossed as 'co-inherence' or 'inter-
penetration'.[110] Here, for example, is the relevant entry, contributed by
H. E. W. Turner, in *A New Dictionary of Christian Theology.* Turner
writes: 'Coinherence (Latin: *circumincessio,* Greek: *perichoresis*) is the
doctrine denoting the mutual indwelling or inter-penetration of the
three Persons of the Trinity whereby one is as invariably in the other
two as they are in the one.' He then proceeds to give us the long history
of this gloss, concluding (as well he might): 'The key to the doctrine is
mysticism rather than the logic of the divine relations'![111]

It is not, however, primarily *perichoresis,* but rather the prevalence
of the language of flow, ecstasy (a standing outside oneself) and indeed
the breaking through a barrier so universally found in exegesis of the
Trinity which has led me to my conclusion. (Of course a woman also
'gives' in the sexual act, but she does not give of herself, of her substance, in quite the sense that a man does.) I give quotations here from
a range of Anglican and Catholic writers on the Trinity. It should not
be thought that those whom I happen to quote are in any way exceptional; the whole point is that they are not. English Anglicans (and
Catholics) have majored on patristics, so it is not surprising that examples of what I wish to draw attention to are readily found in their writings. I shall, however, cite some examples from other traditions as well.

Here is John Macquarrie, commenting on Pseudo-Dionysius on the
Trinity:

Himself a mystic, he imagines a kind of divine ecstasy, in which God comes out of himself in an act of self-emptying or self-giving: 'We must dare to affirm (for it is the truth) that the Creator of the universe himself, in his beautiful and good yearning toward the universe, is through the excessive yearning of his goodness transported outside himself in his providential activities toward all things that have being . . . and so is drawn from his transcendent throne above all things to dwell within the heart of all things, through an ecstatic power that is above being and whereby he yet stays within himself.'[112]

Macquarrie comments: 'Self-transcendence . . . is the capacity to go beyond.' He continues:

> If we accept that in some respects of his being God is involved in time and history . . . then as God fulfils his purposes, he is not just perfecting the world as exterior to himself, but is increasing his own satisfaction and therefore 'surpassing' himself . . .

He concludes that we should 'move toward a more dynamic conception of God . . . as transcending in the sense of constantly coming forth from himself'.[113]

Here again is the Catholic Vernon White, in his *Atonement and Incarnation*, discussing Peter Brown's work. The Trinity, says Brown, consists in two centres of consciousness. White continues: 'In the case of the incarnation . . . there is a harmony and a reciprocal "flow" from one to the other.' Brown comments that the 'flow' is reciprocal 'to the maximum extent compatible with each nature remaining itself'.[114] Again, the Anglican Brian Hebblethwaite writes:

> For Christianity, God is a relational, internally differentiated God, already the fullness of love given and love received, not needing to create in order to love, but nevertheless overflowing in love to new, finite, dependent creatures – ourselves.[115]

And David Jenkins, former Anglican bishop and theologian, writes:

> The Trinity is not only the symbol of this supreme identity . . . The shape of the trinitarian symbol also indicates that in the end identity is not to be had at the cost of other identities but by being the fulfilment of them. For the symbol indicates a dynamic interdependence which is perfect identity and perfect freedom . . . Thus, in the Trinity there is a picture of a total interpenetration of being and activity which provides and sustains a total identity which works precisely for mutual identifying . . . What this picture promises us is that there is a way of my being me which will come about . . . when and as you are you and I am I . . . The Trinity is therefore also the symbol of the perfect society. For it points to that community of relationship

where all will fulfil one another in communion, communication and true communism.[116]

Jenkins' 'in the end' suggests that relationality is something the importance of which needs to be discovered!

We have already seen the language which Arthur McGill employs. McGill was from a Canadian Presbyterian background. And here is the German Reformed theologian Jürgen Moltmann.

> *Love is the self-communication of the good.* It is the power of good to go out of itself, to enter into other being, to participate in other being, and to give itself for other being. If we interpret love as the passionate self-communication of the good, then we have distinguished it plainly enough from destructive passions. Love wants to live and to give life . . . The loving person enters entirely into the other whom he loves, but in that other he is entirely himself. The unselfishness of love lies in the loving person's communication of himself, not in his self-destruction.
>
> *Every self-communication presupposes the capacity for self-differentiation.* The lover communicates himself. He is the one who communicates and the one communicated . . . When we say 'God *is* love', then we mean that he is in eternity this process of self-differentiation and self-identification . . . God loves the world with the very same love which he himself is in eternity. God affirms the world with the energy of his self-affirmation. Because he not only loves but is himself love, he has to be understood as the triune God.[117]

Moltmann, too, quotes Pseudo-Dionysius: 'Love does not permit the lover to rest in himself. It draws him out of himself, so that he may be entirely in the beloved.'[118] And Berdyaev: 'Love as the one that communicates does not yet find the real place of its activity in God himself, but only where there is purely free, primal giving, only where there is pure neediness in the receiver.'[119] Moltmann writes: 'It is in accordance with the love which is God that he should fashion a creation which he rejoices over, and call to life his Other, man [viz. human beings, *den Menschen*] as his image, who responds to him.'[120] We should notice that, significantly, these quotations seem to accord to humanity what is a 'feminine' position.

Clearly such a construal of the doctrine of the Trinity, using this language, is present in a whole range of Christian traditions. It is advanced as though it were somehow axiomatic that love should be understood in these terms. An interesting control experiment here would be whether women who employ the doctrine of the Trinity give it quite the same meaning. Very few women in Christian history have been theologians or have written about the Trinity. Nevertheless there is some evidence to suggest that the way in which women interpret relatilonality within the Triune God is subtly different. What they wish to see reflected is a model of interchange and reciprocity between those who are whole persons in themselves.

Thus Elizabeth Johnson quotes a typical male exegesis of the doctrine as I have characterized it. Walter Kasper writes:

> In the Father, love exists as pure source that pours itself out; in the Son it exists as a pure passing on . . . in the Spirit it exists as the joy of pure receiving. These three modes . . . are in some sense necessary because love cannot be otherwise conceived.[121]

Johnson comments:

> But the experience of mutual love so prized in feminist reflection shows that love can in fact be conceived another way, namely, in a relational pattern of mutual giving and receiving according to each one's capacity and style.[122]

What she wishes to see symbolized is 'genuine mutuality in which there is radical equality while distinctions are respected'. She tells us that 'the idea of the triune God has a powerful affinity' with women's talk of relationality: 'the persons are constituted by their relationships to each other'. When she asks 'how to characterize this relatedness', her response is as follows. 'The mutuality offered in genuine friendship offers one fertile clue. Friendship is the most free, the least possessive, the most mutual of relationships, able to cross social barriers in genuine reciprocal regard.'[123] She quotes Rosemary Ruether: 'Authentic relationship is not a relation between two half selves, but between whole persons . . . We seek a new concept of relationship which is not competitive or hierarchical but mutually enhancing.'[124] That is to say, what Johnson wishes to see is a feminist understanding of relationality characterized as *philia*, not that outpouring of self which is how *agape* is commonly understood within the Christian tradition.[125]

Consider also the words of the Catholic theologian Anne Carr: 'The mystery of God as Trinity, as final and perfect sociality, embodies those qualities of mutuality, reciprocity, co-operation, unity, peace in genuine diversity that are feminist ideals and goals.'[126] Again, we may note the work of Janet Martin Soskice, a Catholic who moves in the same Oxbridge world as many of the men whom I have quoted. In a paper which utilizes the French 'deconstructionist' concept of 'différance', she writes of the Trinity as follows: 'It does let us glimpse what it is, most truly, to be: "To be" most fully is "to-be-related" in difference.' Does this not, we may ask, exemplify exactly what I have described as the feminist understanding of relationality as consisting in two centred selves, existing in a relationship of reciprocity? Martin Soskice further quotes the French philosopher Françoise Collin, commenting that her words must ring true to a theologian within the trinitarian context. Collin, as quoted by Martin Soskice, writes:

> In the beginning, there is difference. This difference is not reducible to duality; there is not, on the one hand, man, and on the other, woman, each having their own additional characteristics. There is in the beginning the not-one which must be allowed free play.[127]

Each within relationship gives the other space.

This strikes me as a very different drawing out of the symbolism of Trinity. Where I should want to question Martin Soskice, however, is as to how, for example, she can allow that such 'male' symbolism as that of the relation between a 'Father' and a 'Son' can be our primary symbol for God. Such a question is particularly pertinent in view of the fact that she is herself so clear as to the centrality of metaphor to our conception of reality. Indeed we may have reason to think that she sees the force of the question. In an article 'Can a Feminist Call God Father?' she asks, engagingly, whether the 'father God' has a future.[128] If I may adopt her vocabulary, I should like to ask how *such* a symbol could be 'turned'?[129] I believe it cannot. It may be relevant to quote a sentence from Antoine Vergote: 'No cure can be effective if it remains captive to the psychological images which preside over the patient's alienation.'[130] What one must question, given that feminists are adapting the doctrine of the Trinity to their purposes, is why it should be *this* model that they wish to adapt. Feminists must surely move on!

Another interesting question arises in this context. If men have written their sexuality as they have experienced it within their social situatedness into their depiction of ultimate reality, may women also be said to have done this? Women have not had access to high culture in the West; it is not they who shaped the concept of God. Nevertheless some women have been mystics. Now women, we may think, know of love as a stillness, a holding, a surrounding. They may embrace others with their love, through caring and nourishing seeking to bring about transformation. In a famous passage Julian of Norwich, a woman mystic living in the late fourteen and early fifteenth centuries, compares the relation of God to the world to the holding of a hazel nut in the palm of the hand.[131] It is tempting to ask what this encapsulates, if not a child in the womb. Nevertheless I think we should be wary of any simplistic correlation. If women are inclined to use nurturative imagery in speaking of God, this too must surely be attributed to the way in which they have interpreted their physicality within society as we have known it.

Let me also give a present-day example which deeply parallels Julian. An Anglican Franciscan at the time that she wrote this, celibate and living in a religious order, Hannah Ward expressed herself as follows:

It struck me very forcefully at a workshop once how closely related was my understanding of my sexuality and my spirituality. We were invited to draw images of both. The image I had of my spirituality was a spherical object, like a globe, resting in the palm of my out-stretched hand. I was still as I held it and it was infinitely lovely. The image I drew to represent my sexuality was a similar object with rays going out from it indicating that it was about relationship, although the rays didn't actually touch anything else. Both images were com-plete in themselves, both had a quality of wholeness, and both 'belonged' to me and in a way *were* me.[132]

Again, to be in relation is to be a centred self who reaches out to another.

How different this is as a model of love! And how crucial that women should be able to find this kind of creativity in their expression of their spirituality! As I shall remark later, much language employed by women seems to have what may be called a 'circularity' about it, as indeed we find here.[133] It has little in common with the language of energies, flow, self-giving and interpenetration which seems to come naturally to men. Thinking theologically, it is in essence a monotheism, rather than the trinitarian expression of a movement between two poles. It is not, of course, the monotheism of a 'transcendent other'; rather is it a unitary conception of that which surrounds another. Interestingly, some women theologians have been attracted to an understanding, found in the tradition, of the world as 'God's body'. God is present in, yet is more than, the material universe, integrally related with it. I think here of the work of Sallie McFague and Grace Jantzen.[134] Such a discussion suggests that, as the grip of Christian orthodoxy weakens and women are freed to express their spirituality in terms that they have chosen, they will do so using profoundly different patterns of thought from those which men have employed.

In this chapter I have suggested that the religious forms which we have known have been a male creation. They have corresponded to the self-understanding of men living within patriarchy. In part, theology has reflected the position which those who have been theologians have occupied in society; they have been privileged people. But theology also bears the stamp of the peculiar place which the boy and the man have occupied within the patriarchal family. Hence it reflects his need to find himself in relation to the father and his feeling of inadequacy. Christian theology is a therapy designed to alleviate fear of the father. Equally, as I shall suggest in the next chapter, though this remains hidden, the drama is played out in relation to the loss of the mother and the desire to regain her. Trinitarianism allows for the resolution of the relation to the father; for the son will one day come to have an equality with him. The nature of the monotheistic God may reflect man's sense of self-sufficiency and his isolation. The doctrine of the Trinity encapsulates his need to overcome the boundary of the self and expend himself in a relation of love for another.

The thought forms of the Judaeo-Christian tradition may indeed have been deeply satisfying to men. But the paradigms which I have described involve the exclusion of women. As we shall see, 'woman', within Christian thought, is a representation of what man needs her to be. She is primordially 'mother'. Woman as daughter, sister, or wife finds no symbolic presence. There is a complete absence of woman as one with whom an adult man might be involved in a relationship of equality. Least of all is a relation between two women, either as mother and daughter, or as two sisters, present. For this does not concern men. Meanwhile the theology may seem to reflect a deep ambivalence on the part of men about their sexuality; hence the sublimation of a longed-for close relationship with another into a non-actualized relation between two, each of which is designated 'male', within a Godhead. In this connection we should remember that both the men who formulated the doctrine of the Trinity in the first place and the overwhelming majority of men who over the ages have cast their lot with a trinitarian spirituality have been celibate.

The problem with which we have been concerned in this chapter has not directly been that of 'woman' – whether women find a place in the Bible, how they are portrayed and so forth. Nor in the first place has it been that God is known by male and not by female metaphors (though it is of course no chance that the monotheistic, transcendent, God has been designated male). The problem is more fundamental than these things. The whole shaping of the religion – the way in which God is conceptualized, the relation between God and humanity, and the internal relations of the Godhead – reflects the problems and the aspirations of men living within patriarchy. The fact that the configuration of God (or Christ) on the one hand and humanity on the other is deeply gendered again reflects the positioning of the male in relation on the one hand to the 'father' and on the other to 'woman', within such a society. It is within this scenario that the representation of woman comes to be that of 'the other', the question to which we shall turn in the next chapter. The problem thus lies much deeper than the simple absence of women, or the way in which they are portrayed. It is rather that

Christian thought forms embody a conceptualization of reality which is firstly patriarchal, and secondly masculinist.

In as far as Christianity has been patriarchal, it has reflected the society in which women too have been situated, mirroring what has also been their world. But in so far as it has reflected what has been a male reality, women may always have been outsiders. Daughters are differently situated from sons: they do not have to set themselves up against the father in order to come into their own. Nor have we any reason to think that the mother/daughter bond has built into it the rivalry between son and (largely absent) father which exists within patriarchal society, where men compete for women and with one another. There is presumably no evidence that daughters feel distant from their mothers as sons do from fathers. The same problem is not in need of resolution which Christianity solves so elegantly by the Son being taken up into God and 'joining' the Father. Nor, since the girl may remain in easy commerce with her mother, does she have the same need to regain her. Again, women have not commonly been involved in sacrificing life, either in war or earlier in the hunt. Rather, their role has been to conserve life.

The feminist theorist Nancy Fraser writes: 'Hegemony . . . expresses the advantaged position of dominant social groups with respect to discourse.'[135] It is the contention of this chapter that the hegemonic control which men have exercised in Western society has resulted in theology, our expression of ultimate meaning, reflecting the needs and aspirations, the terror and the joy of men, as they have experienced what has been their reality. It may further be contended that theology has, in turn, been the 'master' discourse which has exercised a hegemonic power over Western thought, keeping women in their place. Half of humanity has been deprived of writing the way they would envisage their reality, their sexuality and their sense of relationality into our conception of the ultimate. When one comes to consider it, that is no small matter. Moreover, it may be that the structure which men have given to their religion is not that which they themselves might wish for within a different societal ordering.

So, finally, there is this to be said. What if men themselves – could it be? – with the rise of feminism, so that the mother no longer appears inferior in the eyes of the boy child, moreover given the presence rather than the absence of the father within social arrangements which involve equal parenting, will no longer have an Oedipal complex in the form in which Freud describes it? Unless one sees it as biologically endemic to males that, upon learning that the mother is not the 'phallic mother' but 'castrated', they fear that their father will wound them, then one must hope that a different social situatedness from that in which the Oedipus complex has arisen will serve to ameliorate the problem. It may of course still be the case that, since the mother was his first love object, the boy yearns for union with her. (We shall come to a discussion of this in the next chapter.)[136] But even the pain of separation may lessen if there come to be more intimate relations between fathers and sons.

We do not yet know what psycho-social revolution the rise of feminism will cause, but we have reason to think that it will be profound. It may well be then that the paradigms embodied in Christianity will no longer seem natural to men, while women will have come to express God quite otherwise. But when Christian paradigms have faded, will the resulting religion be Christianity? For Christianity cannot simply shed its forms; it is a historical religion which looks back to the biblical religion with its monotheistic transcendent God; its talk of covenant, sacrifice and incarnation; and supremely that relation between Jesus and his 'father' which gave rise, in the course of time, to the doctrine of the Trinity. Reflecting dynamics which no longer pertain and problems no longer in need of resolution, the symbol system of Christian theology will be discarded as irrelevant.

V

Woman, the Other

It was the mother of theoretical feminism, Simone de Beauvoir, who, drawing on Hegel's analysis of the dialectic of master and slave,[1] applied it to the relative positions which men and women have occupied in Western culture. 'She,' wrote de Beauvoir, 'is defined and differentiated with reference to man and not he with reference to her; she is the incidental, the inessential as opposed to the essential. He is the Subject, he is the Absolute – she is the Other.'[2] Moreover for de Beauvoir, as also for her friend Jean-Paul Sartre, what is crucial is that both master and slave see the world through the eyes of the master. For Sartre, notably, our own self-understanding is formed through what others take us to be. Thus within de Beauvoir's framework, woman internalizes man's conception of her; she is formed by her place in a male world. In words that have become well-known, de Beauvoir claims: 'One is not born, but rather becomes, a woman.'[3] Socialization is induced. Women learn what it is that they should be within the ideological context of patriarchy.

Western religion must be understood to be that over-arching framework through which men have projected their understanding of reality. Within this religion man has given woman a place. As many feminists in different schools have pointed out, woman becomes a mirror which allows man to find his own reality. She is the 'other' in relation to which he defines himself as subject. What woman is to be acquires, then, a certain plasticity. It is as though man were to stand in the centre of the room and project what woman represents on to the various walls. She is at the edges of his own reality, reflecting back his image of himself. Woman is a site to be inscribed. But whatever she is, she is always conceived of in relation to man himself. For it is he who is the subject. What I shall consider in this chapter is the way in which the male view of woman is reflected in his religion – and the consequences of this for the lives of actual women.

When one is thinking about 'woman' in Western religion there are two seemingly contrary things to be said (which are, however, parts of a greater whole). In the first place, woman is notably absent. As Luce Irigaray, the French psychoanalyst and philosopher of the current generation, has well said: 'The God whom we know and the ones we have known for centuries are men and they both reveal and conceal the different aspects of man.'⁴ Religion is the sphere which reflects back to man his own reality. He sees God as male, while the father/son relation has been a central concern of Western religion. The religion is simply not about her, nor does it revolve around a relationship between man and woman as equals; let alone having anything to do with woman's projection of her actuality (for example, it does not reflect the mother/daughter relationship). Western religion appears to be about the male reality, a reality in which woman plays a minor part.

Yet appearances are deceptive and the truth more complex. For when we probe deeper it would seem that a good case can be made that actually what is at stake is the power which the idea of woman has over men's lives. Thus some French feminists, learning much from a Lacanian psychoanalytic perspective, have suggested that religion (as indeed culture more generally) is an elaborate construction formed precisely in order to escape the mother. In this case woman, or the concept of the feminine, has been instrumental in the formation of religion. Indeed, one might be inclined to say that nothing witnesses so clearly to the power of woman in men's lives as male religion. But this of course does not help actual women; it profoundly hinders them. For what we are confronted with in the male religion is a male concept of woman which serves to mask the fact that actual women, having their own subjectivity, are nowhere to be seen. The fact that women have to some extent been able to find themselves within the role to which they were assigned within a patriarchal world serves to complicate the matter further.

It was de Beauvoir's insight that man sets himself up as master over against woman, whom he casts as 'slave', using her to project his own notion of himself as the opposite of what he takes her to be. As she expresses it: 'No group ever sets itself up as the One without at once setting up the Other over against itself.'⁵ This insight is clearly similar to what Anglo-Saxon feminists have seen to be operating in mono-theism, which we considered in the previous chapter.⁶ This model is the foundation of Western religion. God is seen as transcendent and as 'male'. Humanity is understood as 'female' in relation to the 'male' God. Thus Israel in relation to YHWH, or the church in relation to the bridegroom who is Christ, are designated 'feminine'. The soul is also feminine (as that which is receptive to God). The highest to which humanity can attain is exemplified by the Virgin Mary; she who is perfectly present for God, declaring in total obedience that not her will but God's should be done. But while man takes up the 'feminine' position in relation to the 'male' God, he repeats the pattern, acting as 'male' in relation to human females. Woman is always at the bottom of the heap. She occupies the place of alterity; unlike God, and unlike man conceived in God's image. Sacred reality is dichotomous and gendered. It is governed by a projection of what 'male' and 'female' should represent.

The current generation of French feminists have moved beyond de Beauvoir, giving us striking readings of Western religion. Julia Kristeva draws attention to what is at stake in monotheism. Returning from China, she writes, of the West:

> No other civilization . . . seems to have made the principle of sexual difference so crystal clear: between the two sexes there is a cleavage, an abyss, which is marked by their different relationships to the Law (religious and political) and which is the very condition of their alliance. Monotheistic unity is sustained by a radical separation of the sexes: indeed, this separation is its prerequisite. For without this gap between the sexes, without this localization of the polymorphic, orgasmic body, laughing and desiring, in the other sex, it would have been impossible, in the symbolic sphere, to isolate the principle of One Law – One, Purifying, Transcendent, Guarantor of the ideal interest of the community.

We should note her words. Without the separation of that which is material and sexual (the polymorphic, orgasmic body, laughing and desiring) so that these things are projected on to 'woman', the purity of the Law (that is to say the law of the father) and monotheistic unity (that which is transcendent, true, and one) would not be possible. Kristeva sees the position given to 'woman' as the condition of the whole. The Lacanian symbolic sphere (culture and above all religion as the guarantor of culture and of the law) is built upon that which it has been convenient to forget or overcome.

Kristeva further draws this out by playing with the Genesis story, showing how its symbolism fits such an analysis of what is at stake.

> The economy of this system requires that women be excluded from the single true and legislating principle, namely The Word, as well as from the (always paternal) element that gives procreation a social value: excluded from knowledge and power. The myth of the relationship between Eve and the serpent is the best summary of this exclusion. The serpent stands for the inverse of God, since he tempts Eve to transgress His prohibition. But it is also this very desire to transgress which Adam represses, which he dares not act out, which is his shame. The sexual symbolism helps us understand that the serpent is that which, in God or Adam, remains outside or beyond the sublimation of the Word. Eve has no relationship other than with that – precisely because she is its opposite, the 'other race'.

When Yahweh says to the serpent, 'I will put enmity between thee and woman, and between thy seed and her seed: it shall bruise thy head, and thou shalt bruise its heel', He establishes the divergence – of 'race', of 'seed' – between God and man on the one hand and woman on the other. Furthermore, in the second part of the sentence, woman disappears altogether into seed: generation. But, even more essentially, Yahweh formulates the code of eroticism between the two sexes as though it were a code of war.[7]

Western religion is tied to the dichotomizing of what is 'male' and what is 'female'; the upper term (the male) comes to be associated with what is good, the lower (the female) with what is problematic, in particular with the sexual.

However, as we have seen, it is the need to escape woman which is fundamental to this structure. Thus Luce Irigaray has pointed to the power which woman continues to exercise over the male through his desire for her. Man may model himself on the father, he may project a God in his image and see God as that which is higher and male. But the vehemence with which he does these things belies the drawing power of the mother. It may then be, as Irigaray suggests, that it is this need to be free of the mother which is the linchpin of the whole. Far from being of no account in Western religion, woman (or the male view of woman) holds the key to its interpretation. Man is shown to hold a schizophrenic view of woman. On the one hand he fears her; on the other desires her. As we shall see, this analysis would correspond well to the construction of the feminine within male religion.

I cite the philosopher and feminist theorist Elizabeth Grosz, who has done so much to interpret and to draw out Irigaray's thought in the realm of religion. Here she encapsulates Irigaray's insight.

The son is unable to accept the debt of life, body, nourishment and social existence he owes the mother. An entire history of Western thought is intent on substituting for this debt an image of the self-made, self-created man. One could go even further and suggest that the idea of God itself is nothing but an elaborate if unconscious strategy for alleviating man's consciousness of and guilt about this debt. As man's self-reflecting Other, God usurps women's creativity and their place as the source of the terrestrial. God (and through Him, man) becomes the creator or mother of the mother. Born of woman's body, man devises religion, philosophy and true knowledge not simply as sublimations of his desire, but as forms of disavowal of this maternal debt.[8]

If this is right, the implications for an analysis of Western culture and religion are extraordinary.

But we should let Irigaray speak in her own words. She writes:

> In order to become men, they continue to consume . . . [the mother],
> draw on her resources and, at the same time, they deny her or dis-
> claim her in their identification with and their belonging to the
> masculine world. They owed their existence, their body, life and they
> forget or misrecognize this debt in order to set themselves up as
> powerful men, adults busying themselves with public affairs . . .[9]

And again:

> Because he fails to leave her a subjective life, and to be on occasion
> her place and her thing in an intersubjective dynamic [that is to
> say, fails to allow woman to be for once the 'subject' and to be an
> 'object' for her] man remains within a master-slave dynamic. He is
> ultimately the slave of a God on whom he bestows the qualities of an
> absolute master. He is secretly a slave to the power of the mother
> woman, which he subdues or destroys.[10]

What Irigaray wishes to see is, by contrast, an inter-subjectivity between
man and woman, each of whom occupies a subject position. That is to
say, precisely that which has not been present within the skewed and
distorted nature of Western culture, in which man has been the subject
and woman 'the other'. It is with such theoretical insights in mind that,
in this chapter, I turn to an analysis of the construct of woman and the
feminine within Western religion.

I shall divide the material into three images of woman: woman as
ideal, woman as slut, and woman as complement to the male. First I
consider woman as ideal. Not surprisingly, woman as ideal is largely
woman as mother. This notion is, of course, encapsulated in the Virgin
Mary, but it is also written into the conception of the 'male' God.
Secondly I consider woman as slut, the schizophrenically constructed
opposite to woman as ideal.[11] Woman here is all that man is not or that
he wishes to forget; that which is contrary to the 'male' God in whose
image man casts himself. Thirdly, woman as complement to the male
consists in a projection of the ideal 'feminine'. She is to hold certain
qualities for humanity as a whole. Thus woman as complement is in one
sense woman as ideal, but the complement can quickly veer over into
the opposite of man, once again woman as slut. In each case, we must
note, woman is represented with reference to what man is – which is
what it is to be a slave. I shall say something in passing about the
effect of this scenario on the lives of actual women, particularly their
lives within the church and the Christian religion. In conclusion, I shall
point to the threat which the rise of feminism represents to this whole
symbolic universe.

I commence, then, with the characterization of woman as ideal. It should hardly surprise us that woman as ideal is almost equivalent to woman as mother. If it is correct that male religion and culture reflects man's need to establish himself over against the pull of the mother, then we should expect him to build back the image of her into his conceptual system. God the father must, of course, be conceptualized as male. He is modelled on the father and serves to legitimize the man's understanding of himself. It is on to this father God, then, that nurturative and protective characteristics are projected. But woman as mother is also represented more concretely in the Virgin Mary, the ideal mother of the son. What is lacking is any sense of woman as an independent agent, the equal of man, involved in a reciprocal relationship with him. As Don Cupitt remarks, one never sees Mary portrayed with her mouth open, laughing or speaking, let alone as a sexual being showing affection for her husband, a subject in her own right.[12] Woman is the mother whom the son needs her to be.

That the mother of Jesus of Nazareth should have become the madonna of Western art and 'mother' of the church must be counted an astonishing cultural phenomenon. It would seem that the figure of the mother, so notably absent from the male monotheism of ancient Judaism, had to be grafted on to Christianity from the cultures of the Mediterranean lands into which that religion spread. Without the mother, the male universe was incomplete. Fascinatingly it has been shown that early icons of the Virgin are almost indistinguishable from representations of the Egyptian goddess Isis, her boy child balanced in like pose on her knee.[13] It may well be that the original naming, within Alexandrian Christianity, of Mary as 'theotokos', the mother of God, was intended to lay stress on the fact that this child had been born of a human mother. But it is hardly surprising that she who had given birth to such a child came to be venerated in her own right.

Consider those extraordinary frescos of huge dimensions from the early fourteenth century by Cimabue, Giotto and Duccio, to which a room in the Uffizi is dedicated. The impact which they made on the worshipper must have been stunning. There she sits, the Queen of Heaven, robed in blue, the colour of the sky. She seems to surround the human child, on whom nonetheless all attention is focused. The cultural historian Marina Warner, in her great book on the cult of the Virgin, writes of another Giotto panel thus:

> The Virgin is serene, sagacious, exquisitely fulfilled as the Christ child on her arm reaches up and touches her cheek with his tiny hand and clutches at the neckline of her dress. She tenderly hovers with delicate tapering fingers to catch him if he struggles too vigorously. Her eyes,

as in so much Marian iconography, gaze out beyond the picture frame to dwell on an inner landscape of the soul, where tragedy and triumph are bound together, and her countenance is therefore wistful. Wistfulness seems also a natural quality of the feminine, a part of modesty and grace, a suitable expression of wonderment at her own beauty and mystery, a kind of hesitancy and humility that is hardly ever present in images of masculine beauty and goodness.

A visitor from another planet could surely be excused for thinking that this was a religion of a mother and her (boy) child.

It is a complete portrayal of the feminine; an image of woman which pervades Western art. Warner comments:

> Myth and ideology [are] camouflaged . . . Myriad assumptions are limpidly and luminously made. Assumptions about role satisfaction, sexual differences, beauty, and goodness are all wondrously compressed in this one icon, just as they are in every artefact produced by the cult of the Virgin Mary.[14]

Powerful she may be, but powerful in relation to her child. That there was indeed ambivalence about the projection of female power is shown by the fate of Piero della Francesca's famous 'Madonna della Misericordia' (in which a dominant Virgin, out of all proportion to the other figures, looks down on the representatives of humanity whom she shelters in her cloak).[15] Initially it was disavowed by the Catholic authorities![16] Woman shall not achieve seemingly independent power. (There is no female figure in the Godhead.)

Nor has the cult of Mary been abandoned with the coming of modernity. The advent of biblical scholarship, which it might have been thought would signal her demise, has not resulted in Catholic theologians ceasing to extol her. To name a few such theologians from the twentieth century, representatives of the most various traditions within Catholicism, Teilhard de Chardin, Hans Urs von Balthasar, Henri de Lubac, even the down-to-earth Karl Rahner, and Latin American 'liberation' theologians, have all participated in that veritable industry called mariology. Indeed, it was after the Second World War that the cult of the Virgin reached its apogee. In 1950 Mary's bodily assumption into heaven became dogma; in 1945 Pius XII proclaimed her Queen; while in 1964 – after the commencement of the Second Vatican Council – she became *Mater Ecclesiae*. (Moreover it was the Protestant Carl Jung – misogynist of psychiatrists if ever there were – who thought fit to commend the papacy for the dogma of the Assumption, pronouncing it 'in every respect timely'.[17])

The cult of Mary is hardly to be explained apart from human

suffering, particularly the suffering of men. (This does not mean that she has failed to be of comfort to women, embodying as she does the feminine, the exemplification of the mother of a son, the role woman in patriarchy was to fulfil.) Gathering up all to herself, Mary provides the love which only a mother can give when the (male) world has done its worst. The representation of woman within Christian iconography as the one who guards, holds and protects must surely be of the greatest interest. She it is who stands grieving at the foot of the cross – *stabat mater dolorosa* — while in the *pietà*s she cradles her dead son in her lap. Not for nothing was it that Teilhard de Chardin came to his conception of the 'eternal feminine' while working as a stretcher bearer in the trenches of the Great War. Furthermore, it was after the horrors of the Second World War that mariology attained to new heights. Indeed, we may note that it is in those countries which have known great suffering, Poland or the countries of Central America, that the Virgin has often seemed to replace the figure of the male Christ in people's affections. These things tell us much about the role of woman in patriarchal culture.

Kristeva asks pertinent questions here. 'What is there,' she asks, 'in the portrayal of the Maternal in general and particularly in its Christian, virginal, one, that reduces social anguish and gratifies a male being . . . ?' Of the proclamation of Mary's assumption, she comments: 'What death anguish was it intended to soothe after the conclusion of the deadliest of wars?'[18] She concludes:

> Man overcomes the unthinkable of death by postulating maternal love in its place – in the place and stead of death and thought. This love, of which divine love is merely a not always convincing derivation, psychologically is perhaps a recall, on the near side of early identifications, of the primal shelter that ensured the survival of the newborn.[19]

For man in trouble, woman is mother.[20]

But as we have said, it is not the Virgin alone on to whom what it is to be 'mother' is projected. God 'the father' has come to possess motherly qualities. Neither in scripture nor in the later tradition has God directly been called 'mother' – until the recent attempts of some Christian feminists to do this.[21] Only the father and God as father writ large can allow the man to acquire the necessary distance, escaping the pull to an identification with the mother. Again, the man models God on himself; and patriarchal culture projects its conception of the lords of its world on to the deity. Nevertheless, given that God is 'male', the attributes of the mother which he must leave behind are woven into the image of the father. Both sexes are then summed up in him; but asymmetrically, so that we have a 'motherly Father', while a 'fatherly Mother' is unthinkable! Kristeva tells us that for Freud likewise the Father of prehistory possesses the sexual characteristics of both parents.[22]

Coming from a psychoanalytic and Lacanian context, Kristeva's comments are informative here. She suggests that the desire for the mother which has been repressed into the unconscious, a desire which was bound up with frustration and absence as the mother was not always available to the child, finds articulation and expression as that desire is projected on to the father God in the realm of the symbolic. Commenting on the words of the Creed ('I believe in God, the Father Almighty'), she writes:

> As an analyst, I find that the Credo embodies basic fantasies that I encounter every day in the psychic lives of my patients. The almighty father? Patients miss one, want one, or suffer from one. Consubstantiality with the father and symbolic identification with his name? Patients aspire to nothing else . . . More than any other religion, Christianity has unravelled the symbolic *and* physical importance of the paternal function in human life. Identification with this third party separates the child from its jubilant but destructive physical relationship with its mother and subjects it to another dimension, that of symbolization, where, beyond frustration and absence, language unfolds. Because of its insistence on the paternal function, Christianity shapes the preconscious formulation of the basic fantasies characteristic of male desire.[23]

That is to say, the elemental desire for the mother before the acquisition of language (what Kristeva names the 'semiotic') finds an outlet at the level of conscious symbolization. As she says, 'beyond frustration and absence, language unfolds'. The concept of the perfect mother (who is so much better than the actual mother) is then attributed to God. She continues:

> Overcoming the notion of irremediable separation, Western man, using 'semiotic' rather than 'symbolic' means, re-establishes a continuity or fusion with an Other that is no longer substantial and maternal but symbolic and paternal. Saint Augustine goes so far as to compare the Christian's faith in God with the infant's relation to its mother's breast. 'What am I even at the best but an infant sucking the milk Thou givest, and feeding upon Thee, the food that perisheth not?' What we have here is fusion with a breast that is, to be sure, succouring, nourishing, loving, and protective, but transposed from the mother's body to an invisible agency located in another world.

This is quite a wrench from the dependency of early childhood, and it must be said that it is a compromise solution, since the benefits of the new relationship of dependency are entirely of an imaginary order, in the realm of signs.[24]

Kristeva speaks thus of a 'fusion with God' on the semiotic (non-artic-ulated, non-linguistic) level. The believer 'aspires to rejoin the body . . . from whom he has been irrevocably severed'. Reassured of 'God's per-manent generosity and grace', he is given a gift of love without any immediate requirement of merit'. There is a '"semiotic" leap toward the other, [a] primary identification with the primitive parental poles close to the maternal container . . .'. It is this dynamic, she says, which 'theology excels at describing'.[25]

That the attribution of motherly qualities to the 'male' God reflects an elemental desire would certainly be suggested by the widespread occurrence of this phenomenon within different traditions and over the course of history. It may well be that women, too, have a need to con-ceptualize God as mother; whether for different reasons is a question it would be fascinating to explore. The basis of the tradition is of course found in the Hebrew scriptures. In Isaiah we read: 'Can a woman forget her sucking child, that she should not have compassion on the son of her womb? Yes, these may forget, yet will I not forget thee.'[26] YHWH here becomes the perfect mother, while in the process actual mothers, with whom he is compared, are denigrated.

This attribution of motherly qualities to God is subsequently taken up in the tradition. Thus Clement of Alexandria writes:

> God is love, and we seek him precisely because of that love. In his ineffable majesty he is our Father; but in his love he has opened him-self up to us and become our Mother. Yes, in his love our Father has become woman, and the greatest proof of this is his Son born of her.[27]

We have already seen Augustine's language in the quotation from Kristeva.[28] In the Middle Ages it was notably Anselm of Canterbury who, in his prayers, spoke of both Christ and the Father as mothers.[29]

We should pause here to consider what has transpired. Human mothers in their biology and in the role which they perform, far from being honoured, have actually been supplanted. It is not simply that, as we have seen, God the Father provides the care which the actual mother gave inadequately. The 'biology' of the father God is apparently such that he has the attributes of a woman, a womb and breasts. The male God has appropriated to himself the characteristics of both sexes. It is the 'male' who, independently of any female partner, performed the act of 'creating' the world. (Indeed it is often said that the creation *ex nihilo* is unlike a fertility rite, which would be associated with woman as powerful and as fecund.) Thus (as Elizabeth Grosz points out)[30] the male God becomes the 'mother' of the mother, displacing woman's natural role. Again biology is denied as, in one of the two creation stories, instead of man coming forth from woman, the 'male' God first creates man and then forms the woman from man! Again the 'male' God is the one who nourishes, providing manna for the children of Israel in the wilderness. And in the eucharist it is Christ (or his representative the male priest) who offers the bread of life.

At times when the Christian tradition has been influenced by Aristotelianism, mistaken biological assumptions have fuelled this attribution of the powers of reproduction to the father God. Consider the following passage from Thomas Aquinas:

> One should . . . note carefully that the fleshly generation of animals is perfected by an active power and by a passive power; and it is from the active power that one is named 'father', and from the passive power that one is named 'mother'. Hence, in what is required for the generation of offspring, some things belong to the father, some things belong to the mother: to give the nature and the species to the offspring belongs to the father, and to conceive and bring forth belong to the mother as patient and recipient. Since, however, the procession of the Word has been said to be in this: that God understands Himself; and the divine act of understanding is not through a passive power, but, so to say, an active one; because the divine intellect is not in potency but is only actual; in the generation of the Word of God the notion of mother does not enter, but only that of father. Hence, the things which belong distinctly to the father or to the mother in fleshly generation, in the generation of the Word are all attributed to the Father by sacred Scripture; for the Father is said not only 'to give life to the Son' [cf. John 5. 26], but also 'to conceive' and 'to bring forth'.[31]

In such a conception the male alone is understood to be potent.[32] But the need that God should be mother would seem to be trans-historical, with roots deep in the male psyche.

The theme of God as a motherly Father is evident not least in Luther. Nothing could be more mistaken than to suppose that Luther characterizes God as a transcendent 'male'. True, the God before whom the sinner stands, unable to justify himself in his sight, may be cast as father. But the God who accepts him, irrespective of his merits, is deeply maternal. Luther has a sense of being one with God, basing his whole sense of identity on the acceptance he is given. It is as though he casts aside all human intermediaries in his desire for direct access to the God who is a mother to him. Thus Luther:

The person who believes in Christ is righteous and holy through divine imputation. He already sees himself, and is, in heaven, being surrounded by the heaven of mercy. But while we are lifted up into the bosom of the Father, and are clad with the finest raiment, our feet reach out below the garment, and Satan bites them whenever he can . . . Thus we are saints and children [of God], but in the spirit, not in the flesh, and we dwell under the shadow of the wings of our mother hen, in the bosom of grace . . . [But] you must draw your tiny feet with you under the garment, otherwise you will have no peace.[33]

One wonders whether in this quotation the medieval image of the Virgin with which Luther must have grown up, her voluminous skirts surrounding and protecting, has not simply been transposed on to God 'the father'.

Nor have men abandoned the attribution of motherhood to the father God in the modern world in which we have learnt the truth about human reproduction. Leonardo Boff, the Latin American liberation theologian, writes as follows of the generation of the Son from the Father within the inner life of the Trinity.

This eternal generation, as the Creed explicitly insists, must not be interpreted as any sort of making or creation – *non factus nec creatus* – but as genuine generation – *genitus* — by the Father. We are to take this expression to the hilt, then. We are dealing with generation in the proper sense of the term.[34]

Boff considers that: 'Put figuratively: the Father "begets" the Son virginally in the maternal-virginal womb of the Holy Spirit.'[35] To what extraordinary ideas men are led in pursuit of their religion!

Among modern Protestant theologians, Jürgen Moltmann has majored on the theme of the 'motherly' Father. Moltmann thinks (quite mistakenly, I believe) that this will aid the feminist cause. Thus he seeks to contrast the singularity of the male God of monotheism with the trinitarianism of Christianity, in which a (motherly) father generates the son. Moltmann writes:

But if the Son proceeded from the Father alone, then this has to be conceived of both as a begetting and as a birth. And this means a radical transformation of the Father image; a father who both begets and bears his son is not merely a father in the male sense. He is a motherly father too. He is no longer defined in unisexual, patriarchal terms but – if we allow for the metaphor of language – bisexually or transexually. He has to be understood as the motherly Father of the only Son he has brought forth, and at the same time as the fatherly Mother of his only begotten Son . . . According to the Council of

Toledo of 675 'it must be held that the Son was created, neither out of nothingness nor yet out of any substance, but that he was begotten or born out of the Father's womb *(de utero Patris)* , that is, out of his very essence.

Thus Moltmann considers: 'It is . . . the doctrine of the Trinity, with the bold statements we have quoted, which makes a first approach towards overcoming sexist language in the concept of God.'[36] By contrast we may think that, in this singular act of male parthogenesis in which the father God arrogates all functions to himself, the need for the female has simply been done away with. Jealous of woman's capacity to give birth, men have projected female qualities on to a God who has no need of a female partner. The male comprehends all within himself.

If it is correct that man sees woman as exemplifying a completion which he lacks, something that we have already considered,[37] then it is not coincidental that he has understood God as somehow exemplifying 'the feminine' in God's completion and unity. Thus the Dominican Victor White, commenting on the dogma of the Assumption of the Virgin and writing in appreciation of Jung's analysis of 'the feminine', comes to the following conclusion.

> Perhaps this definition may lead the Church to a deeper consideration and an ultimate formulation of the mystery of God's motherhood: in her Assumption Mary returns to her source. Not she, but God is the ultimate prototype of motherhood and femininity, even materially . . . Just as Christ, in ascending to heaven, carried us to the arms of God our eternal Father, may it not be that Mary, assumed into heaven, means to lead us to a deeper knowledge and love of God our eternal Mother?[38]

Again, the Anglican theologian V. A. Demant writes:

> If we are pressed to see in the doctrine of the Trinity some clue to the sense that gender . . . must have something corresponding to it in the God-head, one would find in the unconditioned Unity of God something like the feminine in creation, while the differentiated Persons, on the other hand, have each a masculine denomination.[39]

That which is individuated and which has agency is understood as male. Women are complete but inert.

Indeed one might well think that much male mysticism (not something which I have investigated) is characterized by the sense of regaining that greater whole from which one was severed. The man loses his singular identity, which was too great to bear, in that to which he returns. Loss of self is, of course, a common theme of mystical writing.

Nothing would seem to witness more profoundly to the place which the mother plays in the male universe.

At this point we have reached a realm of cultural analysis which it is difficult to know how to plumb. Nevertheless, the following observations may be instructive. In the ancient Pythagorean table of opposites, femaleness was placed on the side of the unbounded, the vague and indeterminate. In more sinister vein, woman has often been linked with that void which is death. Again it is interesting that men give female designations to those entities which represent a greater whole to which they belong; thus countries or ships are feminine. Hurricanes – those wild freaks of nature which cannot be controlled – were always given girls' names, until American feminist protest stopped this!

Considering the depth of such a cultural inheritance, it would seem that any mere tinkering with the symbolism of the Godhead must be beside the point. Or rather we may put it this way. Simply to name God as female, while retaining the conception of a transcendent God, would seem to be too superficial a change which will fail to stick. Given what mother and father represent in our society, this will appear somehow inappropriate. Indeed, to call God 'mother' while that word continues to have the connotations which it has at present, must be detrimental to women. For it fails to symbolize women's wish to be agents, subjects in their own right. On the other hand, were it possible to name God as female, while at the same time conceiving God to have agency and power, that would be revolutionary.

Secondly, I turn to the projection of woman as slut. We may well think this to be closely related to the construal of woman as ideal; the other half of a schizophrenic male splitting.[40] What we should note, however, in considering Western religion, is that we are not simply faced here with some psychological male whim which could be cured. That woman in her sexuality is unclean, the contrary to that which is spiritual, is the corollary of a transcendent monotheism in which God is conceptualized as 'male'. Woman comes to be designated as that which is other than what is true, good and pure. As we have said, humanity itself is conceptualized as 'female' (and as sinful) by comparison with a transcendent deity. Woman then represents that which is closer to nature, of the earth and material, over against man, who is spiritual and more like God. Moreover (note the Genesis narrative), woman is the cause of male temptation, dragging man down. Consequently she must be contained and controlled, in particular be kept outside the sphere of the spiritual, especially in regard to anything which pertains to her bodily functions.

It could, of course, be contended that a transcendent monotheism, indeed one in which God was gendered 'male', need have no such

consequences. Even were it to be held that woman has been placed subordinate to man in the order of creation, it could be said that this need
not involve the denigration of women. Thus Karl Barth admonishes men
to care for their wives.[41] Again, it could be said that it is not a
transcendent monotheism itself which is problematic; that simply in
psychological terms (quite apart from any metaphysical structures) the
fact that man has to separate from the mother is likely to lead to the
denigration of women (as we have seen some psychoanalysts to
believe).[42] I do not think that such arguments hold water. It surely must
be the case that a transcendent monotheism, in which God is gendered
'male', has in fact been influential in Western history. Religion has not
been without import; our ancestors were steeped in it. Indeed, they
understood Christian doctrines (or the creation stories) in the most
literal terms. That the Jewish and Christian traditions could in any way
have sanctioned what has happened is surely the most damning indictment of it. For the record of man's inhumanity to woman has been
startling and terrible. Woman has been understood as other, as beyond
the pale, barred from the human rights which were accorded to man. In
the light of such considerations, we may think that the comments of
male theologians to the effect that we should renew our understanding
of God's 'fatherhood' will not wash.[43]

In spelling out how woman has been designated slut there are a
number of matters to which we should turn our attention. First I shall
consider the use of marriage as a sacred metaphor, both within the
biblical literature and in the later tradition. Secondly, I shall point to the
presence of pornography and sadism in the biblical text and of a profound misogyny within subsequent Christian history. Thirdly, I believe
that we may, inadvertently, have something to learn from mariology.
Finally, I shall turn to the wide-ranging topic – the dimensions of which
I can only indicate – of the actual suffering of women caused by
Catholic teaching on sexual matters. What makes these topics interesting and important is that lines of connection are to be drawn between
them. Metaphors are not without their material effects. It may also, in
reverse, be the case that a loathing of women has given rise to the
cultural construction.

I commence with the employment of the marriage metaphor for the
relationship between God and humanity. It would appear to be a fundamental metaphor within the scriptures. Feminists who are biblical
scholars have in particular drawn attention to the book of Hosea, where
the metaphor structures the text.[44] However, one should recognize that
Hosea is in no way unique. Robert Carroll has pointed to the use of
such sexual symbolism in the book of Jeremiah and it would appear to
be widely dispersed throughout the prophetic literature. In the case of

Hosea, YHWH's relationship to Israel is compared to that of the male prophet Hosea to his unfaithful wife Gomer. YHWH (and Hosea) are cast as good and as rightly expecting the obedience of the female partner. The 'male' is the one who chooses himself a covenant partner, or a wife, as the case may be. Meanwhile the people of Israel are compared to the unfaithfulness of Gomer. It is taken for granted that 'she', whether Israel or Gomer, does not have rights and that 'she' is not expected to show initiative. The female becomes a synonym for that which is weak, sinful, and liable to go astray. Moreover lewd imagery is used for Gomer, who is described as a prostitute and becomes the subject of the male gaze.

The nature of the problem has been well put by Renita Weems in a discussion of the book of Hosea.

> Elevating the marriage metaphor . . . to the level of 'super model' presents serious problems for biblical and systematic theology. In spite of the fact that it functions as a literary device that draws poetic connections between the nature of Israel's crime and YHWH's punishment, and in spite of its versatility in providing important insights into divine-human relations, how are we as biblical theologians to come to grips with the prophet's association of God with sexual violence? In his sagacious attempt to portray the passionate and compassionate side of YHWH, has the prophet/poet risked those insights when the basic premise of his message evolves around the untenable image of violence against a woman? Does the fact that the marriage metaphor is '*only* a metaphor' and the motif of sexual violence '*only* a theme of the metaphor' insulate them from serious theological scrutiny? . . . For in order for the metaphor to make sense, to be exegetically meaningful, the exegete must discern some thread of similarity between the metaphor and the thing signified . . . The problem arises when the metaphor 'succeeds', meaning that the reader becomes so engrossed in the pathos and the details of the metaphor that the *dissimilarities* between the two are disregarded.[45]

This is surely right. As I have already commented in discussing biblical literature, it is what is suggested to the mind at a subconscious level, where it is not in the same way subject to rational scrutiny, which is so peculiarly dangerous.[46]

But it is not simply that the use of such metaphors may lead to a denigration of woman's sexuality. The employment of the marriage metaphor for God's relationship to humanity clearly has deeply hierarchical connotations.[47] On the Dominican Roger Ruston's statement that 'the natural love between man and woman is the climax of God's good creation but also a paradigm of nature being prepared for grace'.

Angela West (herself a Catholic) comments as follows (the reference now is not to the books of the prophets but to the Genesis narrative):

> It sounds nice but the reality, to say the least, is a lot less smooth. The relationship between Yahweh and Israel is, in many respects, the Perfect paradigm of the Impossible Relationship . . . For a start, it [exemplifies] the problem that most women have become familiar with in their relationships with men – that of inequality of power. Love demands an equality – the absence of the subjection of one party to the other is its pre-condition. Yet the relationship between Yahweh and Israel is the epitome of the extreme discrepancy in power . . . Unlike the petty godlings in the pantheons of other Ancient Near Eastern deities, Yahweh was utterly Other and totally omnipotent; clearly not much basis for equality here.[48]

How – one may wonder – is a Christian feminist like West to begin to deal with something like the consequences for the understanding of woman of the way in which the marriage metaphor has been used within the Judaeo-Christian tradition, consequences which she so clearly sees?

The metaphor is present again in the Christian gospel. Most notably, the church is designated as the 'bride' and female partner of the 'bridegroom' who is Christ. This rendition was to become a fundamental metaphor in the Christian tradition. But further, Paul designates his converts 'female' in relation to himself! Thus he writes to the Corinthians that he feels a 'divine jealousy' since they, like a straying wife, have been giving credence to versions of the gospel other than his own, finding fit to compare this behaviour to the temptation of Eve![49] Again, writing to the Romans, Paul compares Christians to a woman who, while she would be an adulteress were she to live with another man during her husband's lifetime, is free to marry again on his death: so too they, being dead to the law, are now married to Christ. (It seems excessively contrived.) The first marriage, moreover, is said to be in the flesh, arousing sinful passions and bearing children to death.[50] It would appear that the conflation of woman with evil humanity, more particularly with perverse sexuality, is the most natural thing in the world.

I move, secondly, to the wider question of the presence of outright sadism and pornography in the biblical text. I can imagine that it could be said that these texts are rarely read in church or synagogue. But that can hardly be the case; the offensive material is so widespread. (Hosea, for example, is undoubtedly read.) There has been considerable feminist writing in recent years on the profoundly problematic nature of the text, which I have no space to consider here.[51] Thus there is regular portrayal of violence against women and a manifestation of disgust at female sexuality. In particular, the continuity between past and present to which scholars have pointed to may be thought to be of interest. Thus for example Hosea has been analysed with the aid of present-day male pornographic literature, in which woman is often compared to the land or to nature, which should be 'tamed' (that is to say raped) by man.[52] Again, attention should be drawn to other related problems (the bias of the narrator and the presence of the male gaze) on which I have already touched.[53]

I give an example of such scholarship which should be better known: the work of Gracia Fay Ellwood. Enumerating what have been found to be the characteristics of men who batter their wives, Ellwood points to the fact that the text exemplifies these same traits. 'Yahweh as a masculine Deity,' she writes, ' . . . shows characteristics of possessive attachment, domination and violence.' While 'Israel, as wife, is the personified recipient of ambivalent feelings of desire for and revulsion against women that seem to characterize patriarchal males everywhere'. There are many examples. I summarize Ellwood here:

> Sadistic tortures are employed, as for example in Ezekiel 32.25 in which the woman's nose and ears are to be cut off. Murder is threatened . . . Overwhelming jealously and possessiveness characterize most batterers . . . Yahweh's jealousy is of this irrational sort; he is sure that his wife will lie with anyone. 'You . . . lavished your harlotries on any passer-by,' he accuses in Ezekiel 16. 15 . . . Yahweh punishes Israel by means of rape in a series of grim passages [cf. Isaiah 3.16–17] . . . There follows a long catalogue of finery that Yahweh will pull off even leaving the woman bald, until 'ravaged, she shall sit upon the ground' (Isa. 3.26). Jeremiah makes a similar point, focusing on Yahweh's jealousy: 'It is for the greatness of your iniquity that your skirts are lifted up, and you suffer violence . . . I myself will lift up your skirts over your face, and your shame will be seen' (Jer. 13.22,26). Sometimes Yahweh threatens gang-rape against Israel . . . Hosea . . . addresses his children (an image of Yahweh addressing individual Israelites) saying, 'Plead with your mother . . . that she put away her harlotry from her face . . . lest I strip her naked . . . and slay her with thirst . . . Now I will uncover her lewdness in the sight of her lovers, and no one shall rescue her out of my hands' (Hos. 2.2–3,10). [Furthermore there is revulsion at women's sexuality.] In Lamentations we find 'all who honoured (Jerusalem) despise her, for they have seen her nakedness . . . Her uncleanness was in her skirts' (Lam. 1.8–9).[54]

And so forth. Clearly this is a problem of major dimensions in the scriptures.

Not the least disturbing aspect of the whole matter is the continuing blindness of male exegetes to the problem. With the notable exception of Carroll, it appears not to have struck them that anything is amiss.[55] Twenty years after the advent of feminist biblical scholarship, it must be a rare academic course or sermon in which the issues are squarely confronted. Patriarchy would appear to be all of a piece, oblivious to the impact of such a naming of the female or its unacceptability. One senses that women are increasingly becoming alerted to these questions. But the hydra is so multi-headed that it must be difficult to know how it could be rooted out of the text and tradition.

Whatever may be the relationship between the biblical text and the subsequent development of Christianity (and presumably Judaism), it cannot be said that the later history has done anything to mitigate the problems. The designation of woman as somehow polluted pervades the tradition.[56] The fanaticism of many of the church fathers has been widely commented upon in recent years. Within the monastic tradition, to relate to God has meant to separate oneself from women. Menstruation has been held to make a woman unclean: I believe that within Eastern orthodoxy it is still the case that a woman is considered unfit to partake of the eucharist during her period. Ceremonies for the 'churching' of women to 'cleanse' them after the birth of a child persisted into the post-war period in English Anglicanism. Campaigning twenty years ago for the ordination of women, I remember receiving a fanatical letter to the effect that it could transpire that a pregnant woman celebrated the eucharist, evidently the height of blasphemy. Within orthodox Judaism, if a woman simply touches the parchment on which the Torah is written that scroll is considered polluted. What more need one say?

Nor has unabashed misogyny been absent. Indeed it has been taken for granted – in the most naive manner – as acceptable. Mary Daly gives us the following story:

> In 1966 two women journalists were barred from entry to a ceremony in the Sistine Chapel. Writing in the *British Weekly*, one of these correspondents, an Anglican, told that she had received an official pass to the ceremony and had been ushered to her seat. Then an Italian bishop said to her: 'This is for the Pope a special day. We must not allow a woman to sully the Sistine Chapter for His Holiness.' She was asked to leave.[57]

Suppose blacks or Jews were to be the victims of such discrimination: there would be an outcry. Nor is this a one-off example. In the same year, in a much publicized gesture of ecumenical friendship, the Archbishop of Canterbury visited the Pope. Commenting on the 'sincere sense of purpose' of the ceremony, *The Times* further reported:

Its spiritual significance was such that the Vatican authorities could not face the thought of permitting women to witness the event and two women journalists found themselves barred.

Apart from this mishap, the proceedings were flawless.[58]

One may be allowed a wry smile. Twenty years later it was to be the ordination of women to the priesthood within the Anglican church which was to dash hopes of ecumenical reconciliation! Far from being a minor matter, the issue of the treatment of women would serve to upset the applecart. I myself have been axiomatically excluded from entering the sanctuary of an Orthodox church, while the man whom I was with (a Catholic priest) was admitted without question. No one appeared to recognize that what happened was in any way hurtful or offensive.

How should one evaluate what is afoot? We must remark that the problem is certainly not 'the problem of women', as it is often cast. It is men's problem and one they need to address. Of course it is widely recognized that a fair proportion of clergy within the Anglican and Catholic priesthood (higher than in the population at large, so surveys have suggested) are homosexual. The tenor of the celebrations which followed the defeat of the measure to ordain women to the priesthood in the Church of England in 1979 (at a time when I was deeply involved) certainly suggested that those who so celebrated despised women. But it may well be that other gay men, counting themselves 'outsiders', comprehend women's plight better than do some heterosexuals. In the case of heterosexual men the problem is clearly their fear of their own sexuality – a problem which is then projected on to women.

There is a long history of this. Thus Augustine (who in the Western tradition was so largely responsible for the coupling of sexuality with sin) tells us that it is not the sexual act itself but the lust with which it is associated that is sinful. In *The City of God* he considers the conjecture that, since it is possible for humans to control the movement of soft flesh (he instances their mouths and faces, and even knows of people who are able to wiggle an ear), it may have been that, prior to the fall, Adam was able to have intercourse without an erection.[59] It is the involuntary movement of the male member which so alarms him. Given his particular struggle prior to his conversion, it is hardly surprising that Augustine should have had such an obsession. If men cannot control their desire, then it is women who must be controlled. To a man afraid of his own body, woman's sexuality must appear alarmingly out of control.[60] Hence the extraordinary way in which the Western church has invigilated the lives of celibate women in particular.

Indeed, thirdly, we may think the lengths to which mariology has been taken to point inadvertently to male fear of normal female sexuality. In the first place the mother of Jesus has to be a virgin. There is, of course, a textual basis for this assertion (I have already drawn attention to the probable confusion in translation which gave rise to this).[61] But even given this textual basis, the elaboration of Mary's virginity within Christendom has been nothing short of fanatical. In the fourth century the idea came to prominence that Mary's hymen had remained intact through the birth of Jesus. In a book on *The Cult of the Virgin Mary*, Michael Carroll writes: 'Let me emphasize . . . that the issue of Mary's *in partu* virginity was a major concern of the early Church, and was an issue addressed by all the great theologians of the period.'[62] This crackpot notion remains Catholic dogma in the twentieth century![63] Again, despite the clear evidence of the Christian scriptures that Jesus had siblings, Mary is said to have remained a perpetual virgin. With the alarming biological discovery that a new human being derives from its female as well as its male parent, Mary herself, were hereditary sin not to be transmitted, had to be declared to have been immaculately conceived! What a crazy muddle celibate males have got themselves into in pursuit of their religion!

So, fourthly and finally, I turn to the vexed subject of Catholic teaching on women and on sexuality (the two, significantly, are usually connected). Human sexuality has not been conceived of as something which is intrinsically good, not even as that which, quite apart from any consideration of procreation, cements the bond between a man and a woman within marriage. Sexual intercourse has been understood to exist for the purpose of procreation. The form in which this has been expressed since the Middle Ages has had Aristotelian overtones: nature has certain purposes or goals. But the idea that male sexuality must be used for the creation of the next generation (so that, for example, there are prohibitions against spilling semen on the ground) goes back to ancient Judaism. If this can be said to have any *raison d tre* in a sparsely populated world, its retention today is quite another matter. In all this, the elementary rights of women have simply been flouted. Thus Thomas Aquinas – whose views in this matter have been so influential – thought masturbation worse than rape (because 'unnatural', in the sense of unable to lead to conception). Indeed on this ground he considers rape, incest and adultery lesser vices than masturbation, homosexuality, anal and oral intercourse, and *coitus interruptus*.[64] Again, he thought deviation from the 'missionary' position in sexual intercourse a serious sin, believing as he did that this made conception more difficult![65]

Nor, apparently, is all this simply a thing of the long-forgotten past.

In a letter to *The Tablet* in 1989, the Benedictine Sebastian Moore reported the following. At a conference on AIDS sponsored by the Vatican, the dean of the 'John Paul II Institute for Marriage and Family Studies', Mgr Carol Caffarra, commented that if a spouse had AIDS the couple was under 'a grave obligation of total abstinence'. However, there could be exceptions to this rule were there to be a danger of adultery and when 'prolonged abstinence gravely harms conjugal harmony'. Condoms could not be used. But the couple could choose to risk infection; for it is reasonable for spouses in their love 'to prefer to safeguard spiritual good (conjugal harmony and holiness of life) rather than the good of life' itself. As Moore remarked, any child so conceived would of course not only stand the chance of being AIDS-infected, but of losing not simply one but both parents at an early age.[66] The letter prompted no expression of outrage in the correspondence column of subsequent issues of *The Tablet*.

The suffering for which the Catholic church must be held responsible on account of its stand on contraception and abortion is beyond any reckoning. Millions upon millions of women, during several generations now and in many of the poorer countries of the world today, have quite unnecessarily (at a time when safe contraception was available) been subjected to 'motherhood' beyond their financial resources and at the expense of their health. Uta Ranke-Heinemann tells a horrendous story of the convolutions through which the Catholic hierarchy (in particular Rome) has gone during the last two centuries in its attempt to stop contraception. Nature's 'intention' in procreation has been upheld, even when 'nature' could not bear the pregnancy, in that the woman would die on account of it.[67] Moreover these things continue today, in the midst of Europe. Other than in women's circles, we have heard little enough of what it has meant in a Catholic country like Poland that, subsequent to the fall of Communism, the state with the support of the church has tightened the law on abortion. Fearing that it would lead to back-street abortions, a woman doctor spoke of the terrible mutilations she has encountered in the course of her practice. One woman had survived intervention by the village blacksmith; many others had irrevocably damaged internal organs.[68] Male religion has been bound up with an authoritarianism which not infrequently has taken the most perverse forms, leaving women (and sometimes small boys)[69] helpless and bewildered.

Nor has male perversity been confined to Catholicism. In 1984 a report, which it had itself commissioned, was presented to the General Assembly of the Church of Scotland, concerning the use of 'motherly' language for God.[70] (We have seen what a long history such an attribution has in fact had.) Refusing even to debate the report, the Assembly agreed, in a substantial vote, to depart from the matter. One man wrote to *The Scotsman* of 'the disgraceful display of masculine paranoia' which he had witnessed. 'I was acutely ashamed to hear foot-tapping and heckling . . . I felt estranged from a horrific rabble . . .'[71] Likewise, a woman commented on the 'raft of openly hostile questions', while '*no one* had any articulate support for the motion that the Church should study the report'.[72] Earlier that same week the Assembly had agreed to ordain a man who had murdered his mother (for which he had served a prison sentence). I had been wholly unaware of this background at the time when this man had been my student. In a quarter of a century of teaching I have had no other experience of a man behaving so preposterously in the class room that other students attempted to control him. He evidently had no way of relating to a woman in a position of authority. Aghast at the church's decision, an Anglican bishop commented to me that he supposed the outcome of that debate would have been different had it been the father who had been murdered.[73]

How should we conclude such a consideration? The whole thing is beyond any comprehension. One half of humanity has visited untold misery on the other half. It has done this not in a limited period of time or in one culture, but – considering only the Western tradition – over two if not four thousand years, and continuing into the twentieth century. This is true of all the great monotheistic religions of the West. (We have not considered the situation pertaining in Islam, where for example the practice of female circumcision affects approximately six million women.) Does this history just represent a malfunctioning of Western religion? Or is it built into it? What should bother us is that this question is rarely given serious consideration. Enlightened Christians (and presumably enlightened people within other religions) seem to think that the problems can simply be overcome. Can they? The question which the analysis that owes to the French feminists raises is whether, far from being a by-product of Western religion, the denigration of women may not be integral to it. In that case male religion has acted as smoke-screen which has served to mask male fear of women and the behaviour which has flowed from this.

In considering whether such an analysis is in fact correct, one further indicator should be considered. The male God has frequently taken on female qualities. But we should also note that there are many instances of what (either by nature or in our culture) are female tasks being built back into the religion, now performed by men. Thus it is women who go through the hard slog of birthing, feeding and cleansing. But men arrogate to themselves the right to perform these elemental things at a symbolic and sacred level. Indeed one might well say that the symbolic actions of most religions consist in them. In an apparent need to forget their natural birth, within Christianity men perform the ceremony of spiritual birth which is baptism. Indeed, the baptismal font has, with intent, been given the shape of a womb.[74] In famous words Cyprian declared: 'We cannot have God as Father without having the church as mother. Out of her womb we are born, with her milk we are fed, through her spirit we are animated.'[75] The (female) church upstages woman. Within Judaism the male child must undergo circumcision, an act which admits him to the (male) community of the Jewish people. Again, while it is women who feed at the breast and do the day-to-day work of preparing food, it is a man who celebrates at the sacred meal which is the eucharist. The tendency to usurp women's roles (perhaps indicating a fear of women's power) would seem to be strong. In the cultic acts of religion, woman is displaced.

I turn now, thirdly, to woman as complement. In discussing the theme of 'complementarity', what we must focus on is the male construct of 'femininity'. Of course this theme is difficult to assess, since women have in some measure accommodated to the role which has been assigned to them within patriarchy. As we have said, woman as slave is socialized to conform. Nevertheless, in discussing 'the feminine' it will quickly become apparent that we are confronted with something which is quite unreal. Feminist women are adamant in rejecting the concept of a 'complementarity' between the male and the female. It does not, of course, follow that were women to come into their own there could not be a new partnership between women and men. A good way then of marking the male concept of 'complementarity' is to note that the female is always to 'complement' the male and never *vice versa*. That is to say, he is subject, while she is 'the other'. As Luce Irigaray puts it in the earlier quotation which I gave from her, he 'fails . . . to be on occasion her place and her thing in an intersubjective dynamic'.

The male notion of 'femininity' is, in effect, a projection by man on to woman of what he finds himself not to be, so that he shall find these things in her. Thus certain qualities like gentleness, receptivity, humility, nurturative abilities and obedience (for example in relation to the 'male' God) are said to be peculiarly feminine. The recipient of this projection may be a woman, woman in general, in symbolic form the Virgin Mary, or the church or humanity in relationship to God. Certain themes come to the fore which clarify that what we have here is a projection. First, man himself is ideally to have these qualities, so that at crucial points we find that it is man who represents 'the feminine'. The construct enables man to explore for himself what he envisages as the female or the maternal. Secondly, we find that the feminine is understood as that which mediates male–male relations, while woman herself is not counted a subject and becomes inessential. Thirdly, for all the adulation of 'the feminine', it is not actually a veneration of women. Actual women have commonly been despised, their most elementary rights flouted. At no point in all this symbolism is woman allowed to develop her own subjectivity, so that she is counted the equal opposite of man.

We may think it to be the gendered world of Catholicism which displays a zest for complementarity. Its most obvious location is mariology. The extent to which Catholicism has distorted its symbolism (for example in the realm of christology) in order to construct a place for the feminine is astonishing. Far from being inclusive of women, this has the effect of making them into a secondary genus alongside the male. Thus one might have thought that the Christian doctrine of the incarnation was that God took on humanity, such that all Christians are equally 'in Christ'. Indeed the development of this doctrine within the patristic period well allowed this, given the sense of (Platonic) 'real universals' which was abroad at the time.[76] Christology is not presumably – or was not intended to be – the divinization of a male human being. But much of Catholicism seems to have two divine people who form a pair, Jesus and Mary. One of them is of course more divine than the other; indeed Mary would have no *raison d tre* apart from her son, exemplifying precisely the theme of the female complementing the male. Women are then exhorted to emulate not Christ but rather Mary, who provides a role model for them!

What we have is then a typology of what it is to be male (which is the norm for humanity) and, by contrast, of what it is to be female. This typology comes complete with its genealogy. Thus Christ is often aligned with Adam, while Mary is aligned with Eve (who sinned). The typology may further be carried through into the Trinity, so that the male Christ is the second person of the Trinity, while woman is represented by the Holy Spirit. In other words, that which has evident agency and is a full 'person' is male, while woman is somehow diffuse, lacking agency and subjectivity. The Latin American liberation theologian Leonardo Boff writes in this vein :

> The divinizer of the *masculine* (with the feminine) is the Word. The divinizer of the *feminine* (with the masculine) is the Holy Spirit. The Christ–Adam and Mary–Eve parallels find their perfect symmetry here. Mary is not beneath Jesus, but beside him. Together they translate absolutely what it means to say that the human being is the image of God.[77]

Moreover, far from such a christology (if it could be called that) being countermanded by the Vatican, as we shall see it exactly accords with thinking which emanates from Rome.[78] Indeed we may suspect it to have deep roots in a Latin Mediterranean (and equally perhaps in Latin American) culture.

Let us consider the gendering of Mary within this situation. Her role is represented as being one of glad obedience to the male God. Whereas in representations of Mary with her boy child on her knee she looks out on the onlooker with steady gaze, in annunciation scenes commonly she demurely bows her head, averting her eyes. (We may note as an exception Donatello's annunciation in Santa Croce, depicting a Mary who is startled but self-confident.) Indeed we should remark on the exaggerated way in which within this typology not only Christ (as her 'partner' and 'opposite') but also the 'Father' God comes to be decisively 'male' in relation to her femininity. She 'receives' from a God, gendered male. Mary and God then come to be conceptualized as an (unequal) fertile pair who conceive a child at long-distance! Thus the Catholic systematic theologian Michael Schmaus, writes of the conception of Christ: 'What is otherwise achieved through the action of a male, was done to Mary by God's omnipotence.'[79] (In medieval art the homunculus which is the baby Jesus [in an age in which it was thought that the new human being came exclusively from the male] is sometimes shown in a shaft of light making for the virgin's ear!) Hence the pertinence of the feminist Christmas card of recent years. Mary responds to a dejected looking angel Gabriel with downturned trumpet: 'Tell him no! Not unless he's wearing a condom!'

So much for the schemata of male theologians who, when it suits them on other occasions, are wont to tell women that the appellation of God as 'father' is 'only' a metaphor, chiding women for finding it unacceptable. God is always the one who takes the initiative, while Mary is self-effacing. Again, Catholic women who dedicate their lives in celibacy to the church are encouraged to see themselves as engaged in a life-long betrothal to the 'bridegroom' who is Christ. Within Catholicism young girls are admonished to model themselves on Mary as mother and as virgin (which is impossible by definition), whereas by contrast it is open to boys to aspire to become priests and so to represent Christ to the people. Marina Warner, who grew up a Catholic and understands only too well the dynamics of this iconography, concludes: 'The Virgin Mary . . . is the instrument of a dynamic argument from the Catholic church about the structure of society presented as a God-given code.'[80] This is scarcely a complementarity of equals in which woman shall determine who she is.

However, Protestantism has not necessarily been better. True, there is no equivalent construct of 'the feminine'. But what we are then left with is an undiluted masculinity. Could it be that there is actually less room within Protestantism for any shifts in what gender represents?

Meanwhile conservative Protestant circles rival Catholicism in the subsidiary and secondary role which they assign to women. What is determinative here is notions of headship and covenant, which gives woman a particular 'place' within an ordered totality. While declaring humanity to be in the image of God, far from following through the obvious symmetry of his argument so that man and woman in Christ have an equality parallel to the equality of the first and second persons of the Trinity, Karl Barth, basing himself on I Corinthians 11. 3 ('The head of every man is Christ; and the head of the woman is the man; and the head of Christ is God'), declares man to be superordinate and woman subordinate.[81] Moreover, in Barth's case, what the female represents is instantiated by the Virgin Mary, the representative of humanity in relation to the (male) God, who alone has initiative. Precisely for Barth the human being does not have in himself (or herself) any goodness which God can take up.[82] Hence Barth writes of Mary: 'It is not as though this non-willing, non-achieving, non-creative, non-sovereign, merely ready, merely receptive, virgin human being as such can have brought anything to the active God of her own, in which her adaptability for God consists.'[83] Catholicism must have difficulty beating this depiction of what, symbolically, is woman's role!

And what of Barth's notion of 'complementarity'? Of the creation of woman from man's spare rib, Barth states:

> What is meant by this statement that woman 'was taken out of Man' is that God willed to complete man of and through himself . . . She is the witness and embodiment of the free favour in which . . . God willed to complete him as man . . . It is, of course, a strange honour. It came by God's initiative and attack. Without even being asked, man had to yield up something of what belonged to him by divine and natural right. He had to allow the infliction upon himself of a mortal wound. For one who was not a lump of dead earth but a living soul it entailed sacrifice, pain and mortal peril as God marched to this climax of His work.

For Barth, because woman 'marks the completion of his creation, it is not problematic but self-evident for her to be ordained for man and to be for man in her whole existence'.[84] So much for a twentieth-century exegesis by an otherwise intelligent male.

We may turn our attention to the complementary function of woman as the intermediary in the father-son genealogy. She forms the necessary and indispensable link. But nothing can disguise the fact it is the male–male relation which is crucial. In biblical religion, it is not that woman and man form their subjectivity within their relationship. Symbolically, in Christianity we find the trinitarian God conceived of as a relation, not between a female and a male pole, but between 'father' and 'son'. When the Son is born, the Virgin Mary is the intermediary between the 'father' God and his 'son'. (In the internal relations of the Trinity, in the absence of any female partner the male God alone generates the son.) Also interesting is the way in which Mary, *qua* mother, models the role of the necessary intermediary between the human and the father God which we may think actual mothers have often performed for their small sons in relation to the distant father. Thus sinners pray to Mary, asking that she will take their cause to the 'male' God.

But as we have said, it is the father/son relationship which counts. It is symbolized in the relations between the 'male' God and his 'sons'. Woman is excluded. As Julia Kristeva has it, with reference to the Hebrew scriptures: 'God, on the whole, speaks only to men.'[85] It is Abraham's relationship to YHWH, not to Sarah, which is crucial, so consolidating the male genealogy YHWH/Abraham/Isaac. In the episode of the near-slaughter of Isaac which we considered,[86] Sarah is not consulted. Indeed Jewish midrash interpreted Sarah's death (immediately following this episode) as resulting from shock that her husband would contemplate a radical obedience to God of this nature.[87] As Carol Delaney, the social anthropologist whom I cited, points out, rather than being the fulfillment of love of kin, love of God is allowed to take precedence over it.[88] The primary male relationship is that to the 'male' God, not that to a woman.

The role of woman as the intermediary who allows a father/son relation is, of course, strongly marked in the Hebrew scriptures.[89] Indeed the characterization of woman as mother (and as little else) may be thought to be prominent within the Jewish tradition in all ages. In the Hebrew scriptures the production of male heirs is woman's chief, if not sole, purpose. The scholar of the Hebrew scriptures Cheryl Exum remarks: 'There is something ludicrous in the preoccupation with producing sons.'[90] Lack of sons is represented as woman's greatest tragedy! It is interesting that none of the many birth stories in the Bible concerns the birth of a daughter. Nor is there the same concern about naming daughters, who are frequently simply mentioned as daughters. Nor of course is there any concern for women's genealogy, whereas the male succession is vital.

The way in which woman becomes little more than a necessary intermediary between the father and the son is highlighted by the British Jewish scholar Naomi Segal. Segal remarks that, whether one looks to Freud, or to the rabbis teaching their male pupils, the pattern is the same.

All seek a male parthenogenetic genealogy that goes only momentarily via the body of the woman: she is the channel that makes the father-son relation possible, briefly difficult, then resolved on the grounds of their agreement to despise and discount her. This is the crucial move of patriarchy: precisely a reversal of the male's brief role in natural reproduction.[91]

As we have seen, Irigaray, too, has drawn attention to the way in which, even for a secular Jewish thinker like Emmanuel Levinas, it is the father/son relation which remains crucial.[92]

In this context we may comment on the fact that it is the male God (and not woman) who is understood to have control over fertility. Thus we should note the significance of the fact that in so many of the biblical stories women are barren. Woman's natural fecundity and ability to produce children is taken from her and placed in the hands of the 'male' God, leaving her impotent in the matter. Again, Rachel's death following the birth of Benjamin has been thought to relate to her failure to perceive YHWH's exclusive control.[93] Thus even in regard to that which most intimately concerns her in her role as child-bearer, woman becomes a pawn in the hands of the 'male' God. Segal makes a thought-provoking observation.

> Monotheism . . . rests on a recuperation in a male deity of creation and providence: womb and breasts . . . This God reroutes nature, awarding late conception to Sarah, Rebecca, Hannah etc., because 'he' is himself a distortion of the sexual difference in nature.[94]

As we have seen before, the 'male' God comes to comprehend all within himself.

Finally, we should pay attention to the way in which a construct of 'the feminine' enables men to explore a side of themselves which is denied under patriarchy. There is a kind of blurring of gender distinctions here as man allows himself to be vulnerable. The result is that woman is displaced. Thus, as we have seen, man characterizes himself as 'female' (obedient, passive and receptive) before the 'male' God. Again Christ, who is male, is often seen as an almost 'feminine' figure in relation to the 'father'. He, like Mary, pleads with the Father for the forgiveness of sins. Obedient to his father, he goes to his death. Likewise the priest has often had a distinctly 'feminine' image. It may be that priests wear clothing modelled on that of the late Roman empire. But there is no reason on earth why it should have been retained, indeed elaborated, as it has been. At the end of the day, then, it is not actually woman, but the man who takes on himself the 'feminine' role in relation to the 'male' God! In the very role to which man has assigned her, woman is undercut.

It is difficult to know how to explore the dynamic at work here. Clearly in some cases it is homosexual. Anyone who looks at those museum cases of ecclesiastical garments from the seventeenth and eighteenth centuries (deriving from the Counter-Reformation) which one sometimes sees on the Continent must surely conclude that they are nothing short of 'camp' – note the velvet shoes with elaborate buckles. But it is also that, within patriarchal society, the Christian religion has often allowed man to develop a side of himself which was otherwise disallowed. Man can enter into a near-symbiotic union with the female, 'mother', church; a substitute for the actual mother if ever there was one. As priest, a man may also take up a 'feminine' position in relation to the 'male' God. Indeed, he may engage in a love affair with God. Kristeva remarks on the fact that in their writings 'Augustine, Bernard of Clairvaux, Meister Eckhart, to mention but a few, played the part of the Father's virgin spouses'. And she remarks: 'Freedom with respect to the maternal territory . . . becomes the pedestal upon which love of God is erected.'[95]

It is in this context that one can understand why it should be so alarming to some men that women should be ordained priests. As a bishop suggested to me, the presence of a real woman threatens male femininity. Significantly again, the fact that feminism is not concerned with the 'complementarity' of male and female seems often to disorient and to dismay men. This has notably been the case within the church. Catholic men, often priests, will tell Christian feminist women that they honour women; that Mary is central to their spirituality. When those women insist that they themselves have not been heard, they are simply represented as being angry. It provokes men's wrath that women should apparently be unwilling to see themselves in 'the feminine' when that notion has been given so high a place in their estimation.[96] But it is perfectly clear that feminism is not about complementarity, in the sense of woman carrying for humanity certain qualities which the macho male world lacks.[97] While men celebrate 'the feminine', actual woman are left standing on the sidelines, increasingly, in this day and age, unable to find anything corresponding to that notion in themselves.

They may waltz with the idea of 'the feminine' and place motherhood on a pedestal, but male ecclesiastical authorities have normally exemplified a singular blindness to the fate of actual women. This again is a good indication that what we have to do with is some masculine ideal, rather than anything connected with women. Indeed, what is worse, ecclesiastical power and biblical injunctions have commonly been employed to undercut any sense that a woman might have of her dignity. Here we are speaking with a vengeance of a world in which the slave comes to take on the master's view of her. Thus, as we have said, women have been exhorted to model themselves on Mary, whose *at* represents a glad and selfless submission to the 'male' God. It has not been for them to control whether they wished to become pregnant again, for motherhood is that for which women are created. Indeed, when women have been abused by men, they have only too often been counselled by male priests and ministers to exhibit the Christian virtues of patience and forbearance, those peculiarly feminine characteristics.

At the outset of the Western Christian tradition, here is Augustine commending his mother Monica.

> When she was old enough [her parents] gave her in marriage to a man whom she served as her lord . . . He was unfaithful to her, but her patience was so great that his infidelity never became a cause of quarrelling between them . . . He had a hot temper, but my mother knew better than to say or do anything to resist him when he was angry . . . Many women, whose faces were disfigured by blows from husbands far sweeter-tempered than her own, used to gossip together and complain of the behaviour of their men-folk. My mother would meet this complaint with another – about the women's tongues. Her manner was light but her meaning serious when she told them that ever since they had heard the marriage deed read over to them, they ought to have regarded it as a contract which bound them to serve their husbands, and from that time onward they should remember their condition and not defy their masters.[98]

Kari Børresen points out that, in contrast to Augustine's position here and elsewhere, the civil marriage contract in the Roman law of the time does not seem to have made any special allusion to the subordination of the wife to the husband.[99]

Nor does an undermining of woman's position through theological precepts belong to the distant past. The way in which supposedly Christian tenets have been employed to this end is something to which Christian feminist women have drawn attention. The American Carole Bohn writes as follows:

> Man's authority to rule over woman is traced to God's intention in [the] account from Genesis 2 and 3 . . . It is quite common for women who seek counsel from their ministers to receive . . . advice such as:
> – Marriage is sacred and you must do whatever you can to hold it together.
> – Your husband is the head of your household; do what he tells you and he won't need to resort to violence.
> – You must have done something to provoke him; go home and mend your ways so he will not need to behave in this manner.

– All of us must suffer; it makes us more Christ-like. Offer up your suffering to Jesus and he will give you strength to endure.[100]

In fact current thinking on the matter of abuse is that, far from it being wise to suffer meekly, not standing up to his behaviour simply encourages the perpetrator to continue.[101]

Many will think that this is clearly a misreading of Christian precepts. What we should note, however, is that the religions of the West have been amenable to such an interpretation. Thus men who abuse their wives not infrequently claim that their wife 'belongs' to them, giving them the right to control her, with violence if necessary.[102] Moreover women themselves – horrifically – may think that they have no right to protest. We remember the woman in a shelter for battered women who maintained 'God punished women more'.[103] Lest any British person should smugly dismiss this as a predicament of fundamentalist America, I should report that a graduate student of mine who has long experience of work in the local women's refuge tells me that such a story is not at all unthinkable here. Jennifer Kerr writes: 'It has been of interest to me that so many incest survivors and abused women speak of their subjection and obedience to men in a context of religious teachings and imagery. God the Father has become quite abhorrent to me after listening to this for years!'[104]

We have considered woman as ideal, as slut and as complement. What is interesting is the way in which it has become apparent that one of these images can flip over into another. Thus woman as slut and as ideal may seem to be counter-faces of male 'splitting' in relation to the mother; a splitting which is then displaced on to other women. Woman as complement quickly translates into giving woman an inferior position to the male, in which she comes to be denigrated. As we consider either the biblical material or later Christian paradigms, what is missing is the sense of woman as an independent agent, having her own subjectivity, the equal of man. But it is such an agent, with such a subjectivity, that, with the rise of feminism, women are rapidly coming to be. In the remainder of this chapter, therefore, I shall in the first place ask whether anything has changed in the outlook of the male (particularly Catholic) ecclesiastical authorities. In the second place I shall say something more about Protestantism. And lastly, I shall direct our attention to the threat which the rise of feminism represents to the male universe which I have described.

I turn, first, to the conceptions of woman emanating from Rome today. Has anything changed? The Vatican took the opportunity of the 'Marian' year of 1988 to issue a comprehensive statement on womanhood, (in)appropriately named *Mulieris Dignitatem*, 'On the Dignity of Woman'. The authorities are, of course, not unaware of the call for change prevalent among Catholic women, not least, so the evidence would suggest, among nuns. Yet their armour is thick. It is as though a certain mind-set is so deeply ingrained that, even though they may speak of the need for a renewed understanding of woman, what we are presented with turns out to be yet more of the same. *Mulieris Dignitatem* may well be said to exemplify every aspect of the male construct of 'woman' and of femininity as I have described it in the course of this chapter – and it takes 116 pages over this!

Consider, then, the following (the italicization is that given in the original). Of the dignity of woman we are told: 'this dignity consists *in the supernatural elevation to union with God in Jesus Christ* which is Mary's; 'she *represents the humanity* which belongs to all human beings, both men and women'. Thus: 'In anything we think, say or do concerning the dignity and the vocation of women, our thoughts, hearts and actions must not become detached from this horizon.' In the scriptures 'we find *comparisons that attribute to God masculine or feminine qualities* . . . Thus even *fatherhood in God is completely divine* and free of the "masculine" bodily characteristics proper to human fatherhood'. The Son is 'joined to the Father by the eternal mystery of divine generation.' There is a 'specific diversity' between man and woman. Consequently 'even the rightful opposition of women to what is expressed in the biblical words "He shall rule over you" (Gen. 3.16) must not under any condition lead to the "masculinization" of women. In the name of liberation from male "domination", women must not appropriate to themselves male characteristics contrary to their own feminine "originality". There is a well-founded fear that if they take this path, women will not "reach fulfilment", but instead will *deform and lose what constitutes their essential richness*. It is indeed an enormous richness . . . The personal resources of femininity are certainly no less than the resources of masculinity: they are merely different.'

Yet further: 'In the tradition of faith and of Christian reflection throughout the ages, *the coupling Adam-Christ* is often linked with that of *Eve-Mary* . . . Mary is "the new beginning" of the *dignity and vocation of women*, of each and every woman . . . *In Mary, Eve discovers* the nature of the true dignity of woman, of feminine humanity. This discovery must continually reach the heart of every woman and shape her vocation and her life.' Thus: 'Virginity and motherhood [are] two particular dimensions of the fulfillment of the female personality . . . *Motherhood is linked to the personal structure of the woman.* . . . While 'by freely choosing virginity [women] . . . realize the personal value of their own femininity by becoming . . . a gift for Christ . . . *One cannot*

correctly understand virginity . . . without referring to spousal love . . .
Women, called . . . to virginity . . . give themselves to the divine Spouse.'
Moreover, 'unless one looks to the Mother of God, it is impossible to
understand the mystery of the Church . . . In this way there is a
confirmation of the profound union between what is human and what
constitutes the divine economy of salvation . . . We cannot omit, in the
perspective of our faith, the mystery of "woman": virgin–mother–
spouse.'

And again: 'The bride *is the Church*, just as for the Prophets the bride
was Israel. She is therefore *a collective subject* and not *an individual
person.*' Of self-giving it is said: 'In this way "being the bride", and thus
the "feminine" element, becomes a symbol of all that is "human" . . . A
woman's dignity is closely connected with the love which she receives
by the very reason of her femininity; it is likewise connected *with the
love which she gives in return . . . Woman can only nd herself by
giving love to others.* Of the Genesis story: 'Our reflections have focused
on *the particular place occupied by the woman* in this key text of revelation.' So in conclusion: 'During the Marian Year *the Church desires
to give thanks to the Most Holy Trinity* for the "mystery of woman"
and for every woman – for that which constitutes the eternal measure
of her feminine dignity.'[105]

Need one say more? A suitable response to the papal pronouncement
might well be thought to be some words taken from the writing of the
French feminist thinker Marguerite Duras:

> It is an extraordinary thing, but men still see themselves as supreme
> authorities on women's liberation. They say: 'In my opinion women
> should do this or that to liberate themselves' – And when people
> laugh they don't understand why. Then they take up the old refrain
> – their veneration of women. Whatever form this veneration of
> women takes, be it religious or surrealist . . . it is still racism. But
> when you point this out to men, they don't understand . . .
>
> We will have to wait until whole generations have disappeared,
> whole worlds of men . . . Men are like old kings who think they are
> still in power when they have ceased to reign. And I think that the
> various other aspects of their retrograde behaviour stem directly from
> their most important regressive stance: they still want to rule.[106]

This is well said. Clearly these celibate males in Rome do not bat an eye-
lid at telling woman who she is.

Despite its assured tone, however, it would seem that the document,
when carefully read, belies something else. It becomes apparent that
the reason for its promulgation is that clear blue water has opened
up between where even Catholic women are today and traditional

teaching. The document represents an attempt to adjust to the modern world, to speak of the 'dignity of woman'. But the Roman authorities are quite unable to do this. That is not surprising if, as I have suggested, the construct of woman is fundamental to the whole Catholic universe. Given, however, the changing self-understanding of women (even those in religious orders) within at least the Western world today, the admonitions of men as to what women shall be simply passes them by. The disjunction is becoming marked.

Symptomatic of the extraordinary change which has come about in Catholic women's self-understanding is writing on 'Mary' emanating from within that tradition. Mary now comes to be the Mary of the Magnificat! How extraordinary, we may say, and how significant, that this revolutionary document – almost the only words that the evangelist puts into the mouth of the historical Mary – over two millennia has played so little part in shaping mariology! In another scenario, the 'Mary' to which Catholic women turn now becomes Mary Magdalene.[107] Again, how significant that it was Mary the Mother of Jesus and not Mary Magdalene whom the church chose to honour! We may note that in fact Jesus' reported remarks to his mother in the episode in which he remained behind in the temple (and she was concerned, as well a mother might be),[108] as also his remarks to her as an adult,[109] were none too kind. They suggest, rather, his sense for the independence of persons and a lack of family bonds. If such an ethic had governed the male relation to women in the church (even if God had been conceptualized using masculine metaphors) we should have had a very different story.

But what of Protestantism? For I do not doubt that many a woman reading this chapter would want to contend that she does not recognize in her own experience that about which I have been speaking. I, too, grew up within Protestantism. In the first instance – by way of justification for the obvious bias of this chapter – it is important to point out that Catholic doctrine (for example in the field of mariology) has served to shape the understanding of women in the West over a much longer period of time; moreover, by far the greater part of Christendom today is Catholic. Nevertheless, there are interesting question to be asked as to whether within Christianity Protestantism does not represent the coming of modernity. What of the interface between Protestantism and feminism?

Protestantism, of course, is such a diverse phenomenon that no generalizations will be wholly satisfactory. Nevertheless, some remarks may be made. In the first place it is quite unclear historically whether the change from Catholicism to Protestantism can be said to have benefitted women. As Catholic women have often pointed out, within

Catholicism women had an essential choice between motherhood or the life of celibacy – and the latter gave women as religious persons a certain independence from the world of men. Within Protestantism, by contrast, the only formal role allotted to women (until their recent ordination) was that of the pastor's wife! It is interestingly the case that the image of woman changed from that of being wicked and liable to seduce man, the cause of evil in the world (which prevailed from patristic times through to the sixteenth century and beyond), to an understanding of woman as wife and mother, the custodian of spiritual values (which we find in full flood by the beginning of the nineteenth century). It may be thought to be a remarkable evolution. How far Protestantism was responsible for this is a good question.

It would also seem to be that Protestantism is to be associated with the rise of individualism in the modern world. But this alliance between Protestantism and modernity may well have been a mixed blessing as far as women are concerned. On the one hand a discourse about the rights of individuals had the effect that in time women, too, came to have rights even within the church, leading eventually to their ordination. On the other hand, Protestant churches have often exemplified the competitive individualism of a band of brothers, an atmosphere which many a woman must surely find alienating. I remember that on the in-service training days that I used to have to conduct for ministers of the Church of Scotland, almost whatever one said would result in feuds between those who had jousted at one another from the same high horses for twenty years or more. What one sometimes hears of Presbytery meetings is no different.

There is, then, something extraordinarily male about Protestantism. One recognizes what the ex-Catholic Marina Warner means when she speaks of that 'sombre-suited masculine world [which is] altogether too much like a gentleman's club'.[110] The woman who is ordained joins the club. It is a world of the 'father' God and his 'sons'. Far from worship providing anything aesthetic which delights the eye, a single individual proclaims the Word of the absent God. She too now stands alone in the pulpit proclaiming the father's Word. One wonders, indeed, whether ordained women are not something of an anomaly within the church? Left to themselves, would it come naturally to women to separate off some of their number, giving them special roles and status on a permanent basis? It may of course be that in time the ordination of women will change the culture. However, it must be said that in those Protestant churches in which women have been ordained for many years now they seem to have had little enough effect. It is still difficult for women even to get positions.

Nor should one underestimate the impact of the Protestant attachment to scripture. As we have seen, from Genesis to the Epistles the secondary status of women is assumed. What effect does it have that, week by week, such literature is read? Christian discourse may also be problematic in more subtle ways. When the church (whether Catholic or Protestant) is held to be a body (rather than a liberal democracy) and the ethos is one of not putting oneself forward but rather of giving oneself in service, it can be difficult to bring about change. Thus in a well-known passage St Paul advocates what may be called an organic notion of the church: of the eye and the ear he asks, 'Where would they be without each other?'[111] Flower-arranging and organizing the Sunday School may then also be said to be essential tasks within the body. It is notable that even Protestant churches have in no way kept pace with the changes in the surrounding society.

It would seem then that both Protestantism and Catholicism are exemplifying the strain of attempting to come to terms with the modern world. I should want to argue that this must necessarily be the case, since in the last resort the gap is unbridgeable. This has been very noticeable in recent years in the realm of language. As society increasingly comes to find gender-inclusive language the only ethical option, what is the church to do? But the task which Catholicism and Protestantism face is essentially different. Whereas Catholicism is stuck with a wholly untenable view of 'woman', Protestantism seems to lack a sense for anything but the masculine. It is difficult to know which tradition confronts the more uphill struggle. The problem, of course, is that Christianity is a religion rooted in an ancient patriarchal society. Whereas there is no inherent reason why the world of politics should not change, in Christianity the church is founded on an ideology which is far from neutral.

But – I shall be asked – what of the many women who fill the pews? Need one be surprised by this phenomenon? I do not find it to controvert anything I have said. There is every indication (as I shall consider in the next chapter) that women tend to be more religious or spiritually inclined than men. In the West, Christianity (or Judaism) have been the only vehicles we know which have carried people's love of God. To break with one's religion is traumatic, as I myself well know. Moreover, one might well say, particularly of more conservative Christianity, that the symbol system of the religion, with its place for 'woman', has made sense to women precisely because it has mirrored their lives under patriarchy. It has served to interpret their world to them. That is what is so invidious. Within patriarchal society the girl too has looked up to her father, so that it has seemed the most natural thing in the world to love the father God. It is he (whether God or the human father) who loves and protects her.

Women are not to be despised for having found their way as best they could within patriarchy. Until very recently patriarchy has been the social reality of all of us. Yet Christianity has in fact been what is sometimes called a 'false consciousness'; it has served to keep women secondary citizens, often with their connivance. As Simone de Beauvoir was the first to acknowledge, there has been a certain complicity on the part of women. But it must be clearly stated that, in conforming to her place within the male reality, woman has undermined her vital interests. Increasing numbers of women are coming to recognize that this is the case. Those who seek to draw one's attention to those women who still darken the church door should have their glance redirected to the many who have found themselves compelled to leave. They have done this, moreover, difficult though the step has been.

Patriarchy is built upon the suppression of women as women. The patriarchal imagination substitutes for woman as the equal of man, a male projection of 'woman'. She is understood with reference to him. There is a failure to allow woman to have her own subjectivity – in the sense that man takes it for granted that he has a subjectivity which is not defined in relation to her. (Though it may well be said that male subjectivity has been defined negatively in relation to man's need to escape and to dominate woman and that therein lies the problem.) Hence women's bid for autonomy is seen as a threat to the whole patriarchal system (which indeed it is). Within patriarchy, men fail to allow women to be genuinely other than themselves. They live in a world in which they are the norm and women's 'otherness' is defined with reference to what they are.

What the male symbolic order lacks (exemplified well by Christianity) is the image of woman as the adult equal of man. Given that for two thousand years the theologians have been men, indeed overwhelmingly celibate men, this need hardly strike us as surprising. The only woman whom such a man knew intimately was his mother, from whom he had often been removed at the tenderest age so that she remained a figure of his imagination. In a very real sense, then, woman as herself goes unrepresented within Christianity. With whom should a present-day woman associate herself? In what ideal should she find her reflection? The religion lacks any place for women who see themselves as strong and independent, agents acting on their own behalf. Christian symbolism reflects – devastatingly for actual women – a failure to recognize women as persons.

Indeed, if the analysis of this chapter is correct, far from representing male maturity, the symbol system of Christianity reflects male inadequacy. As long as men remain cocooned within it they will be quite unable to face or to comprehend the new social reality which has come about. That symbol system simply panders to men's needs. Thus, in considering it, we should ask the following kinds of question. Does it not suggest a separation from the mother which remains inadequate and incomplete? Hence the need to build the mother in ideal form back into the religion. Does it not, in its model of the Virgin Mother who is Mary, depict a wholly unreal relation to a strangely romantic conception of woman? Again, does it not suggest a deep ambivalence on the part of men about their sexuality? Hence the substitution of a sublimated and necessarily unconsummated relationship with a father/mother God for a real relation with another person? Furthermore, does it not manifest a crippling fear, on the part of the boy, of his distant father? Hence the need for the mediation performed by the mother or the elder brother. And finally, does it not suggest the unhealthy power which women have until recently had over the lives of small boys; in a world in which men were essentially absent and he had no close relationship other than with her?

The hope is that in our present age men will come into their own; that man will come to 'himself'. If men's construction of what they call 'the feminine' reflects the fact that they have split off part of themselves, then their appropriation of those attributes which they have not known how to handle would represent a very real healing. Man's religion would suggest that he swings between two scenarios, each of which is equally impossible. On the one hand he sees himself as a lone, isolated, independent and self-sufficient monad. He constructs the transcendent father God in the image of this impossible ideal. On the other hand, knowing that this is untenable and yearning to find another possibility, he projects the ideal of 'the feminine' (which may be in the form of God, the church, or woman) in which he seeks to lose himself and so find a completion which he lacks. What is markedly absent in the symbol system of the religion is the understanding of a self as centred in relation: able to stand on its own, yet existing in reciprocity with others (including persons of the neighbouring sex). In other words, what is lacking is exactly what I have characterized as the feminist ideal.

Meanwhile, in this situation, for women to come into their own is simply the most revolutionary thing that they could do. The appearance on the scene of independent and self-actualizing women must necessarily disrupt the whole symbol system which I have described. She does not fit; there is no place for her. The challenge is that as people, men and women, come to be themselves, with their sexuality as one of their attributes, we should find the multifariousness of persons to be good. It need not follow from the fact that there are manifestly differences that we should set up dualisms around gender (or anything else) which consign some members of humanity to something less than the status of being a full person. It could be possible simply to allow other persons to be themselves!

We may hope that a profound social change of this nature is on the cards. As women come to see themselves and to be accepted as subjects in their own right, we shall lose the sense of woman defined with reference to man. In a world in which there is equal parenting (and in which indeed many women do not have children),[112] we can move away from a construal of woman as simply 'mother'. (We should note the asymmetrical meanings within patriarchy of the expressions 'to mother' and 'to father' a child; reflecting, on the one hand, the assumption that it is mothers who care for children, and, on the other, the mistaken biological assumption that a new child derives exclusively from the male.) As I have said, the advent of social arrangements in which men father (in the sense of looking after young children may in itself bring about a social shift. The mother will no longer represent one from whom an escape needs to be made. Meanwhile the fact that a woman is not constantly tied to looking after her children will allow her to be a person in her own right. She will be recognized as such by the boy. For her part, the young girl will grow up with a role model in the mother (of a very different kind).

We may think that much of this is already coming to pass. There is a marked difference in attitude between the young people whom I teach today from those whom I taught twenty years ago. Given such a shift in social relations, a religion which reflects a past construal of gender can hardly remain unscathed. Indeed, we may think the demise of patriarchy to represent the greatest challenge which a symbol system that reflects a patriarchal ordering has known in four thousand years. For symbol systems both reflect and in turn serve to legitimize social arrangements. If, as I have suggested, the religion which we have known is in particular predicated upon the ordering of the patriarchal family, then the change in family relations (indeed the breakdown of the family) cannot but have the most profound impact. At the same time, a shift away from a hierarchical ordering of social relations will mean that a God who was an extrapolation from the patriarchal lords of the past must be left high and dry. In so far as 'he' stands as the pivot of the system, 'his' demise or irrelevance must unsteady the whole.

One does not topple the patriarchal God by slinging mud at him. The men have slung enough already. The great detractors of religion in the modern world – Feuerbach and Marx (and behind them Hegel); Nietzsche; and in the twentieth century Freud – urged men to appropriate for themselves the qualities which they had projected on to their God. Religion, however, held too strong a grip for their admonitions to be of much effect. They little realized that there would be a wholesale re-ordering of gender relations (though Marx and Engels to some extent advocated this). We may think that it is not through the preaching of a secular ideology 'from above' that change will come about. Rather, it is through the advent of a new basis to society that a revolution is secured. That is what feminism represents – and Western culture is profoundly challenged by it. The very evident absence of woman from the 'place' which she has occupied in the patriarchal imagination constitutes in itself a disruption of the first order.

An interesting question arises. As woman comes into her own, as she too is the creator of culture and of symbol systems, will women require a transcendental in relation to which they can find themselves? It is this question which Luce Irigaray in particular has raised. Irigaray wishes women to create what she calls a gendered and sensible (material, rooted in nature) transcendental, that is to say a horizon, which she thinks must be gendered (this time female) and not divorced from the body (and therefore sensible), in which women may see their reflection and hence establish their subjectivity. Only as this transpires, she believes, will men and women be able to relate to one another as equal opposites across the difference of sex. The very raising of such a question is itself revolutionary. A consideration of it serves to relativize the patriarchal religion which we have known and to show it to be just that. It is no chance that there is such intense interest in Irigaray's work among women working in the philosophy of religion (and – as I discover when I teach her work – among students).[113] Yet Irigaray recognizes the difficulty of effecting such a transcendental. From her background in Lacanian thought she knows how deeply we are trapped within the language and culture which we have. As Elizabeth Grosz has well said: 'Her project is ultimately impossible, but necessary.'[114] In the next chapter I shall attempt to say something of my own, very different, conception as to what the way forward might be.

What I believe we need to confront is that the harm which has been done to women within Christian culture is not simply an aberration. It is not as though that symbol system which is Christianity could simply be purified, after which it would serve us well. The shocking treatment of women, throughout Western history, has been at least in part a con-sequence of that mythological universe which is Christianity. Nor is it possible through a renewed reading of the scriptures to revert to some pristine faith. For the scriptures themselves exemplify the problem. Christianity is not a religion in which the female and the male, women and men, equally find their symbolic place. The only balancing act which it knows is one in which man is the subject and woman is the 'other'. What, however, when women come to conceive of themselves as subjects?

Again, the fault lies in a hierarchical structuring of reality, so that God is above (and gendered male), throwing the concept of humanity into a secondary position. But this is fundamental to a transcendent monotheism. Nor are the postulation of a transcendent male mono- theism and the subordination of women within patriarchy to be separated. The one is the corollary of the other. Men who conceive of God as 'above' and perfect will also project woman as the opposite to that which is good and transcendent. The problem lies in the difference of sexuality being construed as the dualism of gender, understood as a hierarchical difference. Hence Kristeva writes:

> Whatever attacks this radical codification of the sexual difference . . . is attacking – primarily and in the same blow – a fundamental discovery of Judaism that resides in the separation of the sexes and in their incompatibility: in castration if you like – the support of monotheism and the source of its eroticism.[115]

Now feminism represents woman's refusal to conform to the place which she has occupied in the male imagination. Hence Kristeva speaks of Western women 'who are trying to get out from under the thumbs of . . . monotheism'.[116] What when they succeed?

The biblical scholar Norman Gottwald writes:

> Symbol systems claiming to be based on 'biblical faith' will be judged by whether they actually clarify the range and contours of exercisable freedom within the context of the unfolding social process. Symbol systems that blur the intersection of social process and human free- dom – by talking fuzzy nonsense, by isolating us in our private souls, by positing 'unseen' worlds to compensate for the actual world we fear to see, by conditioning us to compete for many small favors instead of cooperating for a few big gains, by cultivating mood and sentiment in place of vision and passion, by instilling resignation in the name of sweetness and sacrifice, by persuading us to accept the humanly unacceptable and to desist from changing what is manifestly changeable, by confirming our fixations to the past and our venture- lessness toward the future, by decrying power while feasting on its benefits – all such symbol systems, however venerable and psychi- cally convenient, are bad dreams to be awakened from, cloying relics to be cast away, cruel fetters to be struck off. They are, in a word, the Canaanite idols that Israel smashed when it smashed the Canaanite kings.

And he adds:

> In this rapidly complexifying and maturing sociocultural transitional

period [which is our age], all forms of religious faith and practice that fail to grasp and to act upon their connection with and dependence upon the cultural-material evolution of humankind are doomed to irrationality and irrelevance, whatever diversionary consolation they offer at the moment.[117]

New wine must burst old skins.

VI

A Future Theism

It was to Friedrich Schleiermacher that it fell to make the first great theological response to modernity. In his youthful *On Religion: Speeches to its Cultured Despisers*[1] and later in more fully-fashioned form in the work of his maturity, *The Christian Faith,*[2] Schleiermacher founded theology on a novel basis. In what is a phenomenological consideration of the nature of the self, he advanced the thesis that the self exists in an immediate connectedness to that which is more than itself. I am in agreement with Schleiermacher that the question as to the nature of that membrane between the self and that which exceeds the self must form the kernel of theology. Accordingly, in this chapter I shall engage in a running debate with him. The fact that in the intervening two centuries there has been no one else who is a suitable partner for such a dialogue is an indication of his stature. That Schleiermacher's way of grounding theology may not be as secure as he supposed, that we have questions which he scarcely entertained, is certainly the case. But it is also the case that I at least hold convictions predicated on evidence of which he – we may suppose as a modern person – took no account! That Schleiermacher did not follow through the implications of his thought as I shall wish to, that as a Christian he would have disagreed with me, I do not doubt. But – if in nothing else – I must agree with Schleiermacher's great opponent of the twentieth century, Karl Barth (who understood his life work as countering all that Schleiermacher stood for), that upon reaching the kingdom of heaven, Schleiermacher will be first among those whom I shall seek out – in order to engage him theologically.[3]

I shall summarize my argument in advance here. In short, what I wish to do is to bring Schleiermacher's conceptualization of the relationship of the self to that which is more than itself to the empirical evidence for religious experience which I shall adduce. It is important that I make myself clear here if I am not to be misunderstood. Although I shall consider Schleiermacher's grounding of theism in an immediate awareness of God (which will enable me in turn to consider his understanding of the self as it is related to what is more than itself), I myself do not want to found my theism on such an intuitive awareness. Perhaps such a grounding of theology has more to commend it than one might think – even this side of Derridean deconstruction. In passing I shall suggest that this may be the case. But I do not want to rest my case for theism on the outcome of such a deliberation. Where I wish to be in dialogue with Schleiermacher is in his *conceptualization* of the self as having an immediate connectedness to that which is more than the self – which he, and I likewise, wishes to name God.

What leads me to be theistic is, as I have indicated, quite other than in Schleiermacher's case. I am theistic on account of certain observations as to the presence of power and love in the world. Thus I speak of the existence of 'another dimension to reality'; of there being more than meets the eye; of there being that on which we can draw. I call this dimension of reality God. In consideration of the evidence for such a dimension to reality, I must look not to Schleiermacher but to what has essentially been an Anglo-Saxon tradition in the study of religious experience. What is significant is that within that tradition, empirical and pragmatic as it is, no attempt has been made to move into the realm of theology, that is to say, to ask after the nature of God, given the evidence which it brings forward. So I repeat, what I wish to do is to bring to the evidence which I believe there to be of the existence of this other dimension of reality Schleiermacher's conceptualization of the self as existing in relation to what is more than itself.

I shall proceed in the following manner. In the first place I shall attempt to clarify what I believe Schleiermacher to be saying. Whether I am pushing him further than he would have wanted to go is an interesting question. That conversation must await the kingdom of heaven. But it would seem to be evident that Schleiermacher has been profoundly misread, both in his lifetime and since. The misreading makes nonsense of his position! What I wish to bring to the fore – and what attracts me to Schleiermacher's conceptualization – is the lack of the possibility of any heteronomy in the human relation to God. In passing, as I have mentioned, I shall attempt to defend Schleiermacher's position against any too easy charge of reductionism or, more particularly, against a deconstructionist critique. These are not matters which, living when he did, Schleiermacher considers in the form in which we know them. It may be that he would have thought that his christology served to secure his position. (Whether, given his founding of theology in a general proposition about the grounding of the human self in what is more than itself, Schleiermacher could legitimately have a christology is, of course, another issue.) But whatever we may think of the reductionist, or deconstructionist, charge, this need not affect my argument since, as I have made clear, I myself do not wish to ground theism in such a direct cognition of God.

I move then, secondly, from Schleiermacher to a consideration of the evidence which, I believe, leads us to speak of that dimension of reality which I name God. I shall give examples from my own life and from the lives of friends and relatives, and I shall draw on the work of the Oxford Religious Experience Research Unit. I again point out, as I have earlier in the book, that while it is the case that, at the macro-level at least, nature and history form a causal nexus, we may need to extend our understanding of what it is that is everywhere and always the case. In turning to the theological question as to how, given the evidence, we should conceptualize that which is God, I revert to Schleiermacher. For Schleiermacher is fascinated by the question of the relationship of the self to that which lies beyond it. Moreover feminist thought of the future may well have much to offer here. By way of further elucidation (and advocacy) of the way in which I am suggesting that God should be conceived, I consider how, given this understanding, what have been major conundrums in Western theology fall away. I look at the 'question of miracles' and at theodicy. I also mention what, within Christianity, has been the doctrine of creation and the idea of eternal life.

Thirdly, I turn to a consideration of what may well be considered to be two major problems with the understanding of God which I am advocating. In the first place I consider whether it is not essential, in particular to the life of prayer, for the relationship with God to be conceived of in dialogical terms. In the second place I consider whether it is not the case that the concept of God (if it is indeed to be a concept of *God*) must necessarily perform a transcendental function. I suggest that I do indeed wish to maintain this. I discuss how such an act of faith that this is the case could comport with the phenomenological depiction of God, rooted in an empirical grounding, which I have given.

Fourthly and finally, I return to the question of a theism which may be adequate for the future. I attempt to trace historically the movement away from an anthropomorphic conception of God which has come to fruition in our time. I wish to take a step further than anything Schleiermacher conceived towards understanding God as intrinsically a part of what we are. I thus suggest that (on multiple counts, ethical and epistemological) we should undertake the major shift of paradigm in our conceptualization of what God is that I have advanced in this chapter.

I turn then in the first instance to a consideration of Schleiermacher's understanding of the relationship of the self to that which he conceived God to be. Schleiermacher came to maturity as the thought of Kant was in the ascendant. He absorbed deeply the Kantian prohibition against speaking of 'knowledge' of God. As has been well said, Kant placed a boulder in the stream of theology, diverting its course. For at least that stream of Protestantism which accepted the Kantian analysis, it would not henceforth be possible to reason from a knowledge of the world to the existence of a God. Schleiermacher attempted to circumvent the prohibition by grounding theology in an immediate awareness of God. In developing such a postulation, Schleiermacher brought together a number of influences: the Platonism which was second nature to him, a certain borrowing from Spinoza (who had in turn been influenced by English Quaker thought), and the Romanticism prevalent in the circles in which he moved. 'You lie directly on the bosom of the infinite world,' said Schleiermacher in his famed *Speeches* of 1799.[4] Religion was to be conceived as 'a life in the infinite nature of the Whole, in the One and in the All, in God, a having and possessing all things in God, and God in all; . . . a revelation of the Infinite in the finite, God being seen in it and it in God'.[5] To be religious is to relate the particular to the whole, while the *Universum* (in his *Speeches* at least Schleiermacher is wary of the word 'God' with its anthropomorphic connotations) is immediately apparent in the particular.

Schleiermacher's *Speeches* were intended to be performative: through their very use of language and imagery to awaken that sensibility to which he wished to draw attention. The book was after all dedicated to the circle of his friends, among whom he was the only clergyman and professing Christian. These 'cultured despisers' of religion, who (as he quipped) had exchanged sayings from the poets for biblical quotations as wall decorations,[6] were in fact through their Romanticism – so Schleiermacher maintained – close to a religious consciousness. Schleiermacher's aim was maieutic. He wished to bring others to a recognition, to allow them to articulate what they already half sensed. (Significantly, Schleiermacher was to say of preaching that he always spoke to faith, not to unfaith.)[7] The idea of religion had come to be tied to an assent to outworn dogmatic propositions – propositions which Schleiermacher agreed were longer tenable – and its essence dissipated. Schleiermacher's founding of theology in human awareness was revolutionary. It could not have occurred other than against the background of the Romantic interest in the subjectivity of the human person and belief in the relatedness of the individual to the whole.

In *The Christian Faith* of 1821/22 (second edition, from which the English is translated, 1830), Schleiermacher systematically worked through this novel basis for theology. True to the philosophical concerns of the age, he commences from a consideration of the faculties (or basic capacities) of the human being. Already in the *Speeches* Schleiermacher had denied that religion belongs to the sphere of knowledge. Furthermore he is scathing about Kant's proposition that religion is to be understood as a kind of appendage to morality.[8] However, he contends, we have a third faculty or fundamental way of being in the world (analogous to Kant's aesthetic sphere), that of feeling or awareness, which for him consists in an openness or receptivity towards the whole. It is to this sphere, Schleiermacher proposes, that religion rightly belongs.

The initial paragraphs of *The Christian Faith* accordingly consist in a phenomenological description of what it is to be a self. Schleiermacher's argument proceeds as follows. In relation to everything in the world, we are aware both of a certain dependence and of a certain freedom. Schleiermacher instances our relation to our parents or our country; but also in relation to a star it must be said that we exert a minute amount of gravity on it and it on us. Our feeling on the one hand of freedom, on the other of dependence, together then constitute the dialogical relationship with the world which there must always be. Schleiermacher refers to it as the realm of the antithesis.

Schleiermacher is then set to make his crucial move. Quite apart from (it is difficult to know how best to express this: behind, before, or more fundamental than) our relation with the world (which, as we have seen, always involves reciprocity), we have, so Schleiermacher maintains, a sense of being simply dependent, a *schlechthinniges Abh ngigkeitsgef hl*. It is that sense, he says, which we should understand by God.[9] The claim here is that we sense ourselves as immediately derived; in our awareness of ourselves we are aware that there is more than what we are, to which we have an immediate connectedness. Schleiermacher expresses what he wants to say in a variety of ways. He speaks of our sense of 'Whenceness', of *Woher*. Again, if we sense ourselves as Being, as *Sein*, it is also the case that we sense ourselves as having-in-some-way-come-to-be, as *Irgendwiegewordensein*. As I have already suggested, such a sensibility is not foreign to his age. Romanticism conceived of the human as profoundly related to that which is more than the self. Whether it is unique to Schleiermacher to speak of this sense of whenceness as being absolute, and further equating God exclusively with this sense, I do not know.

There is a point here which it is crucial to grasp. If my reading is correct, in making such a move Schleiermacher is not putting forward an argument for the existence of God as though, given the nature of human self-consciousness, God were some kind of a noumenal (or mental) 'object' whose existence one could deduce. The whole way in which he goes about his project, arguing that religion does not belong to the sphere of knowledge, tells against this. Schleiermacher is well aware (after Kant) that we could have no knowledge of a such an 'object'. Rather we may say, speaking figuratively, that God is much 'closer' to us than any such 'object' could be. Our awareness of God is given together with our intuiting of ourselves.

By way of clarification of my point, let me take an example of writing which would seem to be none too clear here. Considering Schleiermacher's 'feeling of absolute dependence', Robert Roberts remarks: 'What kind of feeling is the feeling of absolute dependence? Do we have the feeling? If so, when and under what conditions? *Does it imply God? And if so, what God?*' (my italics).[10] However, Schleiermacher states that the awareness *is what we mean by God*. It is not, then, a question as to whether that awareness *implies* God, as though one were obliged to make a move from the awareness itself to (a) God. It is not that Schleiermacher believes there to be evidence, of a subjective nature, which leads us to postulate the existence of God, a God conceived of as in some way set over against the self. On the other hand, neither is it that God simply resides within the self. Rather – as Schleiermacher quite precisely says – in intuiting ourselves, we sense ourselves as immediately connected to that which is more than ourselves, and this is what he intends by the word God.

It follows that, by definition, for Schleiermacher there can be no heteronomy in the relationship to God. God is not, in the requisite sense, an 'other' to the self. Such a reading of Schleiermacher is no more than simply commensurate with what we may think to be the correct estimate both of Schleiermacher as a man and of his intellectual project, set as it is within the context of the Enlightenment. Schleiermacher wished to conceptualize God in a manner which was at once both compatible with what he thought to be the epistemological impossibility of arguing to the existence of a God, and at one with the moral imperative of human autonomy. Were Schleiermacher to be suggesting that God is other than what we are ourselves (that God is to be understood as set over against us) and at the same time stating (as he does) that the relationship is one of absolute dependence, it would constitute a heteronomy with a vengeance! Indeed it would be slavery! Such an interpretation cannot then be right.

I shall come in a moment to what I conceive to be misreadings of Schleiermacher here, but let us first complete the exposition. If my reading of his position is correct, Schleiermacher must differentiate between the relationship in which we are engaged with the world and the way in which we are related to God, which is exactly what he does. These relations are, he tells us, qualitatively different. In regard to the world, we are always placed within the realm of the antithesis: there is a reciprocity. But God, by definition, is not one with whom we interact. God, we may say, is the presupposition of our existing, the foundation of ourselves. There is, then, no sense in which the relationship to God

could be heteronomous. In relation to the world we have both freedom
and autonomy, qualified only by the fact that we always exist within the
realm of the antithesis, in a reciprocal relation with all. Now the whole
point is that God is not in the requisite sense other than ourselves such
that God could qualify our relation to the world. It may of course be
that God is more than what we are individually; but we exist in direct
relatedness to God.

That Schleiermacher conceives of the relation with God as being of a
different order from our relation with the world (and thus as being
qualitatively and not simply quantitatively distinguished – as though
God were one on whom we are absolutely, as opposed to relatively,
dependent) would seem to be further evident from the sentence with
which he immediately follows his explanation as to what he intends by
God. I quote these two sentences.

> As regards the identification of absolute dependence with 'relation to
> God' in our proposition: this is to be understood in the sense that the
> *Whence* of our receptive and active existence, as implied in this self-
> consciousness, is to be designated by the word 'God', and that this is
> for us the really original signification of that word. *In this connexion
> we have rst of all to remind ourselves that, as we have seen in the
> foregoing discussion, this Whence is not the world, in the sense of
> the totality of temporal existence, and still less is it any single part of
> the world* (my italics).[11]

Again, Schleiermacher quite explicitly says that God is not in some sense
an object for us; it is not that God is 'given'. In this he distinguishes the
relation to God from our relation to all that is within the realm of the
antithesis. He writes: 'On the other hand, any possibility of God being
in any way *given* is entirely excluded, because anything that is outwardly given must be given as an object exposed to our counter-
influence, however slight this may be.'[12]

I have mentioned that it would seem that Schleiermacher has failed to
be understood in this fundamental matter of the human relation to God.
The most famous misreading must surely be the first. In his defence
we must remark that Hegel (Schleiermacher's colleague in the Berlin
faculty) was responding to the first edition of *The Christian Faith*, in
which Schleiermacher's intention was more obscure. The fact that
Schleiermacher took the opportunity of the second edition to clarify his
thought in this regard suggests that he wished to distinguish his meaning from what he considered to be a misreading. Alluding to Schleiermacher's proposal, Hegel (who himself understood the relationship to
that concept which is God to be one of reciprocity) quipped: 'If we say
that religion rests on this feeling of dependence, then animals would

have to have religion, too, for they feel this dependence.'[13] But Schleiermacher's whole point is that God is not an 'other' in relationship to us in the way in which a dog is necessarily 'other' than its master. Only in our relation to the world, as in the case of a master and dog, do we exist within the realm of reciprocity. Hegel's remark is irrelevant.

Nor is Hegel alone in such a misreading; this despite the second edition! John Macquarrie writes as follows. 'I do not think I am being presumptuous in saying that it is very hard for people today to experience a feeling of "absolute dependence". Contemporary theology is more likely to stress the responsibility of man . . .', etc.[14] But to make such a statement, suggesting that our responsibility (in relation to the world) could be qualified by an absolute dependence on God, is to turn Schleiermacher's intent on its head. Schleiermacher's identification of God with an immediate awareness (one which is a sense of absolute dependence) places God in another sphere than our (reciprocal) relation with the world: we are left fully autonomous in relationship to the world. For Schleiermacher the scenario which Kierkegaard envisages in *Fear and Trembling* could not, by definition, arise.[15] Precisely because God is not, for Schleiermacher, such an 'object' and does not exist within the realm of reciprocity, the relationship to God cannot, by definition, be heteronomous and our responsibility towards the world remains unqualified. Again we may note that Schleiermacher remarks that religion does not belong to the sphere of ethics; so the relationship to God is not potentially heteronomous for him.

The radicality of Schleiermacher's conception would seem not to have been taken up in subsequent theology. Consider, for example, the thought of Rudolf Otto; for one might expect that he, if anyone, would be Schleiermacher's disciple here. But we find the misreading of Schleiermacher to which I have drawn attention. Otto criticizes Schleiermacher for making the distinction between the relation to the world and the relation to God 'merely that between absolute and relative dependence, and therefore a difference of degree and not of intrinsic quality'.[16] This is surely quite mistaken. Otto may well be thought to be reading Schleiermacher through the spectacles of his own position, in which God is almost a noumenal object. This is all of a piece with Otto's major concern, namely to delineate a phenomenology of our sense of awe. According to Otto, we have a 'creature feeling' before that which is Other than ourselves. Schleiermacher employs no such vocabulary.

What we may well wish to question (given that Schleiermacher speaks of our relationship to God as being immediate) is whether he rightly casts that relationship as a sense of 'absolute dependence'. It may well be that this is acceptable, even helpful, once we have grasped that the relationship with God is of a different order from our relationship with the world. For we can then read this phrase as conveying that in some way we come forth from God: God is not an other, but that which gives us our very sense of ourselves without which we should not be. How one can best express this relation to God is a question. It would seem that in any case it must be expressed as an absolute if one is to capture the sense that it is not reciprocal (and so not relative). And once we understand that God is sensed as our whole intuition of *Woher*, of whenceness, then it becomes natural to describe the relationship as one of dependence.

We have, then, opened up large issues here about which I should like to say something in passing. It may well be thought questionable whether today one could found theology on something which one discovers to be the case about the nature of human consciousness. (I have said that I myself am not arguing that theology should be grounded in an immediate intuition of God.) A damaging critique of Schleiermacher's position was not long in coming. In his *The Essence of Christianity* of 1841, Ludwig Feuerbach proposed that God is simply a human projection.[17] Living as we do after not only Feuerbach but also Freud, we must be aware, as Schleiermacher was not, of the difficulties of protecting what he had to say against an outright reductionism.

However, what I wish to discuss – albeit inadequately, given the space available – is a rather different critique which in recent years has come at an angle to the reductionism of Feuerbach or Freud. Many today are of the opinion that there can be no experience (either of God or of anything else) which is immediate, that is to say unmediated by language or concepts. As Derrida has famously put it, there is nothing outside what he calls 'the trace'. The question I wish to consider, then, is whether Schleiermacher in fact supposes that the awareness of God is prior to any expression of it and whether it is necessary to his position that he should do this. In other words, assuming the Derridean critique is correct (which we may think by no means self-evident), is a theological position such as Schleiermacher's simply unable to get off the ground? As I have indicated, I believe that Schleiermacher's position may well be more sophisticated here than some commentators have supposed.

In formulating an answer to questions arising from this quarter, one might first make the following general observations. Schleiermacher was never one who believed thought to be contextless. Indeed, he must be counted among the progenitors of the discipline of hermeneutics (the science of interpretation). What Schleiermacher attempts to do (in considering, for example, Plato's thought) is to place Plato within his social environment in order to make him comprehensible. Again,

Schleiermacher was fascinated by language and presumably had a deep sense of the inseparability of language from the thought which it conveys. Schleiermacher is interested in family and people (*Volk*) as ethical associations within which we are formed. Indeed *The Christian Faith* opens with a consideration of the church as such an ethical community. It is as though Schleiermacher is saying, 'If you want to understand what the consciousness of God is of which I am speaking, go and be among those who maintain among them Jesus' sense of the Father.' This is no abstract thinker.

But to come to the particular point at issue. It is not that Schleiermacher believes that that higher awareness which is a God-awareness exists in *independence* from the relationship to the world. (It is different *in kind*, as I have discussed.) Were he to hold that consciousness of God is *independent* of the relationship which we have with the world, that would indeed constitute an attempt to make God-consciousness inviolable, the easy target of those who believe that there can be nothing beyond the trace of language and our sensible awareness. But Schleiermacher specifically says that the consciousness of God *always arises in conjunction with a particular determination of our sensibly determined self-consciousness* (that is to say, our consciousness formed within the realm of the antithesis). He writes: 'For it is as a person determined for this moment in a particular manner within the realm of the antithesis that [the person] is conscious of his absolute dependence.'[18] Is this not Schleiermacher's way of saying – had he been given the language – that 'the trace' permeates all?

Again in this regard we should note the following fascinating statement:

> Everything inward becomes, at a certain point of its strength or maturity, an outward too, and, as such, perceptible to others. Thus feeling, as a self-contained determination of the mind . . . will, even *qua* feeling . . . not exist exclusively for itself, but becomes an outward . . . by means of facial expression, gesture, tones, and (indirectly) words; and so becomes to other people a revelation of the inward.[19]

The statement is equivocal. Is Schleiermacher necessarily suggesting that there is that which is inward, which only becomes outward 'at a certain point'? Is he tied to saying this? Were he simply to say (as he was not challenged to say) that there is no inward which does not have an outward expression, then a critique from a Derridean perspective would fall. Clearly Schleiermacher is not speaking of what Derrida charged Husserl with having: a solitary mental life. I do not consider, then, that Schleiermacher is a sitting duck for those who have proclaimed in recent years that there can be no such thing as religious experience, unpolluted by concepts, which could form an epistemological starting point for theology. This must be maintained despite the fact that Schleiermacher is often held to be the fount of such thinking.[20]

Before at least temporarily departing from Schleiermacher, I must revert to the consideration (in the first chapter of this book)[21] of whether, given his epistemological starting point, Schleiermacher has any legitimate way of constructing what is a Christian (as opposed to simply a theistic) position. What I previously questioned was that Schleiermacher could move from the presupposition of universal religious experience to the particularity of Christianity. But there is something else to be considered. Given that Christianity is (one would have thought by definition) a religion of revelation (in that it proclaims a particularity in Christ), it would seem to be a corollary that Christians must in some way speak of God as differentiated from and placed in apposition to the self (though language is inadequate here). Let Barth have his say. 'We cannot reckon, in Schleiermacher, with an ultimate opposition between God and man, between Christ and the Christian . . . How he failed to notice that his result challenged the decisive premise of all Christian theology . . . presents us with a mystery . . .'.[22] Christianity does not, perhaps, necessarily entail an 'opposition' in quite the Barthian sense: I am not at this juncture intending to castigate Schleiermacher for having a christology in which Christ is simply a human possessed of a perfect God-consciousness (that raises other problems). But I must agree with Barth that it is a 'decisive premise' of Christianity that God is other than the self. This follows necessarily from the fact that Christianity is a religion which conforms to Kierkegaard's truth type 'B' (which entails revelation) and not his 'A' (where all that is, is implicit in the world or given with the self).[23] That Schleiermacher himself ardently desired to be a Christian, that as a theologian in his day and age nothing else would have been conceivable to him, is not of course in question.

I turn then, secondly, to a consideration of the basis upon which I myself wish to be theistic. In looking to evidence of a more experiential and empirical nature than anything that Schleiermacher ever adduces, I must move from what has been a German to what has been an Anglo-Saxon tradition in the study of religion. It was F. D. Maurice who, in the nineteenth century, wrote:

My feeling about the relation between English thought and German is generally this: that we must always be, to a considerable extent, unintelligible to each other, because we start from exactly opposite points; we, naturally, from that which is above us and speaks to us;

they, naturally, from that which is within them and which seeks for some object above itself.[24]

The comment is observant. Since Maurice's day, German thought has given rise to phenomenology and existentialism. In relation to our present concern (the study of human religious experience) it is surely no chance that it was the Anglo-Saxon tradition which produced William James.[25] While Schleiermacher commences from the consideration of human faculties, James collects 'evidence' in the external world. Indeed the Oxford Religious Experience Research Unit's project, which I shall shortly consider, may be thought peculiarly English.

In not giving credence to (or at least not mentioning) the effects which I shall wish to consider, Schleiermacher was very much a child of his age. It was not long since educated people had escaped the idea that God was a kind of agent who could poke his finger in the pie at will. Even Sir Isaac Newton, upon discovering that the planets did not follow the orbits which he had calculated, proclaimed this to be evidence for God, who from time to time put them back on course. (Subsequently Neptune was discovered, and the previous 'discrepancy' became explicable.) Living as he did at the turn from the eighteenth to the nineteenth century, Schleiermacher intended to be a modern man, founding a theology which was not incommensurate with what human beings had discovered to be the laws of nature. Indeed, it is in having attempted this that the greatness of his achievement lies. Schleiermacher's God is not a God of the gaps. Denying that there could be interventions, Schleiermacher (in the age of Romanticism) translates the term miracle to mean no more than the order and beauty of the world. 'Miracle,' he writes, 'is simply the religious name for event . . . To me all is miracle.'[26]

Of course there is nothing in this to which I could want to take exception. I have made it abundantly clear that I consider it an *a priori* that theology can have no quarrel with the fact that nature and history form a causal nexus (at least at the macro-level at which we live). There can be no 'interventions', such as a resurrection or a virgin birth would represent. On the other hand, many people hold the conviction that there is more to reality than meets the eye; that there is what I have called another 'dimension'. It may well be that from the eighteenth century until today 'Enlightenment intellectuals' (if one needs a cover term) have been insufficiently willing to grant that there could be that for which we are unable to account. But it is surely the case that many ordinary people (and some intellectuals!) have never doubted that there was a spiritual reality that involved effects which they could not explain. (It would be fascinating to know whether women in particular have retained among themselves a sense for such a reality; a matter which I shall consider further.) To believe this, I must emphasize, in no way contradicts what was discovered in the Enlightenment about the regularity of nature. It is simply to maintain that what is the case (and has been the case always and everywhere) is more extensive than has commonly been recognized.

We do, then, have criteria for judging what kind of putative accounts of 'religious experience' we should consider and what we should categorically deny. Thus as I have said,[27] according to our present knowledge, it is not possible to turn water into wine: wine has carbon atoms and water does not, and such atoms cannot appear from nowhere. Or, to rephrase this, we may say that we know that one man cannot, on one occasion, have turned water into wine. If on the other hand we came to change our minds and to think it possible to effect such a change, it would no longer be counted a miracle that a man had done so in the past and we should expect that others could also do this. Again, we know that it is not possible to walk on water, for the specific gravity of a human being is greater than that of water. But there are other phenomena (as I shall consider) which appear to happen today and which in this sense do not break a law of nature. Moreover there is evidence that these things also took place in the first century. This is, of course, what we should expect to find if nature (whatever it is like) remains the same.

Yet I think that there is also this to be said. Though of course if something is possible it must always be possible, it may be that knowledge or awareness of one or another aspect of reality comes to the fore in certain ages, or is retained within certain groups. To take an example. In the Boston familiar to William James it seems that there were all sorts of groups which knew of the possibility of spiritual healing; the context which gave rise, in more permanent form, to Christian Science.[28] We know of course from the 'New' Testament that there seems to have been healing in the first century and spiritual healing is much in evidence today. Yet there have been times when, or communities (even religious communities) where, the awareness of this possibility has apparently been lost.

Doubtless there are some instances in which it is almost impossible to know what may be possible and what is not. I take a famous example (readers who are not British or who are too young to remember the awe with which this was still regarded in the 1950s must make a leap of imagination here). In 1940 a flotilla of little boats plied back and forth across the English Channel, rescuing the British army from Dunkirk for another day. The Channel, a stretch of water frequently difficult to navigate, stayed uncommonly calm for just long enough. A whole nation was praying. What shall we say? It is an example of a purported miraculous happening which, it is not surprising to find, has been subject to ridicule in discussions of miracles in philosophy of religion! (I shall mention such a discussion later.) Personally I believe that we must remain agnostic in the case of Dunkirk. For water to remain calm is not to break the laws of nature (unlike walking on it or changing it into wine!). Meanwhile we simply do not know how mind and matter may interact (a whole nation was praying).[29]

I come next to an attempt to enumerate the kinds of things that I, at least, am persuaded are possible. It is important to say that I do not think that one converts other people to such an outlook by reciting the kind of 'evidence' which I shall adduce. On the other hand, it is probably important in coming to hold such a conviction that one belongs to a sub-group within society which credits such possibilities. I grew up in a family in which my mother had no doubt as to the power of prayer. And many of my friends (most of whom are women and who, while not necessarily being Christian, have about them a pronounced spirituality) agree with me in crediting what kinds of things are possible. Indeed, they take it for granted that this is how the world is. I wonder whether there is not a good reason why these things tend to be known (and more talked about) to a greater extent within the world of women than in the world of academic theology. On the whole, women enjoy closer personal relations than men and many of these 'phenomena' involve relations between persons. Certainly I have gained a sense for these things at every stage of my life from the community of women.

I have a clear memory of the occasion on which I came to the conclusion that I had to stand by the conviction that there was more to reality than meets the eye. It was an important moment in my life, leading to my giving up the pursuit of a career as a historian and turning to theology. Undertaking as I was a doctoral thesis on the response in Britain to the church conflict in the Third Reich, I went to visit Dr Martin Niemöller. Until his imprisonment Niemöller had been the outstanding spokesman for the Confessing Church. He was internationally known and revered. Acquitted – astonishingly, in the circumstances of the Third Reich – by the German court which tried him, instead of being set free, he was immediately detained again as Hitler's first 'personal prisoner'. Seven years later, on liberating the concentration camp in which he was confined, American soldiers discovered – Martin Niemöller! When I asked him how he, who – if anyone – had publicly represented an alternative Germany, had survived, Niemöller simply replied that all over the world people had been praying for him. And as I walked back to the station in Wiesbaden I realized that I had to credit such an explanation as causal. But such 'causation' is not something which the (secular) historian's net is able to catch.

I turn now to my attempt to enumerate the kinds of things which I think to be the case and which lead me to say that there is that dimension to reality which we call God. First, something that I have already mentioned. There is every evidence that there is a power abroad which allows healing, not only mental but also (remarkably) physical healing. That this is the case seems to have become much more widely acknowledged, at least in Britain during my life-time. Doctors are open to the idea; there is a National Federaton of Spiritual Healers; and many groups and churches practise spiritual healing. Such awareness is in no way necessarily connected with 'religion' as religion is understood in our society. People I have known who count themselves healers have been of very various persuasions. (What they seem to me to have in common is that they are profoundly loving human beings who care deeply about the welfare of others.) I myself have experienced healing which I can in no way deny.

Secondly, it seems that there is available what we may call intuition or clairvoyance. It may be significant that we lack appropriate vocabulary: 'intuition' seems to connote something private and personal (whereas what I wish to draw attention is relational), while 'clairvoyance' sounds mystical, if not magical. Let me illustrate this phenomenon by drawing on an example reported to the Oxford Religious Experience Research Unit.

I was a young married woman with a six month old baby daughter. My husband and I got an evening off to see a film at K— about six miles away. One of the hotel staff had volunteered to baby sit and we set off . . . We had not been long seated in the cinema when a terrible uneasiness overcame me. I could distinctly smell burning. I fidgeted a lot and my husband asked what was the matter. I told him I could smell burning. He said I'd probably dropped a bit of my cigarette. I stooped and had a look on the carpet but no sign of any glow. The smell persisted and eventually I told my husband I was leaving. He followed me reluctantly, muttering something derogatory about women.

As we boarded the bus for home I prayed for it to go faster; at each stop I almost died. At last we were sprinting down the lane leading to the cottage. The smell of burning was now very definite to me though my husband could not smell a thing. We reached the door which I literally burst in. As I did so the dense smoke poured out and a chair by the fire burst into flames. I rushed through to the bedroom and got the baby out while my husband dragged out the unconscious girl. She had fallen asleep in the armchair and dropped her lighted cigarette into the chair which had smouldered for hours.[30] It would be particularly interesting to know in this regard whether the bond (if we may call it that) between a mother and her child is particularly strong.

In relation to what we may call intuition or clairvoyance there are what we may call 'intermediate' cases. (This is something I shall discuss further below.) It may well be that 'knowledge' gained at some level through our senses works in conjunction with information gained more intuitively. My mother once put out a hand to stop a swing which was built into the kitchen door, on which as a small child I was swinging, just as the rope broke. Again, there was an occasion on which she knew by telepathy (if that is what we should call it) that I had been taken violently ill on returning to the United States. But then she may have sensed that I was deeply agitated over whether I should give up my life at Harvard and accept the position which I had been offered in Britain. I supposed (rightly, it would appear) that the decision would determine which side of the Atlantic I should spend my life.

It would seem that people who live with this kind of openness to what is the case can know all manner of things. They may be attuned to comparatively trivial information which is yet significant in the circumstances; as for example what platform number they need if they are not to miss a crucial connection at a railway station on the Continent. I have been thinking of someone who, never having done so before, then telephones me from California. Is it perhaps that these things are more likely to happen when the situation is an emergency or someone needs help? I know of one case when during the war a woman knew to move her bed to the other side of the hall in which she was sleeping. The bomb that fell that night forced off the front door so that it landed where the bed had been. It appears that if we are quiet we can be open in ways that we simply do not begin to comprehend to knowledge otherwise unavailable to us.

So, thirdly, it would appear that if people go forward in trust (or faith), unexpected 'coincidences' occur. Needs will be provided for or a way forward will open up. I find myself wanting to illustrate this by a lovely story I heard some years ago. Unfortunately I failed to keep any reference. The story delighted me, but I did not consider it to be out of character with what I had already concluded was possible. A certain tribe in Zaire had come to hear of the World Day of Prayer – I think it must have been at the time when that day was the Women's World Day of Prayer – and decided to send a delegate. The woman concerned (never, one assumes, having previously been outside Africa) arrived in New York and got into a cab. Speaking French and failing to be understood, she lapsed into her native dialect. The cab driver had come from that part of Africa a few years previously! He took her to an address she had; a neighbour had the key; they telephoned the organizers of the event; and to the considerable astonishment of the other participants she arrived at the proceedings (in upstate New York)! One could cite other examples. Again, we may often feel that cases are what I have called 'intermediate': help has come in a way which, although not impossible, was highly improbable.

It will be useful to those who are unfamiliar with it for me to say something at this stage about the work of the Oxford Religious Experience Research Unit. The importance of the study of religious experience (as, notably, it has been pursued by that body) is that it allows one to put one's own experience in a wider context through the recognition that many other people witness similar things. I believe that the work of the Unit is a fund of raw material for the theologian. It is particularly useful that from the start it has collected evidence of the type which I have mentioned, rather than recording what may be counted bizarre happenings which lie (as I think) outside the bounds of possibility and are rightly to be discounted. William James's task was other. He set out to undertake a study of what people believed had happened to them; and – as he commented in inimitable words – he sought his evidence 'among the extravagances of the subject'.[31] By contrast, an early appeal that material should be sent to Professor Alister Hardy, the founder of the Oxford Unit, published in *The Observer* in 1970, read: 'Professor Hardy . . . is not at present studying the more ecstatic or mystical states, but more general feelings.'[32]

The basic question which the Unit has formulated for use in the surveys it conducts reflects this open-endedness: 'Have you ever been aware of or influenced by a presence or power, whether you call it God or not, which is different from your everyday self?'[33] What is surely remarkable is that (in supposedly secular modern Britain, in which around 12% of the population attend a place of worship on a Sunday) an average of 31% of men and 41% of women respond to this question in the affirmative.[34] (And I have often wondered what I should reply if, coming out of the supermarket, I were to be accosted by someone with a clip board who wanted to know . . .!) Moreover the volume and quality of the material which people have sent in to the Unit is surely impressive. People will tell of an experience which they had half a century ago and which has shaped the course of their life. The published version of extracts from the letters makes profoundly moving reading, and the evidence cited would seem to be difficult simply to dismiss.[35]

We should return to the question of the accreditation of evidence. Of course one should be wary. James remarks quite candidly that if people have a purported 'religious experience', that experience will tend to conform to the type they would expect to have (were they to have an experience), given the sub-group to which they belong. Thus nineteenth-century French peasants witness appearances of the Virgin; Christian Scientists know of healing; while charismatic groups speak with tongues. I believe one's response should be a considered one. One needs to rule out what self-evidently (one may think) is not the case. Thus while people could perhaps be vividly aware of someone who had recently died, I would take it for granted that a woman who lived in ancient Palestine does not appear in flesh-and-blood guise to a group of peasants. On the other hand it may well be that, as I have said, certain possibilities are intrinsic to human beings (as for example healing), 'knowledge' of which comes to the fore at certain times and is held within certain sub-groups. Indeed, may it not be that the expectation that such things are possible, that one has access to insight, or that a healer has power, is prerequisite to their coming to be?

I have said that it must surely be the case that whatever is possible must be at least potentially possible at all times and places. In this respect it is interesting that the evidence that has come to us from first-century Palestine suggests that the same kinds of things were known then as occur today (which is exactly what one would expect to find). Thus there would seem to be strong evidence (I should want to say overwhelming evidence, if one looks at it with unbiassed eyes) that Jesus had about him a power for healing. Indeed, we hear that not only he but those around him could heal,[36] suggesting that – as I have said – people absorb such a capacity from one another, so that the awareness of what powers there are comes to the fore in a particular sub-group. It is even the case that we have no record of his having healed broken bones, something which does not occur today either. Again, those who had known Jesus remembered him to have had the capacity for clairvoyance or intuition. Whether or not he 'saw' Nathanael under the fig-tree, or 'knew' that a colt was tied up ready for him to make his symbolic entry into Jerusalem, exactly as was recited later, is immaterial. Again, it is clear that Jesus lived with a basic trust that vital needs would be provided for and taught others to do the same; such a faith would seem to have been fundamental to his preaching.

In conclusion, I should like to draw attention to the fact that throughout this discussion I could make no reference to the tomes of academic theology. (How that would have surprised me when I deserted the study of secular history for that discipline which I supposed would take account of the way in which I had concluded things must be!) I dare not surmise what relation this may have to the fact that theology has been undertaken by men! But I am clear that the reason why many women whom I know count themselves theists and not atheists is the evidence that, if one lives in a certain way, patterns emerge like those that I have described. Of course I know men who would think a description of religious experience such as that which I have given was true to their experience. (Interestingly, I think that they would explain it in orthodox Christian terms, whereas the women friends of whom I can think would not.) Perhaps there is a distinction between what at least some men credit and the public discipline of theology? If so, then so much the worse for theology! One woman known to me, a scientist of some distinction, with whom I discussed the content of this chapter, telling me that she herself credited all sorts of things which parallel the examples which I have given, commented that, were she to admit to this, it would probably ruin her career! Perhaps it will mine!

That brings us to theology. It is significant that neither James nor Hardy, in the empirical Anglo-Saxon tradition, are prepared to make the move from the phenomena on which they report to the question of what it implies. They are cynical about theology as we have known it. James speaks scathingly of 'scholastic theism';[37] while Hardy, writing an introduction for a colleague's book on the religious experience of children, comments, 'What is important to stress in schools today is that the discussion of religious feelings – I use these words rather than "religion" – is no longer to be dominated by conventional ideas of what constitutes religion, or by theological orthodoxies of one kind or another . . .'[38] The theological question which we must ask is about the step that they fail to take. What does the kind of evidence of which we have been speaking suggest is the case? In other words, theology is a secondary discipline. It does not come to us fully-fledged, as it were out of the blue. Theology must be held accountable to the evidence. At the same time, something cannot be held to be the case which is incompatible with what we now know scientifically to be the nature of the world.

We undertake theology, then, because we come to the conviction that there is another dimension to reality. The theological question is the question as to what this implies. Of course it by no means follows from the kind of evidence to which I have drawn attention that there is a kind of being who has agency, and who brings such eventualities about. Indeed the continued use of the word 'God' may well be misleading if that word is so tied to the belief in such a being that it cannot come to have other connotations. It may be fully explicable that, given that persons are themselves agents, God should have been conceptualized agentially. But it should be noted that even within the Christian tradition this is not the only way in which God has been understood. The theological move from the evidence to what it may be thought to imply will always involve a leap. Nevertheless, the idea of God as an anthropomorphic agent would in fact seem to be rather an unlikely explanation.

It is important here to make clear what I am not saying. The under-standing of God which I am advocating is not a 'God of the gaps'. It is not that I am saying that God is the explanation for the phenomena I have mentioned. Of course it may well be that there is some unitary dimension of all that is which explains the various phenomena of which I have spoken (and perhaps others) which we should name God. But were these things to be explained (suppose, for example, we were to discover how extra-sensory perception works), I should simply say that we had gained a better grasp of that dimension of reality which hitherto we have called God. I think we do recognize this dimension of reality as being loving or somehow a power for good. That that is the case is a kind of faith statement; a matter to which I shall come later. Moreover, I am in no way suggesting that matter is God and I am not a pantheist. What the connection is between mind and matter, whether for example through quantum physics in time we shall arrive at a better understanding of how our mind and body are inter-connected, is a fascinating question. But I am not suggesting that matter is God: it would seem that God is somehow mental, or mind, or spirit. Nor, finally, have I said that God is all that is. Rather, quite pre-cisely, I have suggested that God is a dimension of the totality that is.

What I believe we need to attempt to conceptualize is this. How is it that we should think of the self in relation to that which lies beyond the self? To put this another way and to draw out its complexity: how can we understand there to be that on which we draw, which is evidently greater than ourselves, while we yet remain centred selves? For one would not want to think of the self as 'swamped' by God, nor does that seem to be the case. Nevertheless, we do perhaps need to find ways of speaking of knowing ourselves as 'prompted' by what is more than we are. The supremely difficult question to answer is whether what we name God has agency, or whether all agency lies with ourselves. Perhaps if we come to think differently about the relatedness of the self to that which lies beyond the self, we shall gain greater purchase on this question. It may not be an either/or situation. Rather, as we understand our relatedness to that which is more than what we are, we shall be better able to conceive how we are in tune with a greater purposiveness, so that the question seems to dissolve. Indeed it then becomes a false question to ask whether what I have called 'intermediate' cases are attributable to us or to God, or whether they are somehow 'miraculous': God, we and the world are inter-related.

We need, then, to find ways of conceptualizing that 'membrane' which lies between the self, as we ordinarily think of it, and that which lies beyond the self but to which it is immediately connected. Again, what we need to understand is the process of 'osmosis' between the self and that which is more. We do not want to suggest a self which lacks integrity or which lacks its own agency. Nor, on the other hand, do we want to suggest a self which is simply set in apposition to that which is other than the self. It is in thinking about these matters that I turn to Schleiermacher. For of all theologians of whom I am aware, it is he who is singularly interested in precisely these questions. Indeed it is interesting to note that theological methodology as I have described it is very close to Schleiermacher's procedure. For Schleiermacher, too, theology is a secondary discipline, in his case predicated upon the immediate awareness of absolute dependence.[39] Again, as I have suggested, it was that awareness itself which he intended by God; he did not wish to make a subsequent move and, given the evidence, postulate the existence of 'a God'. How then does Schleiermacher conceptualize the relation of the self to that which lies beyond it?

In the case of the world, Schleiermacher, as we have said, thinks that there is always a reciprocity. I believe that we have a fine sense of Schleiermacher as a man in this regard. He was evidently a person who could both listen and dynamically hold forth. One who had known him wrote after his death:

> While he was engrossed in the most lively conversation, nothing escaped him. He saw everything that was going on about him on all sides; he heard everything, even the softest conversation of others . . . Even in this moment, it often seems to me as if he were there, nearby me, as if he were about to open his firmly closed lips in earnest converse.[40]

It is an engaging picture, at one with his theoretical beliefs.

Consider, further, in respect of Schleiermacher's interest in the crossing of that membrane which surrounds the self, his interest in the nature of human faculties. He sets up a contrast between a remaining-in-self (an *insichbleiben*) and a passing beyond oneself (literally an out-of-oneself-stepping-forth, an *aussichheraustreten*). Schleiermacher thinks that knowing involves both of these. Ethical action clearly involves a stepping beyond oneself. Religion – interestingly, in view of our concern – consists in a remaining in self. In other words, religion is essentially a receptivity. (Of course it may, indeed must, lead in turn to moral action.) The discussion to which I am referring is set out propositionally in *The Christian Faith*.[41] But we should note that in the *Speeches*, too, Schleiermacher comments that religion is 'a surrender, a submission to be moved by the Whole'.[42] And again in memorable words he tells us: 'Seers of the Infinite have ever been quiet souls.'[43]

How then does Schleiermacher conceive of the self's relatedness to that which is more than the self, which is God? Here words must necessarily fail us. Nevertheless, I think one can say that Schleiermacher avoids two extremes, leaving our understanding to lie between them. Thus as I read him, on the one hand Schleiermacher rules out any idea of an atomized (or monadic) self which can be a self in and of itself. The self cannot fully be itself apart from God. As Richard R. Niebuhr well says: 'The fundamental thing that Schleiermacher has to say is [that] . . . religion is an intrinsic element in the self-consciousness of the fully developed man.'[44] For Schleiermacher the self would seem to open out on to that other dimension which is God. The self is not itself except as it must always lead beyond itself. In this sense (and reverting to our earlier discussion as to whether Schleiermacher must fall foul of a Derridean critique), it must be said that Schleiermacher's self in no way attempts to enjoy what Derrida would name 'full presence'. As we observe ourselves, Schleiermacher finds, we have a sense of being (we know ourselves as a *Sein*), but we also have a sense of having in some way come to be (of an *Irgendwiegewordensein*). Again, he tells us that we sense ourselves as having placed ourselves (a sense of *Sichselbstsetzen*), but equally as not having placed ourselves (a sense of *Sichselbstsnichtsogesetzthaben)* which carries the implication that we have been 'placed', or posited, by another.[45]

Yet if we stand in immediate relation to that which is more than we are, it is also the case that our self is determinate, free in relation to the world. This is the other half of the quotations which I have just given: we have a sense of being (of *Sein*) and of having set or placed ourselves. I have already remarked that Schleiermacher was very much a man of the Enlightenment. Furthermore, the only stance which is commensurate with his ethics is that Schleiermacher should see himself as an autonomous agent, standing in a reciprocal relation with the world. As we have said, the relationship with God could never (by definition) qualify his relationship with the world. God is not one towards whom our relation is heteronomous; God is not one who could limit our freedom in the world. In relationship to the world Schleiermacher knows himself as a free agent (within what must always be a reciprocal relation). Thus Schleiermacher knows the self both as determinate (as centred) and yet also as posited (as related). Nor do these two stand in tension, for they relate respectively to the relation to the world and to God. Again we come back to where we started. God is not some kind of an object, not even a 'noumenal object', which could be said to be placed in apposition to myself. It is precisely this feature of Schleiermacher's thought which makes it so difficult to reconcile with Christianity; for Christianity, as a religion of revelation, must always conceive of God as other than the self.

Now it will not have escaped the observant reader that the way in which I characterize Schleiermacher's conception of the self has much in common with how I characterized the feminist ideal in Chapter III. The self both has a centredness in itself and an intrinsic relationality. There is, of course, a major difference. In Schleiermacher's case the leading on to that which is more than itself consists in an openness to God, whereas in my discussion of feminist thought I was speaking of the relationality between persons. Whether one could ever speak of being immediately in relation to another person in the way in which one may speak of being immediately in relation to God would seem to be doubtful. Other persons must always remain in some sense 'other' to ourselves. Nevertheless if we wish to speak of an immediate presence to another through what we call intuition, and indeed conceive of God as that through which we can be present to another in such a way, the distinction between the nature of the relation to God and to another person becomes blurred. Whether feminist thought will in time enrich our ways of thinking about the relational nature of the self in a way which is pertinent for theology must be an interesting question.

Finally in this section, I wish to advocate further the understanding of God which I am advancing by showing how it solves what have been major conundrums in Western theology. I shall consider what is commonly called 'the question of miracles' and the issue of 'theodicy'. (By theodicy is meant the question of the goodness of God – how God can be justified – given the extent of suffering.) Here I must immediately clarify my position in order to avoid misunderstanding. In this chapter I have proceeded in a 'positive' manner, arguing from the belief that there is evidence of another dimension of reality to what consequently our conception of God should be. But it is not that the conception of God which I have advocated conveniently provides a solution to conundrums in theology (although this is the case). Rather, 'negatively', I should have to argue that these conundrums (as I have called them) are so pressing that, on no other count, we must recast our conception of God. That is to say, the lack of any solution within the past paradigm must lead us to think again as to what God is. If we fail to do this, the gap between what we consider moral and our sense of God as good may well be unbridgeable. I am, then, in this chapter wishing to advance two criteria in accordance with which we must fashion our conception of God: one epistemological, the other ethical. First, our conception of God needs to accord with the reasons why we are driven to speak of God in the first place (and must not be incompatible with what we know about the nature of the world). Secondly, the conception of God must be morally tenable.

I hope thus to show that with the conception of God which I am advocating what have been major conundrums within Western theology fall away. First I turn to the 'question of miracles'. In considering so-called miracles it is well for me to narrate an incident which brought home to me how differently I conceive of God from those of a conventionally Christian outlook. The incident has remained with me as it came to be considered theologically. I was driving to the nearest station, some miles from St Andrews, to catch the last train south to Birmingham that night (a journey of some seven hours). I was to give a day school the following day. Suddenly and inexplicably my engine faltered. Realizing that I should not reach the station, I stopped in a lay-by near a shop, a cluster of houses and a hotel, but otherwise out in the country. I cried out to God; trying then to concentrate on God, remaining wholly open and aware. I supposed that perhaps a hundred people would be converging on Birmingham the following day expecting me to be there. During the next few minutes I discovered that the shop's telephone was out of order (only that day!), that apparently no one could be roused in the hotel, and knocking helplessly on doors I was reaching the point where the houses end and the open countryside begins. At that moment a taxi came at snail's pace down the uneven farm track which joins the main road at that point. I ran to it, the driver telephoned for another cab – and I made the day school, at which I then recited these events!

What has remained with me was that there seemed to be two, and only two, alternatives open to my audience: either God 'sends taxis' or it was 'just chance'. Now I do not think in terms of either of these options and that is what I want to explore. It needs to be recognized that the options conceivable to the audience (or at least suggested by those who were vocal) are bizarre. If God 'sends taxis', then we must ask, 'Why does "he" not always do so?' There are cases of rather more consequence than the instance I have related! We have a stunning theodicy problem. But if, on the other hand, all such happenings are 'just chance', then what can it mean to be a religious person who believes that God is actively present in the world? We are caught between a Scylla and Charybdis, as indeed much theology has been. By contrast, I believe that if there is a way out of a situation (and it may be that there is none), then by being open that solution will be found. That is to say (in the case that I am citing), if a friend was about to drive along the road/ a bus was due/ there was someone who could help me, then I should have been likely to be at the right place or to speak to the right person to find that solution (as indeed I was).

What I am suggesting is that that which we call God is in some profound way connected to the rest of reality. One can then be open to God, or, to put it another way, God can be drawn into being in the situation. Any solution which comes about must of course necessarily be within the bounds of possibility. (No taxi dropped from heaven.) And there may well be no way through. To what extent we can bring eventualities about, as opposed to simply being open to what is already there, is a big question. Equally, to what extent God is an agent in such a situation, bringing about what would not otherwise be the case, would seem to be unanswerable. But I do clearly believe that one can be 'in tune' with a wider arena than one's self. It is a fact that we can draw on such a power, or be open to an insight, that I name our connectedness to God. To my mind the most observant comment on the situation was made by my mother, to whom, as I drove her along the same stretch of road a few weeks later, I recited what had happened. She simply said, 'Well done.' Yes, indeed, we should think in terms of our being able to actualize the potentialities which are ours to exercise. But to think in such a way must be ultimately heretical!

Let me now compare my interpretation of this example with the standard treatment of the 'question of miracles'. I take by way of example J. L. Mackie's discussion of the case of Dunkirk, a case to which I have already alluded.[46] Mackie supposes (as also does, for example, Antony Flew in debating the possibility of a resurrection)[47] that if one is to speak of a miracle, there has first be a well-defined law of nature which the purported miracle could then be said to break. As Mackie says, 'literal' (as opposed to 'metaphorical') miracles would be 'genuine supernatural interventions into the natural order'. Referring to Dunkirk, he then concludes: 'even if we accepted theism, and could plausibly assume that a benevolent deity would have favoured the British rather than the Germans in 1940', the explanation of miracle would be improbable.[48]

Now personally (although I am a theist), I cannot conceive of a benevolent deity sitting up there favouring the British rather than the Germans! The mind boggles. Furthermore, I take it for granted that the laws of nature (the causal nexus) cannot be broken. But as I have said, for the sea to remain calm is not to break a law of nature. Moreover the question as to how mind and matter interconnect and whether prayer may not be powerful in such a situation is something we have not begun to grasp and perhaps never shall. Any narrow 'Enlightenment' view of what is the case may well need to be amplified. A recognition that the mind/matter divide in terms of which we have previously conceived of the world is too simplistic would seem to be a likely candidate for a front on which we need to advance in our understanding. Thus whether the people of the allied nations were aided in their winning of the war through being in tune with what was ethically right and through constant prayer may well be an issue which is far from settled. But whatever it is that is possible must always and at all times be at least potentially possible. In that sense there are no miracles. Nor are there interventions or gross breaks in the causal nexus which are not allowed for by randomness at a sub-atomic level.

I turn secondly to the issue of theodicy. Once more, in the terms in which it has been cast, predicated upon the existing conception of God, it is incapable of solution. If God is an agent conceived of anthropomorphically, one who could intervene if 'he' would, then why doesn't 'he'? To such a question there can be no answer. The wrestling with the theodicy issue which has taken place within Judaism after the Holocaust is significant here, given the conception of God in the Jewish tradition.[49] Some, attempting to rescue the notion of such a God, are baffled, while others find themselves forced to abandon such a conception. It is an interesting question whether the Western understanding of God has in any way evolved from anthropomorphism in the modern world, so that theodicy issues become less pressing. The intellectuals of Europe might well ridicule a God who could be called in question by the 1755 Lisbon earthquake, but it is clear that most people (in an age supposed to be the height of deism!) were profoundly shaken. Not far from where I write, the Tay bridge disaster of 1879, in which carriages carrying people returning from church on a Sunday evening fell into the water, caused similar questioning. Langdon Gilkey comments: 'Insofar as all twentieth-century theology shares this dual respect for the causal nexus and for human freedom, it has not been easy for any theology to understand how God *can* be involved in natural and social process.'[50] Has the theodicy issue then eased for believers? If Gilkey is right, only – it would seem – at the cost of making God more distant.

By contrast, the way in which I am conceptualizing that which is God does not allow the theodicy issue, at least in its classical form, to arise. As I have already indicated, that this is the case is not a failure to take suffering seriously. Rather is it that were God to be an anthropomorphic agent who could intervene, the questions raised would be so horrendous that one would have to abandon such a conception of God. Meanwhile, a feminist awareness must give theodicy an added twist. For now the question is not simply why God does not intervene, but how it can be that a supposedly revealed religion has been so detrimental (to say the least) to half the human race. Nor does the 'answer' given to Job constitute a solution. It may well be that a sense for the wonder of the world helps to restore our belief that there is goodness, placing our suffering in a wider context. But simply to give way before God's majesty does not solve the question as to how we can possibly conceive of God. If God continues to be conceptualized as an anthropomorphic agent, 'he' at best remains enigmatic, blowing both hot and cold.

What we must do is to recast our understanding of God, whereupon the question raised by suffering will look different. God is no anthropomorphic agent. The question to be asked in relation to suffering caused by humans is then: 'How can it be that human beings descend to such evil?' Or, if we wish to put this in theistic terms, 'How could they so far desert their God-given nature?' Thus the way in which I am recasting the understanding of God leads to an emphasis on human responsibility. It may well be that there is a question to be asked (for example in relation to the Third Reich) as to whether a force for evil greater any individual may not overtake a nation. But this question must never be phrased in such a way that it appears to take responsibility away from each and every person. The issue becomes one of how humans may be in touch with their deepest selves (if you will, with that which is God in them) so that, as the Quakers have it, the good may be raised up in them and the evil overcome. The classical conception of God credits humans with autonomy and responsibility only at the expense of divorcing God from the human scene. By contrast, the way in which I am conceiving of God suggests that God is involved in the process of persons coming to themselves.

It may be of interest here that Schleiermacher has sometimes been charged with lacking an adequate notion of sin and having an overly optimistic view of human beings. Could it not be that, given his conception of God, the theodicy issue did not arise for him in the form which it must take for one whose God is transcendent and anthropomorphic? Schleiermacher's life was not without eventualities, nor free of pain. As a young man, after a failed love affair with a married woman, he had to leave Berlin and his circle of friends; in his middle age, Napoleon having won the battle of Jena, the theology faculty in which he worked was closed down; and as an older man he lost his only and much loved son. For Schleiermacher religion did not revolve around 'God entering into pain', a 'theology of the cross' of the kind that is fashionable today, as though it were the only adequate answer to the theodicy question. Rather, religion is that which lifts us above the realm of strife and pain in which otherwise we are engaged. To quote him as a young man: 'They are bad spirits and not good that take possession of man, and drive him. [Note the sense of autonomy.] The legions of angels with which the Father provided His Son, exercised no power over Him. They had no cause to help Him in any doing or forbearing [viz. religion is to be distinguished from ethics], *but they poured serenity and calm into a soul exhausted with doing and thinking.*'[51] May it not be that this is the role which a religious sensibility should play?

However, given what I am suggesting, might not an interlocutor recast the theodicy question thus? If God is, as you will have it, a 'dimension' of the whole, why is this not the best of all possible worlds? (I take it that my interlocutor will not ask why God did not create the best of all possible worlds; it will have been understood that God is not, as I think, a kind of agent, so that God creates something other than God's self.) Though the question might appear to be pertinent, it implies a misunderstanding. I am still more radical than the question presupposes. It is not that I conceive that God, while interwoven with creation, retains the upper hand, determining what creation is. All I am wishing to claim is that there is one reality of which we also are necessarily a part, and that within that whole there is that (which we do not fully understand) on which we can draw for healing and so forth. I name the fact that there is that dimension to reality 'God'.

It will, then, be evident that I am envisaging a very real theological shift. I believe that the depth of that shift is a measure of the fact that the theology which we have known has been a masculinist creation conceived within patriarchy. By way of exemplifying this shift I shall take two further instances which will show what it implies in yet further spheres. First, the 'doctrine of creation', on which we have just touched. I remember that when on one occasion I was a member of a panel at a conference on science and religion, it was taken for granted as apparently the lowest common denominator on which we should all agree that God was creator. However, I hold no such presupposition. How could we possibly know which of mind and matter preceded the other, or whether, as might perhaps seem most likely, they have both existed in interrelation with each other 'from the beginning' (whatever that might mean)? Indeed, commencing as I do methodologically from the evidence that there is 'another dimension of reality', it might well be said that a grand statement, such as that God is creator, is the last kind of proposition at which one could arrive! In like manner Schleiermacher, we may note, in writing *The Christian Faith*, placed the doctrine of the Trinity at the conclusion of his book – at the furthest remove from his starting point in human awareness.

Secondly, consider something which may be thought to have been fundamental to theology, both Catholic and Protestant: the idea of eternal life. Interestingly, I frequently find myself asked whether I believe in eternal life: it seems to be a question of major importance to religious people. But in considering as a theologian what God may be, it never crosses my mind to consider eternal life. As with the concept of God as creator, so with that of eternal life, one must ask how we could possibly know what is the case. What does strike me is that the notion of God as creator in some way reflects the concept of a being who exists as separate from and as more powerful than humans. Again, the idea of eternal life may well be said to reflect a concern that a self, conceptualized as a self-subsisting discreet entity, will continue to exist not only in time but through all eternity. Both of these would seem to embody deeply masculinist presuppositions. We may, then, only have begun to unearth the ways in which masculinist paradigms are built into the theology which we have known. Such presuppositions structure both the questions asked and the answers given.

Thirdly, in this chapter I turn to two major questions which, given the understanding of God that I have depicted, should rightly be raised at this point. In the final section I shall return to a further consideration of the question as to how God should be conceptualized. The first question I wish to raise is whether it is not a necessity, not least for the life of prayer, that we should conceive of the relation to God in what may be called I–Thou, dialogical, terms. The second is whether the concept of God, if it is to be a concept of *God*, is not necessarily transcendental. That is to say, must not the concept of God have an over-arching function? Is it not necessary that God-language should be 'horizon' language or the language of ultimacy? (The term 'transcendental' must here be distinguished from 'transcendent'.) It will become clear that I take both of these questions very seriously.

I turn first to the question whether, human beings that we are, we do not have a need to conceptualize the relationship to God in dialogical terms. In particular we must ask: if we do not conceive of God in a way that makes such a relationship possible, what does the life of prayer become? It should be noted that I have phrased the question rather carefully. What we are concerned with here is the human *conception* of God, rather than whatever it is that God is in God's self. Again, we are asking after what may well be a human need, given that, as human beings, we only know of relationships with other human beings which are in some sense dialogical. In considering this question I shall juxtapose the thought of Martin Buber (and in particular Buber's critique of Schleiermacher) with Schleiermacher's thought as I have depicted it. Buber's Jewish conception of God of course conforms to the major Western tradition, in that God is conceived of as an other, in Buber's terminology a 'Thou', in relation to the self.

Evidently referring to Schleiermacher (in that he picks up Schleiermacher's vocabulary), and not without a certain sympathy for his position, Buber writes:

> It has been suggested that the essential element in the relation to God should be seen in a feeling that has been called a feeling of absolute dependence . . . Although the emphasis on and determination of this element is right, the one-sided stressing of this leads to a misunderstanding of the character of the ideal relationship . . .

In its basis the ideal relationship can be understood only as
bi-polar, only as the *coincidentia oppositorum*, as the making-one of
contrasting feelings . . .

Yes, in the pure relationship you have felt yourself to be completely dependent, as you are unable to feel in any other – and
completely free also, as never and nowhere else; creaturely[52] – and
creative. There you did not any longer have one limited by the other,
but both without limit, and both together.

That you need God more than anything you know in your heart at
all times; but do you not know also that God needs you, in the fullness of his eternity, you?[53]

For Buber, then, the relation to God, the Eternal Thou, should be
considered to have the same structure as that to other persons (though
we shall find reason to modify such a bald statement). God is a 'Thou'
in relation to whom I am enabled to become myself. As Buber has it,
when speaking of an I–Thou relation between humans: *'Ich werde am
Du; Ich werdend spreche ich Du*.[54] Buber must rival Heidegger in the
creativity he exercises in relation to the German language! 'I become in
relation to (or because I am in relation to) you: I, becoming, am able
(thus and therefore) to say "You".' The relation to God is likewise conceived of dialogically. God is conceptualized anthropomorphically: God
needs you.

What is someone like me, holding what I have depicted as a Schleier-
macherian position, to think? Before attempting a response, I want to
say that I think this question goes to the heart of the matter. Speaking
personally, I have found it extraordinarily difficult to move away from
the dialogical conception in terms of which I previously thought of my
relationship with God. It has not been easy to bring my prayer life into
conformity with my developing intellectual conviction as to what it is
that God must be. Whatever may have been the case in philosophical
theology, an I – Thou relationship has been of the essence of the life of
prayer within the Western tradition. The point is well made by the
Dominican J. A. DiNoia, who in this passage may be giving a thought-
ful response to my work, given that he has earlier referred to my discussion of this problem in *Theology and Feminism*. DiNoia writes: 'It is
hard to see how it is possible to remain true to the Christian conviction
about God's nearness and presence to us if personal categories for
speaking about this mystery are abandoned.' And he adds: 'To speak of
God in impersonal or suprapersonal terms constitutes not a revision of
Christianity but an alternative to it.'[55] I think that that is perfectly
correct. Indeed I conceive of myself as advocating an alternative to the
Judaeo-Christian tradition, though it may have roots in that tradition.

However, the difference between the two positions may be seen to be less absolute as we progress.

In responding to Buber and DiNoia I should like to make a number of comments – though I may not be able to solve this problem to universal satisfaction. In the first place it is important to draw attention to the fact that there are also gains to be had from problematizing the conception of God as a 'Thou'. For there are ways of conceiving of the relation to God which may be largely lost sight of when God is considered to be set over against me as a 'Thou'. Thus one may think of oneself as being nourished by God, as being upheld by God, as coming 'to' oneself through an 'intunement' with that which is more than one is. Julian of Norwich spoke of God as 'the Ground in whom our Soul standeth'.[56] Furthermore, one may well think of God as being present within the communication which takes place between oneself and another person. Again, one may wish to see others (perhaps in need) as 'surrounded' by God; or one may respond to (as the Quakers would say) 'that of God' in people; or one can be aware that God is present in the healing which persons are able to give to one another. The need to bracket the dialogical language may well allow other ways of thinking to flourish.

In the second place (as I have already suggested), it may well be that a distinction should be drawn between a consideration of what God is (of the kind that a theologian might undertake) and the life of prayer. After all, it is very natural that in prayer people should turn to God as a 'Thou'. I remember my response on the occasion that I mentioned when my car broke down. I called out to God as one would to an other, though I was also attempting simply to be open to what was the case so that I might find a way out of my dilemma. After all, from our earliest childhood we have been structured by I–Thou relationships. The problem then (it may be thought) is not that it may not be useful for us in the context of prayer to think of God as a 'Thou'; that may be inescapable. It arises when this mode of thinking is carried over into an attempt to conceptualize God. For then we have a wholly unrealistic anthropomorphic conception of a God who is a kind of being who exercises agency. Thereupon the conundrums of, for example, 'the question of miracles' and theodicy arise.

Schleiermacher's counsel is extraordinarily wise here. He writes:

> The usual conception of God as one single being outside of the world and behind the world is not the beginning and the end of religion. It is only one manner of expressing God, seldom entirely pure and always inadequate. Such an idea may be formed from mixed motives, from the need for such a being to console and help, and such a God

may be believed in without piety, at least in my sense, and I think in the true and right sense. If, however, this idea is formed, not arbitrarily, but somehow by the necessity of a man's way of thinking, if he needs it for the security of his piety, the imperfections of his idea will not cumber him nor contaminate his piety. Yet the true nature of religion is neither this idea nor any other, but immediate consciousness of the Deity as he is found in ourselves and in the world.[57]

Again:

But it is not necessary that the Deity should be presented as also one distinct object. To many this view is necessary and to all it is welcome, yet it is always hazardous and fruitful in difficulties. It is not easy to avoid the appearance of making Him susceptible of suffering [viz. being acted upon] like other objects. It is only one way of characterizing God, and, from the difficulties of it, common speech will probably never rid itself. But to treat this objective conception of God just as if it were a perception, as if apart from His operation upon us through the world the existence of God before the world, and outside of the world, though for the world, were either by or in religion exhibited as science is, so far as religion is concerned, vain mythology. What is only a help for presentation is treated as a reality. It is a misunderstanding very easily made, but it is quite outside the peculiar territory of religion.[58]

That is surely right. Such an anthropomorphic conception, which is probably not to be avoided, will be welcomed by many. But it must always be hazardous.

In the third place, and following from this, it may well be important for us not simply to rest content with anthropomorphic conceptions. Not least Buber himself differentiates between the I–Thou relation which we may enjoy with others and the manner of the presence of the 'Eternal Thou' to us. The Eternal Thou, it would appear, is present for him with and through our relations with the world. Now in that this is the case, the nature of the relation to God which is conjured up in our minds is in some way akin to Schleiermacher's sense (in his *Speeches*) that we should see the particular as resting in the eternal and the eternal as present through the particular; albeit Buber's context is a Jewish sense of God in God's transcendence drawing near to us, while Schleiermacher's context is that of Platonism. The need to move from an I–Thou relation with God and an anthropomorphic conception of God was put forcefully by John Robinson in the 1960s. Robinson – who fascinatingly had written his doctoral thesis on Buber – considered that 'The conception of God as *a* Being, a Person – like ourselves but supremely above or beyond ourselves – will, I believe, come to be seen as a human projection. (Most people already recognize this in the case of the Devil.)[59] If this judgment is correct, then we are in real trouble if at this point in history we fail to develop other ways of conceptualizing God.

So, finally, there is this to be said. Human beings have long wanted to guard the recognition that God is different in kind from us. If our conception of God bears too great a similarity to ourselves, then God becomes not God, but a 'god'. We have a kind of paganism. Indeed, it is for this reason that I am sceptical of the talk of God (advocated by some Christian feminists and other radical Christians) as, for example, 'our friend'. How is it that this can be God? In the Jewish and Christian traditions the primary way of indicating God's 'godness', of allowing God to be other than we are, has been to speak of God as transcendent. In this case a God conceptualized in deeply anthropomorphic terms – he loves, chastizes, creates, suffers and so forth – acquires the necessary difference from humans through being 'beyond'. God is all that humans are, only much more so; or again, God is the perfection of what they are imperfectly. But if God is conceptualized, as I am advocating, as being different *in kind* from us, so that anthropomorphic language must be deemed inappropriate, then there is no need to conceive of God as set over against us. God may be understood as a dimension, or aspect, of our present creation. We may then consider that in prayer it is we who actualize God in the world (but this is already to anticipate my further reflection on what God may be).

The second major question which I believe should be raised in view of the conceptualization of God that I am advocating is whether the concept of God does not necessarily have 'transcendental' connotations. What I am asking when raising this question is whether God does not form a framework for the rest of our thought. If this is almost by definition the case when one is speaking of God, then is it not quite insufficient – so someone might say – to cast God as a 'dimension' of a greater reality (and no more)? I think that I have increasingly come to see that the idea of God must perform a transcendental function, and it is that which I now wish to explore.

It is important to note the change in my language at this point in the chapter if the nature of the consideration is to be understood. Up till now I have being trying to elucidate (one might say, in positivistic fashion) what those phenomena are which lead us to speak of God and, in consequence, to consider how we should conceptualize God. The question to which I have now turned is that as to whether the *concept* of God does not perhaps perform a transcendental *function*. That is to say, I have changed to a markedly Kantian way of speaking. Kant spoke of the concept of God as a (necessary) 'regulative idea'.[60] To say that one thinks of God as somehow all-embracing, so that one understands all else in relationship to God, must involve a leap of faith: not faith in a paradox which is otherwise a contradiction in terms (such as we considered in relation to Kierkegaard), but a faith that the whole is in some way good or makes sense.

If this is how the concept of God functions, then an atheist is not one who disagrees with a theist over whether a certain being, called God, exists. (Were one to be speaking of the existence or non- existence of a noumenal being, I might well have to class myself as an atheist. But then I notice that there are those who call themselves Christians who equally deny the existence of such a being.[61]) No, the true atheist is not one whose world-view does not include an additional being called God, but one who denies that there is, in an ultimate sense, purpose or meaning. In the light of such a discussion Kant, whom one must otherwise class an atheist, must at the very least be said to have had a profound understanding as to how theism functions. To be truly atheistic is to live in the kind of world which a Jean-Paul Sartre or an Albert Camus depicts. Whereas in the eighteenth century Kant's sense of intrinsic order is such (or his fear that moral chaos would otherwise break out is such) that he believes that we must think our ethical responsibility to exist within a wider framework such that right acting is validated, no such presupposition seems evident to the existentialist atheist. Camus' Dr Rieux of his novel *The Plague*[62] dedicates himself to doing good in a world which makes no sense at all: a much more acerbic outlook.

I turn next to a consideration of the way in which the concept of God may function for me as a transcendental. How could a conviction that the whole is good function in relation to the belief (as I have so far explained it in this chapter) that there is a dimension of reality which we may name God? We should notice that the form in which this question confronts us is different from how it would appear to one who is traditionally theistic or Christian. If one believes, as such a person believes, that God exists independently of the creation, indeed that 'he' is the creator of all else, then it would seem to follow axiomatically that the whole is at some level purposeful and good. (The fact that this is far from evidently the case forms the substance of the theodicy question.) But I am denying that the existence of such a God is the best construal of the evidence. If I wish to postulate, as I do, that at some level there is a goodness, beauty and harmony, then I shall need to postulate that of the whole. There is no 'external' God to guarantee this.

I have suggested that such a proposition must be a kind of statement of faith. Thus I remember very well what was for me what Van Harvey would call a 'paradigmatic' experience[63] in which I was forced to such a conclusion. Aged twenty-one, I went alone to visit what had been the Jewish ghetto in Warsaw. The destruction had been so great that the whole area was simply filled in and built over again at a higher level. Blocks of dreary modern flats now occupied the space and in the centre of the square thus created there stood a monument. A kind of frieze, it showed a procession of people (including children with no idea that anything was amiss) being led away, evidently to captivity and near-certain death. I stood transfixed, oblivious to my surroundings. Suddenly a small girl asked me the time. Having been in Poland several weeks I understood the question, but unable to reply, I bent down so that she could read my watch – and when she done so she scampered off. Then I saw, as I had not, that there were children playing on the concrete, over all that destruction – another generation. And as I left my eyes fell on the blades of grass forcing their way up through the cracks.

To say that at some level the world manifests the capacity to recover is not of course to seek to minimize the extent of human suffering. That would be to live in cloud-cuckoo land. Nor is it to deny the capacity of human beings, in a nuclear holocaust, to reduce our planet to a habitation fit only for insects. But we have not yet done this. We may, then, exercise a kind of hope and faith, a hope and faith without which perhaps we should not delight in life and be empowered to work for change. The evidence of a fundamental goodness (inasmuch as one can speak of that evidence) must consist in the extraordinary way in which there does seem to be healing and renewal. This seems to be true of our minds and our bodies on the individual level. Again, what of the fact that even in my lifetime demonstrably evil regimes – Nazi Germany, Pinochet's Chile and now South Africa – have not finally prevailed? Even on a macro-scale the world of nature seems to have a propensity to right itself, if only we would let it. What is one to think of the fact that in war time more boy than girl babies are born? (It would be fascinating to contrast such an understanding with Kant's wager that ultimately the empirical and the moral world are one.)

One does not quite know whether it is a different question – because the scale is so different – as to whether order, beauty, even 'intention', is built into the universe as a whole. The so-called 'anthropic' principle has of course come in for much discussion in recent years. What are we to think of the fact that the four fundamental forces of the universe, within very narrow limits, have the right ratio to one another such that the universe neither collapsed back into itself nor ran away with itself and in time life could arise? The belief of some that this must lead us to postulate the existence of a God, in some sense separate from the universe as a whole – a twentieth-century 'argument from design' – can surely have no more to commend it than the eighteenth-century belief that the world, considered as a watch, implies the existence of a watch-maker. The argument of Hume's famed *Dialogues on Religion*[64] must surely stand against any such suggestion. But whether order, beauty, symmetry, and even (as I have expressed it) 'intention' (though one does not quite know even how to phrase that) is somehow integral to the whole must be another issue. The belief that this is the case would fit very well with the conviction that within the whole there is that which is a power for good, which I have named God.

Despite my sense that these two things that I wish to say may be cognate, I find the relationship between them the most puzzling question in theology. As I have suggested, they are radically different kinds of proposition: on the one hand, a conclusion (built on less than hard evidence) that there is a dimension of reality on which we cannot quite put our finger; on the other, a faith statement (though it may have an empirical element) about the nature of the whole. Let me again point to the different twist which the question of the relationship between the two has to the way it would be framed by a conventional theist. If God is conceived to be the creator of the universe, then he may also be thought to see the sparrow fall. I find such an understanding of God untenable. (Moreover the problems it creates are, as I have said, pro-found; for a feminist, I should have thought, monstrous.) If, by contrast, one commences, as I wish to, from the experiential evidence that prayer is effective or spiritual healing possible, it is difficult to know quite how that conviction relates to the order, beauty and indeed fundamental goodness of the whole. Yet I remain convinced that for any adequate theism it is insufficient simply to speak of God as a dimension of what is, lacking a sense of God as being transcendental.

The difficulty in bringing together these two disparate things may well be illustrated by the following incident. On the first occasion that (living in Scotland) I climbed a proper mountain and saw the panorama open out before me I was left awe-struck. Returning to the hut of the women's mountaineering club and confronted with the log book (where I was supposed to write that I had climbed Ben so-and-so and crossed such-and-such a saddle), I simply wrote 'I have seen God's universe'. (My remark, so I am told, elicited further comments!) What is the relationship between such a sense and the conviction that prayer is powerful? The closest that we can come to bridging the gap and joining our mental selves to the physical universe is perhaps the sense of a one-ness with all which some experience mystically. Consider the following statement sent to the Oxford Religious Experience Research Unit:

One day as I was walking along Marylebone Road I was suddenly seized with an extraordinary sense of great joy and exaltation, as though a marvellous beam of spiritual power had shot through me linking me in a rapture with the world, the Universe, Life with a capital L, and all the beings around me. All delight and power, all things living, all time fused in a brief second.[65]

Is it that a human being can have such a sense because, at some profound level, we are one with the rest of creation and the whole is good? That, I believe, is the religious vision. John Hick writes: 'What distinguishes the religious experience . . . is the unity of ultimacy and value.'[66]

By way of concluding this chapter I turn, then, fourthly, to an attempt further to refine what I think the future of theism must be if we are to be theistic. I shall set this discussion within a sketch of the developing historical context, a development which parallels the discussion of the breakdown of the possibility of the Christian myth that I traced in the Introduction to this book. In doing this I need to be quite clear what I intend. I am wishing to suggest both that the past conception of God is no longer viable and that there is much about our present situation which may lead to a new conception of spirituality. But in situating this contention historically, I am not intending a kind of relativism, as though I were to think that each age forms a conception of God as it sees fit and it is time now for us to move on. I would hope that this chapter has made this clear enough. I believe that a conception of God like that which I am advocating is truer to the experiential evidence which leads us to speak of God in the first place. I also believe that the past conception which we have had has been profoundly harmful, and that only some conception such as that which I am advocating is morally acceptable for the future. Thus I write legislatively, not simply descriptively.

The immediate response to the recognition in the eighteenth century that nature and history form a causal nexus was to banish God from the stage of history. At the same time the wonder which Newton's discoveries induced in men caused them to conceive of God in the first instance as creator. Deism was born. The author of this intricate machine had set it on its course and left it to its own devices. An attempt was made to substitute more philosophical language for the previous anthropomorphic language for God, which was considered primitive. This shunning of anthropomorphic terms for God is still evident at the end of the century in Schleiermacher's *Speeches,* however much he had departed from the deist's God in other respects. Yet it would be difficult to say that the God of the Enlightenment was other than profoundly masculine! The characteristics which he embodied were those of power and might, self-sufficiency and agency, associated with the male. While studiously avoiding anything so anthropomorphic as the word 'God',

Joseph Addison (d. 1719) in his famous deist hymn 'The spacious firma-
ment on high' still gives his God an 'almighty hand'. At the end of the
century – that century, we should note, in which we are inclined to think
that God is envisaged in non-anthropomorphic ways – William Blake
paints, in 1794, his 'The Ancient of Days', depicting God with a long
white beard, his compass spanning the universe.

In the nineteenth century a certain anthropomorphism returned – had
it ever been lost? But now there is a crucial difference. For it is understood by at least some thinkers that such a God is a human projection.
Dormant in Hegel's discussion of the unhappy consciousness which is
separated from what it would be, this theme comes to fruition in the
mid century in the work of Feuerbach and of Marx. It was to find an
added twist in the early twentieth century in the work of Freud. What
is significant, is that it is taken for granted even by the great atheists of
the modern world that this God, this Father figure, is what God would
be were there to be a God. 'He' – we might well say – constitutes a
reflection of the status of the *paterfamilias*, that social construction
which reached a crescendo in the Germany of the nineteenth century,
the culture from which the atheistic denunciations of such a God came.
(Marilyn Chapin Massey points interestingly to a much more 'feminine'
understanding of the divine, nascent in the Romanticism of the early
century, which comes to be lost.[67])

Indeed, in the late twentieth century we still seem not to have escaped
a profoundly masculinist conception of God. In this regard I have
pointed to the work of certain Anglo-Saxon philosophers of religion.[68]
The language of creeds, prayers and liturgy still clearly conveys that
God is male. Hence the feminist resistance. What is now rapidly being
overcome, I am arguing, is any social basis which supports such an
understanding of God. With the rise of feminist sensibilities and the
coming of women into their own, the disjuncture between people's
ethical beliefs and the Christian conception of God has simply become
too great. If the hierarchical relation between men and women has been
reflected in a dichotomous conception of the relationship between God
and humanity, then the demise of the one must lead to a destabilizing of
the other. If we are not to lose all sense of a spirituality, we must find
ways to move on. We shall need a profound paradigm shift from the
God we have known.

The seeds of that shift may well lie in our past. There will be a certain
continuity with the Western tradition. It would be difficult indeed to
step right outside our culture. Thus I find Schleiermacher's thought
provocative. (It would not surprise me if someone from a Catholic background were similarly to raid Thomas Aquinas.)[69] While Schleiermacher
shares with deism that nature is fundamental to his theology (more

particularly is this true of the *Speeches*), it is nature very differently conceived. Now it is not nature as a mechanism, but rather (in the age of
Romanticism) the sense of wonder which arises from its contemplation
that leads him to be theistic. Schleiermacher's God is the polar opposite
to that of the deists. Far from being a kind of object who is removed
from the scene, his God is closer to us than any such 'object' could be.
It is in returning to our selves in self-observation that we recognize that
our being opens out on to that which is more than are we. But Schleiermacher, hardly surprisingly, did not carry through the radicality of his
insight that spirituality is intrinsic to the human person. (Indeed much
of *The Christian Faith* is much more conventional than one might
expect from the opening paragraphs.) If we now take a further step, that
is because we live in a different age.

Today there is a whole cultural context within which such a shift can
take place. What has happened in the women's movement in recent
years and more generally within society since the 1960s is that people
have begun to take 'spirituality' into their own hands. They crave
healing in their lives; they seek to be both centred and connected; and
they find themselves compelled to respond to the natural beauty of the
world. All of these involve a certain spirituality. There has been an
'anthropomorphic' shift, not in the sense of conceiving of God as an
anthropomorphic agent (such a view is increasingly confined to the
Christian churches), but in the yearning for a humane spirituality,
centred on the human person. Many have turned to the East, hoping
there to discover a practice which will allow them to find themselves.
While I do not wish to disparage this (indeed I think that there is something to be gained from meditative practice), it would seem that Eastern
spirituality lacks elements which are crucial to this generation of
women. For Western women at this moment in their history are seeking
not to lose the self but to come into their own as articulate agents.

That further step – beyond anything of which Schleiermacher conceived – must be to claim that in being most fully ourselves we are also
realizing God in the world. We need to overcome the dichotomy,
fundamental to the major tradition of Western thought, whereby God's
greatness is at the expense of our weakness, while God's goodness casts
us in the role of sinners. Rather, God should be conceived to be the fullness of our potentialities, if also more than what we are individually and
perhaps collectively. As I have suggested, there is ceasing to be any
social basis for a hierarchical construal of reality (a construal which
moreover has always been gendered). Thus the overcoming of heteronomous relationships within society will lead to the dismantling of the
patriarchal God. Meanwhile women are rapidly discovering their very
humanity, which is to say also their spirituality. They will no longer

tolerate being disjointed, separated from their true selves, with a projection of a God set in apposition to what they themselves are. The
coming of women into their own will lead to their appropriation of their
spirituality.

The evidence suggests that people have found that they can draw on
the resources of God, direct healing towards others, and find empowerment in their lives. Maybe in time we shall attain to greater understanding of how we are connected to that which is more than ourselves,
of how extra-sensory perception (and therefore also prayer) works, of
how body and mind are inter-connected. But what we must commence
upon without delay – and we may think women in particular to have
already commenced upon – is the bringing of our conception of God
into line with those effects which lead us to speak of the spiritual. We
shall need a much more dynamic understanding of God: as energy, light,
power, love and healing. These things themselves should be understood
to be what God is: something to which we have access. Drawing on that
potential which we have as human beings, we must name those powers
which are ours. Indeed it may be that it is only as we come 'to' ourselves
that we shall learn to honour the creation. The kind of theism which
I am advocating may be thought to have profound ecological and
political implications. We need to find our place in the world and to feel
at home in it, rather than looking, as we have in Western history, to an
'external' God and a life 'beyond'.

But is the understanding of God which I am advancing comfort-
less? It may well be that every person desires a 'Father God' (or the
matriarchal equivalent), a God conceived of in our image and designated by parental metaphors. It should be noted here that though I
believe that it is imperative for us to overcome anthropomorphic
metaphors which suggest a 'being' separate from what we are, the way
in which I am speaking of God is far from simply abstract and philosophical. We may understand God as that which gives us illumination,
which allows us to heal in ourselves, and which passes between us and
those whom we love. God is both that which connects me to the greater
whole and that which enables me to be my true self. What this model of
God rules out are such attitudinal stances as those of worship and
obedience; that is to say, hierarchical modes of being. It is these that I
believe we need to overcome. That we may glory in the wonder of the
universe is of course quite another matter. Equally, we should seek to
follow our moral precepts. But we have lost the hierarchical, heteronomous, framework in which worship of, and obedience to, an anthropomorphically conceived 'other' could make sense. I should find such an
outlook incompatible with my ethical precepts, or simply with my way
of being in the world.[70]

What I have suggested in this book is that the lack of fit between the world in which we live and the conception of God which we have inherited has reached breaking point. Many modern people (and perhaps in particular many feminists), while seeking to have a certain spirituality in their lives, have been left without any notion of 'God'. But of course it is not just feminism nor simply our ethical sensibilities which have caused the crisis. What we now know about the universe makes it inconceivable to people that there is an anthropomorphic agent who is somehow other than the world. In our age we cannot hold to the kind of static conception which was still possible in the eighteenth century. What can it mean to imply – even metaphorically – that God is somehow 'outside' space or 'before' time? That which is God must come to be understood as a dimension of what is: something intimately connected with what we are. The Christian myth has become untenable and must be shed. If feminism has given that myth the final jolt as being ethically suspect, it is also that its world-picture can no longer be ours. The sad thing is that so many cling to this myth when they know they can no longer believe it because there seems to be nowhere other than the Christian church to go. However, women in particular are increasingly breaking free of Christianity. I can think of no major feminist thinker who is a Christian.

Meanwhile it may well be that feminist theory is providing Western religion with the paradigms that we shall need if we are to conceptualize that which is God. The masculinist conception of the self as it has led to a certain conception of God which has been modelled upon it, and the masculinist dichotomous gendering of social reality and of religion as legitimizing this, have arrived at an impasse. What I have described in broad terms as the feminist conception of centred selves in relation may not simply conform to our ethical beliefs, but enable a paradigm of interconnectedness which we can bring to theology. As we have seen, feminists have often wished to speak of the self as having 'permeable' ego boundaries. Given such a model, it becomes easier to conceive of that which is more than what we are, yet with which we stand in the most intimate relation. Perhaps it is too early to say what the fruitfulness of feminist paradigms for theology will be. But we may hope that we shall find ways of speaking which comport both with our ethics and with the experiential evidence which leads us to speak of God.

For we may well surmise that if, as spiritual people, we fail in any way to be able to conceptualize God, we shall be left stranded. Hence the importance of the work of the theologian. What impresses me, however, is that, though little systematic theology has as yet been written from the kind of perspective which I am advocating, it is clearly coming.

Consider the following remarks by Linell Cady, an American theologian alongside whom I trained at Harvard:

> It has often been noted that our conceptions of the human person and of God are dialectical, each being mirror images of the other . . . The vision of human being and the moral life sketched out above does not lend support to traditional theism with its focus on an independent, transcendent divine being. I have been using love as a primary metaphor for depicting the orientation of human life that most facilitates the emergence of greater being and value. Incarnating this spirit is analogous to what traditionally has been understood as love of and relationship to God. However, important differences render the latter expression misleading. Most basically, the self does not relate to an independent divine being but embodies the spirit of the divine. Nor should this be understood as the creative work of God operating in human life, insofar as that formulation suggests the activity of an independent agent operating on or through humans . . . From [the] perspective [which she is advocating] the self is no substantial entity, complete and defined, but a reality always in the process of being created through the dynamic of love, which continually alters its boundaries and identity.[71]

This statement – using somewhat different vocabulary from mine – contains elements which profoundly parallel much that I also wish to say.[72]

Upon publishing his *Speeches* – the first major work of theology to take cognizance of modernity – Schleiermacher was accused by his friend Friedrich von Schlegel of having a rather 'skinny' God.[73] I am sure that some Christians would think the same of my God! However, this would constitute a misunderstanding. It is not that they have a 'thick' God (who can apparently do all sorts of things) whereas I by comparison have a 'thin' God (limited and powerless). (As a matter of fact my God can do rather a lot of things.) Rather, it is that I have wiped the slate clean of an anthropomorphically conceived God, be 'he' more, or less, powerful. By contrast, when I speak of 'theism' I intend to designate a conviction that there is more to reality than meets the eye; that there are powers on which we may draw; that we are profoundly connected with what is in excess of what we are. I believe that we need to dare to undertake a paradigm shift in our conceptualization of what God is. If this does not come about, then I fear that the idea of God will have an ever-diminishing hold on people's minds. Whether we should continue to use the word 'God' for what I intend is a valid question which I have yet to consider.

VII

Spirituality and Praxis

What of the lived life as the context in which there can be an openness to the dimension of reality which, in the previous chapter, I have called God? What is the relationship between living in certain ways and the ability to draw on the power and the love which, we may think, is always seeking to enter our lives? Are there particular practices which would seem to be prerequisite to such a spirituality? These are enigmatic questions. It is very difficult to know how to answer them. Nevertheless, it will immediately be apparent that if the kind of theology which I have described is not to be left hanging in the air, it is important to ask after the nature of the life within which it will be situated. Theology bears a quite different relationship to life when it is held to arise immediately out of experience from when, for example, it is held to be predicated upon an 'objective' revelation. It is these questions which I shall attempt to address in this final chapter.

Let me turn immediately to this last matter, the different relationship of a theology of experience to praxis from that of a theology of revelation. Considering this will help to elucidate the kinds of questions that I wish to pursue. It may, of course, be said that every theology arises out of human experience. It will be clear that I myself think that this is so. Even in the case of a religion such as Christianity, in which certain doctrines are passed down from one generation to another, the way in which those doctrines are shaped in a particular generation will owe much to the circumstances in which the Christian church is set. What I am drawing attention to here then is rather the difference in the claims that are being made. Christians hold that there is something 'objective' about what they believe; that it has been revealed. I am claiming a very different kind of objectivity, namely that theology must be rooted in our experience, which is in some sense true to the way things are. Indeed, I should deny that there is anything 'objective' about male dogma.

We shall understand the import of the difference here better by taking a concrete case. Let us use as an example of a theology of revelation perhaps the obvious one in the twentieth century, that of Karl Barth. Barth's claim was that theology should be independent of the cultural circumstances of human beings. If one knows anything of the history of the German church and German culture in the twentieth century one can well understand why he had such a stance. Indeed it is clear why his position met with such resonance among those to whom he proclaimed it. Because of the peculiar circumstances of the development of the church within Germany, by the early years of this century Protestantism had come to be tied to German nationalism in a sense in which this was not the case, for example, in England.[1] Every soldier who marched into battle in the First World War did so with *Gott mit uns*, God with us, on his buckle. No wonder that Barth, who had been alarmed to see his former theological teachers declare in favour of the war policy of the Kaiser, proclaimed that the Word of God came *senkrecht von oben*, vertically from above.

Again, consider the power of Barth's theology in the circumstances of National Socialist Germany. In his famous reply to Emil Brunner of 1934 simply headed *Nein!*, Barth declared that there was no *Anknüpfungspunkt*, no joining point, either negative or positive, which the Word of God required in the world to latch on to.[2] That is to say, there was no way in which we could prepare ourselves for God's coming. It was neither that we had first to be good and open to God (a positive joining point), nor was it that we had first to be in despair and in need of God (a negative joining point) for God to reveal God's self. Theology was sealed off as far as possible from human culture. Barth's work, from his famous 1918 commentary on Paul's letter to the Romans (second edition 1921), proclaimed itself to be exegesis of the text. In fact I should want to give it a very different reading. I have already commented on the way in which the *Zeitgeist* was reflected in Barth's work.[3] But one can see why a proclamation of the objectivity of God's Word could give the pastors of the Confessing Church, which arose under National Socialism, the possibility of opposing the elision of Christianity and German culture. In 1934 the German Christians were draping altars with swastikas.

Barth is perhaps the extreme case of a theologian declaring the basis of theology to be independent of human culture. However, one should note that in one way or another Christians, by definition, believe something other than my claim that theology is predicated upon our experience. For they believe that God has revealed God's self; as I said in Chapter I, this is the basis on which Christianity is founded. Of course Christians for the most part recognize that revelation is in and through human culture, that the circumstances of the first century are reflected in the scriptures, for example. That is not at issue. But it would seem to be impossible for a Christian to say simply what I have said, namely that whatever God may be, God is a dimension of reality which is present equally to every age, which is for us to discern. Of course I also believe that our discernment of God and our formulation of what God may be is tempered by culture.

It would seem that there are internal Christian differences here. In my experience, Christians belonging to the Reformed (Presbyterian) tradition in particular want to proclaim the objectivity of a whole structure of dogmatic beliefs before there can be any consideration of an experiential dimension. By contrast I have found Catholic Christians often profoundly open to the idea that someone like myself has a spirituality and an awareness of God, quite independently of holding to belief in Christian doctrines (which I do not). These differences which I have observed do not surprise me. Catholicism has a 'high' doctrine of creation and, since Vatican II in particular, has been wide open to the idea that God could be revealed outside the Catholic church and indeed the Christian religion. Calvin and his latter-day disciple Barth (indeed Barth more than Calvin, it would seem, given the consideration of the doctrine of creation in the first book of the *Institutes*) wish to guard against any general revelation apart from Christian specificity.[4] I might well think that Barth is turning in his grave at what I am propounding![5]

However, here I want to make a different point, namely how peculiarly masculinist (conforming to a male reality) it strikes me as being that theology should be tied to purportedly 'objective' creeds, so that it is largely divorced from the worlds of experience and spirituality. Why should what it is to be religious consist in subscription to a set of beliefs, formulated as a set of propositions about what is the case? I realize that to question this is to mount a major challenge to what religion has been for many people in the West. Nevertheless I declare that this is masculinist (though it does not by any means reflect where all men find themselves). Thus I have noticed that if one says that theology should be grounded in human spiritual awareness, this is held to be 'simply too vague', unacceptably 'subjective', or just 'waffle' – or so it is implied. It is as though for someone to hold such a position is actually threatening. It is easier, so it would seem, to subscribe to a set of doctrines which are declared to be truth; it need affect one's life less. At least, this is how I read this response with which I have frequently met.

It is an interesting question whether women, because they are in a different social situation, are on the whole open to the idea that theology should be grounded in our own experience in a way in which men are not. If it is true that women are much more closely in touch with one another, as they would seem to be in our society, then it becomes perfectly natural for them to engage in conversation about spiritual matters in the widest sense. Men, given their different personal circumstances, seem baffled. Now this question is important methodologically. If God is known, as I have suggested, for example through the power of prayer, so that people can be healed, or become cognizant of things which they would not otherwise know, then this requires that people should have the kinds of relationships with one another through which these things may come about. If I cannot ask my friends to pray for me when I need help, then I cannot know the power of such prayer. Again, the fact that I have a conviction that there is a spiritual dimension of reality which I call God owes not a little to the fact that I find that my friends think likewise. I assume that many of us first learn how to be open to that dimension of reality which is God from our mothers and maintain it during our lives through the profound friendships which we have with others.

Yet it has been men who have had the power to declare what religion shall be. Theology has then been equated in the West with holding a certain set of beliefs. Now I should want to say that that set of beliefs is moulded by male experience. I devoted Chapters IV and V of this book to a consideration of this. Far from being 'objective', the forms which Christian theology has taken have reflected the situation and needs of men. Its paradigms evince the structure of male desire. If one wants some kind of 'objectivity' in theology, surely the only criterion could be the question of what seems to be true to the evidence that there is that dimension of reality which we call God. It is this which should be a controlling influence as we try to think out what God may be. I embarked upon such a quest in the previous chapter. Meanwhile we should note the horrendous history which we have had of men trying to control what it is that women should think. It is sometimes suggested that in the witch craze of early modern times what was at stake (in part) was that women had retained among themselves knowledge, for example, of the healing power of herbs, so that as healers they posed a challenge to the power of the (male) church. Women had an alternative wisdom. Meanwhile in my generation until recently it has been almost impossible to teach anything other than Christian theology in a theology faculty at a university.[6] Until the present, women have been denied the possibility of thinking out how they wish to conceptualize what 'God' may be. Indeed, slaves that they have been in a patriarchal world, they have not even understood that there was such a question.

Yet is it not the case that men, too, have been short-changed by the gulf which there has been between academic theology and spirituality? Many of our academic faculties are wildernesses in this regard. Indeed, I want to go further and to ask how one could spend one's life thinking about what God may be if one behaves in a way which is wholly incommensurate with an elementary sense of ethical and spiritual values. As is well known, theology faculties have often been the scene of the fiercest academic wrangles, sometimes extending over people's whole careers. Indeed I have to say that some of the worst behaviour which I have witnessed (thinking now internationally) has been on the part of Christian feminists. Perhaps there is greater insecurity among those who hold a minority position? Is this how one is to excuse it? It seems to me crucial that one is all of a piece (as far as this is humanly possible) in what one believes and who one is.

In these circumstances it is not at all the done thing to speak in an academic context of the experiences that make one count oneself other than an atheist. Yet to admit to these things, to speak of them openly in the classroom, allows students (who have often chosen to study theology for a reason) the possibility of integrating their new learning with their own spirituality. Of course theology must remain an academic subject; that is not in question. I am simply denying that the best way to pursue the tasks of theology is in a vacuum, sealed from experience. Were I to become an atheist (which I cannot imagine), I should want to do something else with my life than to be a theologian. It is interesting that in recent years it has often, though not always, been those of a 'left-wing' disposition who have turned theology into a political and social cause, substituting a rhetoric of liberation for any idea of a personal spirituality. Meanwhile it is Evangelicals (or those who have come from an Evangelical background) who are the most ready to acknowledge the kinds of experiences which I cite in the previous chapter! Of course, there are also those (among them my friends) for whom spirituality and social concerns are integrated. But in the case of women, at least, they tend to have moved outside Christianity and are not to be found in theology faculties!

I come now to the central matter of this chapter. Let me pose again the question which I asked at the outset. Are there certain ways of being in the world which would seem to be prerequisite to gaining awareness of that dimension of reality which I have called God? Or to put this another way, what is the relationship between praxis, the praxis of one's life, and spirituality? I am genuinely puzzled as to the answer to this question. I notice that many people who claim to see the hand of God in events would definitely believe that one had to subscribe to a certain set of beliefs before one could be a channel for that power which is God. Thus Christian Scientists appear to think that holding to their outlook on the world is a prerequisite to being able to heal. Those who speak with tongues (a phenomenon which I myself have witnessed) presumably think this a manifestation of Christian belief. But I want to ask a wider question, one less tied to belief systems. Does one in some way have to be a certain kind of person if one is also to draw on God's power?

I shall devote much of this chapter to a consideration of several what I shall call 'practices'. It may be that there are certain ways of being (which one can in a sense learn or foster in one's life) which enable one to be better open to that which is God. One would think that this is very likely the case. People whom we count saintly, in any tradition, do seem to have something in common. Indeed what strikes me as remarkable is that, far from holding like beliefs, people who have about them a spirituality seem to subscribe to widely differing beliefs. Thus I have mentioned that spiritual healers whom I have known have had the most varied outlooks – near-Buddhist, Christian, agnostic. Perhaps this is what one should expect. But it does raise questions again about the relationship between theology and that evidence which compels one to speak of God in the first place. In fact I think it to be the case that those who are in some sense spiritual persons recognize this in others, from whom they may diverge greatly in the matter of belief.

Let me commence my investigation by framing my question negatively. Are there certain ways of being which one might think profoundly inimical to being a spiritual person? That is to say, are there vices which seem so contrary to how one thinks a spiritual person should behave that one is left stunned? I think that I should want to name one: domination of other life. I should include here both domination of other persons and exploitation of the animal creation. Surely a spiritual person, absolutely fundamentally, has to let other life live? I am not saying that anything other than vegetarianism and pacifism is incompatible with spirituality. (Personally, I am not a vegetarian, though I eat little meat; and I am convinced that there are circumstances – as for example in the last world war – when it was necessary to fight.) But a disregard for the beauty and integrity of other life, an inclination to stamp it out, does seem to me to be contrary to what I could count a true spirituality. In these circumstances patriarchy rates as a first-order crime. Indeed, what should one say of the fact that men so often have tried to impose their religious convictions on others?

To put this positively: compassion for others is surely a hallmark of the spiritual life. Those who are truly spiritual people seem to have the ability to let others grow and blossom in their presence. They foster human becoming. Such a judgment has strong links with a practice which I shall describe in this chapter, the ability to attend to others and to listen. It is because the feminist movement has, at its best, allowed people to flourish and to find new life that one might be inclined to say that it manifests a spirituality. Spiritual practices rightly engaged in (so that they have not become obsessive) would seem to free people for openness to others. This is what one would expect if such practices enable people to acquire a 'centred' self.

With these preliminary observations in mind, I turn to a consideration of certain specific practices. I choose three which I shall call 'attention', 'honesty' and 'ordering'. I am sure that this list is in no way
exhaustive, but the choice seems obvious for my purposes. Let me
repeat what I am asking in choosing these practices. I am not simply
seeking to consider what the good life consists of, or what are the
greatest virtues. I want to pose the question whether there are specific
practices which will better enable one to be open to that dimension of
reality which is God. It is difficult to know whether the practices themselves should be called 'spiritual'. It would not be nonsensical to say that
they are, in that a lack of them would seem to be profoundly incompatible with spirituality. But what interests me here is that it would seem
that they are a *sine qua non* if one is to realize in one's life that which
is God. I hardly need say that of course there are many who practise the
things that I shall describe who would count themselves atheists.

I commence with 'attention', something which has been much discussed in philosophical circles in recent years. How interesting, indeed
significant, that, given how few women are philosophically trained, the
development of the notion of attention is almost exclusively attributable
to women! The idea is rooted in the first place in writing of Simone
Weil's. [7] It was, however, Iris Murdoch who gave it academic credence
through her discussion in *The Sovereignty of Good*.[8] More recently this
way of thinking has been developed, notably, by Martha Nussbaum. I
want to reflect for a moment on the fact that women have been the ones
who have developed the notion of attention philosophically, and it is a
matter to which I shall return. It surely arises from women's social
situatedness. Women have been the ones who have needed to attend, in
a world in which they were not the dominant sex. But what may have
been born of necessity has surely been turned to advantage. It enables a
much richer life.

In seeking to characterize attention (or attending) I shall quote from
a range of authors, men and women and in different traditions. What I
want to do is to give some sense of attending as a way of being in the
world. It is, I believe, an ethical stance, and one which is closely allied
to what it might mean to have a spirituality. It involves listening to and
watching both oneself and others. It can also involve allowing oneself to
be affected by art or great literature, or being observant of nature. By
being attentive one is able to grow and change and so make appropriate
response when response is called for. Attending involves not being
swallowed up by circumstances but keeping a certain critical distance,
while also being deeply involved, in the sense of caring for that to which
one attends.

The mode of attention is thus a complex one. It is in a sense duplex.

Thus Annette Kuhn speaks of attentiveness as a 'passionate detachment'.[9] In the context of speaking of an acute observation of nature, Annie Dillard comments: 'Pure devotion to any object . . . is at once a receptiveness and a total concentration.'[10] The person who attends is drawn into the particularity of that which confronts them. Attention, Iris Murdoch tells us, allows a process of 'deepening or complicating'. Martha Nussbaum likewise writes: 'Our highest and hardest task is to make ourselves people "on whom nothing is lost".'[11] Attentiveness must always involve the observation of detail. The attentive person is open to the wonder of the world or the intricacy of particular human circumstances.

It is clear that for all the thinkers whom I mention the act of attending is a profoundly ethical matter. It is a practice through which the one who attends changes. This is very evident in Murdoch's writing.[12] Daniel Hardy comments, albeit in a slightly different context:

> The two-sided effect of attention-giving must be taken seriously. One side is that, while it distances the questioner from that which he experiences, it does not altogether separate him from it . . . The other side is that the attending 'dignifies' the one who attends, giving him importance as an active subject so that he is not simply a passive recipient of his experience. If and when the truth emerges from his attending, it is truth for him – within, not only external to him; and he is capacitated by it – he is not as he was before . . . It should also be seen that this process of attending is not simply intellectual, it is an active proceeding along paths chosen.[13]

The process of attending involves the whole person.

Clearly this is a very different understanding of ethics from one in which ethical behaviour is thought to consist in making decisions in accordance with abstract and impersonal norms which are simply brought into play in the case at hand. The action which the person takes will be tempered by the particular circumstances to which he or she is responding. What we have been able to discern becomes crucial. To say this is by no means to suggest that there are no circumstances in which justice demands that we take no account of the particular situation which pertains. But most of our acting in the world is vastly more subtle than simply taking a series of abstract decisions. What we have become is, then, integrally involved in what we do. That is to say, the notion of attending suggests the importance of what has become known as 'virtue ethics' in recent years, rather than simply pursuing a Kantian, deontological, ethics.

Murdoch puts it this way:

If we consider what the work of attention is like, how continuously

it goes on, and how imperceptibly it builds up structures of value
round about us, we shall not be surprised that at crucial moments of
choice most of the business of choosing is already over.[14]

While Nussbaum writes:

> Progress comes not from the teaching of an abstract law but by lead-
> ing the friend, or child, or loved one – by a word, by a story, by an
> image – to see some new aspect of the concrete case at hand . . .
> Giving a 'tip' is to give a gentle hint about how one might see.[15]

Indeed we may remark on the fact that great teachers – not least Jesus
of Nazareth – have used the vehicle of parables and stories to convey
their message.

We should note, then, that such an ethic of attention is profoundly
contextual. No wonder it has appealed to women if what Carol Gilligan
has to say of the way in which women commonly think about ethical
matters is correct.[16] In the context of discussing Murdoch's writing,
Josephine Donovan comments:

> Women more than men appear to be willing to adopt a passive mode
> of accepting the diversity of environmental 'voices' and the validity of
> their realities. Women appear less willing to wrench that context
> apart or to impose upon it alien abstractions or to use implements
> that subdue it intellectually or physically. Such an epistemology pro-
> vides the basis for an ethic that is non-imperialistic, that is life-
> affirming, and that reverences the concrete details of life.[17]

That women think like this is (as I have said) certainly due to the social
situatedness in which they have commonly found themselves. Women
are used to being at the centre of a family, at the hub of the life of a
crowded office, or caught up in the melee of a social work department
– that is to say in circumstances in which there are various and conflict-
ing demands and in which they see it as their task to make life somehow
possible for all who are involved. Women have had to learn the skill of
mediating between the varied needs of people.

I have not undertaken sufficient research to know whether men's
writing on attending differs from that of women! In any case it would
be almost impossible to ascertain whether any conclusions are to be
drawn from the random examples which have come my way. What one
does find in male writing which impresses me is a concentration on the
skills needed for communication and listening. One might take the
following examples. Kierkegaard comments that 'the ear is the most
spiritually determined of the senses'.[18] I have been fascinated by this
passage written by Rowan Williams, a theologian, spiritual writer and

now an Anglican bishop. Would I, I wonder, read this passage differently if I thought it had been written by a disadvantaged woman (one whose powers of communication had been stunted through her life circumstances) from the way in which I read it knowing that it comes from a man possessed of many talents to whom the world has offered every opportunity? Has it been more difficult for men to communicate, since they are less willing to listen to one another, than it has been for women? Williams writes:

> My obscurity to myself, yours to me, and mine to you, are not *puzzles,* waiting for fruitful suspicion to uncover the real script, Marxian, Freudian, sociobiological (though all these stories may be true, need finding out). They are to do with the inescapability of taking time. 'I do not really know myself' must be heard as 'I don't yet know what to say; how to speak so that others listen and answer and build up in their words a way for me to go on speaking so that others may answer; how to become a partner in the world.' The sense of a choked or imprisoned or elusive interiority is, on this account, a sense of skills not yet learned and nourishment not given, of not knowing what it might be to be *heard* and so set free.[19]

I admire this passage for its candidness. Again, Hans-Georg Gadamer writes: 'Anyone who listens is fundamentally open. Without this kind of openness to one another there is no genuine human relationship. Belonging together always also means being able to listen to one another.'[20] Attentiveness involves a mutuality and reciprocity. It must break down hierarchical relationships. To think that they do not need to be listened to represents an unwarranted *hubris* on the part of any human being.

It need hardly be said then that speaking and being listened to is profoundly therapeutic. People heal and open out when they are attended to. I remember how I used to say (in the days when I still counted myself an insider to the Christian church) that, rather than symbolizing God as an eye (I had in mind that single eye which terrifyingly looked down on medieval worshippers from the chancel wall), we should envisage God as an ear. For I had the sense that God hears us into being. A (male) theologian said to me, 'What about listening to God?'. But I cannot imagine what it would mean to listen to God (other than to be on the right wavelength, so that one is profoundly aware of what is going on in one's environment, in the way that I described in the previous chapter). I suppose he meant that one should read the scriptures! On the other hand, I remember that a woman, meeting me again at a conference years later, leaned across the dinner table and commented (to the considerable astonishment of others who were present): 'I remember you! You are the person who said that God is an ear!' She had evidently carried it with her. Should we not see God as an environment which (who?) enables us to be ourselves and so to heal?

Indeed, given what the past has been, it is peculiarly healing when men listen to women. Most women, I am convinced, have almost no idea how to express themselves at any depth in the presence of a man; it is such a rare eventuality for a man to listen to one. (Indeed, many women who get divorces – it is said – could not stand a situation in which they were not being 'heard' any longer, while the man may well have had no understanding that anything was amiss.) On social occasions at which the men whom I have been seated next to, or to whom I have been introduced, do not know how to stop talking, I have sometimes played a game in which I see how long I can keep them talking without it occurring to them that they should perhaps find out something about me. On one occasion I did this at a Harvard University reception for foreigners. I noted that of those to whom I spoke, of many nationalities, the men completely dominated the conversation in the most ridiculous way, while the women in every case also asked me about myself. How delightful it is, then, to find men who can also listen to one! What women have missed out on!

The possibility of attending to others at any deep level surely depends on who one has become. It is for this reason that the thinkers I have quoted draw attention to the fact that attending is an ethical matter. Being able to listen to others is a corollary of having achieved a certain centredness oneself. Until people know and have come to be at peace with themselves they simply will not be able to be 'present' to others. In this sense attention-giving is a spiritual practice, or derives from the spiritual practice which one keeps in one's life. Anne Klein, the specialist in Tibetan Buddhism whom I quoted earlier,[21] describes what is involved in the practice of self-awareness. It consists, she says, in a 'calm abiding'.[22] It is fundamentally non-judgmental, leading in an unforced manner to change and growth. Attending, or 'observing awareness' as Klein names it, involves having a certain integration oneself. It requires considerable maturity. That is why it is a spiritual practice, one which can be cultivated.

What one wishes that one could get some grasp on is the relationship between being acutely observant of the world and being open to that dimension of reality which I have named God. All that can be said is perhaps that those people who have a profound spirituality about them do also seem to be people who are observant of the world and other people. We should suspect a spirituality which seemed to be simply focussed on a person's God, while that person was thoughtless about other people. If there is a training involved in openness to that which is

God, it must surely consist in the first place in being present to others on a mundane level. It is this kind of question which I believe to be crucial for theology and yet which is rarely asked. Seeing, awareness, intunement, must surely at some deep level be one. In fact I think one finds that it is only on days when one is at peace that one is receptive in the way that I described in the previous chapter. That is hardly surprising.

A discussion of attention as a practice leads quite naturally to the discussion of honesty. By 'honesty' I intend here not simply not telling lies (that is relatively easy), but what one might call a complete integrity. That is to say, being honest will involve, for example, not exaggerating, or not weighting the evidence in one's favour in a disagreement. For one who is an academic it must involve reading carefully (with attention, one might say) and representing the view of others accurately. Indeed honesty involves also seeing oneself in a true light. Commenting on the well-known words in *Hamlet*, 'to thine ownself be true; . . . thou canst not then be false to any man',[23] Lionel Trilling comments: 'If sincerity is the avoidance of being false to any man through being true to one's own self, we can see that this state of personal existence is not to be attained without the most arduous effort.'[24] Honesty is a spiritual practice.

I believe I learnt much about honesty as a practice from the Society of Friends (Quakers) among whom I worshipped as an Attender for many years. That is exactly how Quakers think of honesty: as a practice, something which can be cultivated and which is fundamental to the spiritual life. To be honest comes to be integral to one's whole self-understanding. Indeed being honest in this sense can help one gain a sense of oneself. That is not to say that one is never threatened. And one knows full well that it is at times that one feels threatened that one is tempted to be 'economical' with the truth. But even here there are practices which one can learn, such as pausing for a moment before replying. Honesty, then, would seem to involve having a fundamentally friendly attitude towards others rather than a tendency to take an oppositional and defensive stance. It must also be said that (perhaps particularly in the case of women) it should entail the ability to be forthright about one's own strengths and talents.

Honesty and attention to oneself are clearly inter-related. It is not surprising that those who are interested in attending should also have been concerned for an overcoming of what Murdoch calls 'personal fantasy'. She writes:

The chief enemy of excellence in morality (and also in art) is personal fantasy: the tissue of self-aggrandizing and consoling wishes and dreams which prevents one from seeing what is there outside one.[25]

And, taking up Murdoch's thought here, Sara Ruddick observantly comments:

> Fantasy is reverie designed to protect the psyche from pain, self-induced blindness designed to protect it from insight. It is the dreams one invents or is driven by to assuage pain and achieve desires, irrespective of the intentions and projects of others.[26]

Honesty then is related to the adequacy of one's acceptance of oneself.

But what of the stance of those who say that in this post-Freudian age we should realize that we cannot fathom our own motives, let alone those of anyone else? What of those who say that after Derrida we should know very well that we can never achieve the kind of 'full presence' to ourselves or others which the kind of honesty I have described must imply? Such a line of argument, if put forward in response to what I have said about honesty, should be seen for the red herring which it is. Of course we must always to a certain degree be obscure to ourselves, and others will be even more obscure to us. Of course it is the case that human beings are constantly in flux and changing. (Were this not the case, we could never let others surprise us.) But the fact that we may be difficult to fathom surely cannot be a reason for slacking in our attempts to observe ourselves and understand others. (Personally, I do not remember anyone having listened to me more closely than Derrida himself on the occasion on which I read a paper in his presence. His work could be said to consist in attending to what is present.)

I now turn to my third example of a practice which I think fundamental to a life which is centred and spiritual, which I have called 'ordering'. By 'ordering' I simply intend having a certain control over one's time and one's affairs. For someone like me it will mean keeping my desk and my diary straight, answering correspondence and dealing with administrative matters promptly, and planning ahead what I shall do when. Indeed procrastination becomes the greatest sin! I believe ordering to be not just a personal idiosyncrasy in which some people may choose to engage but a social discipline. This becomes evident if one considers its contrary, scattiness. Scattiness is the most selfish of vices, disrupting the lives of others. If I do not order the books for the library in time, they will not be available when my students need them. If I do not give the information he needs to my chair of department, he must spend time chasing it. Those of us who enjoy full employment have come to live in a relentless world in which one person's inefficiency needlessly affects others.

Ordering is clearly a skill which has been crucial in the lives of many women. For women have had to be adept at keeping a complex life afloat, juggling different demands on their time and energy. If one considers the Greek concept of *eudaemonia*, which consists in a certain flourishing, for many women such flourishing consists in being at the centre of a many-faceted existence over which they exercise a reasonable control. Ordering, then, is a foundation for living. It is about creating space and time and freedom in our lives for the things which really matter. One may well think that ordering their environment is peculiarly important to many women. Maybe I am gender-biassed. If I see a man's room in considerable chaos I think nothing of it. If I see a woman's room in the same state I wonder what is making her so unhappy! Women like to pace themselves, to organize the space around them and to create, even in small ways, a sense of serenity and beauty.

At this point I am sure that it will be asked, 'But what of spontaneity?' Indeed, 'What of exercising some mercy towards those who are less organized than oneself?' I do not think that these are valid objections. I have said nothing of a regimentation which has come to rule one's life. It is because one is reasonably in control that one is free to be spontaneous! If my lecture is prepared, then I am free to drop everything when a friend telephones. Nor have I suggested that one should not care for others, even though this may well be time-consuming, or that one should be reluctant to turn to others for help. It tends, however, to be those people who are already coping with all that comes their way who are able to take on yet more when the need arises. A person drowning in the chaos of her own life is unlikely to be free in herself to be present to another. Whether one is merciful is a different issue from whether one is organized.

However, I find myself moved here by a delightful and provocative article by Janet Martin Soskice entitled 'Love and Attention'.[27] Martin Soskice, a theologian with a full-time job and the mother of two, makes the criticism that traditional teaching on the spiritual life reflects a lack of any conception as to what it means, for example, to be responsible for the care of young children. One's life is constantly fractured, as the best-laid plans must be scrapped. Is what I have called ordering a discipline which is viable only in the privileged lives of those of us who are single? (It is, of course, the case that over the years spiritual injunctions have flowed almost exclusively from the pens of those whose lives have been remote from the turmoil which is the lot of many women!) I am inclined to think that, on the contrary, the scenario which Martin Soskice places before me precisely exemplifies the need for women to have some control over their lives if we are not to be wholly frustrated. In discussing ordering I am scarcely envisaging a life which is vacant or removed from the world.

Given that we may think that many women crave a certain order in their lives, it is invidious that they have so often been at the beck and call of men. Only too often women's lives have circled around those of men, clearing up after them, typing that memo after hours which could have been thought about weeks ago, or racing to the shops for something they could not guess they would need. It is not for men to charge through life leaving a trail of disorder in their wake. Particularly does it behove those in positions of authority (usually men) to understand that 'subordinates' will want to plan their lives. For a person not to have reasonable charge of her work is, in effect, for her to be a slave. It is to be hoped that as women come to be in positions of authority they will retain a memory of what it was like to be on the receiving end of unwarranted demands. We are, after all, speaking of nothing more than being attentive to the lives of others.

But why should ordering be so important to a life which has a certain spirituality about it? We should notice that in fact an ordering of time and space has been a marked characteristic of the most diverse spiritual traditions. Buddhist practice consists in large part in being centred and therefore in control of one's affairs. Catholic monasticism has taken to extremes an ordering of one's whole way of life. The Muslim day is ordered by definite times of prayer. And it was a Quaker, J.C. Whittier, who last century gave us that line which I have carried with me from Christianity: 'And let my ordered life confess the beauty of thy peace.'[28] Traditionally human beings have kept the sabbath, or have had set times for prayer, meditation, or to go on retreat. Today many people attempt exactly the same in their lives, even if it only consists in going to a yoga class, taking long walks or tending their garden, even simply using the time it takes to drive to work to mull things through. We cannot live without a framework which brings us back to base.

It would seem to be perfectly clear then that unless a life has a certain coherence the wheels will simply spin. We need time to dwell, not simply to exist. Now and again we must return to ourselves, becoming focussed. The Quakers speak of 'centring down'. I have one friend who takes three months silent Buddhist retreat each autumn! It is fascinating to watch her in her kitchen (when not on retreat!). She goes immediately and without hesitation to the next thing that she needs. It is as though she has near-total presence to the matter at hand. So to be at peace with oneself is surely of the essence of a life which has a spirituality about it. A certain ordering is fundamental to this. Unless one has dealt with the clutter in one's life, one can scarcely enjoy the sense of having arrived. Ordering is a vehicle which allows us, day by day, to deal with the demands of the present and to face the future with confidence.

In a more directly spiritual sense, then, it may be thought that both honesty and ordering, as I have described them, are crucial spiritual practices. Honesty involves clarity and directness. Indeed, those whom we consider saints commonly possess a certain transparency. If people are not present to themselves, we may think they can scarcely be open to that which is God. Meanwhile chaos in one's life will prevent the establishment of that peace which allows one to become centred. There may, of course, be exterior chaos. The skill in learning to live is to allow that chaos to remain exterior. Finally, it is only as there is a pattern to our lives that we shall find time to sit down and be quiet – or whatever it is that we do to maintain our lives, other than simply on a material level. Peoples' spirituality takes many forms. But the basic skills which are needed to enable the spiritual life are surely not dissimilar.

We may note with interest the profound interconnection between the three practices of attending, honesty and ordering which I have discussed. Perhaps this is exactly what we should expect to find. (I am not clear as to the relationship between a discussion of whether life-practices are ultimately one and the philosophical discussion of whether the virtues are one.) Consider, then, these practices. What would seem to be crucial to their exercise is that one has a certain 'centredness' in oneself. It is as one is so present to oneself that one is free to attend to others. Attending, whether to other people or to the world of nature or the arts, allows one to grow in complexity and maturity. Self-observation enables one to know oneself. It is out of this centre that one acts. A basic honesty allows an integrity to one's life. As one achieves a confidence and knowledge of oneself, one is the better able to order one's life. The freedom which one achieves allows one to be present to others. A many-faceted life over which one exercises some control gives one a sense of serenity. One has a sense of being 'at home' with oneself and in tune with the world. Such a life has a balance and stability which allows one to meet difficulties. A certain trustfulness is present in it which allows one to face the future.

Furthermore, we should notice what the character of the virtues which enable the practices of which I have spoken is likely to be. These practices clearly presuppose that one has a strength in oneself. It requires a level of self-integration to attend to oneself and to others; it would seem that only as one is fearless does one have the possibility of a deep honesty; to order one's life demands self-control. The practices involve having a sense of oneself. One respects both oneself and others. The virtues which these practices imply are then certainly at least courage, a love of others and a belief that one is oneself valuable, and the ability if need be to stand alone for what one considers to be the truth. Again, one might say that the traits which might enable the world which I am envisaging are forthrightness, self-confidence and belief in the importance to human beings of self-realization. We should note that the so-called 'virtues' which I have not mentioned are precisely those which, in particular, have so often been enjoined upon women within Christianity. I am thinking of self-sacrifice, humility and obedience.

It is clear, then, that the question as to which virtues and their attendant practices one will pursue is a highly political matter. As Alasdair MacIntyre, notably, has pointed out, virtues and practices are situated within a life context.[29] When certain practices and virtues are held up before people as worthy of emulation, their lives will take a particular shape. Changes in estimation as to what is to be deemed right, good and proper allows people to become different persons. Such a transition has come about through the advent of the women's movement. What was previously preached to women is now seen to be harmful, calculated to perpetuate a hierarchical and gendered society. We are concerned here with a profound education in self-understanding which has taken place in the lives of many women. Women now look askance at what they formerly thought virtuous. Well do I remember as a teenager singing 'Love so amazing, so divine, demands my life, my soul, my all'; trying to take on board what that meant for my projected life.[30] I should now immediately be sceptical. To say this does not of course mean that one should never choose to be self-sacrificial.

How different, then, is the spirit of the women's movement from what has commonly been the outlook of Christianity. For, rightly or wrongly, from the earliest times Christian discipleship has been thought fundamentally to demand self-denial, even self-denigration and self-flagellation (either in actuality or metaphorically). Within Christianity, human beings are enjoined to understand themselves in the first instance as sinners. The incarnation has been interpreted as a willing divestment of power on the part of the Lord of history, while the crucifixion has been cast in terms of sacrifice. But given the circumstances which women have known, what help is such a religion likely to be to them – other than to provide an interpretation of their lot and to give them the patience to endure? Indeed, how could it be useful to women to have held up before them, as the basic icon of their religion, the appalling picture of a naked and bleeding man impaled on an executioner's gibbet? As women come to place themselves at the centre of their spirituality they will surely leave such imagery behind.

The basic incompatibility between feminism and Christianity thus consists in a difference in their ethos. In Christian terms, as Eleanor Haney has pointed out, to place oneself at the centre is understood as a manifestation of the sin of pride. I have already indicated the misrepresentation by men of the feminist concern for self-actualization and self-recognition (because the context has not been understood).[31] For women commonly conceive of the self relationally. If in the past spiritual guidance has come disproportionately from men, it is interesting that in recent years books of daily readings by women for women have appeared on the scene. The popularity of Anne Wilson Schaef's *Meditations for Women Who Do Too Much*[32] or Anne Dickson's *A Book of Your Own*[33] would seem to suggest that they have touched a chord. Fundamental to these books are the kind of virtues and practices which I have described: the need to pace one's life, to have a good sense of oneself, to forgive oneself, and to keep the web of one's relations with others in a state of repair. It would be fascinating to know whether men, chancing on these books, found that they spoke to their condition! But that there is wisdom for women to share is evident.

I have spoken of the different ethos of feminism from that which has been to the fore in Christian culture. Nevertheless, I think it to be of the deepest significance that, when one considers the nature of spiritual practices, it becomes clear that humanity across all times and ages (and both sexes) holds a great deal in common. While the systems of thought and belief of different religions may seem to be poles apart, the practices which are enjoined on believers are by no means so disparate. It follows that it will not be surprising to find that, while a person may reject the Christian myth, she will wish to continue, perhaps in somewhat different form, certain practices which allow of a spirituality in her life. Many feminist women of whom I know seem to have reached such a position.

Some remarks of David Hay, who has been closely associated with the Oxford Religious Experience Research Unit, are of interest in this matter. Comparing the practices of Buddhism and Christianity, Hay comments that here are two great religious traditions which grew in isolation from one another, in worlds which are 'about as distant, both geographically and ideologically, as it is possible for two great cultural systems to be'. Yet at the level of practices they hold much in common. Hay names the following:

> The requirement to be silent; the requirement to be still; the requirement to be aware or receptive; the requirement to lead a celibate life, at least for a time; the requirement to follow the rule of a spiritual director or meditation master; the requirement to abide by the ethical norms of one's culture.[34]

Clearly these requirements resonate with those which I have wished to discuss: the need to be silent or still; the importance of being aware or receptive (attentiveness); and the importance of ethics, which I have treated under the heading of honesty. But what of the two which I have omitted: the requirement to follow a spiritual director and the requirement to lead a celibate life? There may be some worthwhile observations to be made here.

Consider first the question of spiritual direction. I believe that one should be deeply suspicious of the efficacy of women going to men (for spiritual directors, priests and ministers have commonly been men) as spiritual directors. Such relationships can only be set in a context which is far from neutral within a patriarchal society. Very often they have simply involved power play. What women need is justice, not consolation. A man who has sexist presuppositions about the 'natural' ordering of society, or the relationships which should pertain within marriage or in the workplace, will give advice which has the effect of undermining a woman in her pursuit of rights and recognition. It may be deeply insidious that men have set themselves up as the counsellors of women. Faced, for example, with a decision over abortion or divorce, a woman had best be empowered to take her own needs seriously. Only too often, we must think, women have been given the most inappropriate advice. And in a patriarchal world they have listened to it.

That there may be profound problems in women looking to men for 'spiritual direction' is something which has been recognized by women whose religious position is much more conservative than is mine. I quote a comment in the (British) *Catholic Women's Network Newsletter*:

> Most spiritual directors, most authors of spiritual books, most theologians, all confessors, many counsellors, have been men. Men are ignorant of specifically feminine approaches to the spiritual life and therefore usually propose for women male spiritual practice plus the ideal of the eternal feminine! Women have rarely been alerted to the vices which may be more characteristic of them. Moreover, men tend to stress the intellectual over the affective approach to God and emphasize method in prayer over intuition. Their model is Christian warfare, asceticism rather than mysticism, submission rather than personal initiative. At Confirmation we were invited to become 'soldiers of Christ' and conquering self became an objective.[35]

One may also consider here the character of the female saints, including the Virgin Mary, who have been held up for women's emulation. Women have commonly been admonished to exercise humility and to be self-effacing; in effect, yet again, to serve the world of men.

Part of the problem with spiritual direction as it has been practised within a masculinist culture has clearly been its non-egalitarian presuppositions. Why should one human being direct the life of another in a non-reciprocal way? If, for women, the ethical and spiritual task is to come into our own, then it is peculiarly difficult to know how this could be learnt within what is in effect a hierarchical relationship. Spiritual wisdom may be something which essentially we must learn for ourselves. This is not to say that one will not need spiritual counsellors; others – perhaps of one's own sex – to whom one can turn. We all need people to listen to us and to reflect back to us what we are saying. It may well be that such a relationship with another human being should be formalized and that one should pay for such help. But that is another issue, which need not basically affect the egalitarian mode. In comparing the Socratic paradigm with that of the revelation of the God in history, Kierkegaard rightly remarks that a Socratic relationship is the true relation between human beings. Anything else is a matter of one person, inappropriately, setting himself or herself up as a 'god' for the other.[36] Indeed it would seem that relationships through which one truly learns are always, to some degree at least, reciprocal. It has been found that patients make progress when they are also able to serve those who counsel them. Individuals who refuse such reciprocity may well be highly dangerous. The same should be said of social institutions (the confessional or some kinds of psychotherapy) which deny this.

Yet if feminist women may well wish to place question-marks against spiritual direction, it is also the case that women in the women's movement have developed precisely modes of listening to and enabling one another. That is what consciousness-raising has been about. Also significant in this regard is the development among women of the practice of 'mentoring'. A 'mentor' is a more senior woman (for example in industry) who gives a younger woman a helping hand, discussing strategies and appropriate courses of action with her. Given that women are still not part of the male network, that they come to the work situation with different expectations, and that often there are no patterns for them to follow in the way that there are for men (for women are breaking new ground), mentoring can be extraordinarily beneficial.[37] How difficult it is for a woman to know whether the fact that she looks askance at male behaviour at work is simply a personal idiosyncrasy, or reflects much deeper presuppositions about human relationships which are at variance with those of her male colleagues! When should she mount a challenge and when does she stand no hope of changing the culture? One needs mentors, allies and friends if one is not to feel quite alone.

Hay also mentions celibacy. Here again I think that there are interesting observations to be made. I write as one to whom the sense that one's relationship with God might indeed preclude an intimate relationship with a member of the opposite sex (if, as I am, one is heterosexual) is not at all foreign. I well remember the astonishment that was caused when the Quaker meeting to which, in my mid-thirties, I had

gravitated was to set up groups to discuss human sexuality and I said
that the 'most pressing question' I should like to consider was celibacy!
By celibacy here – let us be clear – I mean the absence of a sexual relationship on account of one's relationship with God. What a farce that,
in our society, that word should have come to connote anything less
than this! Celibacy follows from the way in which one conceptualizes
the human relationship to God. (This is something on which I am
intending to write further in the context of a discussion of the different
conceptions of this relationship pertaining in Lutheran and Catholic
thought.)[38] If God comes no longer to be conceived of as a 'Thou',
placed in apposition to oneself, for whom anthropomorphic metaphors
are appropriate, then celibacy fails to make sense. (What one's sexual
ethics should be is quite another matter.) But whether or not a person's
understanding of her or his relationship to God involves celibacy, it is
presumably the case that all human beings need some time to be apart
if they are to lead centred and spiritual lives.

However, I must move on. Given my previous experience, I do not
doubt that many of my readers (particularly perhaps feminist readers)
are impatient to raise another matter. Am I not wishing to promote
what they will call, pejoratively, a 'personal spirituality' at the expense
of the political? In speaking to this question let me first once again
remind readers of the aim of this chapter. I am wanting to ask, however
elusive the answer may prove to be, whether there are certain ways of
being in the world, certain practices, which will enable one to be aware
of that dimension of reality which is God. I am not for a moment seeking to deny the importance of the political. I should not know what it
meant to be a spiritual person who was not also politically engaged
through her very spirituality.

I believe, then, that there is this to be said – and that it needs saying.
Coming to be oneself and serving others are not mutually exclusive.
This is something feminists, of all people, should know. As we become
older, perhaps rightly we become more hesitant about rushing in to help
others. We find that we ourselves are only truly helped by those who
have a deep integrity. Indeed, one supposes that the reason why some
people who speak so much about serving others in fact behave so
destructively is that they lack an adequate sense of themselves. They
need first to heal. A person who is all over the place will hardly be
observant of others. Again, a prophetic religion which thunders 'Thus
saith the Lord' may well simply leave people passively in the pews doing
nothing. Such a religion serves to disempower people. In this day and
age, indeed, it may strike them as offensive. What we value in our
present society is self-realization, not obedience to a higher power.
People need to be told that they have strengths. By contrast with such a

religion, feminism has commenced with the empowering of individuals in community.

Nor should we fail to notice that those who have been counted sages and religious leaders, far from seeing social action as an alternative to the spiritual quest, have predicated the former upon the necessity of the latter. This would seem to be true of the most diverse thinkers across the ages. I quote Plato, placing words in the mouth of Socrates:

> In reality justice . . . is not a matter of external behaviour, but of the inward self and of attending to all that is, in the fullest sense, a man's proper concern. The just man does not allow the several elements in his soul [reason, spirit and desire] to usurp one another's functions; he is indeed one who sets his house in order, by self-mastery and discipline coming to be at peace with himself, and bringing into tune those three parts, like the terms in the proportion of a musical scale . . . Only when he has linked these parts together in well-tempered harmony and has made himself one man instead of many, will he be ready to go about whatever he may have to do.[39]

Quite so. It is such a sense, derived from the thought of the ancient world, which has been taken up in the development in recent years of so called 'virtue' ethics, to which I have drawn attention.

At the other end of the philosophical spectrum – or so we might think – and after an interval of two and a half millennia, here is perhaps the greatest philosopher of the twentieth century, Martin Heidegger. 'Resoluteness' in the English translates *Entschlossenheit*, a gathering up of oneself, a determinateness. The context is a discussion of authenticity, of *Eigentlichkeit*: literally a coming to 'own' oneself, as Heidegger plays with the German word *eigen*. I quote from Heidegger together with a commentary on the passage by George Steiner.

> 'Resoluteness brings the self right into its current concernful being-alongside what is ready-to-hand, and pushes it into solicitous being with others.' Heidegger is arguing that possession of self and rejection of 'theyness' [inauthenticity/ going along with the crowd] do not, as they seem to in Kierkegaard or Nietzsche, cut off the individual from social responsibility. They make him more apt to take such responsibility upon *himself* (a term which as we have seen, comports a full realization of identity and autonomy). This idea that *Dasein* [the human being] can transcend alienation through personal authenticity, that true authenticity entails active involvement with others . . .[40]

The relationship to others is understood to be inseparable from that to oneself. It does not negate this insight that Heidegger's personal behaviour in the years after he wrote *Being and Time* left so much to be desired. Precisely – one might say – had he but followed his own injunction that one should not submerge one's identity in 'the crowd', Heidegger might have shown more perspicacity and resolution in the face of National Socialism.

It may very well be that, in a passage like this, Heidegger owes much to Luther. We should not forget that a few years before he wrote *Being and Time* Heidegger had been lecturing on . . . what? The New Testament, Augustine and Luther! He knew Luther intimately, something often not reckoned with by Heidegger scholars who, philosophers not theologians, are frequently not conversant with Luther's thought. For Luther 'person' always precedes 'works'; or, as he will have it, picking up the words of John's Gospel, the good tree bears good fruit. Again, seeking another example, Luther refers back to Aristotle (otherwise the arch-enemy): a workman makes work like himself.[41] For Luther it is not that we shall become good through doing good works (the medieval Catholic concept of the *habitus*). Luther knew full well that seeking to be good enough to win God's acceptance could only land one in despair. Rather is it as one accepts oneself (in Luther's terms, trusts that one is accepted by God irrespective of one's merits) that this newfound security will lead to spontaneous love and acceptance of others. Indeed only in this way will service of others be freely given, rather than calculated to boost one's self-estimation.

Meanwhile, across the theological divide, but from the same century as Luther, here are words of John of the Cross:

> Let those, then, who are singularly active, who think they can win the world with their preaching and exterior works, observe here that they would profit the Church and please God much more, not to mention the good example they would give, were they to spend at least half of this time with God in prayer, even though they may not have reached a prayer as sublime as this. They would then certainly accomplish more, and with less labour, by one work than they otherwise would by a thousand. For through their prayer they would merit this result, and themselves be spiritually strengthened. Without prayer, they would do a great deal of hammering but accomplish little, and sometimes nothing, and even at times cause harm.
>
> God forbid that the salt should begin to lose its savour, for however much they may appear to achieve externally, they will in substance be accomplishing nothing; it is beyond doubt that good works can be performed only by the power of God.[42]

Need one say more? A concern for one's own growth is not simply the birthright of every human being. Coming into one's own is, in truth, prerequisite to the service of others.

There is one further matter which I think it appropriate that we should consider. It is philosophical in nature and yet of considerable practical import. In the previous chapter I drew attention to the question of the relationship between (on the one hand) the conviction that there is, as I put it, a dimension of reality which is God; and (on the other) the faith that the universe as a whole makes some kind of sense, that is to say the word God has a transcendental function.[43] I believe that a closely allied question arises in conjunction with the discussion of practices and virtues which I am pursuing in the present chapter. If we are to pursue these ways of being and acting, is it important that we should conceive there to be a framework within which our doing so makes sense? In conjunction with the previous discussion I have already mentioned that there are of course those (I instanced existentialist atheists) who exhort us to continue to do the good in what they conceive to be a senseless universe. What, as a theist, should one think in this respect?

Clearly an obvious conversation partner here is Kant. I shall summarize, as best I can in short compass, his argument in his so called 'second' critique, *The Critique of Practical Reason*.[44] Kant conceives that to act morally is to obey the categorical imperative; that is, in short, to ask oneself how it would be were everyone to do that which one is oneself now contemplating. To act ethically must, of course, be to act independently of any reward or harm which might accrue to one in the process. Nevertheless Kant believes – as he spells it out in the second half of that book – that if we are not to be undermined in our right doing, we must conceive that in so acting we are doing so in a world in which our action conforms to the ultimate nature of things. We postulate a *summum bonum*, in which happiness will be commensurate with virtue. Evidently this state of affairs does not pertain in our world (in which we may say the good man Job sits on his ash heap). Thus we must also postulate the concept of eternal life: that is to say, a state in which, first, we shall be able to act in conformity with our moral precepts (which at present we singularly fail to do), and secondly, we shall be commensurately rewarded. We must then, finally, also postulate the concept of God, i. e. that which will square the circle, so that virtue and happiness coincide and the *summum bonum* is attained.

It is important that I give some critique of Kant here, or I am sure I shall be told (in view of the line of argument which I wish to pursue) that I am nothing more than a thorough-going Kantian! There are a number of respects in which I find Kant's position problematic. In the first place it should be clear from what I have already said in this chapter that I by no means subscribe without further ado to a Kantian, deontological ethics. I am much attracted to virtue ethics, in which the character of the ethical agent is decisive. Furthermore – and this is pertinent to our present concern – I do not employ the word God simply to designate a transcendental function. Rather, in the first instance it connotes for me certain effects in the world which I believe to be the case. Thirdly (as have many), I find Kant's outlook too individualistic. While not wanting to subtract from individual responsibility, it seems to me a deeply masculinist proposition to think that I, as an individual self, embark on a quest for self-improvement, extending not simply throughout my life but extrapolated in my imagination into all eternity! This is to say nothing of the fact that I shall apparently be individually 'rewarded', whatever that may mean, for my achievement!

Of course I am not the first to raise such criticisms. Writing little more than a decade after Kant, in his *Speeches* of 1799, Schleiermacher is very clear that morality must be independent of any ulterior motive. As he expressed it in the 1821 edition: 'Morality can be quite moral without therefore being pious.'[45] For Schleiermacher (as also for Camus) ethics must stand on its own feet and could only be subverted through any hint of an ulterior motive. We must be clear that Kant did not intend so to subvert ethics. His is a carefully crafted argument. Nevertheless he walks on a knife edge. Indeed I might find the way in which Kant develops the question he has posed so off-putting that I failed to notice its importance. For I do think that there is something important to be said here, which Kant places before our eyes (perhaps in garb which we may dislike).

Is it not the case that one who is a theist believes – perhaps as a matter of faith – that right acting and human goodness conform to the very nature of the way in which things are? I cannot put this better than by giving a quotation from someone who has considered many cultures, the social anthropologist Clifford Geertz:

> The heart of this way of looking at the world, that is, of the religious perspective, is, so I would like to argue, not the theory that beyond the visible world there lies an invisible one . . .; not the doctrine that a divine presence broods over the world . . .; not even the more diffident opinion that there are things in heaven and earth undreamt of in our philosophies. Rather, it is the conviction that the values one holds are grounded in the inherent structure of reality, that between the way one ought to live and the way things really are there is an unbreakable inner connection.[46]

That is very interesting. If this is so, then as a corollary it must follow that it is peculiarly evil to destroy another's framework of meaning. Yet we may think that those things which destroy people's framework of meaning – torture (whether mental or physical), betrayal of their trust, even simply the lack of validation which they may rightly expect from others – are commonplace in our world. Commensurately with this, we should have unbounded admiration for those who, in excruciating circumstances, are able to retain a grasp on basic human values, often enabling others to do likewise. In our generation we think of the faith of Nelson Mandela, maintained during those long years of imprisonment. Then there is the extraordinary story of Victor Frankl, who in later years as a psychoanalyst was to advocate a form of therapy (logotherapy) in which the understanding that a sense of purpose is fundamental to a human life is foremost. The first draft of *Man's Search for Meaning* was taken from Frankl upon his arrival in Auschwitz.[47] He lived it out. Frankl relates how, after a particularly harrowing episode, he spoke in the dark to a silent gathering of prisoners, reciting to them Nietzsche's words *'was mich nicht umbringt, macht mich stärker'* (what does not bring me down/kill me, makes me stronger).[48]

Indeed, it seems to me that in more mundane circumstances it has often been women who have held together a framework of meaning for themselves and others. It was Julian of Norwich who gave us those oft-recited words 'All shall be well, and all manner of thing shall be well.'[49] I am reminded, too, of the woman who, speaking after a meeting with Ronald Higgins (the campaigner who, during the 1970s and 1980s, attempted to bring to public awareness the multiple collision courses on which our world is set), commented, 'You have given us the cross . . . but where is the encompassing circle?'. Higgins responded that he did not know the answer, but that he had begun to see the significance of the question.[50] Again, I am reminded here of those extraordinary pictures by the German artist Käthe Kollwitz, living at the end of last century and the beginning of this. Her mother figures reach out to surround the children whom they embrace, protecting them from war and devastation. In each case there is the image of the circle. Julian of Norwich holds a hazel nut in the palm of her hand; Higgins' interlocutor asks after the surrounding circle; Kollwitz's mothers encircle. Even Irigaray's little girl dances in circular motion, creating safe space.[51] We may think this sense for holding things together to be a profoundly religious sensibility.

In concluding this chapter I wish to return to the discussion on which, in a slightly different guise, I embarked at its outset. How is the relationship between God and the self differently conceived within different theological paradigms? In order to consider this question, I shall designate three types of theology. That I may better convey some concrete sense of each mode of theological discourse, I shall mention a

particular thinker in conjunction with each. Nevertheless it is important
to stress that I do not wish to suggest that the thinker whom I mention
conforms in every respect to what I shall say about the paradigm. Let
us, then, consider three different types of theology: first, a theology of
revelation; secondly, theology as history; and thirdly, a theology predicated upon experience. It will not surprise readers that I shall seek to
commend the last of these.

Consider then, first, a theology of revelation and, as a theologian who
conforms to type, Karl Barth. In a theology of revelation, God is by
definition other than the world, revealing God's self in the world. It is of
course the case that (as in Barth's theology) the 'distance' between God
and humanity may be traversed by a doctrine of incarnation. Like
Irenaeus here, Barth conceives of humanity as taken up into the fullness
of God, in his case through a trinitarian doctrine in which the second
'person' of the Trinity takes on what it means to be human. Nevertheless
the basic sense – even in the later Barth – is that of God's otherness to
humanity. In the early Barth there is a disjuncture. God pronounces a
resounding 'No' to humanity; only in Christ is a 'Yes' imposed on that
'No'. It is not that humanity in itself has worth; in and of itself humanity
is not able to relate to God. The theological move is thus a disruption of
the human reality. Now it may well be thought that the theme of God's
difference from the world (and consequently also the concept of revelation) is fundamental to the Judaeo-Christian tradition. In this book we
have considered Kierkegaard, who is the fount of this type of theology in
the modern world. Kierkegaard's truth of revelation is precisely other
than human truth and (apart from revelation) unknown to humankind.[52]

Let us contrast with this that mode of theological thought in which
theology is history. Here the obvious candidate for our consideration is
of course Hegel. In this paradigm God (or in Hegel's case spirit/mind,
Geist), becomes in a sense history; 'he' (or it) works 'himself' (or itself)
out in history. History itself takes on a purposefulness as it moves
towards a climax or *telos*. In this mode of theological discourse, history
is *par excellence* a grand narrative. Marxism is its secular equivalent. It
will not surprise us, then, to find that theologies of liberation have often
learnt much from this paradigm. They may also have a transcendent
God; but then so did Augustine, who has a theology of history.
However, it is not that this theological mode is tied to left-wing politics;
as becomes clear when we consider that Wolfhart Pannenberg's is a
theology of history.[53] As in the case of a theology of revelation, so also
theology understood as history would seem to be fundamental to the
Judaeo-Christian tradition. The God of the Hebrew scriptures is bound
up with the unfolding history of a nation. Christians look forward to an
eschaton, seeking to bring about the reign of God on earth.

Now I have already suggested that intrinsic to both these theological types there are profound problems of theodicy. In relation to a theology of revelation, the question arises – if God transcends history and has the power to intervene in history (the presupposition of this model) – why then has the lot of humanity not been otherwise? Why, in particular, has the situation of women – in all times and cultures – been what it has? Moreover, how can it be that (as may be thought to be the case), the supposed revelation has in *any* sense served to legitimize sexism if that revelation is indeed from God?[54] But the problem of theodicy to which a theology of history gives rise is no less acute. If a theory of progress seemed valid in the nineteenth century (the century of Hegel and of Marx), that optimism met its death on the battlefields of the First World War. My own father, a young soldier in that war, spent a night on the floor of the church of the Holy Nativity in Bethlehem, beside him a dying man, whose bloody boots my father was to inherit. I believe that my father was the one member of his school class, who had signed up together, to return from that war. As we approach the end of the twentieth century, far from thinking that there is to be a final consummation in glory, we are more likely to fear that the world will end in a nuclear holocaust or in ecological degradation. Again, women must ask – if God or spirit be bound up with history – how is it that the circumstances of women have been what they have? At least on a grand scale, 'history' has left women out.

But what I more especially wish to draw attention to here is that neither a theology of revelation nor theology as history place human beings at the centre of the stage. Consider, first, a theology of revelation. Truth (the truth of revelation) is not found within the self (or the world). It is other than the self; precisely, it is revealed. (There is a fundamental distinction, which we considered, between what Kierkegaard names 'A' and what he names 'B', the truth of revelation.) Thus in the act of salvation a self which is essentially devoid of truth has to be broken open, so that now it bases itself not on itself but on God. As St Paul classically states this: 'I am crucified with Christ, nevertheless I live; yet not I, but Christ lives in me.'[55] Such a theological structure is fundamental to Protestantism. (As in so much, Schleiermacher is the exception here.) Consider, secondly, a theology of history. In this case the problem is not that the self has to base itself on that which is other than itself, but rather that there is little concentration on the individual self at all. The individual is submerged in history. The person knows salvation only as he or she is caught up in a greater whole which will be redeemed, and that scarcely in that person's lifetime!

Fundamental to feminism, however, is a concern for the individual.

Feminists believe that it is the transformation of individual lives which is crucial. Far from wishing to deny the self, or to say that an individual should be broken open and based on someone or something other than herself, feminists have wished to affirm the self. Feminists will that women should come into their own. In theological terms, feminism might well be said to be aligned with a 'high' doctrine of creation. Feminists believe, not in the undoing of the self, castigating a person for her pride, but rather in building up what is already given. Feminists will therefore look askance at a doctrine which advocates turning away from the self to God. They will be sceptical about the contention that the self is only itself when it is based on that which is not the self, namely God. Again, it may be that feminists believe that the cause of women is embedded within history, even that women are – as Mary Daly will have it – the 'final cause'.[56] But in looking to the grand sweep of history to right what is wrong, feminists refuse to avert their eyes from the cause of the individual here and now. Change comes about as the lives of individuals change. Moreover it is through the changed lives of individuals that change is secured. (Marxism may well have floundered in not sufficiently taking into account the need for a trans-formed subjectivity.) The personal is the political. Feminists must, then, be profoundly suspicious of a movement which, in its quest for some future goal, by-passes the individual.

There is, however, a third way in which God, humanity and the rela-tionship between God and humanity can be conceptualized. It is that which I have sought to commend in this book. Let us call it a theology which is predicated upon human awareness. If a theology of revelation is encapsulated by the mention of Barth and a theology of history by the mention of Hegel, with whom should we associate the theology which I would have? Is it Plato? It is no chance that both Schleiermacher and Murdoch incline to be Platonists. Nevertheless, I am cautious. In the first place I live the other side of the critique of Platonism by Nietzsche, Heidegger and Derrida. Thus I am not enamoured of the idea that there is a 'real world' (Nietzsche's turn of phrase)[57] which lies 'beyond'. My interest in Schleiermacher lies not in his attempt to reach through the transient world to that which is ultimate (a theme present in the *Speeches),* but in his sense that the human self opens out immediately on to that which is more than itself. Secondly, as a feminist one must be suspicious of any such endeavour. For, as we have seen, in Western history women have been cast as 'the other' to that which is considered somehow spiritual and higher. If I mention Plato, I must do so, then, with the deepest reservations. In the history of Christian thought, there is perhaps no figure (and for good reason) who captures exactly what I would say (and for good reasons). Schleiermacher comes closest, but in the remainder of *The Christian Faith* he veers off into a much more conservative mode.

A theology of experience, as I have called it, places the human self centre-stage. God is known with and through the self. 'Salvation' within such a theology must mean healing, which indeed is the etymological derivation of that word. In a theology of revelation (we may note), almost by definition there is a heteronomous relationship to God. Truth is embodied in the revelation, or in the scriptures, or back in history. In a theology of history, it is the greater whole rather than the individual which counts. By contrast, in a theology of experience the individual comes into her or his own. We are not of course speaking here of individuals in isolation; it is often the case that persons are aware of God through their relationships with other people. But there can be no heteronomy in relation to God. The methodological starting point for such a theology is our awareness. Theology is predicated upon our recognition as to what is the case. Such a theology affirms, rather than seeking to overcome or to deny, that which is already given. Moreover, what is notable about such a religious position is that it in no way requires the Christian myth.

As I reach the conclusion of this chapter and draw this book to a close, one question remains. I have endeavoured to explain what I understand by God and, in this chapter, to relate this to a life which might be designated spiritual. But am I justified in naming that which I do 'God', and is a life such as I describe rightly called 'spiritual'? That I should indeed be employing the terms 'God' and 'spiritual' is the essence of the argument of this book. I have made the accusation that men have formulated their religious understandings through the creation of a particular system of thought, a system of thought which it is no longer possible to credit and which must necessarily distort human relationships. But, I have argued, there is no need for human awareness of that dimension of reality which is God to be thus captured by this myth. Such an awareness does not need to be expressed through a rigid and intricate system of belief.

The need to jettison the myth has been with us for some time. (Indeed, harmful as it has been, one must regret that it ever came into existence.) With the coming of modernity in the eighteenth century, it became untenable. Christians, in part, recognize this. They have in succession discarded the literal meaning of Genesis, then the Virgin Birth, now many discount the resurrection as a flesh-and-blood event. However, they have often sought to move sideways, saying that although it is not literally true, Christianity may be retained as a 'true myth'. What has happened with the rise of feminism is that this move has become unavailable. Feminism has made it evident that Christianity, far from being a true or helpful myth, is a profoundly harmful myth. It has served, and still serves today, to legitimize the inferior place of women in society. The Christian myth now appears as a projection of patriarchy, calculated to justify a patriarchal order to both women and men. Nor, indeed, does the concept of a transcendent monotheism remain unscathed. Given the hierarchy which is intrinsic to it and the model of the human self which it reflects, it is at variance with our values. Finally, a God conceived of as somehow set apart from the universe flies in the face of what scientifically has come to be our understanding of reality. It is time to move on.

In this post-Enlightenment age, human beings must place themselves at the centre of their world. We should not, of course, see ourselves in isolation, but rather as having a profound connectedness to all else that is. Only in this way shall we care for the planet and learn responsibility towards the rest of creation. But to place ourselves at the centre in this way is not to exclude God, since God is to be understood not as set over against us but as one with our self-realization. We may think that which we have named God to be a dimension of all that is: something which we may recognize, on which we can draw, and which allows us to be all that we have it in us to become. Feminists may well be at the forefront of the theological revolution which is coming. For feminism brings new paradigms to the theological endeavour. We shall need ways of speaking of connectedness and relationality which, while leaving us with our full autonomy, allow us to conceptualize the self in relation to that which is more than the self. Moreover women can have no stake in the previous order.

I may believe that we need to discard as untenable the Christian myth and the theological system which is Christian doctrine. But I do not doubt that, in all ages as also in ours, there have been many who have lived with an awareness of God. I clearly think the word God to have a reference. It is not simply to be 'de-mythologized', nor is human spiritual awareness to be translated without remainder into ethics. The word God must refer to a dimension of reality which has always been the case. We may not in future require a grand narrative like the one we have known in Judaism and Christianity. But we shall need to find ways of speaking of that which is God. Though the myth of former times must be jettisoned, some of the past ways of speaking may be useful to us, and we must formulate others.

We must move away from a myth which is held to be objective and true and which, in turn, governs us. Nor may there be the givenness of a transcendent God 'above' the world, by which all else is to be measured. We shall have to sit much more loosely to dogmatic beliefs. Indeed many within the churches are doing just that. There is no need to predicate one's spirituality upon a myth which, first, is no longer believable and, secondly, is situated in past patriarchal history, heavily imbued with its values. It is within ourselves that our spirituality needs to be centred: in our response to the world, our experience and our attentiveness. Spirituality is more fragile, more fleeting, than the attempted objectification would suggest. Moreover to associate what it is to be religious with believing the myth may well be to fail to come into our own. Spirituality must be bound into the matrix of our being what we are and our acting as we do. Inasmuch as there is an objectivity in religion, it must surely be that 'objectivity' which consists in healed lives.

After Christianity there will be – people; people set in the midst of the glory and the wonder of our world. We must trust that the fact that the Christian myth has reigned for so long will not deter us from an exploration of those spiritual resources which are ours. Murdoch writes: 'But someone may say, we shall have to live now with *spirit* and without *absolute* and be thankful if we still have spirit and if that too is not withdrawn from us.'[58] To have that, truthfully, is enough.

Notes

Introduction: A Shift of Paradigm

1. I. Kant, 'Beantwortung der Frage: Was ist Aufklärung?', in *Was ist Aufklärung?,* ed. E Bahr, Stuttgart: Philipp Reclam jun. 1975, 9. My translation.
2. Horace, *Epistles*, I, 2, 40.
3. D. Bonhoeffer, *Letters and Papers from Prison. The Enlarged Edition*, ed. E. Bethge, London: SCM Press 1971 and New York: Macmillan 1972. See the letters from 16 July onwards, 359–62. The context of Bonhoeffer's remarks is certainly also Lutheran thought, in which human 'religiousness' constitutes a false approach to God.
4. Kant, 'Aufklärung?' (n. 1), 9.
5. I. Kant, *Religion within the Limits of Reason Alone*, reissued New York: Harper Torchbooks 1960.
6. From the Greek 'other law', as opposed to 'autonomy', being a law to oneself.
7. T. Greene, 'Introduction', *Religion within the Limits* (n. 5), xxix n.
8. For further consideration of this theme, cf. my article 'On Autonomy and Heteronomy', in *Swallowing a Fishbone? Feminist Theologians Debate Christianity,* ed. D. Hampson, London: SPCK 1996, 1–16.
9. Cf. J. Donovan, *Feminist Theory: The Intellectual Traditions of American Feminism,* New York: Frederick Ungar Publishing Co. 1985, 21.
10. J. S. Mill, 'The Subjection of Women', in *Three Essays on Liberty, Representative Government and the Subjection of Women*, London: Oxford University Press 1975, 478.
11. H. G. Wells, *Experiment in Autobiography*, London and New York: Macmillan 1934, quoted by W. A. Visser 't Hooft, *The Fatherhood of God in an Age of Emancipation,* Geneva: WCC 1982, 48.
12. *Syllabus Errorum*, X, LXXX.
13. Cf. Visser 't Hooft, *Fatherhood* (n. 11), 147.
14. Sex Discrimination Act 1975, chapter 65, part II, 19, Ministers of religion, etc.; 21, Mineworkers.
15. The title of a book by Juliet Flower MacCannell.
16. There is so much writing here that it is difficult to know what to specify, but see e. g. I. M. Young, 'Impartiality and the Civic Public: Some Implications of Feminist Critiques of Moral and Political Theory', and S. Benhabib, 'The Generalized and the Concrete Other: The Kohlberg-

Gilligan Controversy and Feminist Theory', both in *Feminism as Critique,* ed. S. Benhabib and D. Cornell, Minneapolis, MN: University of Minnesota Press 1987.

17. G.W.F. Hegel, *Phenomenology of Spirit* (1807), trans A.V. Miller, London and New York: Oxford University Press 1977, 111–19.

18. De Beauvoir is influenced here by her friend Jean-Paul Sartre's existentialism, so that it is for woman to become, like man, a *pour soi* rather than remaining an approximation to that which is *en soi.*

19. See e. g. the work of Nancy Chodorow and Carol Gilligan discussed below, 100–4, or equally the interest on the part of women in the ethics of 'attention', discussed in Chapter VII.

20. *Octagesima Adveniens,* xxx.

21. See below, 35.

22. Stephen Hawking now apparently posits such a singularity at the 'beginning'.

23. Not least the findings of the Oxford Religious Experience Research Unit would seem to suggest this. See below, 228.

24. A. MacIntyre, *After Virtue: A Study in Moral Theory,* London: Duckworth 1981, 245.

25. 'Recoiling from Reason', review of MacIntyre, *After Virtue, The New York Review of Books,* 7 December 1989, 41.

I. Christian Particularity

1. See below, 26.

2. Thus because I have mentioned that there is a causal nexus, Iain Torrance supposes that I am a determinist ('Is Christianity Irredeemably Sexist?', in R. Holloway [ed.], *Who Needs Feminism? Men Respond to Sexism in the Church,* London: SPCK 1991). Torrance writes: 'Daphne Hampson tells us that she cannot believe that the causal nexus of nature can be broken. Because of this she rules out unique events as an impossibility.' Yes indeed. But Torrance then continues: 'Every event in the world is necessary, and as such, can be traced back to a sufficient and necessary cause. Now, let us apply this to the child born at Bethlehem. If you take the view that the causal chain cannot be broken, and that all events are necessary, . . . then the baby *had* to be a boy. . . It was a set up. If you look at the world through the eyes of Daphne Hampson then there is something very sinister in the birth of that boy baby' (79–80). But I should never dream of saying that every event in the world is necessary! I do not think that the fact that Jesus was a boy was any more determined than is the case with any other child! Indeed I cannot conceive that God could intervene in this kind of way (that is just my point). Moreover Torrance concludes that I am a deist (presumably because I have said that I do not believe that God intervenes in nature). But the form which my theism takes has nothing in common with deism, as Chapter VI will make clear. Whether or not she has picked up this misreading in Torrance I do

not know, but Julie Hopkins has now proclaimed that I am a 'hard determinist' (*Towards a Feminist Christology: Jesus of Nazareth, European Women and the Christological Crisis*, London : SPCK 1995, 65). One could wish that writers would attempt to check with authors whose work they describe that at least they have understood them.

3. See below, 236–7.

4. I find it astonishing how frequently authors confuse the two senses of particularity, moving from what I have called particularity in the second sense to the claim that there has been a particularity in the first sense in history, without apparently noticing the step they have taken. The problem pervades, for example, Colin Gunton's *The One, The Three and the Many: God, Creation and the Culture of Modernity*, Cambridge: Cambridge University Press 1993. Thus Gunton writes: 'It is often said that one of the intellectual drawbacks of Christianity is its elements of particularity. The fact that so much of the faith's content is linked to a particular human figure, and behind him a particular national history, and indeed that neither of them has any manifest world-historical importance, generates what is called the scandal of particularity' (180). Now if Gunton wants to call what he has mentioned 'the scandal of particularity' (which is not what I have called 'the scandal of particularity'), that is fine. It may indeed have been offensive to the Greeks, or may be offensive to some today, that Christianity is tied to the particularities of the history of Christ's life. As far as I am concerned, that is not a problem (or at least not the problem that I am considering here; it may cause ethical problems for feminists). But Gunton then immediately continues: 'It has often appeared to the rational mind that there is something inherently problematic about a faith that is, unlike so many of the philosophies and religions of the world, not a general teaching but the proclamation of historical particularities as the centre of an account of God's being and activity.' That is indeed a 'scandal of particularity' in the sense in which I am employing that term. I could not conceive that, as this sentence implies, God could be related to certain events in history in a sense in which God is not potentially present in all events.

5. Cf. Hopkins, *Towards a Feminist Christology* (n. 2), 76.

6. Cf. D. Hampson, *Theology and Feminism*, Oxford and Cambridge, MA: Basil Blackwell 1990, 50.

7. Cf. F.D.E. Schleiermacher, *The Christian Faith*, ET of the second German edition, ed. H.R. Mackintosh and J.S. Stewart, Edinburgh: T. & T. Clark 1928; paperback ed., New York: Harper and Row 1963, in particular § 11, 91f.

8. See Don Cupitt's interesting comments on this in 'The Christ of Christendom', in *The Myth of God Incarnate*, ed J. Hick, London: SCM Press and Philadelphia, PA: Westminster Press 1977, 133–47, and Stephen Sykes' response, 'The Incarnation as the Foundation of the Church', in *Incarnation and Myth: The Debate Continued*, ed. M. Goulder, London: SCM Press and Grand Rapids, MI: Eerdmans 1979,

115–27. My sense is that after the Enlightenment and in the nineteenth century (slightly later in English Anglicanism than in German Protestantism) there did come to be a different understanding of what it is to be a person, which caused a difficulty for christology which had not previously been present.

9. Cf. (since we are considering him) Bultmann's well-known denial that we have any such access in the Introduction to his *Jesus* of 1926, ET *Jesus and the Word*, New York: Charles Scribner's Sons 1958.

10. Karl Barth was to remark, in my view correctly, that Christ fits 'desperately badly' into Schleiermacher's theology (*Protestant Theology in the Nineteenth Century*, London: SCM Press 1972, 432).

11. Schleiermacher, *The Christian Faith* (n. 7), 93.

12. Heb. 4. 15.

13. For what follows see in particular Bultmann's famous 1941 essay 'New Testament and Mythology', in H. W. Bartsch (ed.), *Kerygma and Myth: A Theological Debate*, London: SPCK 1952 and New York: Harper and Row 1961, and in S. M. Ogden (ed.), *New Testament and Mythology and Other Basic Writings*, Philadelphia, PA: Fortress Press and London: SCM Press 1985, and his *Jesus Christ and Mythology*, New York: Charles Scribner's Sons 1958 and London: SCM Press 1960.

14. S. Kierkegaard, *Philosophical Fragments* (1844), *Kierkegaard's Writings* VII, ed. and trans. H. and E. Hong, Princeton, NJ: Princeton University Press 1985; or *Philosophical Fragments*, translated by D. Swenson and revised by H. Hong, Princeton, NJ: Princeton University Press 1967.

15. Kierkegaard, *Philosophical Fragments* (n. 14), Hong and Hong, 13; Swenson, 16.

16. S. Kierkegaard, *Concluding Unscientific Postscript to the Philosophical Fragments*, trans. D. Swenson, Princeton, NJ: Princeton University Press, 1941, 219, and trans. H. and E. Hong, *Kierkegaard's Writings*, Vol. XII. I, Princeton, NJ: Princeton University Press, 243, 245: 'The immediate relationship to God is paganism . . . If God could have permitted a direct relationship, [the human] would doubtless have taken notice. If God, for example, had taken on the figure of a very rare and tremendously large green bird, with a red beak, sitting in a tree on the mound, and perhaps even whistling in an unheard of manner – then the society man would have been able to get his eyes open . . . All paganism consists in this, that God is related to man directly, as the obviously extraordinary to the astonished observer' (Swenson, 218–9).

17. Cf. S. Kierkegaard, *Practice in Christianity* (1850), *Kierkegaard's Writings* XX, ed. and trans. H. and E. Hong, Princeton, NJ: Princeton University Press 1991; or in *Training in Christianity*, trans. W. Lowrie, Princeton, NJ: Princeton University Press 1944, 28–34.

18. J. Martin Soskice, 'Turning the Symbols?', in *Swallowing a Fishbone? Feminist Theologians Debate Christianity*, ed. D. Hampson, London: SPCK 1996, 22.

19. Quoted by A. Flew, *Did Jesus Rise from the Dead?: The Resurrection*

Debate, ed. T. Miethe, San Francisco: Harper and Row 1989, 7.

20. J.I.M. Packer, in Miethe (ed.), *Did Jesus Rise from the Dead?* (n. 19), 145.
21. M. Green, 'Jesus and Historical Scepticism', in *The Truth of God Incarnate*, ed. M. Green, London: Hodder and Stoughton and Grand Rapids, MI: Eerdmans 1977, 112–13.
22. I Cor. 1. 23.
23. J. Polkinghorne, *One World: The Interaction of Science and Theology*, Princeton, NJ: Princeton University Press 1986, 76.
24. Ibid., 75.
25. J. Polkinghorne, 'Contemporary Interactions between Science and Theology', *Modern Believing*, NS, Vol. xxxvi, no. 4 (October 1995), 37.
26. K. Ward, *Religion and Revelation*, Oxford: Clarendon Press 1994.
27. Ibid., 292; J. Polkinghorne, *Science and Creation*, London: SPCK 1988, 76–83, 83.
28. Ibid., 292.
29. Quantum physics would presumably have nothing to say about the claim that a certain human being was conjoined in one 'person' with a second and divine nature: that must be a faith statement.
30. Cf. for example T.V. Morris, *The Logic of God Incarnate*, Ithaca and London: Cornell University Press 1986.
31. H. McCabe, 'The Myth of God Incarnate', *New Blackfriars*, Vol. 58, no. 687 (Aug. 1977), 353.
32. M. F. Wiles and H. McCabe, 'The Incarnation: An Exchange', *New Blackfriars,* Vol. 58, no. 691 (Dec. 1977), 543.
33. D. Bonhoeffer, *Christology*, London: Collins and New York: Harper and Row 1971.
34. This information was given to me by Franz Hildebrandt.
35. J.A.T. Robinson, *The Human Face of God*, London: SCM Press and Philadelphia, PA: Westminster Press 1973. Works by the other authors are discussed in the text.
36. G.W.H. Lampe, *God as Spirit*, Oxford: The Clarendon Press 1977, 111, 23–4.
37. J. Hick, *The Metaphor of God Incarnate*, London: SCM Press 1993, 26.
38. A. Schweitzer, *The Quest of the Historical Jesus: A Critical Study of Its Progress from Reimarus to Wrede*, London: A. & C. Black and New York: The Macmillan Company 1950.
39. J. Macquarrie, *Jesus Christ in Modern Thought*, London: SCM Press and Philadelphia, PA: Trinity Press International 1990, 375, 382, 376, 385.
40. J. Hick and P. F. Knitter (eds.), *The Myth of Christian Uniqueness*, London: SCM Press and Maryknoll, NY: Orbis 1987.
41. W. Cantwell Smith, 'Idolatry: In Comparative Perspective', in Hick and Knitter (eds.), *The Myth of Christian Uniqueness* (n. 40), 63f.
42. See below, 237–9.
43. In the same volume, the American theologian Langdon Gilkey comments that we must today confront the issue of other world religions, just as the

American Medical Association has to face acupuncture. But no: Christianity is a myth which must be discarded; acupuncture is a way of treating sickness – seemingly sometimes successful – which needs to be investigated and which may or may not be capable of assimilation into the (Western) rational paradigm. Meanwhile it would not seem to be too complimentary to other world religions to compare them to acupuncture! Cf. id., 'Plurality and Its Theological Implications', in Hick and Knitter (eds.), *The Myth of Christian Uniqueness* (n. 40), 49.

44. M.F. Wiles, *Theology* LXXXI (Jan. 1978), 4–14, reprinted in id., *Explorations in Theology* 4, SCM Press 1979, 64–5.

45. Id., 'Christianity without Incarnation?', in *The Myth of God Incarnate* (n. 8), 1–10.

46. See below, 52–8.

47. Id., 'Does Christology Rest on a Mistake?', in *Christ, Faith and History*, ed. S. Sykes and J. Clayton, Cambridge: Cambridge University Press 1972, 10.

48. F.H. Bradley, *The Presuppositions of Critical History* (1874), ed. and with an introduction and commentary by L. Rubinoff, Chicago, IL: Quadrangle Books 1968, 100–1.

49. W. Pannenberg, *Jesus – God and Man*, Philadelphia, PA: Westminster Press and London: SCM Press 1968.

50. I am not myself a biblical scholar and must rely here on the work of others; in particular I acknowledge my indebtedness to a correspondence with Sarah Coakley.

51. C.F.D. Moule, *The Origin of Christology*, Cambridge: Cambridge University Press 1977.

52. Macquarrie, *Jesus Christ and Modern Thought* (n. 39), 405–9: 409.

53. H. Küng, *On Being a Christian*, London: Collins and New York: Double-day 1977, 349.

54. Augustine, *The City of God* XXII, 8, ed. D. Knowles, trans. H. Bettenson, Harmondsworth: Penguin Books 1972, 1042–3.

55. Cf. Frances Young, 'Two Roots or a Tangled Mass?', in *The Myth of God Incarnate* (n. 8), 89.

56. J.L. Houlden, review of W.J. Abraham, *Divine Revelation and the Limits of Historical Criticism*, *Journal of Theological Studies* XXXIV, April 1983, 378.

57. For Jewish thought on the resurrection, which both pre-dates and post-dates the belief which grew up that Jesus had been raised, see M. Greenberg, 'Resurrection', *Encyclopaedia Judaica* 14, Jerusalem: Keter Publishing House 1972, 95–103.

58. Matt. 1.23.

II. Continuity and Discontinuity

1. Cf. my *Theology and Feminism*, Oxford and Cambridge, MA: Basil Blackwell 1990, 7f.

2. See above, 14.

3. Cf. Bede Griffiths, *A New Vision of Reality: Western Science, Eastern Mysticism and Christian Truth*, London: Fount Paperbacks 1992, 166–7. 'The infinite, then, is manifest in Jesus, in this historic person . . . Jesus was born in that historic context and was recognized to be the fulfilment of all these roles as God's revelation on earth. That is the understanding of Jesus within the Hebrew context . . . It is really an extraordinary thing that it should be of the essence of Christian faith that Jesus was crucified under Pontius Pilate at a particular time in history and under a particular Roman governor. This kind of thing is absolutely alien to Hinduism or Buddhism. When Krishna or Rama, or Buddha in the Mahayana, lived is of no account whatsoever; they are manifestations of the eternal, not confined to any time or place. Jesus, on the other hand, manifests the infinite God in historic time and place . . . There are many ancient myths of the god who dies and rises again but these are symbolic figures and their meaning is deep but different. Jesus' death, on the other hand, is not simply symbolic . . . On that historic death and on the resurrection the whole Christian faith centres.'

4. S. Dowell, review article of *Theology and Feminism, Feminist Review* 38, Summer 1991, 95–100.

5. R. R. Ruether, 'Is Feminism the End of Christianity? A Critique of Daphne Hampson's *Theology and Feminism*', *Scottish Journal of Theology* 43, 390–400.

6. Ibid., 399.

7. Cf. for example Ruether's *Sexism and God-Talk. Toward a Feminist Theology*, Boston, MA: Beacon Press 1983 and London: SCM Press 1983, a work in which one might expect Ruether to have said that she too believes that there is such a God. The exception is the concluding words of the book in which, referring to Divine Wisdom, Ruether writes: 'She comes; She is here'. Perhaps it is easier to affirm the existence of wisdom than of the (male) God of the tradition?

8. Cf. in particular Chapter III, 'Concretion'.

9. Cf. E. Fuchs, 'Who is Hiding the Truth? Deceptive Women and Biblical Androcentrism', in A. Yarbro Collins (ed.), *Feminist Perspectives on Biblical Scholarship*, Chico, CA: Scholars Press 1985, 137–44; ' "For I have the Way of Women": Deception, Gender, and Ideology in Biblical Narrative', in J. C. Exum and J. W. H. Bos (eds.), *Reasoning with the Foxes: Female Wit in a World of Male Power*, Semeia, no. 42, 1988, 68–83.

10. Cf. Cheryl Exum's writing on the David/Bathsheba story, 'Raped by the Pen', in *Fragmented Women: Feminist (Sub)versions of Biblical Narratives, Journal for the Study of the Old Testament* Supplement Series 163, Sheffield: Sheffield Academic Press 1993, 174–5, 188–9. See also her 'Bathsheba, Plotted, Shot and Painted', in *Plotted, Shot and Painted: Cultural Representation of Biblical Women*, Gender, Culture, Theory 3, Sheffield: Sheffield Academic Press (forthcoming).

11. For further discussion of these matters cf. my *Theology and Feminism* (n. 1), 56–7.

12. J. Macquarrie, *Jesus Christ in Modern Thought*, London: SCM Press and Philadelphia, PA: Trinity Press International 1990, 420–2.

13. For a discussion as to why this may be, see below, 172.

14. D.E. Nineham, *The Use and Abuse of the Bible*, London: Macmillan 1976, 259.

15. R. Bauckham, 'The Book of Ruth and the Possibility of a Feminist Canonical Hermeneutic', *Biblical Hermeneutics* (forthcoming).

16. J. Ochshorn, *The Female Experience and the Nature of the Divine*, Bloomington, IN: Indiana University Press 1981. Cf. *Theology and Feminism* (n. 1), 98. See below, 127.

17. For an analysis of Jesus' attitude to women and his parables cf. *Theology and Feminism* (n. 1), 87–90.

18. For the situation of women in the time of Jesus, see J. Jeremias, *Jerusalem in the Time of Jesus: An Investigation into Economic and Social Conditions during the New Testament Period*, London: SCM Press 1969 and Philadelphia, PA: Fortress Press 1975, Ch. xviii, 'The Social Position of Women'.

19. Dowell, 'Review Article' (n. 4), 98.

20. Cf. P. Trible, *Texts of Terror*, Philadelphia, PA: Fortress Press 1984.

21. Ibid., 1–2.

22. E. Schüssler Fiorenza, *In Memory of Her: A Feminist Theological Reconstruction of Christian Origins*, New York: Crossroad and London: SCM Press 1983, 31.

23. Ibid., xiv, xix, 350.

24. Cf. *Theology and Feminism* (n. 1), 33–7.

25. Cf. *Theology and Feminism* (n. 1), 34–5. In her recent work Schüssler Fiorenza seems even more reluctant to face issues of truth. Cf. *Jesus – Miriam's Child, Sophia's Prophet: Critical Issues in Feminist Christology*, New York: Continuum and London: SCM Press 1995.

26. E. Schüssler Fiorenza, *But She Said: Feminist Practices of Biblical Interpretation*, Boston: Beacon Press 1992, 7.

27. S. Brooks Thistlethwaite, 'Every Two Minutes: Battered Women and Feminist Interpretation', in *Feminist Interpretation of the Bible*, ed. L.M. Russell, Oxford and New York: Basil Blackwell 1985, 99.

28. See n. 10.

29. Ibid., 5.

30. L. Irigaray, 'Equal to Whom?', *differences*, Vol. 1, no. 2, 1989, 74–5, 73. For further discussion of Irigaray on women's need for a transcendental, see below, 209.

31. J. Armstrong, *The Idea of Holiness and the Humane Response. A Study of the Concept of Holiness and Its Social Consequences*, London: George Allen and Unwin 1981.

32. Irigaray, 'Equal to Whom?' (n. 30), 73–4.

33. A.O. Dyson, *The Immortality of the Past*, London: SCM Press 1974.

34. Ibid., 3–4.
35. Ibid., 4 –5.

III. *Feminist Ethics*

1. R. Poole, *Towards Deep Subjectivity*, New York and London: Harper Torchbooks 1972, 140, 141, 142, 145.
2. There has been much feminist art criticism, which I cannot discuss here. In particular there has been consideration of the fact that the 'gaze is male': that is to say, it is assumed that the person who views the work is male – it is created with him in mind. That this is the case is well illustrated by my example!
3. M. Kemp, 'Cities and Citizens in Italian Renaissance Art', talk in St Andrews, 24 January 1992.
4. M. McCarthy, *The Stones of Florence*, New York and London: Harcourt Brace Jovanovich nd., 21.
5. E. Hutton, *Florence and Northern Tuscany with Genoa*, New York: The Macmillan Company, 1925, 165–6. On the prevalence of the theme of woman's death in Western literature cf. E. Bronfen, *Over Her Dead Body: Death, Femininity and the Aesthetic*, Manchester: Manchester University Press 1992.
6. Ibid., 166.
7. Cf. his gaunt Mary Magdalene, unfortunately damaged by the flood, almost the sole female statue in that city of male statues; and his Annunciation, see below, 194.
8. Cf. E. Borsook, *The Companion Guide to Florence*, London and Glasgow: Fontana, Collins, revised ed. 1973, 47. Francesco the Herald, in a discussion in 1504 as to where Michelangelo's David should be placed, suggested that it should replace the Judith, which was 'a deadly sign and inappropriate in this place because . . . it is not fitting that the woman should slay the man' (B. A. Bennett and D. C. Wilkins, *Donatello*, Oxford: Phaidon 1984, 85).
9. See below, 191–2.
10. See below, 137.
11. Marion McNaughton. See below, 138.
12. S. Bordo, 'Feminism, Postmodernism, and Gender-Scepticism', in *Feminism/Postmodernism*, ed. L. Nicholson, New York and London: Routledge 1990, 141 (italics removed from original).
13. N. Chodorow, 'Toward a Relational Individualism: The Mediation of Self through Psychoanalysis' (1986), in *Feminism and Psychoanalytic Theory*, New Haven and London: Yale University Press 1989, 159. Also in T. Heller et al. (ed.), *Reconstructing Individualism: Autonomy, Individuality and the Self in Western Thought*, Stanford, CA: Stanford University Press 1986.
14. N. Chodorow, *The Reproduction of Mothering: Psychoanalysis and the Sociology of Gender*, Berkeley, Los Angeles and London: University of

California Press 1978. Chodorow's position is further developed in a series of papers, published both before and after *The Reproduction of Mothering* and collected as *Feminism and Psychoanalytic Theory* (n. 13). Good summaries of Chodorow's position are given in I. M. Young, 'Is Male Gender', and J. Flax, 'Patriarchal Unconscious ' (see nn. 56 and 41 respectively).

15. N. Chodorow, 'Gender, Relation and Difference in Psychoanalytic Perspective' (1979), in *Feminism and Psychoanalytic Theory* (n. 13).
16. R. Brunswick, 'The Pre-Oedipal phase of the Libido Development', in R. Fliess (ed.), *The Psychoanalytic Reader*, New York: International Universities Press 1940, 231–53. Quoted by Chodorow, 170.
17. Chodorow, 'Gender, Relation and Difference' (n. 15), 110.
18. N. Chodorow, 'Feminism, Femininity and Freud', in *Feminism and Psychoanalytic Theory* (n. 13), 177.
19. See, for example, Chodorow, 'Gender, Relation and Difference' (n. 13), 109 n. 14.
20. R. Stoller, in J. Strouse (ed.), *Women and Analysis: Dialogues on Psychoanalytic Views of Femininity*, New York: Dell Publishing Co. 1974. The article was first published in French the previous year. See also M. Rawlinson, 'Psychiatric Discourse and the Feminine Voice', *Journal of Medicine and Philosophy*, Vol. 7, no. 2, 1982, 153–77.
21. Ibid., 403–4, 407.
22. Ibid., 407, 408, 410, 411.
23. Ibid., 408–9.
24. N. Fraser, 'The Uses and Abuses of French Discourse Theory', in N. Fraser and S. L. Bartky (eds.), *Revaluing French Feminism: Critical Essays in Difference, Agency and Culture*, Bloomington and Indianapolis, IN: Indiana University Press 1992, 182.
25. R. Fairbairn, *Psychoanalytic Studies of the Personality*, London and Boston: Routledge and Kegan Paul 1952, 66–7.
26. C. Gilligan, *In a Different Voice: Psychological Theory and Women's Development*, Cambridge, MA and London: Harvard University Press 1982; reissued with a new preface, HUP 1993. The literature on this work is extensive: in favour, against, and critiquing those who are against. Some of the most interesting work is by women in other fields who apply Gilligan to their discipline; see L. Code (a philosopher), 'Experience, Knowledge and Responsibility', in M. Griffiths and M. Whitford (eds.), *Feminist Perspectives in Philosophy*, Bloomington and Indianapolis: Indiana University Press 1988, and S. Benhabib (a political theorist), 'The Generalized and the Concrete Other', in *Feminism as Critique*, ed. S. Benhabib and D. Comell, Minneapolis, MN: University of Minnesota Press 1987. For more recent work of Gilligan's see *inter alia* the interesting essay on Freud, 'The Conquistador and the Dark Continent: Reflections on the Psychology of Love', *Daedalus: Journal of the American Academy of Arts and Sciences*, Summer 1984 (issued as Vol. 113, no. 3 of the *Proceedings of the American Academy of Arts and*

Sciences); *Psyche Embedded: A Place for Body, Relationships, and Culture in Personality Theory* (coauthored with L.M. Brown and A.G. Rogers, Harvard University Laboratory of Human Development 1988, given to me by the author and not to my knowledge otherwise published); *Mapping the Moral Domain: A Contribution of Women's Thinking to Psychological Theory and Education*, ed. C. Gilligan, J.V. Ward and J. McLean Taylor, Cambridge, MA: Harvard University Press 1989; *Meeting at the Crossroads: Women's Psychology and Girls' Development* (coauthored with L.M. Brown, Cambridge, MA: Harvard University Press 1992). For appreciation, see for example L. A. Blum, 'Gilligan and Kohlberg: Implications for Moral Theory', *Ethics* 98, University of Chicago, April 1988, 472–91. For critique see J. Broughton, 'Women's Rationality and Men's Virtues: A Critique of Gender Dualism in Gilligan's Social Research', and D. Nails, 'Social Scientific Sexism: Gilligan's Mismeasure of Man', *Social Research*, Vol. 50, no. 3 (Autumn 1983), 597–642 and 643–64 respectively. The criticisms have been well summarized by Celia Kitzinger in an article in *The Higher*, 4 March 1994. See also 'Viewpoint: On "In a Different Voice": An Interdisciplinary Forum', L.K. Kerber et al., in *Signs: Journal of Women in Culture and Society*,Vol. 11, no. 2, 1986, 304–33. S. Hekman, *Moral Voices, Moral Selves: Carol Gilligan and Feminist Moral Theory*, Oxford: Polity Press 1995 is an interesting appraisal.

27. Cf. *A Different Voice* (n. 26), 2.
28. Cf. Susan Bordo's excellent article 'Feminism, Postmodernism, and Gender-Scepticism', in L. Nicholson (ed.), *Feminism/ Postmodernism* (n. 12), 133–56. Bordo shows the extent to which more recent feminists have read their own agenda into Chodorow's and Gilligan's work.
29. Gilligan, *A Different Voice* (n. 26), 163.
30. Ibid., 40.
31. Ibid., 167.
32. Ibid., 45.
33. Ibid., 42.
34. Ibid., 46–47.
35. S. Freud, 'The Interpretation of Dreams', in *Works,* standard ed., London: Hogarth Press 1953, Vol. IV, 257.
36. Review of J. Hoyland (ed.), *Fathers and Sons,* London: Serpent's Tail 1992, *The Times Literary Supplement*, 24 April 1992.
37. See the discussion below 147–9 of the happier resolution within Christianity than within the Oedipus myth.
38. S. Freud, 'Beyond the Pleasure Principle' (1920), in *Works*, standard ed., Vol. xviii, 14–16.
39. L. Irigaray, 'The Gesture in Psychoanalysis', in *Between Feminism and Psychoanalysis*, ed. T. Brennan, London: Routledge 1989, 127–38: quotation 132,133,134.
40. S. Benhabib, 'The Generalized and the Concrete Other' (n. 26), 84. See also her collection of essays *Situating the Self: Gender, Community and*

Postmodernism in Contemporary Ethics, Cambridge: Polity Press 1992, in which this essay is reproduced.

41. J. Flax, 'Political Philosophy and the Patriarchal Unconscious: A Psycho-analytic Perspective on Epistemology and Metaphysics', in S. Harding and M. Hintikka (eds.), *Discovering Reality. Feminist Perspectives on Epistemology, Metaphysics, Methodology, and Philosophy of Science,* Dordrecht, Holland, Boston and London: D. Reidel Publishing Co. 1983, 267.

42. L. Irigaray, *Speculum of the Other Woman* (1974) trans. Gillian Gill, Ithaca, NY: Comell University Press 1985, 181,182.

43. Benhabib, 'Generalized and Concrete Other' (n. 26), 84.

44. Cf. also Jacques Derrida's analysis of Rousseau's sense of the maternal presence: *Of Grammatology,* Baltimore and London: The Johns Hopkins University Press 1974, 145–6.

45. Viz. she is not the culturally privileged one. In Lacan's thought the phallus is understood as the signifier of signifiers, that which differentiates between the realm of culture, law (the law of the father which prohibits incest) and indeed language, and the realm of the subconscious which is somehow feminine. Only indirectly is there a biological reference.

46. Ibid., 85.

47. S. Bordo, *The Flight to Objectivity. Essays on Cartesianism and Culture,* Albany, NY: SUNY, 1987, 58.

48. See below, 176–81.

49. Benhabib, 'Generalized and Concrete Other' (n. 26), 85.

50. See below, 141. Cf also 171

51. Gilligan, *A Different Voice* (n. 26), 10.

52. See below, 260–5.

53. G.W.F. Hegel, *Phenomenology of Spirit,* trans. A. V. Miller, Oxford and New York: Oxford University Press 1977, 111–19.

54. C. Whitbeck, 'A Different Reality: Feminist Ontology', in *Beyond Domination,* ed. C. Gould, Totowa, NJ: Rowman and Allanheld 1984, 69.

55. S. Benhabib, *Critique, Norm and Utopia: A Study of the Foundations of Critical Theory,* New York: Columbia University Press 1986, 89.

56. I.M. Young, 'Is Male Gender Identity the Cause of Male Domination?', in *Throwing Like a Girl,* Bloomington, IN: Indiana University Press 1990. See also R. Gottlieb, 'Mothering and the Reproduction of Power: Chodorow, Dinnerstein, and Social Theory', *Socialist Review,* Vol. 14, no. 77 (October 1984), 93–119.

57. See below, 151–3.

58. J. Flax, *Thinking Fragments: Psychoanalysis, Feminism and Post-modernism in the Contemporary West,* Berkeley, Los Angeles, Oxford: University of California Press 1990, 230.

59. I.M. Young, 'The Ideal of Community and the Politics of Difference', in *Feminism/Postmodernism,* ed. L. Nicholson (n. 12), 301. I sometimes think that the reason why American feminism is so hung up on 'hetero-geneity' is that American public life has been much less tolerant of

difference and diversity than has British.

60. Flax, *Thinking Fragments* (n. 58), 233.
61. Cf. J. Grimshaw, 'Autonomy', in *Feminism and Psychoanalysis: A Critical Dictionary,* ed. Elizabeth Wright, Oxford: Basil Blackwell, 1992; 'Autonomy and Identity in Feminist Thinking', in *Feminist Perspectives in Philosophy*, ed. Griffiths and Whitford (n. 26).
62. Flax, *Thinking Fragments* (n. 58), 219.
63. Ibid., 220.
64. For recent debate around these issues cf. S. Benhabib, J. Butler, D. Cornell and N. Fraser, *Feminist Contentions: A Philosophical Exchange*, New York and London: Routledge 1995.
65. J. Benjamin, *The Bonds of Love, Psychoanalysis, Feminism and the Problem of Domination*, New York: Pantheon Books 1988, 294.
66. Fraser, 'Uses and Abuses' (n. 24), 182. Fraser gives a fine critique of Lacan and of Kristeva in this regard. Diana Meyers argues, of both object relations theory and French feminist psychoanalytic perspectives, that they 'cannot deliver a feminist account of agency' ('The Subversion of Women's Agency in Psychoanalytic Feminism: Chodorow, Flax, Kristeva', in *Revaluing French Feminism*, ed. Fraser and Bartky [n. 24]).
67. See below, 207–9.
68. Benjamin, *Bonds of Love* (n. 65), 49–52: quotation, 49.
69. Ibid., 32n.
70. Ibid., 63n.
71. Ibid., 77–8.
72. Cf. 305 n. 106.
73. J. Mitchell, *Psychoanalysis and Feminism*, New York: Pantheon and London: Allen Lane, 1974.
74. Benjamin, *Bonds of Love* (n. 65), 130–1, 126.
75. Benhabib, 'Generalized and Concrete Other (n. 26), 87.
76. Ibid., 94.
77. A. Klein, 'Finding a Self: Buddhist and Feminist Perspectives', in C.W. Atkinson, C.H. Buchanan and M.R. Miles (eds.), *Shaping New Vision: Gender and Values in American Culture*, The Harvard Women's Studies in Religion Series 5, Ann Arbor, MI and London: UMI Research Press 1987, 191–218: quotation 193. See also her 'Presence with a Difference: Buddhists and Feminists on Subjectivity', *Hypatia*, Vol. 9, no. 4 (Fall 1994), 112–30.
78. Klein, 'Finding a Self' (n. 77), 193, 196, 197.
79. E. Haney, 'What is Feminist Ethics? A Proposal for Continuing Discussion', *Journal of Religious Ethics* 8, 1980, 115–24.
80. Ibid., 118–19, 120, 122.
81. See above, 101.
82. Whitbeck, 'A Different Reality' (n. 54), 76.
83. See for example S. Ruddick, *Maternal Thinking: Towards a Politics of Peace*, Boston: Beacon Press 1989 and London: The Women's Press 1990.
84. For working-class Britain cf. B. Campbell, *Wigan Pier Revisited: Poverty*

and Politics in the 80s, London: Virago 1984.

85. Of the University of Miami. Lecture at the University of Toronto, 22 October 1991.

86. Radio interview held in conjunction with the publication of P. Stevenson and U. Padel, *Insiders,* London: Virago 1988. See also pp. 10, 99, 131, 156, 190 of this book, which is an eye-opener.

87. J. Baker Miller, *Toward a New Psychology of Women,* Boston: Beacon Press 1976; second ed. with new foreword 1986, 111, 25, 113–14.

88. Ibid., 119.

89. I. Kant, 'Beantwortung der Frage: Was ist Aufklärung?', in *Was ist Aufklärung?,* ed. E. Bahr, Stuttgart: Philipp Reclam jun. 1975, 9. My translation.

90. J. Viorst, 'Men: The Silent Majority', *Redbook,* 1984, reproduced in (British) *Good Housekeeping,* Vol. 127, no. 6 (June 1985), 72–3, 228.

91. See above, 94.

92. A. McCollum, *The Trauma of Moving. Psychological Issues for Women,* London: Sage Publications 1990.

93. V. Woolf, *A Room of One's Own* (1929), London: Triad Grafton 1977, 35–6.

94. P. Deutscher, ' "The Only Diabolical Thing About Women . . .": Luce Irigaray on Divinity', *Hypatia,* Vol. 9, no. 4 (Fall 1994), 88–111: quotation 91.

95. Plato, *Symposium,* trans. Walter Hamilton, Harmondsworth: Penguin Books 1951, 64–5.

96. Flax, 'Patriarchal Unconscious' (n. 41), 246.

97. L. Irigaray, J'*aime à toi,* Paris: Grasset 1992, quoted by Deutscher, 'Diabolical Thing' (n. 94), 110.

98. M. Massey, *Feminine Soul: The Fate of an Ideal,* Boston: Beacon Press 1985, 186.

IV. *Christian Idolatry*

1. N. Fraser, 'The Uses and Abuses of French Discourse Theories for Feminist Politics', in id. and S.L. Bartky (eds.), *Revaluing French Feminism: Critical Essays on Difference, Agency, and Culture,* Bloomington and Indianapolis, IN: Indiana University Press 1992, 188.

2. L. Feuerbach, *The Essence of Christianity* (1841), trans. George Eliot, NY and London: Harper Torchbooks 1957.

3. Cf. in particular *Totem and Taboo* (1913), trans. James Strachey, NY: W. W. Norton & Co. 1950, 154–5; *The Future of an Illusion* (1927), trans. W D Robson-Scott, revised and newly ed. James Strachey, NY: Doubleday Anchor 1964, 30–5, 68–9; *Moses and Monotheism,* trans. Katherine Jones, London: The Hogarth Press and Institute of Psychoanalysis 1939.

4. J. Bowker, *Licensed Insanities: Religions and Belief in God in the Contemporary World,* London: Darton, Longman and Todd 1987, 12.

5. J. Mackey, 'The Use and Abuse of Mary in Roman Catholicism', in R.

Holloway (ed.), *Who Needs Feminism? Men Respond to Sexism in the Church,* London: SPCK 1991, 99.

6. Ed. A. Richardson and J. Bowden, London: SCM Press 1983.

7. *Summa* I pars Q. 1a. 3,2: '*Deus est actus purus non habens aliquid de potentialitate*' (God contains no potentiality, but is sheer actuality). This understanding is also that of Plato. See, for example, the *Symposium*, where Diotima tells Socrates: 'He [the man who has been guided in the mysteries of love] will see it [the eternal beauty] existing alone with itself, unique, eternal, and all other beautiful things as partaking of it, yet in such a manner that, while they come into being and pass away, it neither undergoes any increase or diminution nor suffers any change' (trans. Walter Hamilton, Harmondsworth: Penguin Books 1951, 94).

8. L E. Goodman, *Monotheism: A Philosophic Inquiry into the Foundations of Theology and Ethics,* Totowa, NJ: Allanheld, Osmun & Co. 1981, 1.

9. R. Swinburne, *The Coherence of Theism*, Oxford: The Clarendon Press 1977, 1.

10. R. Gale, *On the Nature and Existence of God*, Cambridge: CUP 1991, 318–19.

11. Ed. J. Hastings, Edinburgh: T. & T. Clark 1921, Vol. XII, 261–87: quotations 261 col. 1, col. 1–2.

12. Cf. Nicholas Lash's critique of the passage I quote from Swinburne in *Easter in Ordinary: Reflections on Human Experience and the Knowledge of God,* Charlottesville,VA: The University Press of Virginia and London: SCM Press 1988, 98. Elsewhere, having referred to Swinburne's definition which I give and to the work of the Oxford Religious Experience Research Unit, Lash writes: 'I happen to think, however, that it would be idolatrous to worship any particular entity, however unusual, impressive, elevated, or unmeasurable by natural science' ('Considering the Trinity', *Modern Theology*, Vol. 2, no. 3, 1986, 191).

13. R.R. Ruether, *New Woman/ New Earth: Sexist Ideologies and Human Liberation*, New York: Seabury Press, A Crossroad Book 1975, 74.

14. R. Gross et al., 'Roundtable Discussion: Feminist Reflections on Separation and Unity in Jewish Theology', *Journal of Feminist Studies in Religion*, Vol. 2, no. 1 (Spring 1986), 128–30: quotation 128.

15. Gross, 'Roundtable Discussion' (n. 14), 129–30.

16. Cf. D. Hampson, *Theology and Feminism*, Oxford and Cambridge, MA: Basil Blackwell 1990, 153–4.

17. See my somewhat fuller treatment in the article I have contributed on 'Monotheism' to P.B. Clarke and A. Linzey (eds.), *Dictionary of Ethics, Theology and Society*, London: Routledge 1996, 582–5.

18. Lecture by the social anthropologist Malcolm Ruel at The Modern Churchman's Union conference, 1987.

19. S. Howell, *Society and Cosmos: Chewong of Peninsula Malaysia,* Oxford and Singapore: Oxford University Press 1984.

20. J. Ochshorn, *The Female Experience and the Nature of the Divine*, Bloomington, IN: Indiana University Press 1981.

21. The standard work here is Raphael Patai, *The Hebrew Goddess*, 3rd enlarged ed., Detroit, MI: Wayne State University 1990.

22. See below, 176-81.

23. S. de Beauvoir, *The Second Sex* (1949), Harmondsworth: Penguin Books 1972, 205-6.

24. E.L. Mascall, *Women Priests?*, London: The Church Literature Association 1972, 10.

25. J. Kristeva, *About Chinese Women*, New York: M. Boyars Publishers, distributed Kampman & Co. 1974, 22. Also in Toril Moi (ed.), *The Kristeva Reader*, trans. Séan Hand, New York: Columbia University Press 1986.

26. J. Derrida, 'How to Avoid Speaking: Denials', in H. Coward and T. Foshay (eds.), *Derrida and Negative Theology*, Albany, NY: SUNY 1992, 134.

27. F. Nietzsche, *The Gay Science*, trans. Walter Kaufman, New York: Vintage Books 1974, 143, pp. 191-2.

28. See Chapter VI.

29. This re-writing was a group effort! Reported in the Quaker Women's Group Newsletter, Nov. 1987.

30. D. Heller, *The Children's God*, Chicago and London: University of Chicago Press 1986. See also Eric Marshall and Stuart Hample, *Children's Letters to God*, New York: Simon & Schuster 1966.

31. See above, 94.

32. W. Storrar, *Scottish Identity: A Christian Vision*, Edinburgh: The Handsel Press 1990, 9.

33. See below, 190-1.

34. Cf. Luke 1. 52.

35. See above, 58-60.

36. D. Nicholls, *Deity and Domination: Images of God and the State in the Nineteenth and Twentieth Centuries*, London and New York: Routledge 1989. Nicholls thinks that belief in God's transcendence may be a ground on which earthly tyrants are resisted, but it is also the case that earthly power has been patterned upon a hierarchical ordering of divine reality. Belief in God's immanence on the other hand, while overcoming the latter problem arising from transcendence, may serve to legitimize the status quo.

37. A. Lorde, 'The Master's Tools Will Never Dismantle the Master's House' (1979), in *Sister Outsider: Essays and Speeches*, Trumansburg, NY: The Crossing Press 1984, 110-13.

38. A.N. Whitehead, *Process and Reality: An Essay in Cosmology*, corrected ed. by David Ray Griffin and Donald W. Sherburne, London: The Free Press 1978, 351.

39. Cf. for example Sheila Davaney (ed.), *Feminism and Process Thought: The Harvard Divinity School/Claremont Center for Process Studies Symposium Papers*, New York and Toronto: The Edwin Mellen Press 1981.

40. L.E. Hahn (ed.), *The Philosophy of Charles Hartshorne*, LaSalle, IL: Open Court, 1991, 177.

41. J. Levenson, *Creation and the Persistence of Evil: The Jewish Drama of Divine Omnipotence*, San Francisco: Harper and Row 1988, 141–3, 145, 143, 148.

42. See below, 195.

43. Cf. Carol Gilligan's discussion above, 93–5.

44. Cf. Gen. 22.

45. S. Spiegel, *The Last Trial*, trans. J. Goldin, New York: Schocken Books 1969, xvii, quoted by C. Delaney, 'The Legacy of Abraham', in R. Gross (ed.), *Beyond Androcentrism: New Essays on Women and Religion*, Missoula, Montana: Scholars Press 1977, 217.

46. Ibid., Delaney, 231–2.

47. *Kierkegaard's Writings* VI, ed. and trans. H. and E. Hong, Princeton, NJ: Princeton University Press 1983; or trans. Alastair Hannay, Harmondsworth: Penguin Books 1985.

48. One wonders quite how the ethics of the Abraham and Isaac story differs from the proposition attributed to Hitler's minister of justice that whatever the Führer says is right is right.

49. N. Segal, 'Reading as a Feminist: The Case of Sarah and Naomi', *The University of Leeds Review*, Vol. 32, 1989/90, 50.

50. N. Noddings, *Caring. A Feminine Approach to Ethics and Moral Education*, Los Angeles and London: University of California Press 1986, 43.

51. See above, 100–1 and below, 260–5.

52. M. McNaughton, 1992. Private circulation; reproduced with permission.

53. R. Niebuhr, 'Man as Sinner', Chapter VIII of *The Nature and Destiny of Man*, Vol. 1, *Human Nature* (1941), New York: Charles Scribner's Sons 1964, Ch. VII. Niebuhr shows the understanding of sin as in the first place pride to be the major Christian understanding in the Augustinian tradition, footnote, pp. 186–7. See also my discussion of the feminist critique of Niebuhr, *Theology and Feminism* (n. 16), 121–6.

54. Ibid., 180. Cf. Isa. 14. 12, 13, 14, 15: 'How art thou fallen from heaven, O Lucifer, son of the morning! How art thou cut down to the ground . . . For thou has said in thine heart, I will ascend into heaven, I will exalt my throne above the stars of God . . . I will be like the most High. Yet thou shalt be brought down to hell.'

55. Cf. Ex. 20. 5; 34. 14, etc.

56. Cf. Delaney's comment that authority becomes omnipresent but invisible, above, 137.

57. L. Irigaray, 'Questions to Emmanuel Levinas', in M. Whitford (ed.), *The Irigaray Reader*, Oxford and Cambridge, MA: Basil Blackwell 1991, 179.

58. For Irigaray on 'the divine' see E. Grosz, *Sexual Subversions: Three French Feminists*, Sydney: Allen and Unwin 1989, chs. 4, 5; 'Irigaray and the Divine', Sydney: Local Consumption, Occasional Paper, 9; P. Deutscher, ' "The Only Diabolical Thing about Women . . .": Luce Irigaray on Divinity', *Hypatia* special issue, *Feminist Philosophy of*

Religion, Vol. 9, no. 4, Fall 1994. See also below, 209.

59. Ibid., 187.
60. C. Delaney, 'Legacy of Abraham' (n. 45), 218.
61. Cf. *Violence and the Sacred*, trans. P. Gregory, Baltimore: Johns Hopkins University Press 1977.
62. L. Irigaray, 'Women, the Sacred and Money', *Paragraph,* Vol. 8 (Oct. 1986), 7.
63. Cf. Karl Barth, *Church Dogmatics*, IV/1, *The Doctrine of Reconciliation*, ed. G. W. Bromiley and T. F. Torrance, Edinburgh: T. & T. Clark, § 59.
64. There was, however, a medieval debate as to whether so perfect a work as the incarnation can be thought to have been dependent on human sin.
65. Irenaeus, *Against Heresies*, IV. xx. 4.
66. Athanasius, *De Incarnatione Dei*, 54.
67. See the further consideration below, 192, 195–6.
68. For further writing of mine on this theme see my 'On Power and Gender', *Modern Theology,* Vol. 4, no. 3 (April 1988), 243–50; reprinted in E. Stuart and A. Thatcher, *Christian Perspectives on Sexuality and Gender,* Leominster: Gracewing/Fowler Wright and Grand Rapids, MI: Eerdmans 1996, 125–40.
69. A.C. McGill, 'Self-Giving as the Inner Life of God', Ch. IV of *Suffering: A Test of Theological Method*, Philadelphia, PA: Westminster Press 1982, 79, 81, 82.
70. Cf. *Philosophical Fragments*, 26 (Hong and Hong), 32 (Swenson).
71. A good account of this is given in A.M. Ramsey, *From Gore to Temple*, London: Longmans 1960, 36.
72. See my discussion of this theme in *Theology and Feminism* (n. 16), 155, and my further debate with Sarah Coakley in D. Hampson (ed.), *Swallowing a Fishbone? Feminist Theologians Debate Christianity*, London: SPCK 1996, 120–2, 169–70.
73. R. R. Ruether, *Sexism and God-Talk. Toward a Feminist Theology*, Boston, MA: Beacon Press 1983 and London: SCM Press 1983, 137.
74. K. Bloomquist, '"Let God be God": The Theological Necessity of Depatriarchalizing God', in Carl E. Braaten (ed.), *Our Naming of God: Problems and Prospects of God-Talk Today*, Minneapolis, MN: Augsburg Fortress 1989, 45–60; quotation 58–9, quotation from Heyward, *The Redemption of God*, 212.
75. D. Bonhoeffer, Letter to Eberhard Bethge from Tegel, 16 July 1944, *Letters and Papers from Prison: The Enlarged Edition*, ed. Eberhard Bethge, London: SCM Press 1971 and New York: Macmillan 1972, 361; J. Moltmann, *The Crucified God*, London, SCM Press 1974.
76. P. Ricoeur, *The Conflict of Interpretations: Essays in Hermeneutics*, Evanston, IL: Northwestern University Press 1974.
77. Ibid., 470, 471 respectively.
78. Ibid., 491.
79. Ibid., 492–93, 493 respectively.
80. *The Mystery of Salvation: The Story of God's Gift*, The Doctrine

Commission of the Church of England, Church House Publishing 1995, 18–19.

81. For different soteriological motifs which have existed within Christendom, see Gustaf Aulén, *Christus Victor: An Historical Study of the Three Main Types of the Idea of the Atonement* (1930), trans. A.G. Hebert, London: SPCK and New York: Macmillan Publishing Co. 1969.

82. Cf. Anselm's *Cur Deus Homo*.

83. B. Harrison and C. Heyward, 'Pain and Pleasure: Avoiding the Confusions of Christian Tradition in Feminist Theory', in J. Carlson Brown and C. R. Bohn (eds.), *Christianity, Patriarchy and Abuse: A Feminist Critique*, New York: The Pilgrim Press 1989, 148–73: 153.

84. *The Guardian*, 3 September 1990.

85. R. Nakashima Brock, 'And a Little Child Will Lead Us: Christology and Child Abuse', in Carlson Brown and Bohn (eds.), *Christianity, Patriarchy and Abuse* (n. 83), 51–2.

86. Cf. Rom. 8. 28f.

87. J. Levenson, *The Death and Resurrection of the Beloved Son: The Transformation of Child Sacrifice in Judaism and Christianity*, New Haven and London: Yale University Press 1993, 220.

88. Redmond recites the case of the elevation in 1950 to sainthood of an eleven-year-old girl who had been 'martyred' rather than submit to an attempt to rape her.

89. S. Redmond, 'Christian "Virtues" and Recovery from Child Sexual Abuse', in Carlson Brown and Bohn (eds.), *Christianity, Patriarchy and Abuse* (n. 83), 73–4.

90. Ibid., 78–9.

91. Nakashima Brock, 'Little Child' (n. 85), 52.

92. K. Bloomquist, 'Sexual Violence: Patriarchy's Offence and Defense', in Carlson Brown and Bohn (eds.), *Christianity, Patriarchy and Abuse* (n. 83), 67.

93. W. A. Visser 't Hooft, *The Fatherhood of God in an Age of Emancipation*, Geneva, WCC: 1982. See especially Ch. 14, 'Divine Fatherhood without Paternalism'.

94. 'Correspondence between Henrietta Visser 't Hooft and Karl Barth', Appendix 1, in Susannah Herzel, *A Voice for Women: The Women's Department of the World Council of Churches*, Geneva: WCC 1981, 160–6.

95. K. Barth, *Dogmatics in Outline*, (1947) trans. G.T. Thomson, London: SCM Press 1966, 43.

96. T.F. Torrance, 'The Christian Apprehension of God the Father', in Alvin F. Kimel, *Speaking the Christian God: The Holy Trinity and the Challenge of Feminism*, Grand Rapids, MI: Eerdmans and Leominster: Gracewing 1992, 130.

97. R. Hamerton-Kelly, *God the Father: Theology and Patriarchy in the Teaching of Jesus*, Philadelphia, PA: Fortress Press 1979, 18. Cf above, 148.

98. R. Hamerton-Kelly, 'God the Father in the Bible and in the Experience of Jesus: The State of the Question', in J.-B. Metz and E Schillebeeckx (eds.), *God as Father?*, *Concilium* 143, 96, 100.

99. A. C. McGill, 'Self-Giving' (n. 69), 67, 70, 76–8. Emphasis in original.

100. J. Zizioulas, *Being as Communion: Studies in Personhood and the Church*, London: Darton, Longman and Todd 1985.

101. C. Gunton, *The Promise of Trinitarian Theology*, Edinburgh: T. & T. Clark 1991.

102. See the quotations from Irenaeus and Athanasius above, 143.

103. Liturgy of the Scottish Episcopal Church, 1977. That church has historically been influenced by Eastern forms, for example in its eucharistic prayer.

104. Gunton, *The Promise of Trinitarian Theology* (n. 101), 29, 174.

105. Cf. the discussion in Chapter III.

106. Cf. Erikson's work ('Genital Modes and Spatial Modalities', Part I, Ch. 4 of *Childhood and Society*, 2nd ed. revised and enlarged, New York: W. W. Norton & Co. 1963; 'Womanhood and the Inner Space' (1968) and his response to feminist criticism, 'Once More the Inner Space: Letter to a Former Student' (1973), both in J. Strouse [ed.], *Women and Analysis: Dialogues on Psychoanalytic Views of Femininity*, New York: Dell Publishing Co. 1974), which suggests that boys and girls, given building blocks, arrange them in scenes which correspond to their differing sexuality. See also Iris Marion Young's important critique 'Throwing Like a Girl: A Phenomenology of Feminine Body Comportment, Motility and Spirituality', in *Throwing Like a Girl* (n. 56). I find myself basically in agreement with Young's critique of Erikson's general position, thinking likewise that social factors are crucial. Nevertheless in the case of the doctrine of the Trinity I find it difficult to think that men's interpretation of their physicality within the context of the culture we have known is in no way relevant.

107. L. Feuerbach, *The Essence of Christianity* (n. 2), 70. Feuerbach finds that the mother comes in through the back door again in the form of the virgin. But – one might comment – she is not a natural mother, and a sexual relation with a woman is not present symbolically.

108. R. Braidotti, *Patterns of Dissonance: A Study of Women in Contemporary Philosophy*, trans. E. Guild, Cambridge: Polity Press 1991, 255.

109. Quoted on the title page of L. Hurcombe (ed.), *Sex and God: Some Varieties of Women's Religious Experience*, New York and London: Routledge & Kegan Paul 1987.

110. I owe this discussion of etymology to E. Johnson, *She Who Is*, New York: Crossroad 1992, 220.

111. *Dictionary of Christian Theology* (n. 6), 112.

112. Dionysius, *The Divine Names*, IV. 13; J. Macquarrie, *Jesus Christ in Modern Thought*, London: SCM Press and Philadelphia, PA: Trinity Press International 1990, 379–80.

113. Ibid., 380.
114. V. White, *Atonement and Incarnation: An Essay in Universalism and Particularity*, Cambridge: Cambridge University Press 1991, 75.
115. B. Hebblethwaite, *The Ocean of Truth: A Defence of Objective Theism*, Cambridge: Cambridge University Press 1988, 5.
116. D. Jenkins, *The Contradiction of Christianity*, London: SCM Press 1976, 158–9.
117. J. Moltmann. *The Trinity and the Kingdom of God*, London: SCM Press and San Francisco, Harper and Row 1981, 57.
118. Ibid., 58.
119. Ibid, quoted from I. A. Dorner, *Die Unver nderlichkeit Gottes*, Leipzig 1883, 355.
120. Ibid.
121. Walter Kasper, *The God of Jesus Christ*, trans. Matthew O'Connell, New York: Crossroad Publishing Company 1988, 308–9, quoted by E. Johnson, *She Who Is* (n. 110), 196.
122. *She Who Is* (n. 110), 196.
123. Ibid., 216–17.
124. R. R. Ruether, *New Woman/ New Earth: Sexist Ideologies and Human Liberation*, New York: Seabury Press, A Crossroad Book 1975, 26, quoted by Johnson, *She Who Is* (n. 110), 218–19.
125. Cf. Eleanor Haney's discussion, above, 109–11.
126. A. E. Carr, *Transforming Grace: Christian Tradition and Women s Experience*, San Francisco: Harper and Row 1988,156–7.
127. J. Martin Soskice, 'The Trinity and "The Feminine Other"', *New Black-friars*, Vol. 75, no. 878 (Jan. 1994), 2–17: quotation 16.
128. J. Martin Soskice, 'Can a Feminist call God "Father"?', in T. Elwes (ed.), *Women s Voices: Essays in Contemporary Feminist Theology*, London: Marshall Pickering 1992, reprinted in A. Kimel (ed.), *Speaking the Christian God*, 81–94: quotation, 94.
129. Cf. the essay which Martin Soskice has contributed to D. Hampson (ed.), *Swallowing a Fishbone?* (n. 72), 'Turning the Symbols'.
130. Quoted by C. E. Scott, 'The Pathology of the Father's Rule: Lacan and the Symbolic Order', in E. Wyschogrod, D. Crownfield and C. A. Raschke (eds.), *Lacan and Theological Discourse*, Albany, NY: SUNY 1989.
131. *Revelations of Divine Love*, ed. G. Warwick, London: Methuen 1958, First Revelation, Ch. V, 10.
132. H. Ward, 'The Lion in the Marble: Choosing Celibacy as a Nun', in L. Hurcombe (ed.), *Sex and God* (n. 109), 84.
133. See below, 279.
134. S. McFague, *Models of God: Theology for an Ecological, Nuclear Age*, Philadelphia, PA: Fortress Press and London: SCM Press 1987, 69–78; *The Body of God: An Ecological Theology*, Minneapolis, MN: Fortress Press and London: SCM Press 1993; G. Jantzen, *God s World, God s Body*, London: Darton, Longman and Todd, 1984.
135. N. Fraser, 'The Uses and Abuses of French Discourse Theories for

Feminist Politics', in Fraser and Bartky (eds.), *Revaluing French Feminism* (n. 1), 179.

136. See above, 91–2.

V. *Woman, the Other*

1. G.W.F. Hegel, *Phenomenology of Spirit*, trans. A.V. Miller, Oxford and New York: Oxford University Press 1977, 111–19.

2. S. de Beauvoir, *The Second Sex* (1949), Harmondsworth: Penguin Books 1972, 16. De Beauvoir also makes reference to Emmanuel Levinas here. Cf. Genevieve Lloyd's discussion of the significance of the fact that it was Sartre's rendering of Hegel which influenced de Beauvoir, *The Man of Reason*, London: Methuen 1984, 93–6.

3. *The Second Sex*, (n. 2), 295.

4. L. Irigaray, 'Divine Woman', Sydney: Local Consumption Occasional Paper no. 8, 1986, 12. This essay is reproduced in slightly different form as 'Divine Women' in *Sexes and Genealogies*, trans. Gillian Gill, New York: Columbia University Press 1993 (1984), 55–72.

5. *The Second Sex*, (n. 2), 17.

6. See above, 125–6.

7. J. Kristeva, *About Chinese Women* (1974), trans. A. Barrows, London: Marion Boyars Publishers Ltd 1977, 19, 21. Chapter II of this work appears in another tanslation in Toril Moi (ed.), *The Kristeva Reader*, trans. Séan Hand, New York: Columbia University Press 1986, 138–59. I have incorporated some elements of this latter translation.

8. E. Grosz, *Sexual Subversions: Three French Feminists*, Sydney: Allen and Unwin 1989, 120–1.

9 L. Irigaray, 'Etablir une généalogie de femmes', *Maintenant* 12, 28 May 1979, 44, quoted by Grosz, *Sexual Subversions* (n. 8), 121.

10. I have taken part of the quotation which I give from each of two different translations of this article: L. Irigaray, 'Sexual Difference (1984)', in *An Ethics of Sexual Difference*, trans. C. Burke and G. Gill, London: The Athlone Press 1993, 10, and in M. Whitford (ed.), *The Irigaray Reader*, Oxford: Basil Blackwell 1991, 169.

11. Cf. the remark attributed to Picasso: 'Women are either goddesses or doormats' (programme on Picasso on BBC channel 2 on 12 February 1994). It may be that this dichotomous cultural construction has been particularly rife in Catholic cultures.

12. D. Cupitt, *The Last Philosophy*, London: SCM Press 1995, 79.

13. Lecture with slides by Gail Corrington at Harvard Divinity School in 1988–89. Cf. her *Her Image of Salvation: Female Saviors and Formative Christianity*, Gender and Biblical Tradition Series, Louisville, KY: Westminster John Knox Press 1992, 173.

14. M. Warner, *Alone of All Her Sex. The Myth and the Cult of the Virgin Mary*, New York: Vintage Books 1983, 335–6.

15. An illustration is given in Warner (n. 14) opposite page 197.

16. J. Kristeva, 'Stabat Mater', in Toril Moi (ed.), *The Kristeva Reader*, Oxford and New York: Basil Blackwell 1986, 160–85: quotation, 170.

17. C. Jung, *Answer to Job*, trans. R F. C. Hull, London: Routledge & Kegan Paul, 1954, 159; see also 56–9.

18. Kristeva, 'Stabat Mater' (n. 16), 163, 169 respectively.

19. Ibid., 176.

20. A male colleague and priest, who had no idea I was writing on this theme, recently asked in my hearing why it was that men who were dying or otherwise in extremity, in his experience, always called out for their mothers. It would be fascinating to know whether this is common, and not in the case of women.

21. That God is frequently given 'female' attributes, while never directly named as Mother, in the biblical material is the conclusion of an intensive study undertaken by the Church of Scotland, while the significance of this goes unrecognized: A. Lewis (ed.), *The Motherhood of God: A Report by a Study Group appointed by the Woman's Guild and the Panel on Doctrine on the invitation of the General Assembly of the Church of Scotland*, Edinburgh: The Saint Andrew Press 1984.

22. Cf. Kristeva's critique, *Tales of Love*, trans. L. S. Roudiez, New York: Columbia University Press 1987, 26.

23. J. Kristeva, *In the Beginning was Love: Psychoanalysis and Faith*, trans. A. Goldhammer, New York: Columbia University Press 1987, 39–40.

24. Kristeva, *In the Beginning* (n. 23), 24. Quotation from Augustine, *Confessions*, trans. E. B. Pusey, New York: Dutton 1951, IV. 1.

25. Ibid., 25, 26, 25, 26, 24.

26. Isa. 49. 15.

27. *Quis Dives Salvetur?*, PG 9, 641–4. Quoted by Leonardo Boff, *The Maternal Face of God: The Feminine and its Religious Expressions* (1979), trans. R.R. Barr and J.W. Diercksmeier, San Francisco: Harper & Row 1987 and London: Collins 1989, 85.

28. See above, 177.

29. *The Prayers and Meditations of St Anselm*, trans. B. Ward, Harmondsworth: Penguin Classics 1973, 152–4.

30. See above, 172.

31. *Summa Contra Gentiles*, Vol. 4, trans. and with an introduction by C. J. O'Neill, Notre Dame: University of Notre Dame Press 1975, 90.

32. Note the Latin '*vi*' root, meaning potent, which we find in vim, vigour, virile, etc. and the Latin word for man, '*vir*'.

33. Quoted by Gerhard Ebeling, *Luther: An Introduction to his Thought*, trans. R. A. Wilson, London: Fontana 1972, 163–4 (WA 39, I. 521. 5–522. 3).

34. Boff, *Maternal Face* (n. 27), 85–6.

35. L. Boff, *Trinity and Society*, trans. Paul Bums, Tunbridge Wells: Burns and Oates 1988, 147.

36. J. Moltmann, *The Trinity and the Kingdom of God: The Doctrine of God*, London: SCM Press 1981, 164–5. Quotation from the Council of

Toledo, J. Denzinger, *Enchiridion Symbolorum*, 26th ed., Freiburg 1947.
37. See above, 91–2.
38. V. White, 'The Scandal of the Assumption', *Life of the Spirit* 5, 1950, 211–12. Quoted by Boff, *Maternal Face* (n. 27), 87.
39. V.A. Demant, 'Why the Christian Priesthood is Male', *Women and Holy Orders: Report of the Archbishop's Commission*, appendix C, London: Church Information Office 1966, 101.
40. See above, 40, 107.
41. Cf. for example *Church Dogmatics*, III/4, *The Doctrine of Creation*, Edinburgh: T. & T. Clark 1961, 170. According to the eye-witness account of someone known to me, Barth treated Frau Barth like dirt. His relationship to Charlotte von Kirschbaum certainly makes one wonder what he thought to be the elementary rights of his wife.
42. See above, 90.
43. See above, 153–4.
44. Cf. T.D. Setel, 'Prophets and Pornography: Female Sexual Imagery in Hosea', in L.M. Russell (ed.), *Feminist Interpretation of the Bible*; R. Weems, 'Gomer: Victim of Violence or Victim of Metaphor?', in K.G. Cannon and E. Schüssler Fiorenza (eds.), *Semeia 47, Interpretation for Liberation*. M.K. Wakeman, 'Biblical Prophecy and Modern Feminism', in R.M. Gross (ed.), *Beyond Androcentrism: New Essays on Women and Religion*, Missoula, Montana: Scholars Press 1977, 67–86, has a rather different analysis. P. Bird, ' "To Play the Harlot": An Inquiry into an Old Testament Metaphor', in P.L. Day (ed.), *Gender and Difference in Ancient Israel*, Minneapolis, MN: Fortress Press 1989, 75–94, claims of this sexual metaphor that: 'Its female orientation does not single out women for condemnation; it is used rather as a rhetorical device to expose men's sin. By appealing to the common stereotypes and interests of a primarily male audience, Hosea turns their accusation against them. It is easy for patriarchal society to see the guilt of a "fallen woman"; Hosea says, "You (male Israel) are that woman!"' (89). This is surely quite beside the point; which is that the female is denigrated while the male is seen as good. It does not help to say that male Israel has behaved like a woman while characterizing woman in these terms; that simply reinforces how woman is perceived.
45. Weems, 'Gomer: Victim' (n. 44), 100.
46. See above, 62–3.
47. See also the discussion of covenant as a metaphor, 136ff.
48. A. West, 'Genesis and Patriarchy', *New Blackfriars*, Vol. 62 (Jan. 1981), 28.
49. II Cor. 11. 2.
50. Rom. 7.
51. A reader might well begin with the work of Cheryl Exum, see Chapter II, n. 10.
52. See for example Drorah Setel's work on Hosea above (n. 44).
53. See above, 63.

54. G. F. Ellwood, *Batter My Heart*, Pendle Hill Pamphlet 282, Pendle Hill, PA: Pendle Hill Publications 1988, 7–17.

55. For a male scholar's comment on this (something which has often been pointed out by feminist women) see Francis Watson, *Text, Church and Word: Biblical Interpretation in Theological Perspective*, Edinburgh: T. & T. Clark 1994, 156. Renita Weems exempts Robert Carroll on Jeremiah.

56. On the whole extraordinary history see in particular Uta Ranke-Heinemann's documentation in *Eunuchs for the Kingdom of Heaven: Women, Sexuality and the Catholic Church* (1988), trans. P. Heinegg, Harmondsworth and New York: Penguin Books 1991.

57. *The Catholic Citizen*, Vol. LII, no. 5, 5 May 1966, 39. Quoted in M. Daly, *The Church and the Second Sex* (1968), San Francisco and London: Harper Colophon Books, Harper and Row 1975, 141.

58. *The Times*, 24 March 1966. These sentences do not appear in the article in all editions of the paper.

59. Augustine, *Concerning the City of God against the Pagans*, trans. H. Bettenson, Harmondsworth: Pelican Books 1972, Book XIV, ch. 24. This would seem to be somewhat faulty reasoning, since presumably male beasts had no part in the Fall!

60. Cf. the comment of Julia Kristeva above, 171.

61. See above, 49.

62. M. Carroll, *The Cult of the Virgin Mary*, Princeton, NJ: Princeton University Press 1987.

63. Ranke-Heinemann, *Eunuchs* (n. 56), 341–4.

64. *Summa* II/II q. 154 a 11, a 12.

65. Ranke-Heinemann, *Eunuchs* (n. 56), 197.

66. *The Tablet*, 20 Janury 1990.

67. Ranke-Heinemann, *Eunuchs* (n. 56), 288–95.

68. Material circulated by Margaret Collier-Bendelow, of the European Society of Women in Theological Research, in the attempt to enlist support from other women for a protest to be mounted.

69. Lest it should be thought that the problem only concerns Catholicism, or the sadism only practised on women, it is worth noting the following report of his time as headmaster of Repton by a former pupil of Geoffrey Fisher, later to become Archbishop of Canterbury. 'He never flogged me, thank goodness, but I was given a vivid description of one of these ceremonies by my best friend at Repton, whose name was Michael. Michael was ordered to take down his trousers and kneel on the Headmaster's sofa with the top half of his body hanging over one end of the sofa. The great man then gave him one terrific crack. After that, there was a pause. The cane was put down and the Headmaster began filling his pipe from a tin of tobacco. He also started to lecture the kneeling boy about sin and wrongdoing. Soon, the cane was picked up again and a second tremendous crack was administered upon the trembling buttocks. Then the pipe-filling business and the lecture went on for maybe another thirty

seconds. Then came the third crack of the cane. Then the instrument of torture was put once more upon the table and a box of matches was produced. A match was struck and applied to the pipe. The pipe failed to light properly. A fourth stroke was delivered, with the lecture continuing. This slow and fearsome process went on until ten terrible strokes had been delivered, and all the time, over the pipe-lighting and match-striking, the lecture on evil and wrongdoing and sinning and misdeeds and malpractice went on without a stop. It even went on as the strokes were being administered. At the end of it all, a basin, a sponge and a small clean towel were produced by the Headmaster, and the victim was told to wash away the blood before pulling up his trousers.' The writer comments of this Headmaster. 'I would sit in the dim light of the school chapel and listen to him preaching about the Lamb of God and about Mercy and Forgiveness and all the rest of it and my young mind would become totally confused. I knew very well that only the night before this preacher had shown neither Forgiveness nor Mercy in flogging some small boy who had broken the rules' (Roald Dahl, *Boy: Tales of Childhood*, Harmondsworth: Puffin Books 1986, 145–6). As Archbishop of Canterbury, Fisher was involved in the revision of canon law and the system of ecclesiastical courts to enforce it. He described this enormous undertaking to his biographer William Purcell as follows: '[It formed] the most absorbing and all-embracing topic of my whole archepiscopate . . . With the instincts of a headmaster I knew that it was absolutely essential to the well-ordering and self-respect of the Church of England to have canons which could and should be obeyed. The lack of order had become quite dreadful' (Purcell, *Fisher of Lambeth*, 1969, 206–7, quoted by D.L. Edwards, *Tradition and Truth*, Hodder and Stoughton 1989, 14–15). Of course sadism is found throughout human history. What is significant about these reported events (which there is no reason to doubt are the case) is first that such a man could be elevated to the highest ecclesiastical office in the land, and secondly that as recently as forty years ago facts such as these did not come out into the open.

70. The Report presented to the General Assembly is to be found in 'Woman's Guild/Panel on Doctrine Study Group on the Motherhood of God', *The Church of Scotland: Reports to the General Assembly, 1984*, 91–116. The Working Party had put in two years work. See also n. 21.

71. Richard Frazer, *The Scotsman*, 24 May 1984.

72. Kathleen Miller, *The Scotsman*, 24 May 1984.

73. Nor did I find it edifying that my male colleagues at that time, who as far as I know had never lifted a little finger to further the cause of women, fell over themselves in their support of this man's cause. Not being a member of the church, I said nothing.

74. A. Dietrich, *Mutter Erde*, 3rd ed., Berlin 1925, 114, quoted by J. Moltmann, *God in Creation: A New Theology of Creation and the Spirit of God*, trans. M. Kohl, London: SCM Press and San Francisco: Harper and Row 1985, 302.

75. *De unitate ecclesiae* c. 6.
76. See above, 64.
77. L. Boff, *Maternal Face* (n. 27), 95.
78. See below, 201.
79. M. Schmaus, *Mariology*, 107. Quoted by Ranke-Heinemann, *Eunuchs* (n. 56), 32.
80. Warner, *Alone of All Her Sex* (n. 14), 338.
81. K. Barth, *Church Dogmatics*, III/2, *The Doctrine of Creation*, Edinburgh: T. & T. Clark 1960, 309–16, 324; see also III/4, 1961, 163–81.
82. See below, 255.
83. K. Barth, *Church Dogmatics*, I/2, *The Doctrine of the Word of God*, Edinburgh: T. & T. Clark, 1956, 191–2.
84. K. Barth, *Church Dogmatics,* III/ 1, *The Doctrine of Creation*, Edinburgh: T. & T. Clark, 1958, 302–3.
85. Kristeva, *Chinese Women* (n. 7), 17.
86. See above, 137–8.
87. Cf. C. Exum, '"Mother in Israel": A Familiar Story Reconsidered', in Russell (ed.), *Feminist Interpretation* (n. 44), 77–8.
88. C. Delaney, 'The Legacy of Abraham', in R. Gross (ed.), *Beyond Androcentrism* (n. 44), 221. Cf. also above, 141.
89. For an analysis of the Hebrew Bible in this regard see Esther Fuchs, 'The Literary Characterization of Mothers and Sexual Politics in the Hebrew Bible', in A. Yarbro Collins (ed., *Feminist Perspectives on Biblical Scholarship,* Chico, CA: Scholars Press 1985, 117–36.
90. C. Exum, '"Mother in Israel": A Familiar Story Reconsidered', in L. Russell (ed.), *Feminist Interpretation* (n. 44), 79.
91. N. Segal, 'Feminism and Theology – My Interest', Notes for a panel held at the 'Shadow of Spirit' Conference, King's College, Cambridge, dated 24 July 1990.
92. L. lrigaray, 'Questions to Emmanuel Levinas', in M. Whitford (ed.), *The Irigaray Reader*, Oxford: Basil Blackwell, 1991, 178–89. See above, 140–1.
93. E. Fuchs, 'The Literary Characterization of Mothers and Sexual Politics in the Hebrew Bible', in Yarbro Collins (ed.), *Feminist Perspectives* (n. 89), 123.
94. 'Feminism and Theology' (n. 91).
95. Kristeva, 'Stabat Mater' (n. 16), 162.
96. Cf., for example, the words of Cardinal Bernard Law of Boston, that among radical feminists there was a 'difficulty in accepting complementarity, because of an assumption that equality and difference are fundamentally incompatible with one another' (*The National Catholic Reporter*, 24 March 1989).
97. See above, 116. See also my 'Theological Integrity and Human Relationships', *Feminist Theology*, no. 2 (Jan. 1993), 42–56: discussion of 'complementarity', 46–9; and Rosemary Ruether's excellent discussion in *Sexism and God-Talk*, Boston: Beacon Press and London: SCM Press

1983, 112, 189–92.

98. Augustine, *Confessions* IX, 9, trans. R.S. Pine-Coffin, Harmondsworth: Penguin Books 1961, 194–5.

99. Kari Elisabeth Børresen, *Subordination and Equivalence. The Nature and Role of Woman in Augustine and Thomas Aquinas*, Washington DC: University Press of America 1981, 95–6.

100. C. Bohn, 'Dominion to Rule: The Roots and Consequences of a Theology of Ownership', in J. Carlson Brown and C.R. Bohn (eds.), *Christianity, Patriarchy and Abuse: A Feminist Critique*, New York: The Pilgrim Press 1989, 105–7.

101. See for example A. Adams, *Bullying at Work. How to Confront and Overcome It*, London: Virago 1992, 102.

102. Ginny NiCarthy, *Getting Free*, Seattle: Seal Press 1984, 7, quoted by Bohn, 'Dominion to Rule' (n. 100), 115 n. 5.

103. See above, 73–4.

104. Note; quoted with permission.

105. *Mulieris Dignitatem: Apostolic Letter of the Supreme Pontiff John Paul II on the Dignity and Vocation of Women on the Occasion of the Marian Year*, London: Catholic Truth Society 1988, 13, 17, 28, 29, 39, 40, 45, 46, 64, 68, 78, 84, 85, 94, 109, 114.

106. From an interview in *La création étouffée* [Smothered creativity], which contains interviews with creative women (1973). Quoted by E. Marks and I. de Courtivron (eds.), *New French Feminisms: An Anthology*, Amherst, MA: The University of Massachusetts Press 1980, 111–13: quotation 112.

107. Cf. R. Ruether, *Mary – The Feminine Face of the Church*, London: SCM Press 1979, 73–4, which makes this switch, and on Mary Magdalene, Michèle Roberts, *The Wild Girl*, London: Methuen 1984. See also Els Maeckelberghe, *Desperately Seeking Mary: A Feminist Appropriation of a Traditional Religious Symbol*, Kampen: Kok Pharos 1992.

108. Luke 2. 49.

109. Cf. Luke 11. 28; Mark 3. 31f., and parallels.

110. Warner, *Alone of All her Sex* (n. 14), 338.

111. I Cor. 12. 12–30.

112. According to recent surveys, approximately 40% of American women between the ages of 18 and 44 do not have children (M. S. Ireland, *Reconceiving Women: Separating Motherhood from Female Identity*, New York: Guilford Press 1993). In such a world the understanding of woman as in the first instance 'mother' must cease to make sense.

113. When the feminist philosophy journal *Hypatia* had an issue on the philosophy of religion, they were apparently flooded with articles on Irigaray. I myself am expecting to write on her work elsewhere.

114. E. Grosz, 'Philosophy, Subjectivity and the Body: Kristeva and Irigaray', in C. Pateman and E. Grosz (eds.), *Feminist Challenges: Social and Political Theory*, Boston: Northeastern University Press 1987, 135.

115. Kristeva, *Chinese Women* (n. 7), 23.

116. J. Kristeva, 'La femme, ce n'est jamais ça', interview in *Tel Quel*, Autumn 1974, in Marks and de Courtivron (eds.), *New French Feminisms* (n. 106), 139–40.

117. N. Gottwald, *The Tribes of Yahweh: A Sociology of the Religion of Liberated Israel, 1250–1050 BCE,* Maryknoll: Orbis Books and London: SCM Press 1979, 708, 709.

VI. *A Future Theism*

1. F.D.E. Schleiermacher, *On Religion: Speeches to its Cultured Despisers*, trans. J. Oman, New York: Harper and Row 1958. In general I have used this translation, of the third German edition (1821), rather than the more recent translation by Richard Crouter of the first edition of 1799. I find it preferable to do this given my purpose. However, in a number of instances I have noted that a word or phrase is present also in the earlier edition. On the various editions, see the discussion in Crouter's Introduction, 57f.: *On Religion: Speeches to its Cultured Despisers*, Cambridge: Cambridge University Press 1988.

2. F.D.E. Schleiermacher, *The Christian Faith*, second ed., ed. and trans. H. R. Mackintosh and J. S. Stewart, Edinburgh: T. & T. Clark 1928, reprinted New York: Harper and Row, Harper Torchbook ed. 1963.

3. Cf. E. Busch, *Karl Barth: His Life from Letters and Autobiographical Texts*, London: SCM Press 1976, 409, 494.

4. Schleiermacher, *Speeches* (n. 1) 1831, 43 (1799, 113).

5. Ibid., 36.

6. Ibid., 1.

7. Cf. R.R Niebuhr, Introduction to the Torchbook ed. of *The Christian Faith* (n. 2), xv.

8. Cf. 'The Nature of Religion', *Speeches,* 31: 'Piety cannot be an instinct craving for a mess of metaphysical and ethical crumbs.' For a discussion of Kant, see below, 277–8.

9. Here I must depart completely from Nicholas Lash's reading of Schleiermacher in *Easter in Ordinary. Reflections on Human Experience and the Knowledge of God*, Charlottesville, VA: The University Press of Virginia and London: SCM Press 1988. Lash wishes to place Schleiermacher within what he calls 'an interpretative or "hermeneutical" tradition of theological discourse'. Thus when Schleiermacher says, of Protestant Christians, that the 'feeling of absolute dependence is for us the really original signification of that word', Lash, italicizing the 'for us', writes as follows: 'He is, in other words, simply stating that this is, or should be, the way in which Christians use the word "God": they use it to designate the "whence" of the feeling of absolute dependence. The remark, therefore, is what Wittgenstein would have called a "grammatical" remark; it does *not* constitute an *empirical* claim of any kind. To put it another way . . . Schleiermacher is indicating one of the *rules* according to which the word "God", which we have inherited, is appropriately to be used' (127).

On the contrary, I believe there can be no reason to suppose anything other than that Schleiermacher is making a phenomenological claim, predicated upon an empirical observation of our self-awareness, which he finds to include a component of 'derivedness'. In this Schleiemiacher may be seen (as has often been remarked of his work) to be carrying to its logical conclusion what he conceives to be the Reformation project of founding religion in a subjective awareness.

10. R. Roberts, 'The Feeling of Absolute Dependence', *The Journal of Religion*, Vol. 57, 1977, 252–66: quotation, 252.

11. Schleiermacher, *Christian Faith* (n. 2), §4. 4.

12. Ibid., §4. 4.

13. G.W.F. Hegel, *Lectures on the Philosophy of Religion*, Vol. 1, ed. P.C. Hodgson, Los Angeles and London: University of California Press, 1984, 279–80, note: quotation, 279.

14. J. Macquarrie, *Thinking about God*, London: SCM Press 1975, 164.

15. See above, 137–8.

16. R. Otto, *The Idea of the Holy*, trans. J. W. Harvey, Oxford and New York: Oxford University Press 1958, 9.

17. L. Feuerbach, *The Essence of Christianity* (1841), trans. G. Eliot, New York and London: Harper Torchbooks 1957.

18. Schleiermacher, *Christian Faith* (n. 2), §5. 3.

19. Ibid., §6. 2.

20. Thus I find myself sceptical about the thrust of Wayne Proudfoot's *Religious Experience*, Berkeley, Los Angeles and London: University of California Press 1985. It seems to me that Proudfoot forces Schleiermacher's thought into a straitjacket which is not true to its complexity. Schleiermacher is not seeking to answer the question which, in the 1980s, Proudfoot asks of him. Moreover I have suggested (pp. 220–2) that a position such as Schleiermacher's is not necessarily vulnerable to a 'Derridean' critique. It might well be that Otto's position is much more vulnerable, and I certainly should not want to couple Schleiermacher with Otto here. Thus Otto's famous statement, 'The reader is invited to direct his mind to a moment of deeply-felt religious experience, as little as possible qualified by other forms of consciousness. Whoever cannot do this, whoever knows no such moments in his experience, is requested to read no farther' (*The Idea of the Holy* [n. 16], 8), might indeed be an endeavour (of the type Proudfoot finds illegitimate) to speak of direct cognition of the noumenal. See also here the debate which has taken place in *Religious Studies* following Steven Katz's 'Language, Epistemology and Mysticism', in S. Katz (ed.), *Mysticism and Philosophical Analysis*, London: Sheldon Press, 1978. Katz claims that: 'There are NO pure (i. e. unmediated) experiences' (26). After Leon Schlamm's endorsement of Otto's position ('Numinous Experience and Religious Language', *Religious Studies* 28, 1992, 533–51), L. Philip Barnes argued that Otto's position is untenable in the light of a post-Wittgensteinian understanding of the nature of language and experience. ('Rudolf Otto and the Limits of

Religious Description', *Religious Studies* 30, 219–30). Note that Barnes couples Schleiermacher with Otto (221). Barnes comments: 'Otto writes in places as if religious feelings can be isolated from religious concepts without loss of meaning' (223), whereas Barnes wishes to argue that 'There is no privileged domain where religion can retreat to' (224); and again, 'Against Otto, feelings do not provide independent, *nonconceptual* (and sufficient) epistemic grounds for the existence of objects in the external world' (225). Nicholas Lash's position in *Easter in Ordinary* (n. 9) is cognate with this. See also Melissa Raphael's interesting 'Feminism, Constructivism and Numinous Experience', *Religious Studies* 30, 511–26, in which she argues that, far from being immune from concepts, 'religious experience is conditioned from the outset by patriarchal conceptualizations of ultimate value and by sex-role differentiation in the practice of religion' (513). I think that this is clearly right; see for example my discussion of the Trinity, above, 155–62. Finally I wish to say that I think that George Lindbeck polarizes too sharply what he calls an 'experiential expressive' and a 'cultural-linguistic' model of religion *(The Nature of Doctrine. Religion and Theology in a Post-Liberal Age,* Philadelphia, PA: Westminster Press 1984). I find it possible both to say that religion is a response to something which is experiential and also to acknowledge that that experience can never be separated from our linguistic and cultural matrix.

21. See above, 17–19.
22. K. Barth, *Protestant Theology in the Nineteenth Century: Its Background and History* (1952), London: SCM Press 1972, 473.
23. See above, 22.
24. Quoted in F. Maurice (ed.), *The Life of Frederick Denison Maurice*, Vol. I, London 1884, 468.
25. W. James, *The Varieties of Religious Experience: A Study in Human Nature*, New York and London: Collier Macmillan Publishers 1961.
26. Schleiermacher, *Speeches* (n. 1), 88.
27. Cf. the discussion in Chapter I above of the fact that there cannot be particularity in this sense.
28. Cf. James' discussion, *Varieties* (n. 25), lectures 4 and 5, 78–113.
29. Whether developments in quantum physics, for example, will change our idea of what is possible it will be interesting to see. Danah Zohar has suggested, provocatively, that consciousness is a quantum system which is our 'wave' aspect, while our physical selves are our 'particle' aspect *(The Quantum Self. A Revolutionary View of Human Nature and Consciousness Rooted in the New Physics,* London: Bloomsbury 1990). Cf. R. Penrose, *The Emperor s New Mind*, Oxford: Oxford University Press, 1989, 226 (in a chapter on quantum theory): 'Perhaps, also, the phenomenon of consciousness is something that cannot be understood in entirely classical terms.'
30. A. Hardy, *The Spiritual Nature of Man: A Study of Contemporary Religious Experience*, Oxford: Clarendon Press 1979, 46.

31. James, *Varieties* (n. 25), lecture 20, 377–8.
32. Hardy, *Spiritual Nature* (n. 30), 18.
33. Ibid., 126.
34. Ibid., 127.
35. For books which have been produced by the Unit's many collaborators see for example the following: Hardy, *The Spiritual Nature of Man* (n. 30); E. Robinson, *The Original Vision*, Oxford: Religious Experience Research Unit, Manchester College, Oxford 1977; T. Beardsworth, *A Sense of Presence: The Phenomenology of Certain Kinds of Visionary and Ecstatic Experiences Based on a Thousand Contemporary First Hand Accounts*, Oxford: The Religious Experience Research Unit, Manchester College 1977; D. Hay, *Religious Experience Today: The Facts*, London: Mowbray 1990; and M. Maxwell and V. Tschudin, *Seeing the Invisible. Modern Religious and Other Transcendent Experiences*, London: Arkana, Penguin Group 1990.
36. Cf. Mark 6. 13; Acts 3.
37. James, *Varieties* (n. 25), 'Postscript', 404.
38. Robinson, *The Original Vision* (n. 35), 5.
39. Schleiermacher, *Christian Faith* (n. 2), §3. 2, 6–7.
40. H. Steffens, *Was Ich Erlebte*, Vol. V (1842), 141f., quoted by W. Dilthey, *Leben Schleiermachers*, 2nd ed., 1922, 548, quoted and trans. by R. R. Niebuhr, *Schleiermacher on Christ and Religion: A New Introduction*, New York: Charles Scribner's Sons 1964, 75.
41. Schleiermacher, *Christian Faith* (n. 2), §3. 3, 8.
42. Schleiermacher, *Speeches* (n. 1), 37.
43. Ibid., 55 (1799, 108).
44. Introduction, Torchbook ed. of *The Christian Faith* (n. 2), xii.
45. Schleiermacher, *Christian Faith* (n. 2), §4. 1,13.
46. See above, 224–5.
47. Terry L. Miethe (ed.), *Gary Habermas and Antony Flew, Did Jesus Rise from the Dead?*, San Francisco: Harper and Row 1987, 35.
48. J.L. Mackie, *The Miracle of Theism: Arguments For and Against the Existence of God*, Oxford: Clarendon Press 1982, 27–8.
49. See the helpful survey in D. Cohn-Sherbok, *God and the Holocaust*, 1990 St Paul's Lecture (pamphlet), available from The London Diocesan Council for Christian–Jewish Understanding, St Botolph's Vestry, Aldgate, London EC3N 1AB.
50. L. Gilkey, Re*aping the Whirlwind: A Christian Interpretation of History*, New York: The Seabury Press, A Crossroad Book 1976, 225.
51. Schleiermacher, *Speeches* (n. 1), 59–60, my italics (1799, 111).
52. A reference to Rudolf Otto's 'creature feeling'.
53. M. Buber, *Ich und Du*, Heidelberg: Verlag Lambert Schneider, eighth ed. 1974, 97–9. My translation.
54. Ibid., 18.
55. 'Knowing and Naming the Triune God: The Grammar of Trinitarian Confession', in A.F. Kimel (ed.), *Speaking the Christian God: The Holy*

Trinity and the Challenge of Feminism, Grand Rapids, MI: Eerdmans and Leominster: Gracewing 1992, 186.

56. *Revelations of Divine Love*, ed. G. Warwick, London: Methuen, 1958, ch. CLVI, 135.

57. Schleiermacher, *Speeches* (n. 1), 101.

58. Ibid., 50.

59. J. A. T. Robinson, *Exploration into God*, London: SCM Press 1967, 36.

60. I find it of interest that there is a literature stemming from thinkers who are by no means conventionally religious who want to argue that the idea of God does and must perform such a function. I am thinking, for example, of the work of Gordon Kaufman (in many of his writings) and more especially of Stewart Sutherland's *God, Jesus and Belief: The Legacy of Theism*, Oxford and New York: Basil Blackwell 1984.

61. Consider for example Herbert McCabe's essay 'Creation', *New Blackfriars*, Vol. 61, no. 724 (1980), reprinted in *God Matters*, London: Geoffrey Chapman 1987.

62. A. Camus, *The Plague*, trans. S. Gilbert, Harmondsworth: Penguin Books 1960.

63. Cf. V. A. Harvey, *The Historian and the Believer*, New York: Macmillan 1966 and London: SCM Press 1967, 257.

64. D. Hume, *Dialogues Concerning Natural Religion*, New York: Hafner Press and London: Collier Macmillan 1948.

65. Hardy, *Spiritual Nature* (n. 30), 1.

66. M. Goulder and J. Hick, *Why Believe in God?*, London: SCM Press 1983, 41.

67. M. Chapin Massey, *Feminine Soul: The Fate of an Ideal*, Boston: Beacon Press 1985.

68 See above, 123ff.

69. Cf. H. McCabe, *God Matters* (n. 61), 46: 'At the heart of every creature is the source of *esse*, making it to be and to act (STIa,8,1,c). As is well known, Aquinas carries this through to its logical conclusion and insists that it must be just as true of my free acts as of anything else. To be free is to be independent of others. God is not, in the relevant sense, other.' (I disagree that being independent of others is a good definition of 'freedom'.)

70. For further discussion of this point cf. my 'On Autonomy and Heteronomy', in D. Hampson, *Swallowing a Fishbone? Feminist Theologians Debate Christianity*, London: SPCK 1996, 1–16.

71. 'Relational Love: A Feminist Christian Vision', in P. M. Cooey, S. A. Farmer and M. E. Ross (eds.), *Embodied Love. Sensuality and Relationship as Feminist Values*, San Francisco: Harper and Row 1983, 144–5.

72. I should comment here that, in attempting to follow my thought, people will sometimes tell me that what I am talking about is what Christians call 'the Holy Spirit'. I have sometimes accepted this as a rough translation in order to make myself comprehensible. However, I am increasingly clear – perhaps as I have become more radical – that this is not correct. When

Christians speak of the Holy Spirit they mean that which is God, in their sense, and which descends to (I want to write invades) creation. By contrast, I am saying something about the way in which things are; I am not in any sense wishing to conjure up the idea of anything which is separate from or 'more than' the creation, which then comes to reside in the creation. I do agree that spirit language helps if it conveys that the immanent/ transcendent distinction in God-language is overcome. Such a distinction presupposes a deeply atomized view of the self and a polarity between the self and what else there is; so God is either caught up within the self, or else placed in juxtaposition to the self.

73. Cf. S. Sykes, *Friedrich Schleiermacher*, Makers of Contemporary Theology, Richmond, VA: John Knox Press and London: Lutterworth Press 1971, 20.

VII. *Spirituality and Praxis*

1. Cf. M. D. Hampson, 'The British Response to the German Church Conflict, 1933–39', unpublished Oxford D. Phil. 1974, chapter 1.
2. The debate is reprinted in K. Barth and E. Brunner, *Natural Theology*, trans. Peter Fraenkel, London: Centenary Press 1946.
3. See above, 153.
4. Thus it would seem doubtful that Barth's rather than Brunner's reading of Calvin in the famous debate to which I allude is correct.
5. In the 1960s I held a very different position, declaring at a meeting in Berlin of the organization Christian Movement for Peace (Christliche Friedensdienst/ Movement Chrétien pour la Paix), held shortly after the erection of the Berlin Wall, that it was not possible that the church of God should '*untergehen*' (go under). A young Swiss woman, Christina Barth, was present at that meeting; when I questioned her, she told me that Herr Professor Karl Barth was her great-uncle. She later informed me that she had repeated to him the essence of the speech which I had had the courage to make, which doubtless met with his approval. Later that summer I attended her wedding, in a small village church not unlike that at Safenwil, the parish in which Barth's *Römerbrief* was written. The entire Barth family (other than Karl Barth, who was by that time not well) was assembled. It gave me a marvellous insight into that brand of Reformed Christianity.
6. Thus I have spent the greater part of my career so far teaching (against my will) a course on 'Church and Sacraments' and (though I did not mind it so much since I learnt much from it) one on 'Christology'. These things are now no more.
7. Cf. for example *Waiting on God*, London: Collins, Fontana 1959. I am, however, less than happy with Weil's understanding, which seems too passive, when she writes for example: 'Attention consists of suspending our thought, leaving it detached, empty and ready to be penetrated by the object . . .' (72).

8. I. Murdoch, *The Sovereignty of Good*, London: Routledge & Kegan Paul 1970.

9. A. Kuhn, *Women's Pictures: Feminism and Cinema*, London: Routledge & Kegan Paul 1982, quoted by Lorraine Code, 'Experience, Knowledge and Responsibility', in M. Griffiths and M. Whitford (eds.), *Feminist Perspectives in Philosophy*, Indiana University Press: Bloomington, IN 1988, 196.

10. A. Dillard, *Pilgrim at Tinker Creek*, Toronto, New York, London: Bantam Books 1975, 83; London: Jonathan Cape 1975, 83.

11. Murdoch, *Sovereignty of Good* (n. 8), 31. M. Nussbaum, ' "Finely Aware and Richly Responsible": Literature and the Moral Imagination', in A. J. Cascardi (ed.), *Literature and the Question of Philosophy*, Baltimore and London: The Johns Hopkins University Press 1987, 167–91: 169, and in M. Nussbaum, *Love's Knowledge: Essays on Philosophy and Literature*, New York and Oxford: Oxford University Press 1990, 148–67: 148. The quotation comes from Henry James.

12. Cf. *Sovereignty of Good* (n. 8), especially 22f.

13. D. Hardy, 'Man the Creature', paper presented to The Society for the Study of Theology meeting in Edinburgh, spring 1975, 4.

14. Murdoch, *Sovereignty of Good* (n. 8), 37.

15. M. Nussbaum, 'Finely Aware', (n. 11), 184/160.

16. See above, 100.

17 J. Donovan, *Feminist Theory: The Intellectual Traditions of American Feminism*, New York: Frederick Ungar Publishing Co. 1985, 173.

18. S. Kierkegaard, *Either/Or*, Vol. 1, Princeton, NJ: Princeton University Press 1971, 66.

19. R. Williams, 'The Suspicion of Suspicion: Wittgenstein and Bonhoeffer', in R. H. Bell (ed.), *The Grammar of the Heart: New Essays in Moral Philosophy and Theology*, San Francisco: Harper & Row 1988, 36–53: quotation, 50.

20. H.-G. Gadamer, *Truth and Method*, London: Sheed and Ward 1975, 324.

21. See above, 109.

22. A. Klein, 'Finding a Self: Buddhist and Feminist Perspectives', in C. W. Atkinson, C. H. Buchanan and M. R. Miles (eds.), *Shaping New Vision: Gender and Values in American Culture*, The Harvard Women's Studies in Religion Series 5, Ann Arbor, MI and London: UMI Research Press 1987, 206.

23. W. Shakespeare, *Hamlet*, act I, scene 3, lines 79–80.

24. L. Trilling, *Sincerity and Authenticity*, Cambridge, MA: Harvard University Press 1972, 5–6.

25. Murdoch, *Sovereignty of Good* (n. 8), 59.

26. S. Ruddick, *Maternal Thinking*, Boston, MA: Beacon Press 1989 and London: The Women's Press 1990, 120.

27. J. Martin Soskice, 'Love and Attention', in M. McGhee (ed.), *Philosophy, Religion and the Spiritual Life*, Cambridge: Cambridge University Press 1992, 59–72.

28. From the well-known hymn which begins 'Dear Lord and Father of mankind'. On Whittier (1807–1892) see Norman Mable, *Popular Hymns and their Writers*, London: Independent Press 1945, 192–4.

29. A. MacIntyre, *After Virtue. A Study in Moral Theory*, London: Duckworth 1981.

30. Isaac Watts (1674–1748), 'When I survey the wondrous cross', the well-known hymn.

31. See above, ooo.

32. A. Wilson Schaef, *Meditations for Women Who Do Too Much*, San Francisco: HarperCollins 1990.

33. A. Dickson, *A Book of Your Own*, London: Quartet Books 1994.

34. D. Hay, *Religious Experience Today: Studying the Facts*, London: Mowbray, 1990, 8.

35. Elizabeth Lord, SUSC (autumn 1985).

36. S. Kierkegaard, *Philosophical Fragments* (1844), *Kierkegaard's Writings*, VII, ed. and trans. H. and E. Hong, Princeton, NJ: Princeton University Press 1985, 10–11.

37. See the outstanding book by Lily Segerman-Peck, *Networking and Mentoring: A Woman's Guide*, London: Piatkus 1991. I shall not forget the first time that I went through appraisal at work, insisting, as was my right, that I should go outside my department to be appraised by a senior woman. In concluding the interview she commented 'well done'. No one, in fifteen years, had ever said anything like that before.

38. Cf. my forthcoming book to be published by Cambridge University Press.

39. Plato, *The Republic*, trans. F. M. Cornford, Oxford: Clarendon Press 1941, 138–9.

40. G. Steiner, *Heidegger*, Fontana Modern Masters, Collins: Glasgow 1978, 105. Steiner is commenting on the early Heidegger of *Being and Time* (1927). He does not give a page reference.

41. M. Luther,' The Freedom of a Christian' (1520), in J. Dillenberger (ed.), *Martin Luther: Selections From His Writings*, Garden City, NY: Anchor Books 1961, 70; *The Ethics of Aristotle (Nichomachean Ethics)*, trans. J.A.K. Thomson, revised H. Tredennick, London: Penguin Books 1976, 91.

42. John of the Cross, 'The Spiritual Canticle', Stanza 29, in K. Kavanaugh (ed.), *John of the Cross: Selected Writings*, The Classics of Western Spirituality, London: SPCK 1987, 270–1.

43. See above, 244ff.

44. I. Kant, *Critique of Practical Reason*, trans. L. W. Beck, New York: The Bobbs-Merrill Company 1956.

45. F. D. E. Schleiermacher, *On Religion: Speeches to its Cultured Despisers*, trans. J. Oman, New York: Harper & Row 1958, 29. In 1799 he had written: 'We should do everything with religion, nothing because of religion' (*On Religion: Speeches to its Cultured Despisers*, ed. and trans. Richard Crouter, Cambridge: Cambridge University Press 1988, 110).

46. C. Geertz, *Islam Observed: Religious Development in Morocco and*

Indonesia (1968), Chicago and London: The University of Chicago Press 1971, 97.

47. V. Frankl, *Man s Search for Meaning. An Introduction to Logotherapy*, Part I, trans. I. Lasch, Boston: Beacon Press 1962, 106. Cf. 12–13.

48. Ibid., 82. Nietzsche in fact gives this sentence in the plural: F. Nietzsche, ed. K. Schlechta, Vol. 3, Darmstadt: Wissenschaftliche Buchgesellschaft 1966, 603.

49. Julian of Norwich, *Revelations of Divine Love*, ed. G. Warwick, London: Methuen 1949, 'The Thirteenth Revelation', 56.

50. R. Higgins, *The Seventh Enemy. The Human Factor in the Global Crisis*, London: Hodder and Stoughton 1982, 272.

51. See above, 21–5.

52. See above, 96–7.

53. Cf. for example *Jesus — God and Man*, Philadelphia: Westminster Press and London: SCM Press 1968. See above, 45–6.

54. See above, 237.

55. Gal. 2. 20.

56. Daly here plays with Aristotelian terminology: M. Daly, *Beyond God the Father: Toward a Philosophy of Women s Liberation*, Boston: Beacon Press 1973 and London: The Women's Press 1986, ch. 7.

57. F. Nietzsche, 'How the "Real World" at last Became a Myth: The History of an Error', *Twilight of the Idols*, Harmondsworth: Penguin Books 1990, 50.

58. I. Murdoch, *Metaphysics as a Guide to Morals*, London: Chatto & Windus 1992, 467.

Index

Addison, Joseph, 249
Anselm, 149–50, 178
Apollinarius, 18, 19
Aquinas, Thomas, 124, 179, 189, 249
Aristotle, 8, 276
Armstrong, John, 78
Athanasius, 143, 155
Augustine, 48, 157, 177, 188, 198, 199, 276, 280
Aulén, Gustaf, 304 n.81

Baker Miller, Jean, 113
Balthasar, Hans Urs von, 175
Barnes, L. Philip, 315–16 n.20
Barth, Christina, 319 n.5
Barth, Karl, 79, 132, 142, 153, 183, 195, 212, 222, 254–5, 280, 289 n.10, 319 n.5
Bartlett, Tony, 150–1
Bauckham, Richard, 66–7
Beard, Mary, 95
Beethoven, Ludwig van, 53
Behhabib, Seyla, 98–101, 108
Benjamin, Jessica, 105, 106–8
Bernard of Clairvaux, 198
Bird, Phyllis, 309 n.44
Bloomquist, Karen, 145–6, 153
Boff, Leonardo, 180, 193
Blake, William, 249
Bohn, Carole, 199
Bonhoeffer, Dietrich, 1, 8, 35–8, 146
Bordo, Susan, 88, 99
Børresen, Kari, 199
Bowker, John, 121–2
Bradley, F.H., 45
Braidotti, Rosi, 159
Brooks Thistlethwaite, Susan, 73
Brown, Peter, 161
Brunner, Emil, 255
Brunswick, Ruth, 90
Buber, Martin, 240–3
Bultmann, Rudolf, 17, 19–21, 27, 35, 48, 49, 289 n.9

Cady, Linell, 253
Caffarra, Mgr Carol, 190
Calvin, John, 136, 142, 256
Campbell, Beatrice, 298 n.84
Camus, Albert, 245, 278
Carr, Anne, 163
Carroll, Michael, 189
Caroll, Robert, 183, 187
Cellini, Benvenuto, 86
Chicago, Judy, 71
Chodorow, Nancy, 90–1, 96, 97, 102
Clement of Alexandria, 178
Clements, Ronald, 123
Coakley, Sarah, 291 n.50
Cobb, John, 133–4
Cohn-Sherbok, Dan, 317 n.49
Collier-Bendelow, Margaret, 310 n.68
Collin, Françoise, 164
Cupitt, Don, 174, 288 n.8
Cyprian, 192

Daly, Mary, 187, 282
Darwin, Charles, 9, 22, 26
De Beauvoir, Simone, 7, 127, 169–70, 206
De Chardin, Teilhard, 175, 176
De Gouges, Olympe, 3
Delaney, Carol, 137, 141, 196
Della Francesca, Piero, 175
De Lubac, Henri, 175
Demant, V.A., 181
Derrida, Jacques, 6, 128, 220–2, 233, 266, 282, 297 n.44
Descartes, René, 98–100
Deutscher, Penelope, 116
Dickson, Anne, 271
Dillard, Annie, 261
DiNoia, J.A., 241–2
Donatello, xiii, 86, 87, 88, 194, 294 n.7
Donovan, Josephine, 262
Dowell, Susan, 58–60, 70, 132
Duras, Marguerite, 202
Dyson, Anthony, 80–1

Eckhart, Meister, 198
Ellwood, Gracia Fay, 186
Engels, Friedrich, 5, 209
Erikson, Erik, 107, 158
Exum, J. Cheryl, 75, 196, 292 n.10

Fairbairn, Ronald, 93
Feuerbach, Ludwig, 4, 120, 158–9, 208, 220, 249
Fisher, Geoffrey, 310–11 n.69
Flax, Jane, 98–9, 103–5, 116
Flew, Antony, 236
Frankl, Viktor, 279
Fraser, Nancy, 92, 105, 119, 167
Frazer, Richard, 311 n.71
Freud, Sigmund, 4, 89–96, 107, 120, 147–9, 154, 167, 177, 196, 208, 220, 249
Fuchs, Esther, 292 n.9

Gadamer, Hans-Georg, 263
Gale, Richard, 124
Gandhi, Mahatma, 44
Geertz, Clifford, 278
Gilkey, Langdon, 237, 290–1 n.43
Gilligan, Carol, 93–5, 96, 100, 115, 131, 138, 262
Giotto, 174
Girard, René, 141, 149
Goodman, Lenn Evan, 124
Gottwald, Norman, 210
Green, Michael, 29
Griffiths, Bede, 291–2 n.3
Grimshaw, Jean, 104
Gross, Rita, 125–6
Grosz, Elizabeth, 172, 179, 209
Gunton, Colin, 156, 288 n.4

Hamerton-Kelly, Robert, 154
Haney, Eleanor, 109–11, 270
Hardy, Alister, 228, 230
Hardy, Daniel, 261
Harrison, Beverly, 150
Hartshorne, Charles, 133–4
Harvey, Van, 245
Hay, David, 271
Hebblethwaite, Brian, 161
Hegel, G.W.F., 7, 22, 101, 106, 107, 169, 208, 218–9, 249, 280–1
Heidegger, Martin, 275, 282
Heller, David, 130–1
Heyward, Carter, 150
Hick, John, 38, 39, 248

Higgins, Ronald, 279
Hildebrandt, Franz, 36, 290 n.34
Hitler, Adolf, 36, 38, 225
Hobbes, Thomas, 98
Hopkins, Julie, 287–8 n.2
Houlden, J.L., 48
Howell, Signe, 127
Hoyland, John, 95
Hume, David, 247
Husserl, Edmund, 221

Ireland, Mardy, 313 n.112
Irenaeus, 143, 280
Irigaray, Luce, 75–6, 79, 96–9, 116, 140–2, 169, 172–3, 192, 197, 209, 279

Jacklin, C.N., 117–18
James, Henry, 320 n.11
James, William, 223, 224, 228–9, 230
Jantzen, Grace, 165
Jenkins, David, 161
Jeremias, Joachim, 293 n.18
John of the Cross, 276
Johnson, Elizabeth, 163
Johnson, Ernest, 112
Julian of Norwich, 164, 242, 279
Jung, Carl, 175, 181

Kandinsky, Vasily, xiv
Kant, Immanuel, 1–2, 10, 115, 214, 216, 244, 246, 277–8
Katz, Steven, 315 n.20
Kaufman, Gordon, 318 n.60
Kemp, Martin, 86
Kerr, Jennifer, 200
Klein, Anne, 109, 264
Kierkegaard, Søren, 2, 21–9, 35–6, 53, 137, 142, 144, 219, 222, 262, 273, 280, 281
Kirschbaum, Charlotte von, 309 n.41
Kollwitz, Käthe, xiv, 279
Kristeva, Julia, 119, 127–8, 171–2, 176–8, 196, 198, 210
Kuhn, Annette, 260
Küng, Hans, 47

Lacan, Jacques, 92, 105, 122, 297 n.45
Lampe, G.W.H., 38, 39, 42
Lash, Nicholas, 300 n.12, 314 n.9, 316 n.20
Law, Bernard, 312 n.96
Levenson, Jon, 135–6, 151
Levinas, Emmanuel, 140–2

Lindbeck, George, 316 n.20
Locke, John, 6
Lorde, Audre, 133
Luther, Martin, 54, 179–80, 276

McCabe, Herbert, 34, 318 nn.61, 69
MacCannell, Juliet Flower, 286 n.15
McClelland, David, 94
Maccoby, E.E., 117–18
McCollum, Audrey, 115
McFague, Sallie, 165
McGill, Arthur, 30, 143–4, 155, 162
McGlone, Jeanette, 117
MacIntyre, Alasdair, 11, 270
McNaughton, Marion, 138–40, 294 n.11
Macquarrie, John, 38, 40, 47, 64–5, 160, 219
Mackey, James, 122
Mackie, J.L., 236
Maeckelberghe, Els, 313 n.107
Mandela, Nelson, 279
Marion, Jean-Luc, 128
Martin Soskice, Janet, 29, 163–4, 267
Marx, Karl, 4, 208, 209, 249, 281
Mascall, Eric, 127
Massey, Marilyn, 117, 249
Maurice, F.D., 222–3
Meyers, Diana, 298 n.66
Michelangelo, 4, 86
Mill, John Stuart, 3
Miller, Alice, 152–3
Miller, Kathleen, 311 n.72
Mitchell, Juliet, 107
Moltmann, Jürgen, 146, 162, 180–1
Moore, Sebastian, 190
Morris, T.V., 290 n.30
Moule, C.F.D., 46
Münter, Gabriele, xiv
Murdoch Iris, 260–2, 265–6, 282, 285

Nagel, Thomas, 100
Nakashima Brock, Rita, 151, 152
Newman, John Henry, 29
Newton, Isaac, 223, 248
Nicholls, David, 132–3, 301 n.36
Niebuhr, Reinhold, 140
Niebuhr, Richard R., 233
Niemöller, Martin, 225
Nietzsche, Friedrich, 4, 128, 208, 279, 282
Nineham, Dennis, 66
Noddings, Nel, 138
Novak, David, 136

Nussbaum, Martha, 11, 260–2

Ochshorn, Judith, 68–9, 127
Origen, 48
Otto, Rudolf, 219, 315 n.20, 317 n.52

Packer, James, 29
Padel, Una, 299 n.86
Pannenberg, Wolfhart, 45–6, 48, 280
Patai, Raphael, 300 n.21
Paul VI, 8, 187
Paul, St, 143, 145, 151, 185, 205, 255, 281
Penrose, Roger, 316 n.29
Picasso, Pablo, 307 n.11
Pius IX, 4
Pius XII, 175
Plato, 22, 72, 116, 220–1, 275, 282, 300 n.7
Plumb, J.H., 80–1
Polkinghorne, John, 31–3, 34
Poole, Roger, 84, 102
Proudfoot, Wayne, 315 n.20
Pseudo-Dionysius, 160, 162

Rahner, Karl, 175
Ramsey, Michael, 187
Ranke-Heinemann, Uta, 190
Raphael, Melissa, 316 n.20
Rawls, John, 100
Redmond, Sheila, 152
Ricoeur, Paul, 147–9, 154
Roberts, Michèle, 313 n.107
Roberts, Robert, 217
Robinson, John A.T., ix, xii, 38, 243–4
Rousseau, Jean-Jacques, 6, 98–9
Ruddick, Sara, 266
Ruel, Malcolm, 300 n.18
Ruether, Rosemary Radford, 58–60, 125, 132, 145, 163, 313 n.107
Ruston, Roger, 184

Sartre, Jean-Paul, 92, 169, 245, 287 n.18
Savonarola, Girolamo, 87
Schlamm, Leon, 315 n.20
Schlegel, Friedrich von, 253
Schleiermacher, Friedrich, 2, 17–19, 35, 39, 42, 142, 212–23, 232–4, 238–43, 248, 249–50, 253, 278, 281, 282–3
Schmaus, Michael, 194
Schüssler-Fiorenza, Elisabeth, 69–76, 293 n.25
Schweitzer, Albert, 40

Segal, Naomi, 138, 196, 197
Segerman-Peck, Lily, 321 n.37
Shakespeare, William, 35, 62
Shorter, Aylward, 123–4
Smith, Wilfred Cantwell, 40–1
Socrates, 22, 275
Spinoza, Baruch, 215
Starhawk, 159
Steiner, George, 275
Stevenson, Pru, 299 n.86
Stoller, Robert, 91–2
Storrar, William, 131–2
Sykes, Stephen, 288 n.8
Sutherland, Stewart, 318 n.60
Swinburne, Richard, 124

Taylor, A.E., 124
Torrance, Iain, 287 n.2
Torrance, T.F., 153–4
Trible, Phyllis, 71, 72
Trilling, Lionel, 265
Turner, H.E.W., 160

Vergote, Antoine, 164
Viorst, Judith, 115

Visser 't Hooft, W.A., 153
Visser 't Hooft, Henrietta, 153

Ward, Hannah, 165
Ward, Keith, 32, 33–4
Warner, Marina, 174–5, 194, 204
Weems, Renita, 184
Weil, Simone, 260, 319 n.7
Wells, H.G., 3
West, Angela, 184–5
Wiles, Maurice, 35, 38, 41–3, 63
Whitbeck, Caroline, 101, 109, 111, 113
White, Vernon, 161
White, Victor, 181
Whitehead, Alfred North, 133
Whittier, J.C., 268
Williams, Rowan, 262–3
Wilson Schaef, Anne, 271
Winnicott, D.W., 90, 107
Wollstonecraft, Mary, 3
Woolf, Virginia, 116

Young, Iris Marion, 102, 103

Zizioulas, John, 156
Zohar, Danah, 316 n.29